ARTIFICIAL INTELLIGENCE

SECOND EDITION

Patrick Henry Winston
Professor of Computer Science
Director, Artificial Intelligence Laboratory
Massachusetts Institute of Technology

ADDISON-WESLEY PUBLISHING COMPANY
Reading, Massachusetts • Menlo Park, California
London • Amsterdam • Don Mills, Ontario • Sydney

Library of Congress Cataloging in Publication Data

Winston, Patrick Henry.
    Artificial Intelligence.

    Includes bibliographical references and index.
    1. Artificial Intelligence. I. Title
Q335.W56   1984   001.53'5   83-19691
ISBN 0-201-08259-4

Reprinted with corrections, July 1984

Reproduced by Addison-Wesley from camera-ready copy supplied and approved by the author.

EFGHIJ–DO–898765

Acknowledgments

The cover design is by Karen A. Prendergast. The fonts are Almost Computer Modern. The book was prepared using Donald E. Knuth's TEX, with help from Daniel C. Brotsky. The book design is by Marie McAdam. Margaret Pinette handled production. Dikran Karagueuzian also helped enormously.

Many people read this book and contributed valuable suggestions. Of these people, the following require special mention for their careful attention to the entire book: Peter Andreae, J. Michael Brady, Kenneth D. Forbus, W. Eric L. Grimson, Ellen C. Hildreth, Karen A. Prendergast, and especially, Boris Katz. Other people making particularly valuable suggestions include these: Robert C. Berwick, Bruce Buchanan, Bradley H. Dowden, Carl E. Hewitt, Tomás Lozano-Pérez, Ryszard S. Michalski, Jack Minker, and Demetri Terzopoulos.

Most of the ideas in this book were developed with long-sustained help from the Defense Advanced Research Projects Agency and the Office of Naval Research. The visionary people in such agencies, particularly Marvin Denicoff and Robert Kahn, made the field of Artificial Intelligence possible.

Preface

The field of Artificial Intelligence has changed enormously since the first edition of this book was published. Subjects in Artificial Intelligence are de rigueur for undergraduate computer-science majors, and stories on Artificial Intelligence are regularly featured in most of the reputable news magazines.

Part of the reason for change is that solid results have accumulated. In the early days, most researchers in the field were content with *illustrations* that showed ideas at work on simple, blocks-world problems, without showing the limits of those ideas. As the field matured, there came to be a gradual shift toward *demonstrations*, showing that there are ideas that are powerful enough to handle problems of practical interest. Now, having achieved a degree of respectability, more people are building systems for *experiments* as they hypothesize answers to truly hard problems that defy superficial speculation.

Of course, in this book, the emphasis is on illustrations, often from the blocks world, because the book's purpose is educational. But do not confuse the emphasis in a textbook with the emphasis of the field. Artificial Intelligence is a serious subject, one that inquires into the deepest of the classical problems inherited unsolved from fields like psychology, linguistics, and philosophy.

USES

This book is modular, so that the material can be selected and ordered to resonate with personal preferences and time constraints. Much of the book is suited to individuals wishing to learn about the key ideas on their own.

The book was designed, however, to support classroom instruction. Most instructors will use the book as a one-term introduction to key ideas, concentrating on the first eight chapters, because those chapters examine basic ideas like matching, goal reduction, constraint exploitation, search, problem solving, logic, and control. These can be followed by selected topics from the chapters that deal with language understanding, image understanding, and learning.

For more complete immersion, other instructors will use this book in one term and *LISP* in the next, taking advantage of the correspondence between the ideas explained in this book and the programs exposed in *LISP*.

Another alternative is to treat the ideas and the programs that support them simultaneously, teaching material from both books together. One way to do this is to treat the ideas in this book in lecture mode and the programs in *LISP* in small-group mode. Again, this takes two terms.

A companion instructor's manual contains exercise solutions, sample syllabuses, and sample examinations.

CHANGES

The subjects covered in this book are roughly those in the first edition, but this book is stronger in the following ways:

- The focus has moved toward principles and away from case studies.

- I deal explicitly with my view of how Artificial Intelligence work should be done and how it should be judged.

- There are new chapters on logic and learning, inasmuch as readers of *Artificial Intelligence* demanded them. The chapters on programming have emigrated into a new book, *LISP*, coordinated with this one.

- There are explicit procedures. The procedure language is English, so as to require no tangential study, but the English is arranged in procedure-like style, so as to offer greater precision than ordinary language.

- Old material has been purged and new material added to bring things up to date. All surviving material has been rewritten and rearranged to improve clarity and coherence. The most radical changes are in the chapters on control, representation, language, vision, and problem solving. The problem-solving chapter, for example, now treats design and analysis systems, providing explanations of representative successes like XCON, THE DIPMETER ADVISOR, MYCIN, and ACRONYM.

- There are more problems. Many introduce important contributions to the field such as Mitchell's version-space learning procedure, Morevec's reduced-images stereo procedure, and the Strips problem solver.

CORRESPONDENCES

Here is how this book and *LISP* are coordinated:

- Terry Winograd's block-movement system, introduced here in *Description Matching and Goal Reduction*, is described in chapter 13 of *LISP*. In subsequent chapters in *LISP*, the block-movement system is used to illustrate rules for good programming, introspective question answering, and data-driven programming.
- Search, introduced here in *Exploring Alternatives*, is covered in chapter 11 of *LISP*.
- Rule-based analysis, introduced in *Problem Solving Paradigms*, is covered in chapter 18 of *LISP*.
- Theorem-proving, introduced in *Logic and Theorem Proving*, is treated, lightly, in chapter 17 of *LISP*.
- The frames idea, introduced in *Representing Commonsense Knowledge*, is treated in chapter 22 of *LISP*.
- Transition trees for natural language analysis, in *Language Understanding*, is treated in chapters 19, 20, and 21 of *LISP*.
- Feature-space oriented pattern recognition, a minor topic in *Image Understanding*, is handled in chapter 10 of *LISP*.

P.H.W.

Contents

5   CONTROL METAPHORS   133

CONTROL CHOICES   133

Where Is Knowledge about Procedures Stored? • What Process Decides
Which Procedures Act? • How Are Computational Resources Allocated?
• What Kind of Procedures Are There? • How Do Procedures Commu-
nicate? • MOVER Generalizations Illustrate Fancy Control Options

MEANS-ENDS ANALYSIS AND GPS   146

The Key Idea in GPS Is Operating To Reduce Differences • Procedure
Preconditions Force Recursion • Normally GPS Does Forward Chaining
Rather Than Backward Chaining • GPS Involves Depth-first Search •
Deferring Recursion Gives GPS Some Planning Ability • GPS Incorporates
Powerful Problem-Solving and Control Ideas • GPS Is Not a Modern
Control Structure • Control Ideas Are Seductive

6   PROBLEM-SOLVING PARADIGMS   159

GENERATE AND TEST   160

Generate-and-test Systems Often Do Identification • Generators Should
Be Complete, Nonredundant, and Informed • Analyzing Mass Spectrograms Illustrates Generate-and-test • ACRONYM Finds Objects

RULE-BASED SYSTEMS FOR SYNTHESIS   166

A Toy Synthesis System Bags Groceries • XCON Configures Computer
Systems • Rule-based Systems Can Be Idiot Savants

8   REPRESENTING COMMONSENSE KNOWLEDGE   251

10   IMAGE UNDERSTANDING   335

1

The Intelligent Computer

This book is an introduction to the field that has come to be called Artificial Intelligence. The purposes of this first chapter are to explain why knowing about Artificial Intelligence is important, to outline the field, and to give some examples of the progress that has been made.

THE FIELD AND THE BOOK

There are many ways to define the field of Artificial Intelligence. Here is one:

- Artificial Intelligence is the study of ideas that enable computers to be intelligent.

But what is intelligence? Is it the ability to reason? Is it the ability to acquire and apply knowledge? Is it the ability to perceive and manipulate things in the physical world? Surely all of these abilities are part of what intelligence is, but they are not the whole of what can be said. A definition in the usual sense seems impossible because intelligence appears to be an amalgam of so many information-representation and information-processing talents.

1

Nevertheless, the goals of the field of Artificial Intelligence can be defined as follows:

- One central goal of Artificial Intelligence is to make computers more useful.

- Another central goal is to understand the principles that make intelligence possible.

The purpose of this book is to serve two groups of people. Computer scientists and engineers need to know about Artificial Intelligence in order to make computers more useful. Psychologists, linguists, and philosophers need to know about Artificial Intelligence in order to understand the principles that make intelligence possible.

Because this book focuses on basic ideas, almost none of it requires special background such as computer programming experience or advanced mathematical training.

Making Computers Intelligent Helps Us Understand Intelligence

The perspective of Artificial Intelligence complements the traditional perspectives of psychology, linguistics, and philosophy. Here are some reasons why:

- Computer metaphors aid thinking. Work with computers has led to a rich new language for talking about how to do things and how to describe things. Metaphorical and analogical use of the concepts involved enables more powerful thinking about thinking.

- Computer models force precision. Implementing a theory uncovers conceptual mistakes and oversights that ordinarily escape even the most meticulous researchers. Major roadblocks often appear that were not recognized as problems at all before beginning the cycle of thinking and experimenting.

- Computer implementations quantify task requirements. Once a program performs a task, upper-bound statements can be made about how much information processing the task requires.

- Computer programs exhibit unlimited patience, they require no feeding, and they do not bite. Moreover, it is usually simple to deprive a computer program of some piece of knowledge in order to test how important that piece really is. It is impossible to work with animal brains with the same precision.

Note that wanting to make computers *be* intelligent is not the same as wanting to make computers *simulate* intelligence. Artificial Intelligence excites people who want to uncover principles that all intelligent information processors must exploit, not just those made of wet neural tissue instead of dry electronics. Consequently, there is neither an obsession with mimicking human intelligence nor a prejudice against using methods that seem involved in human intelligence. Instead, there is a new point of view that brings along a new methodology and leads to new theories.

One result of this new point of view may be new ideas about how to help people become more intelligent. Just as psychological knowledge about human information processing can help make computers intelligent, theories derived purely with computers in mind often suggest possibilities about methods to educate people better. Said another way, the methodology involved in making smart programs may transfer to making smart people.

Intelligent Computers Are More Useful Computers

Do we really need to make our computers smarter? It seems so. As the world grows more complex, we must use our energy, food, and human resources wisely, and we must have high-quality help from computers to do it. Computers must help not only by doing ordinary computing, but also by doing computing that exhibits intelligence.

It is easy to think of amazing applications for intelligent computers, many of which seem like science fiction by yesterday's standards. Here are a few:

- In business, computers should suggest financial strategies and give marketing advice. Moreover, computers should schedule people and groups, refer problems to the right people, summarize news, and polish draft documents, freeing them of grammatical errors.

- In engineering, computers should check design rules, recall relevant precedent designs, offer suggestions, and otherwise help create new products.

- In manufacturing, computers should do the dangerous and boring assembly, inspection, and maintenance jobs.

- In farming, computers should control pests, prune trees, and selectively harvest mixed crops.

- In mining, computers should work where the conditions are too dangerous for people, and they should recover the manganese nodules from the bottom of the sea.

- In schools, computers should understand their students' mistakes, not just react to them. Computers should act as superbooks in which microprocessors display orbiting planets and play musical scores.

- In hospitals, computers should help with diagnosis, monitor patients' conditions, manage treatment, and make beds.

- In households, computers should give advice on cooking and shopping, clean the floors, mow the lawn, do the laundry, and deal with maintenance.

Some of these things are being done now. Others are close. Still others will require a lot more work. All are possible.

The Book Covers the Basic Ideas of the Field

To understand Artificial Intelligence or to work in the field, one must understand basic ideas about matching, goal reduction, constraint exploitation, search, control, problem solving, and logic. Chapters 1–7 of this book define and explain these basics:

Chapter 1, The Intelligent Computer. Some representative successes are discussed and some criteria for judging success are listed.

Chapter 2, Description Matching and Goal Reduction. This chapter explains one procedure that does geometric analogy problems by description matching and another procedure that manipulates toy blocks by goal reduction. The chapter's purpose is to demonstrate the importance of good representation and to introduce some particularly useful problem-solving tools early on.

Chapter 3, Exploiting Natural Constraints. Once essential facts are well described, constraints may emerge that make problem solving easy. This is true of problems in basic algebra, for example. In this chapter, one example shows how symbolic constraint propagation aids line-drawing analysis. Another example shows numeric constraint propagation at work in nets using financial spreadsheet systems. Still another shows numeric constraint propagation in arrays using sparse barometer information to make elevation maps. All this leads to the introduction of dependency-directed backtracking, by which compatible choices are found efficiently. The chapter concludes with a discussion of the critical role of representation and constraint in doing good work in Artificial Intelligence.

Chapter 4, Exploring Alternatives. Sometimes there is no way to solve a problem without exploring some alternative routes to a solution. Useful examples are the problems involved in traversing various kinds of mazes, discovering new concepts, finding optimal ways of arranging inherently sequential tasks, and playing games like checkers and chess.

Chapter 5, Control Metaphors. Control concerns the process of passing information and attention around a computer problem-solver's collection of procedures. In this chapter, the focus turns directly to the question of attention, and we consider, among others things, the General Problem Solver paradigm.

Chapter 6, Problem-solving Paradigms. There are a number of basic paradigms behind problem solvers. One is the generate-and-test paradigm. The DENDRAL system for mass spectrogram analysis is a generate-and-test system. Another problem-solving paradigm is the rule-based-system paradigm. XCON, a rule-based synthesis system, lays out computer-system components; MYCIN, a rule-based analysis system, diagnoses infectious diseases.

Chapter 7, Logic and Theorem Proving. Logic involves truth values, rules of inference, and techniques for proof. We will look at two popular logic-oriented techniques: resolution theorem proving and truth maintenance. Along the way, we experience the problem of keeping knowledge up to date, popularly known as the frame problem.

Given that the basic ideas of chapters 1–7 provide some of the information-processing strength needed to produce intelligent behavior, the next question is how to combine them to do something that is intelligent. Chapters 8–12 address this question by concentrating on how computers can be made to know commonsense things, to understand human language, to see the world, and to learn.

Chapter 8, Representing Commonsense Knowledge. Powerful representation is an essential ingredient of intelligence. To help you understand representation issues, the chapter begins by drawing a distinction between syntax and semantics. Thus equipped, we explore semantic nets, a popular mechanism for recording relations, and we encounter inheritance, defaults, demons, and perspectives. Next, we move on to representing story knowledge, dealing with frames and standard stereotypes. Finally, the chapter shows how primitive-act frames enable some story paraphrase recognition, and it shows how abstraction units enable some story summarization.

Chapter 9, Language Understanding. For a computer to deal with written language, it is necessary to translate sentences into an internal description suited to solving problems. This can require many representations such as parse trees, thematic-role frames, and various kinds of semantic structures. To get started, we examine context-free parsers, transition-net parsers, and wait-and-see parsers. Next, we consider the issues involved in building thematic-role frames. And finally, we think about transition-net semantic grammar systems for practical language interfaces such as INTELLECT and LIFER.

Chapter 10, Image Understanding. Better representation is the key to computer understanding of visual images as well as to computer understanding of language. Among the popular representations are the primal sketch, the $2\frac{1}{2}$-D sketch, and the generalized-cylinder model, which makes things about volumes explicit. The chapter starts with edge finding and binocular stereo, describes how shading interacts with surface orientation, and finally, explains feature-space pattern-recognition systems for practical identification and location, mentioning CONSIGHT in particular.

Chapter 11, Learning Class Descriptions from Samples. Here we begin to look at learning, both computer and human. We start with an enumeration of various induction heuristics that enable learning about object classes. Next, we examine some specific procedures that use the induction heuristics, procedures that often perform better than people.

Chapter 12, Learning Rules from Experience. To close the book, we see how to learn grammar rules by analyzing impasse-causing sentences, and we see how to learn rulelike principles by recognizing analogies between precedents and exercises, just as people do in learning about management, political science, economics, law, medicine, and life in general.

One reason to be optimistic about future progress in all of these areas is that basic ideas find frequent application. Thus the basic ideas are a channel for cross fertilization. A good idea about vision soon supports progress on expert problem solving, and vice versa.

Moreover, there is help from outside. Many disciplines contribute ideas to this new field. Since intelligence requires so many strengths, the problems faced in many established disciplines intersect the natural concerns of people doing Artificial Intelligence. Mathematics, psychology, linguistics, philosophy, computer science, and many kinds of engineering have important things to say.

WHAT COMPUTERS CAN DO

Having seen the ideas to be examined in this book, let us look at some representative examples of what computers can do once they are programmed using such ideas. Be cautious, however! It is as easy to become a rabid believer as it is to remain dogmatically pessimistic. Much remains to be discovered, and when talking about what computers can do, it is often appropriate to preface claims with, "To some extent ...." In most cases, basic research is only now becoming engineering practice.

Computers Can Solve Difficult Problems

An early program, written by James R. Slagle, operated in the world of integral calculus.[1] Computers can do arithmetic at unbelievable speed, of course. Slagle showed they can do much more, accepting integration problems and producing answers like this:

$$\int \frac{x^4}{(1 - x^2)^{\frac{5}{2}}} dx = \sin^{-1} x - \tan(\sin^{-1} x) + \frac{1}{3} \tan^3(\sin^{-1} x)$$

Slagle's program is simple enough to serve as a programming example even though it comfortably handles problems from university-level examinations. Subsequent programs, like one by Joel Moses in the MACSYMA system, do even better because they have more and better knowledge. No human can compete with them.

Much more recently, programs have been written that solve mechanical problems. Faced with the spring-loaded reducer valve in figure 1-1, a program by Kenneth D. Forbus produces the following explanation for what happens when the pressure rises in the output port:

What happens when ...

When the pressure in the output port, Out, rises, the increasing pressure pushes the diaphragm, D, up and closes the auxiliary valve, A. The pressure in the auxiliary valve's output chamber falls, the pressure in the piston steam port falls, and the piston moves up and closes the main valve. The pressure in the main valve's output chamber falls, causing the pressure in the output port to fall. Note that when the pressure in the output port rises, it causes the system to act so that the pressure in the output port falls. This means the system exhibits negative feedback.

Computers Can Help Experts Analyze and Design

Some programs are intended to help physicians analyze certain kinds of disease. One, MYCIN, by Edward Shortliffe, specializes in certain bacterial infections. Another, CADUCEUS, by Harry E. Pople, Jr. and Jack D. Myers is for internal medicine. The performance of both programs is moving toward the level of human specialists.

Another powerful analysis program, by Gerald J. Sussman and Richard M. Stallman, is for understanding electronic circuits. Their program, EL, reaches conclusions about a diagram like the one in figure 1-2, using humanlike reasoning, rather than brute-force attack on the network equations.

---

[1] References are listed at the end of the chapter.

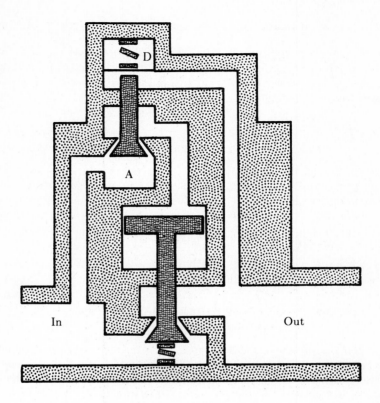

Figure 1-1. A spring-loaded reducer valve that reduces high-pressure steam at 1200 psi to low-pressure steam at a constant pressure of 12 psi. A program can explain how such mechanisms work. Courtesy of Kenneth D. Forbus.

An advantage lies in the system's ability to talk about what it has done in terms human engineers can understand.

Another analysis program, PROSPECTOR, developed by Richard O. Duda, Peter E. Hart, and Rene Reboh, helped to discover a promising new extension to an existing molybdenum deposit near Mount Tolman in Washington.

Programs for analysis are complemented by others for engineering design. Figure 1-3 shows an integrated-circuit chip designed with help from a program. Another representative design program used in the computer business is XCON, originally called R1, developed cooperatively by John McDermott at Carnegie-Mellon University, Arnold Kraft and Dennis O'Connor at the Digital Equipment Corporation, and their associates. XCON decides how to configure the various modules in a computer system.

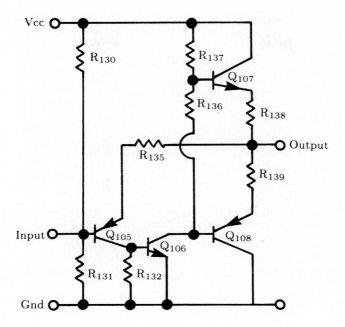

Figure 1-2. Circuit-understanding programs use humanlike reasoning to determine network voltages and currents. They explain complicated electronic devices in terms that are understood easily by electrical engineers. Adapted from "Heuristic Techniques in Computer Aided Circuit Analysis," by Gerald J. Sussman and Richard M. Stallman, *IEEE Transactions on Circuits and Systems*, vol. CAS-22, no. 11, November, 1975, copyright 1975 by the Institute of Electrical and Electronics Engineers, New York. Used with permission of the Institute of Electrical and Electronics Engineers.

Computers Can Understand Simple English

There are now several programs that are capable of handling questions expressed in English. One of these, INTELLECT, developed by Larry R. Harris, answers English questions like the following:

• I wonder how actual sales for last month compared to the forecasts for people under quota in New England?

Another program, LIFER, developed by Gary G. Hendrix, was originally specialized to answering questions in the world of ships:

• How many Spruance class ships are there?

• Who is the captain of the Kennedy?

• What is the length of Old Ironsides?

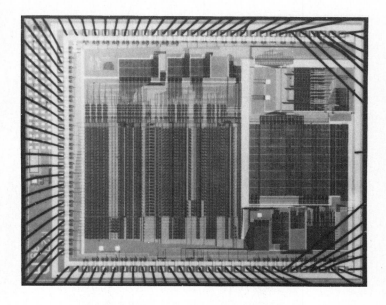

Figure 1-3. An integrated circuit designed with the help of an intelligent program. Courtesy of John Batali, Edmond Goodhue, Christopher Hanson, Howard E. Shrobe, Richard M. Stallman, and Gerald J. Sussman.

Computers Can Understand Simple Images

Equipped with television cameras, computers can see well enough to deal with certain limited worlds. From drawings of a blocks world, for example, they make conclusions about what kinds of objects are present, what relations exist between them, and what groups they form. A program by David Waltz notes that the line drawing in figure 1-4 depicts eight objects, including three that form an arch in the middle foreground. It further observes that to the left of the arch is a wedge, and to the right is a distorted brick with a hole, and a three-object tower stands in the background.

Unfortunately, it is much harder to work with images from a camera than to work with prepared drawings. Promising progress has been made, nevertheless. Figure 1-5, for example, shows a pair of aerial images, and figure 1-6 shows a contour map produced from the images using two procedures: a binocular stereo procedure based on the ideas of David Marr, Tomaso Poggio, and W. Eric L. Grimson; and a surface-reconstruction procedure based on the ideas of Grimson and Demetri Terzopoulos.

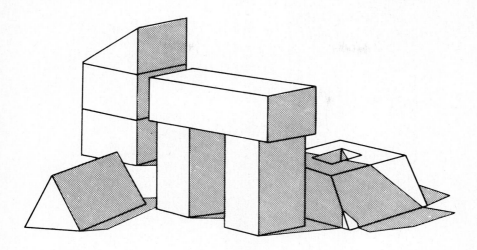

Figure 1-4. A drawing-understanding program uses knowledge about possible vertex configurations to analyze lines. Typical drawings have cracks, shadows, boundaries, concave lines, and convex lines. Adapted from *The Psychology of Computer Vision*, edited by Patrick H. Winston, copyright 1975 by McGraw-Hill Book Company, New York. Used with permission of McGraw-Hill Book Company.

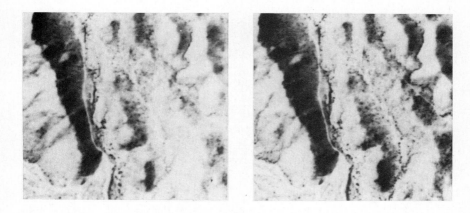

Figure 1-5. A stereo aerial image pair. The two pictures are arranged so that you can see depth yourself with the aid of a stereoscopic viewer. Courtesy of W. Eric L. Grimson.

Figure 1-6. A contour map produced from the aerial images in figure 1-5. Courtesy of W. Eric L. Grimson.

Computers Can Help Manufacture Products

It is fortunate that computers will eventually do work that people dislike—jobs that are dirty, dangerous, demeaning, hopelessly boring, or poorly rewarded. As society advances, such jobs must be done by flexible, intelligent robots or by an armamentarium of special-purpose machines using brute-force methods. So far, the special-purpose machines dominate. Hardly anyone has shoes made to order, even though one person's two feet are rarely the same size. Tailor-made suits have similarly given way to the standard item off the rack.

To move from special-purpose machines to flexible, intelligent robots requires many capabilities. One of these is reasoning about motion in space. Faced with moving the small brick from one place to another in the cluttered environment shown in figure 1-7, a spatial-reasoning program by Rodney A. Brooks and Tomás Lozano-Pérez decides that it can move the brick through the gap between the obstacles after rotation.

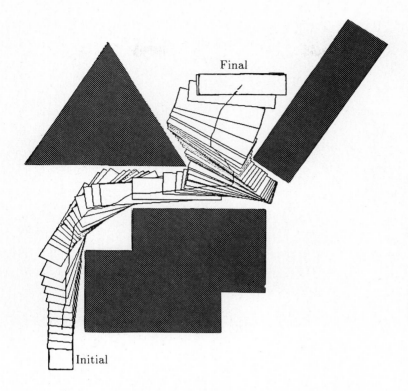

Figure 1-7. A simple spatial-reasoning problem. The solution is to rotate the brick as it is moved through the strait between the obstacles. Courtesy of Rodney A. Brooks and Tomás Lozano-Pérez.

Another requirement is the capability of dealing with force and touch information. A program developed by W. Daniel Hillis can distinguish among screws, washers, cotter pins, and other small objects using information from touch sensors. The touch sensors can be carried by fingers like the tendon-actuated one, developed by Steven Jacobsen and John E. Wood, shown in figure 1-8.

Computers Can Learn from Examples and Precedents

Several programs now demonstrate learning talent. One of my programs learns new concepts from sequences like the one shown in figure 1-9 for learning about arches. Another, INDUCE, by Ryszard S. Michalski, learns to distinguish between the upper trains and the lower trains shown in figure 1-10. In a practical application, the train-recognition program learned criteria for recognizing more than a dozen soybean diseases, producing results superior to human specialists. Since a considerable fraction of the

Figure 1-8. A tendon-actuated finger. The construction of such fingers requires sophisticated materials. Courtesy of Steven Jacobsen and John E. Wood.

world's population relies on soybeans for survival, accurate soybean-disease diagnosis is extremely important.

Another kind of learning program, by me, deals with precedents and exercises like those captured by the following brief descriptions:

Macbeth

This is a story about Macbeth, Lady Macbeth, Duncan, and Macduff. Macbeth is an evil noble. Lady Macbeth is a greedy, ambitious woman. Duncan is a king. Macduff is a noble. Lady Macbeth persuades Macbeth to want to be king because she is greedy. She is able to influence him because he is married to her and because he is weak. Macbeth murders Duncan with a knife. Macbeth murders Duncan because Macbeth wants to be king and because Macbeth is evil. Lady Macbeth kills herself. Macduff is angry. Macduff kills Macbeth because Macbeth murdered Duncan and because Macduff is loyal to Duncan.

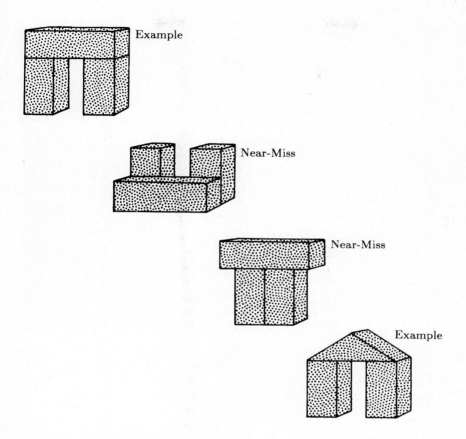

Figure 1-9. One concept-learning program learns about arches from a series of examples and near misses. The program decides that an arch is a brick or wedge that must be supported by two bricks that cannot touch.

An Exercise

> Let E be an exercise. E is a story about a weak noble and a greedy lady. The lady is married to the noble. Show that the noble may want to be king.

Told by a teacher that *Macbeth* is to be considered a precedent, the program forms a rule to the effect that the weakness of a nobleman and the greed of his wife can cause him to want to be king. The same program can learn what things look like from functional definitions, some background knowledge, and particular examples.

Still another learning program, by Douglas B. Lenat, one more oriented toward teacher-free discovery, deals with concepts like multiplication, factorization, and prime number. It demonstrates that a program can invent

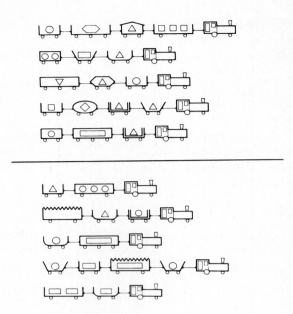

Figure 1-10. Another concept-learning program describes the upper trains as those having a short car with a closed top; it describes the lower ones as those having either two cars or a car with a jagged top. Courtesy of Ryszard S. Michalski.

mathematics that even professional mathematicians find interesting and exciting. In particular, Lenat's mathematical discovery program stumbled across the obscure idea of maximally divisible numbers, even though the program's author, and evidently most other mathematicians, had never thought about maximally divisible numbers before. The distinguished mathematician Ramanujan had, however, so Lenat's program is in good company.

Computers Can Model Animal Information Processing

Many psychologists do Artificial Intelligence because they want to understand animal perception and cognition from an information-processing point of view. Programs join animals as test subjects, with behavior differences between programs and animals becoming as interesting as behavior itself. Part of the research focuses on vision, hearing, and touch, and part addresses human problem solving.

CRITERIA FOR SUCCESS

Any field must have criteria for determining if work has been successful. In some fields, the criteria are firmly established. Criteria for success in Artificial Intelligence are not so firmly established because the field is still young, it is extremely broad, and much of it does not seem susceptible to conventional mathematical treatment.

Still, we need some working criteria for judging results, even if the criteria prove transient. Consequently, let us demand good answers to these questions before we take some particular work in Artificial Intelligence to be successful:

- Is the task clearly defined?

- Is there an implemented procedure performing the defined task? If not, much difficulty may be lying under a rug somewhere.

- Is there a set of identifiable regularities or constraints from which the implemented procedure gets its power? If not, the procedure may be an ad hoc toy, capable perhaps of superficially impressive performance on carefully selected examples, but incapable of deeply impressive performance and incapable of revealing any principles.

All of the examples cited in this chapter satisfy these criteria: all perform clearly defined tasks; all involve implemented procedures; and all involve identified regularities or constraints.

SUMMARY

- Artificial Intelligence has tremendous applications in many socially relevant areas. Leaders in a wide variety of fields need to know its ideas.

- As a means for studying intelligence, working with computers and with computer-based metaphors offers certain clear advantages. Results are more likely to be precise, to provide bounds on the amount of information processing required, and to be testable experimentally.

- Intelligent behavior can be displayed along several dimensions. This is made possible by strength in information-processing capability associated with certain basic areas. These areas include matching, goal reduction, constraint exploitation, search, control, problem solving, and logic.

- Finally, computers already can do many things that seem to require intelligence.

REFERENCES

Artificial Intelligence has a programming heritage. To understand the ideas introduced in this book in depth, there is a need to see some of them embodied in program form. A coordinated book, *LISP* [1981], by Patrick H. Winston and Berthold K. P. Horn, satisfies this need. Another good book is *Artificial Intelligence Programming* [1980], by Eugene Charniak, Christopher K. Riesbeck, and Drew V. McDermott.

In mathematics, the first symbolic integration program was done by James R. Slagle [1963]. Richard Bogen et al. describe MACSYMA, a system for aiding mathematicians [1975]. MACSYMA contains SIN, a powerful symbolic integration program developed by Joel Moses [1967].

The explanation of the pressure-reducing steam valve was produced by a program written by Kenneth D. Forbus based on theoretical work by Johan de Kleer [1979]. It was done, in part, to support the Steamer Project. See the paper by Albert L. Stevens, R. Bruce Roberts, Larry S. Stead, Kenneth D. Forbus, Cindy Steinberg, and Brian C. Smith [1981]. For more recent work on mechanism understanding, see the work of Kenneth D. Forbus [1981, 1982].

MYCIN is described by Edward Shortliffe in *MYCIN: Computer-based Medical Consultations* [1976]. CADUCEUS is described by Harry E. Pople, Jr. [1982].

In their book, *Applications of Artificial Intelligence for Chemical Inference: The DENDRAL Project* [1980], Robert Lindsay, Bruce Buchanan, Edward A. Feigenbaum, and Joshua Lederberg describe the DENDRAL program for analyzing mass spectrograms [1969]. Richard M. Stallman and Gerald J. Sussman explain EL and their work on humanlike electronic circuit analysis [1977].

For information on the PROSPECTOR program for dealing with geological data, developed principally by Richard O. Duda, Peter E. Hart, and Rene Reboh, see Hart, Duda, and M. T. Einaudi [1978] and see A. N. Campbell, V. F. Hollister, Duda, and Hart, [1982]. For information on the XCON system for configuring computers, developed cooperatively by groups led by John McDermott at Carnegie-Mellon University and Arnold Kraft and Dennis O'Connor at the Digital Equipment Corporation, see McDermott [1982]. For work on expert systems in general, see *Building Expert Systems* [1983], edited by Frederick Hayes-Roth, Donald A. Waterman, and Douglas B. Lenat.

In natural language understanding, early, famous work was done by Terry Winograd in a blocks-world domain [1972] and by William A. Woods in the moon-rocks domain [Woods and Ronald M. Kaplan 1971]. For a description of INTELLECT, see Larry R. Harris [1977]. For a description of LIFER, a system built with related technology, see Gary G. Hendrix, Earl D. Sacerdoti, Daniel Sagalowicz, and Jonathan Slocum [1978].

For a treatment of line-drawing analysis, see the work of David Waltz [1972, 1975]. For a description of the Marr-Poggio binocular stereo program, see *Vision* [1982], by David Marr, and see *From Images to Surfaces* [1981], by W. Eric L. Grimson. For treatments of surface reconstruction, see Grimson [1980, 1981] and see the more recent work of Demetri Terzopoulos [1983].

In robotics, for work on spatial reasoning, see Tomás Lozano-Pérez [1980, 1983] and see Rodney A. Brooks [1983]. For work on recognition by touch, see W. Daniel Hillis [1981, 1982].

In learning, the work mentioned on class-oriented learning is by me [1970, 1975] and by Ryszard S. Michalski [Michalski and Chilausky 1980, Michalski 1983]. The work on learning by precedents and exercises and on form and function is by me and my associates [1980, 1982; Winston, Thomas O. Binford, Boris Katz, and Michael R. Lowry, 1983]. The work on mathematical discovery is by Douglas B. Lenat [1977, 1982].

For modeling of human problem solving, see *Human Information Processing* [1972], by Peter H. Lindsay and Donald A. Norman, *Human Problem Solving* [1972], by Allen Newell and Herbert A. Simon, and *The Psychology of Human-Computer Interaction* [1983], by Stuart Card, Thomas P. Moran, and Allen Newell. In the area of teaching people thinking see *Mindstorms* [1981], by Seymour Papert.

In another direction, in his book *Computer Power and Human Reason* [1976], Joseph Weizenbaum argues persuasively that there are areas of human activity in which computers should not be involved, no matter how intelligent they may become, because they lack humanlike experience.

Finally, there are now a number of other textbooks on Artificial Intelligence. Like this book, each of the others adheres to a particular approach or perspective. Elaine Rich, for example, paints a broad picture, recognizing that Artificial Intelligence is a diverse field [*Artificial Intelligence*, 1983], Nils J. Nilsson, on the other hand, takes the view that Artificial Intelligence is a kind of applied logic [*Principles of Artificial Intelligence*, 1980]. Margaret A. Boden concentrates on psychological issues [*Artificial Intelligence and Natural Man*, 1977]. Bertram Raphael offers a particularly easy-to-read survey [*The Thinking Computer*, 1976]. Earl Hunt stresses pattern recognition and theorem proving [*Artificial Intelligence*, 1975].

Finally, *The Handbook of Artificial Intelligence* [1981], by Avron Barr, Edward A. Feigenbaum, and Paul R. Cohen, is a generally useful reference.

2

Description Matching
And Goal Reduction

This chapter's primary purpose is to introduce the role of *representation* in Artificial Intelligence. The secondary purpose is to introduce two important problem-solving paradigms by explaining two venerable, famous procedures. One of these procedures solves geometric-analogy problems, illustrating the use of the *describe-and-match* paradigm. The other solves blocks-manipulation problems, illustrating the use of the *goal-reduction* paradigm. Both examples show that simple descriptions, cloaked in appropriate representations, can produce appropriate problem-solving behavior. The representation used in the analogy example involves sets of relations describing objects; the representation used in the blocks-manipulation example involves tree-like structures, usually called AND/OR *trees*, that describe how goals relate to one another.

THE KEY ROLE OF REPRESENTATION

Coarsely speaking, a *representation* is a set of conventions about how to describe a class of things. A *description* makes use of the conventions of a representation to describe some particular thing. Chapter 8 will expand on the nature of representation and description; for now, informal definitions are adequate.

Theoretical Equivalence Is Different from Practical Equivalence

In some uninteresting theoretical sense, all computer-based representations are equivalent. This is so because computer-based representations are embedded ultimately in the symbolic structures available in a computer language like LISP and thence down into arrangements of bits in memory. Consequently, any representation that can be used to represent arrangements of bits can indirectly bear the information in any other representation.

In a practical sense, however, some representations emphasize things that are important to solving a class of problems. One scheme, therefore, is more powerful than another because it offers more convenience to the user even though, theoretically, both can do the same work. *Convenience*, however, is perhaps too weak a word. In general, the much greater perspicuity and the inherent thinking advantages of powerful representations enable progress that would be impossibly difficult with anything less adequate.

Good Representations Facilitate Problem Solving

Finding the appropriate representation can be a major part of a problem-solving effort. Consider, for example, the following children's puzzle:

The Farmer, Fox, Goose, and Grain

A farmer wants to move himself, a silver fox, a fat goose, and some tasty grain across a river. Unfortunately, his boat is so tiny he can take only one of his things across on any trip. Worse yet, an unattended fox will eat a goose, and an unattended goose will eat the grain, so the farmer must not leave the fox alone with the goose or the goose alone with the grain. What is he to do?

Described in English, the problem takes a few minutes, because the constraints on the moves are implicit, not explicit, and because there are many irrelevant details. English is not a good representation.

Described better, however, the problem takes no time at all, for everyone can draw a line from the start to the finish in figure 2-1 instantly. Yet drawing the line solves the problem because the *nodes* in the net shown represent safe arrangements of the farmer and his things on the banks of the river, while the *links* between the nodes represent possible crossings. The drawing is a good representation.

To make such a diagram, the first step is to make nodes for each arrangement. Since there are two possible places for the farmer and his three things, there are $2^4 = 16$ possible arrangements.

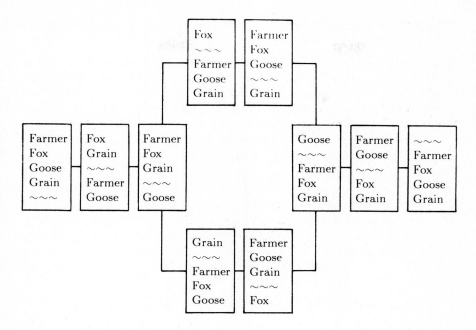

Figure 2-1. The problem of the farmer, fox, goose, and grain. The farmer must get his fox, goose, and grain across the river, represented by the wavy line, from north to south. His boat will hold only him and one of his three things. Foxes eat geese, and geese eat grain.

Only ten nodes describe viable arrangements, however, since the rules about who can eat what forbid the nodes describing the following:

- The farmer is on one side; the fox, the goose, and the grain, on the other.

- The farmer and fox are on one side; the goose and the grain, on the other.

- The farmer and grain are on one side; the fox and the goose, on the other.

To complete the diagram, the last step is to make links for each allowable boat trip. For each pair of nodes, there is a link if the two nodes meet these conditions: first, the farmer changes sides; and second, at most one of the farmer's things changes sides. Since there are ten nodes, there are $\frac{10 \times 9}{2} = 45$ unordered pairs, but of these, only ten are linked. Evidently the node-and-link description is a good description with respect to the problem posed, for it is easy to make, and once we have it, the problem is simple.

Good Representations Support Explicit, Constraint-Exposing Description

One reason that the node-and-link representation worked well with the farmer, fox, goose, and grain problem is that *it makes the important things explicit*. There was no bothering with the color of the fox or the size of the goose or the quality of the grain; instead, there was an explicit statement about safe arrangements and possible transitions between arrangements.

The representation also is good because *it exposes the natural constraints inherent in the problem*. Some transitions are possible; others are impossible. The representation makes it easy to decide for any particular case: a transition is possible if there is a link; otherwise it is impossible.

To highlight the advantage of making the important things explicit, we are about to study a procedure for doing analogy problems. Similarly, to highlight the importance of exposing natural constraints, we are about to study a blocks-manipulation procedure.

First, however, here is a list of desiderata for good representation, starting with the two just introduced:

- Good representations make the important things explicit.

- They expose natural constraints, facilitating some class of computations.

- They are complete. We can say all that needs to be said.

- They are concise. We can say things efficiently.

- They are transparent to us. We can understand what has been said.

- They facilitate computation. We can store and retrieve information rapidly.

- They suppress detail. We can keep rarely used information out of sight, but we can still get to it when necessary.

- They are computable by an existing procedure.

ANALOGY INTELLIGENCE TESTS

Geometric analogy problems like the one in figure 2-2 are typical of those that appear in human intelligence tests and typical of those solved routinely by an easily described procedure named ANALOGY. The problem is to select an answer figure, X, such that A is to B as C is to X gives the best fit. Or said another way, we want to find the rule describing how C becomes some X that most closely matches the rule describing how A becomes B. The key to doing such problems lies in good descriptions of the rules. Once we have such descriptions, working the problems becomes a simple matter of matching rule descriptions together and keeping track of some measure of similarity.

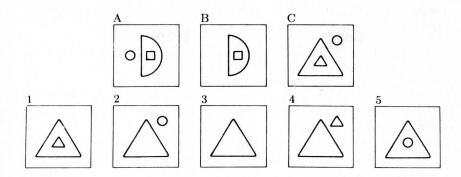

Figure 2-2. An easy problem for ANALOGY.

The ANALOGY procedure calls upon three others:

To work analogy problems using ANALOGY:

1   Describe the rule that transforms the A figure into the B
    figure and the rules that transform the C figure into the
    various answer figures, the Xs.

2   Match the A-to-B rule to each of the C-to-X rules and
    describe the differences.

3   Select the C-to-X rule that is most like the A-to-B rule.
    Announce the corresponding X as the correct answer.

As you move through this book, you will see many other procedures expressed in this numbered-step, English-like form. Let us call this form
structured English.[1] Let us agree that structured English consists of these
things:

- Steps and substeps, denoted by numbers. Thus step 2.3 is the third
  substep of the second step.

- Choices, denoted by letters. Thus choice 2.3b is the bth choice involved
  in step 2.3.

- Iterations, denoted by words like *until* and *for each*.

The use of these elements of our structured English is best understood by
studying what they do as they are encountered.

---

[1] I use the term *structured* because, like structured programming languages, this
     structured English has no *go-to* form.

Analogy Problems Are Solved by the Describe-and-match Method

The rules describe how one figure, the source, becomes another, the destination. The rules have three parts:

- A description of the source figure in terms of how the subfigures in it relate to one another. The possible relations are ABOVE, LEFT-OF, and INSIDE.

- A description of the destination figure, again in terms of how the subfigures relate to one another.

- A description of how the subfigures in the source figure are altered to become subfigures in the destination figure. Typically, a subfigure may become smaller, larger, rotated, reflected, or some combination of these things. Also possible are additions and deletions of subfigures.

Figure 2-3 shows a typical rule that has been translated from the form ANALOGY would use internally to a form that is easy for people to read. Note that the labels m and n appear in both figures and in both descriptions. Placing these labels correctly is the job of a preliminary matching operation that identifies similar subfigures.

Also note that the changes in the relations of the subfigures are implicitly described by the source and destination figure descriptions, part 1 and part 2 of the rule description. Changes in individual subfigures are given directly, however, and those changes are described in part 3. Soon we will see how ANALOGY uses all three parts to find solutions, but first we need to assure ourselves that the descriptions can be derived from the drawings.

As shown in figure 2-4, ANALOGY uses a simple procedure to compute spatial relationship between two subfigures. ANALOGY computes the center of area of each of the two subfigures, imagines diagonal lines through the center of area of one of them, and notes which sector contains the center of area of the other subfigure. Since the relations used are symmetric, it is not necessary to note both left and right relations.

To decide whether INSIDE, rather than either LEFT-OF or ABOVE, is the existing relation, ANALOGY first makes sure that the subfigures do not touch. Then ANALOGY constructs a line from any point on one figure to the drawing boundary as shown in figure 2-5. If the imaginary line crosses the second figure an odd number of times, then the second figure surrounds the first. Happily, this method involves only rapidly computable line-crossing formulas, and it works even if the figures are extremely convoluted.

We have seen how relations among subfigures are specified by part 1 and part 2 of each rule. The example in figure 2-6 is contrived so as to involve only part 1 and part 2. Part 3 is not relevant because no subfigures are altered in the move from the source figure to the destination figure. It

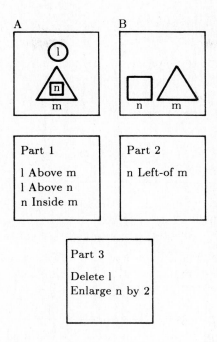

Figure 2-3. Rule descriptions consist of three parts. Two describe relations between subfigures, and one describes how subfigures change.

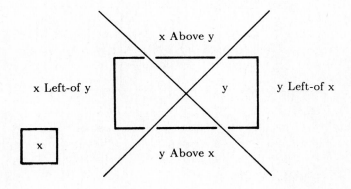

Figure 2-4. Relations between subfigures are determined by comparing centers of area. Here the square is in the area associated with LEFT-OF relative to the rectangle.

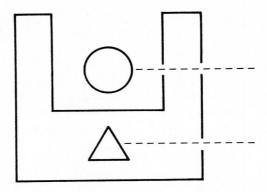

Figure 2-5. One subfigure is inside another if a line drawn to infinity crosses the boundary of the potentially surrounding subfigure an odd number of times. Thus the triangle is inside; the circle is not.

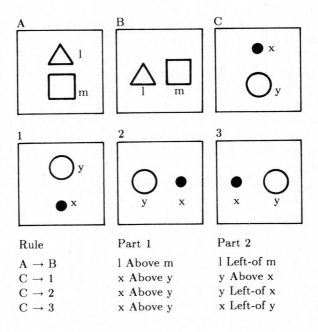

Rule	Part 1	Part 2
A → B	l Above m	l Left-of m
C → 1	x Above y	y Above x
C → 2	x Above y	y Left-of x
C → 3	x Above y	x Left-of y

Figure 2-6. Since the subfigures do not change size or orientation, only relations among subfigures are relevant in this problem; subfigure changes are not. Comparison of the rule descriptions verifies that 3 is the best answer.

is clear that the rule that best matches the A-to-B rule is the C-to-3 rule, since if we associate l with x and m with y, the two match exactly.

Note however that there is no a priori reason to associate l with x rather than with y. In going from the source figure to the destination figure, we want to be sure that squares go to squares, circles to circles, triangles to triangles, and so on. But this need to match one subfigure to a similar one does not hold in comparing two rules. In the example, answer-figure 3 is to be selected even though the subfigures in A and B are a triangle and a square, whereas in C and in all the answer figures, the subfigures are a circle and a dot. In general, ANALOGY's matching procedure must try all possible ways of associating the variables together when matching rules. In the example, we can match l with x and m with y, or we can match l with y and m with x.

This one-for-one association of variables implies that the number of subfigures that move from the source figure to the destination figure must be the same in both of the two rules being matched. This is true also of the number of additions and deletions. Any attempt to match two rules for which the numbers are different fails immediately.

If n subfigures move from the source figure to the destination figure in each of two rules being compared, there will be $n!$ ways of associating the variables together in searching for the best way to match the rules. More generally, if n_1 subfigures move, n_2 are added, and n_3 deleted, in going to the destination figure, then $n_1! \, n_2! \, n_3!$ is the number of possible associations. Each must be tried.

In our previous example, we concentrated on part 1 and part 2 because there is no possible influence from part 3 of the transformation rules. Similarly, for the problem in figure 2-7, we concentrate on part 3 alone. Since there is never more than one subfigure, there can be no relations between subfigures, and part 1 and part 2 can contribute nothing to the results. Using part 3 generates an immediate solution since only answer-figure 1 corresponds to a simple $45°$ rotation with no scale change.

Scoring Mechanisms Rank Answers

How should ANALOGY measure the similarity of two rules? So far the problems have been so simple that the best answer rule matches the A-to-B rule exactly. But if an exact match cannot be found, then a procedure must rank the inexact matches. One way to do this is to count the number of matching elements in the two rules involved in each match, as shown in figure 2-8.

In order to tune the counting a bit, various possibilities found in part 3 of the rule can be weighted less strongly than the elements in part 1 and part 2. If each match of elements in part 1 and part 2 counts one point, then the numbers shown in figure 2-9 work out well experimentally for adding

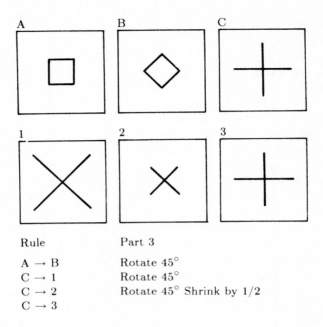

Rule	Part 3
A → B	Rotate 45°
C → 1	Rotate 45°
C → 2	Rotate 45° Shrink by 1/2
C → 3	

Figure 2-7. Since each figure has only one subfigure, only subfigure changes are relevant in this problem; relations between subfigures are not. Comparison of the rule descriptions verifies that answer-figure 1 is the best answer.

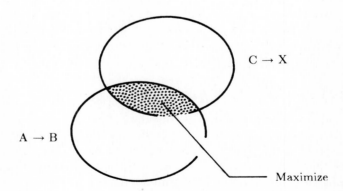

Figure 2-8. Rule similarity is measured by degree of overlap. Answers are determined by finding the C-to-X rule with the maximum number of elements in common with the A-to-B rule.

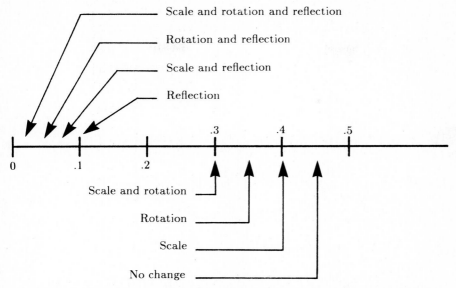

Figure 2-9. Change-description contributions to similarity scores are weighted by the type of change description involved.

part 3 items into the total rule-comparison score. A radically different set of numbers could reflect a different judgment about how the various possibilities should be ordered. The given set is biased toward rotations and against reflections, but another set might indicate the opposite preference. The corresponding variations on ANALOGY would occasionally disagree with one another about the answers!

Of course, it is possible to elaborate our measure of similarity in other directions. Suppose, for example, that S_{AB} is the set of elements in the A-to-B rule and S_{CX} is the set of elements in the C-to-X rule. Then $S_{AB} \cap S_{CX}$ is the set of elements that appear in both rules, $S_{AB} - S_{CX}$ is the set appearing in the A-to-B rule but not in the C-to-X rule, and $S_{CX} - S_{AB}$ is the set in just C-to-X. With these, we can invent formulas involving set intersections and set differences:

$$
\begin{aligned}
\text{Similarity} =\; & \alpha \times \text{Size}(S_{AB} \cap S_{CX}) \\
& - \beta \times \text{Size}(S_{AB} - S_{CX}) \\
& - \gamma \times \text{Size}(S_{CX} - S_{AB})
\end{aligned}
$$

where α, β, and γ are weights, and Size is the function that computes the number of elements in a set. If $\beta = 0$, $\gamma = 0$, and $\alpha = 1$, the formula reduces to counting the common elements. If β and γ are not the same, the formula gives asymmetric similarity judgments, allowing, for example,

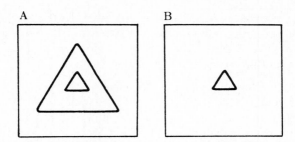

Figure 2-10. Ambiguity is introduced when subfigures have the same shape. In this illustration, the large triangle may have been deleted; alternatively, the small one may have been deleted and the large one shrunk.

the A-to-B rule to be more similar to the C-to-X rule than C-to-X is to A-to-B.

Be skeptical about such formulas, however. A procedure that depends on a lot of weights is a suspicious procedure. Using weighted sums is only one way to combine evidence. As a representation for importance, a set of weights is not explicit and exposes little constraint.

Ambiguity Complicates Matching

So far the subfigures in the source and destination figures have been individual and distinct, and there has been no problem in deciding how to form the rule describing the transformation. But in cases like the one in figure 2-10, there is ambiguity. Which of the two triangles has disappeared? Surely the larger one is gone. But has the smaller one been deleted and the larger shrunk?

In fact, neither explanation can be judged superior without considering the other figures given in the problem. Consequently, ANALOGY should construct two rules, one corresponding to each way the triangles in the source figure can be identified with triangles in the destination. In general, for each source and destination pair, there may be many rules, and for each rule there may be many ways of matching it against another rule. For some typical problems, as many as 40 or 50 rule-pair associations are candidates for the highest matching score.

Good Representation Supports Good Performance

Examine figure 2-11. It shows some examples drawn from intelligence tests that are well within the grasp of the ANALOGY procedure. In the first example, 3 is the correct answer. Actually, 3 is the only answer figure that the procedure seriously considers, because 3 alone among the answer figures has the same number of subfigures as B has. Remember that requiring the same number of subfigures is an indirect consequence of permitting a match only between rules for which the numbers of movements, additions, and deletions are the same.

In the second example, the most reasonable theory about the rule for going from A to B is that the inside subfigure is deleted. The C-to-3 rule is the same, and 3 would be selected. But note that for the A-to-B rule, another theory would be that the outside figure is deleted and the inside one enlarged. Given this theory, the correct answer would be 4. But since subfigure movement descriptions involving change in scale score less than those in which there is no change at all, then 3 is the best answer, with 4 a close second. Answer 4 would be the clear winner if 3 were not present.

In the third example, the A-to-B rule could be described as either a rotation or a reflection, with 2 being the best answer if the process prefers rotations and with 1 being the best answer if it likes reflections better. ANALOGY prefers rotations, and judges 2 to be best.

Analogy Problems Are Solved by the Goal-reduction Method

The ANALOGY procedure solves analogy problems in three steps: rule description, rule matching, and rule selection. Said another way, the procedure achieves the goal of finding a solution by achieving three subgoals. Each of these subgoals, in turn, can be divided still more finely into lower-level subgoals.

The graphical way of showing the relation between goals and subgoals is shown in figure 2-12, where the goals are arranged in a *goal tree*. The goal tree has *nodes*, corresponding to goals. When one goal is attacked by creating several other goals, those other goals are arranged directly underneath, connected by *branches*. The goals underneath are called *immediate subgoals* or *children* with respect to the goal above; the goal above is called the *immediate supergoal* or *parent* with respect to the goals below. The top node, the one with no parent, is the *root* node.

Sometimes the process of achieving a goal by achieving subgoals is called *goal reduction*, and sometimes the process is called, equivalently, *problem reduction*.

Not much is gained by looking at ANALOGY from the point of view of goal reduction, because the particular goal tree involved is simple and is always the same no matter what the actual problem is like. Consequently, we move on to look at another situation where the goal tree is, in contrast, extremely illuminating.

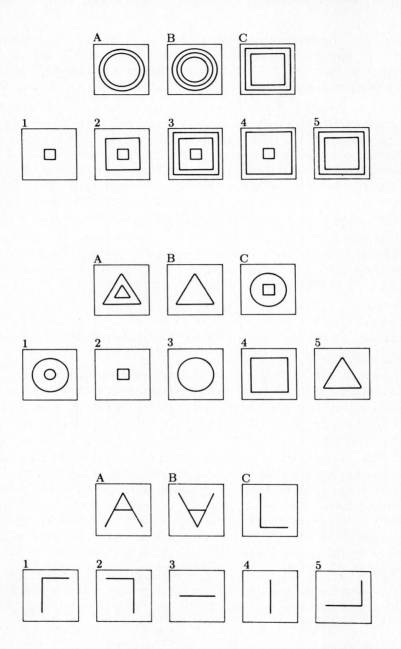

Figure 2-11. Some problems successfully solved by ANALOGY.

MOVING BLOCKS

We now look at MOVER, a procedure that solves problems and answers questions about its own behavior. MOVER works with collections of blocks like the one shown in figure 2-12. MOVER's purpose is to obey commands issued by a person. We limit our attention to simple commands:

Put ⟨block name⟩ on ⟨another block name⟩.

To obey, MOVER must plan a motion sequence for a one-armed robot that can pick up only one block at a time.

Goal-oriented Procedures Act Like a Group of Specialists

MOVER works by using a number of simple procedures that each specialize in achieving just one kind of goal. Conveniently, the names of these procedures are good mnemonics for what they do:

- PUT-ON arranges to place one block on top of another block. All action starts with a request to PUT-ON. It works by finding a specific place on the target block and by moving the traveling block.

- PUT-AT places one block at a specific place. The place must be specified by a set of coordinates. PUT-AT works by grasping the block, moving it to the specified place, and ungrasping it.

- GRASP grasps blocks. If the robot is holding a block when GRASP is invoked, GRASP must arrange for the robot to get rid of that block. Also GRASP must arrange to clear off the top of the object to be grasped.

- CLEAR-TOP does the top clearing. It works by getting rid of everything on top of the specified object.

- GET-RID-OF does the getting rid of. It works by putting objects at locations on the table.

- UNGRASP lets go of whatever the hand is holding.

- GET-SPACE finds space on the top of target blocks for traveling blocks to go. To do its job, it uses either FIND-SPACE or MAKE-SPACE.

- FIND-SPACE finds space. If there is no room on a target block, FIND-SPACE gives up.

- MAKE-SPACE helps out when FIND-SPACE gives up. MAKE-SPACE can do better because it can get rid of blocks that are in the way.

- MOVE-OBJECT moves objects, once they are held, by moving the hand.

- MOVE-HAND moves the hand.

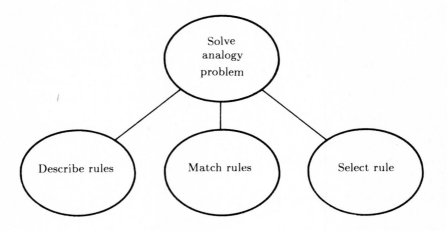

Figure 2-12. A simple goal tree. Analogy problems are solved by dividing them into three subproblems: rule description, rule matching, and rule selection.

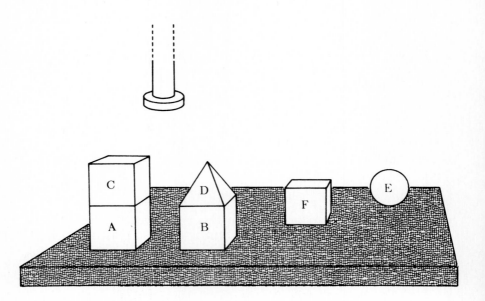

Figure 2-13. MOVER is a procedure for planning motion sequences in the blocks world, a world of bricks, pyramids, balls, and a robot manipulator.

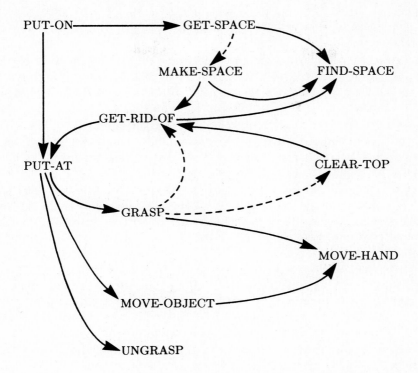

Figure 2-14. A set of specialists for moving blocks. Solid lines indicate help requests that are always made; dashed lines indicate requests that are occasionally made.

Figure 2-14 shows how the specialists fit together. Now let us look at a simple scenario to see how the specialists work together. Imagine that there is a request to put block A on block B, given the situation shown in figure 2-13. Plainly, the following sequence suffices:

Grasp D.

Move D to some location on the table.

Ungrasp D.

Grasp C.

Move C to some location on the table.

Ungrasp C.

Grasp A.

Move A to some location on B.

Ungrasp A.

The question is, How can MOVER find the appropriate sequence. Here is the answer:

First, PUT-ON asks GET-SPACE for some coordinates for A on top of B. GET-SPACE tries FIND-SPACE, but FIND-SPACE gives up because D is in the way. GET-SPACE then appeals to MAKE-SPACE, hoping for a better answer.

MAKE-SPACE asks GET-RID-OF to help by getting rid of D. GET-RID-OF obliges by finding a place for D on the table, using FIND-SPACE, and by moving D to that place using PUT-AT. Let us skip the details of how PUT-AT manages to get D to its new place.

With D gone, MAKE-SPACE, using FIND-SPACE, now finds a place for A to go on top of B. Recall that MAKE-SPACE was asked to do this by GET-SPACE because PUT-ON has the duty of putting A on B. PUT-ON can proceed now, asking PUT-AT to put A at the place just now found on top of B.

PUT-AT, sensibly enough, asks GRASP to grasp A. GRASP wants to use MOVE-HAND immediately to get to A, but GRASP realizes that it cannot grasp A because C is in the way. GRASP asks CLEAR-TOP for help. CLEAR-TOP, in turn, asks GET-RID-OF for help, whereupon GET-RID-OF arranges for C to go on the table using PUT-AT.

Note that PUT-AT, at work placing A on B, eventually produces a new job for PUT-AT itself, this time to put C on the table. When a procedure uses itself, the procedure is said to *recurse*. Systems in which procedures use themselves are said to be *recursive*.

With A cleared, CLEAR-TOP is finished. But if there were many blocks on top of A, not just one, CLEAR-TOP would appeal to GET-RID-OF many times, not just once.

Now GRASP can do its job. Once the hand is in the correct position and A is grasped, PUT-AT asks MOVE-OBJECT to move A to the place previously found on top of B. MOVE-OBJECT does this, uneventfully, with a request to MOVE-HAND. Finally, PUT-AT asks UNGRASP to let A go, which again happens, uneventfully.

Goals and Subgoals Form a Tree

The scenario was a bit hard to follow because one specialist made goals for another to achieve, which in turn made goals for another to achieve, and so on for several levels.

The multilevel goal tree in figure 2-15 illustrates what happened. Clearing the top of A is shown as an immediate subgoal of grasping A. Clearing the top of A is also a subgoal of putting A at a place on top of B, but not an immediate subgoal.

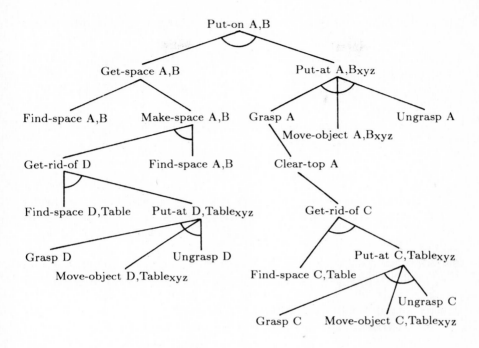

Figure 2-15. A goal tree. Branches joined by arcs are under AND nodes; other branches are under OR nodes.

Note that some goals are satisfied only when all of their immediate subgoals are satisfied. The nodes corresponding to these goals are called AND *nodes*, and they are marked by placing arcs on their branches.

All other goals are satisfied when any of their immediate subgoals are satisfied. The nodes corresponding to these goals are called OR *nodes*, and they remain unmarked. For example, it is possible to find a place with either FIND-SPACE or with MAKE-SPACE, so when FIND-SPACE succeeds, there is no need to use MAKE-SPACE.

Since goal trees are always mixtures of AND nodes and OR nodes, they are often called AND/OR *trees*.

When enough subgoals are achieved to achieve the supergoal at the top of an AND/OR tree, the tree is said to be *satisfied*. To be more precise, of course, we need to lay out a set of testing procedures in detail.

Here are two of the necessary procedures; one tests a single AND node, and the other, a single OR node:

To determine if an AND node is satisfied:
1   Form a queue of the AND node's child nodes.
2   Use AND/OR on the AND node's child nodes until:
   2a   AND/OR finds a child node that is not satisfied. Announce that the parent node is not satisfied.
   2b   AND/OR determines that all of the child nodes are satisfied. Announce that the parent node is satisfied.

To determine if an OR node is satisfied:
1   Form a queue of the OR node's child nodes.
2   Use AND/OR on the OR node's child nodes until:
   2a   AND/OR finds a child node that is satisfied. Announce that the parent node is satisfied.
   2b   AND/OR determines that none of the child nodes are satisfied. Announce that the parent node is not satisfied.

Both use a procedure named AND/OR, a procedure that merely channels action back to the AND and the OR procedures:

To determine if an AND/OR node is satisfied:
1   Determine if the node is satisfied without recourse to subgoals. If so, announce that the node is satisfied. Otherwise determine if the node is an AND node or an OR node, and then:
   1a   If the node is an AND node, use the AND procedure to determine if the node is satisfied.
   1b   If the node is an OR node, use the OR procedure to determine if the node is satisfied.

With AND/OR in hand, it is a simple matter to test an entire AND/OR tree, for we merely use AND/OR on the root node, permitting the various procedures to call upon one another, as necessary, to work their way down the tree.

AND/OR Trees Enable Introspective Question Answering

MOVER is able to build illuminating AND/OR trees because the specialists and their names have a tight correspondence to identifiable goals. Indeed, MOVER's AND/OR trees are so illuminating, they can be used to answer questions about *how* and *why* things have been done, giving MOVER a certain talent for introspection into its own behavior.

Suppose, for example, that we have put A on B, moving other objects according to the illustrative scenario, producing the goal tree shown in figure 2-15.

Further suppose that someone asks, How did you clear the top of A? Plainly, a reasonable answer is, By getting rid of C. On the other hand, suppose the question is, Why did you clear the top of A? Then a reasonable answer is, In order to grasp A.

These examples illustrate general strategies. To deal with *how* questions, identify the goal involved in the AND/OR tree and report the immediate *subgoals*. To deal with *why* questions, identify the goal and report the immediate *supergoal*.

PROBLEM SOLVING AND UNDERSTANDING KNOWLEDGE

From the examples in this chapter, it is clear that basic questions must be answered before any problem solver can be built. Here are some of those basic questions:

What Kind of Knowledge Is Involved?

Does a task require specialized knowledge, or does it succumb to broadly applicable ideas? If broadly applicable ideas work, what are they? What are the most powerful ideas anyway?

How Should the Knowledge Be Represented?

Some knowledge requires embedding in a collection of procedures. Other knowledge meshes well with the features of sophisticated knowledge-representation languages. Still other knowledge is best captured by using formal logic. There are many possibilities.

How Much Knowledge Is Required?

After learning what kind of knowledge is involved in a task, the next question is, How much? Are there forty facts or four hundred or four thousand? Do a dozen basic methods cover most cases? The tendency is to overestimate grossly. There is a one-two-three-infinity phenomenon; for after we see that a task is reasonably complicated, we suppose that it is unimaginably complicated. But little knowledge is required to do many tasks with human-level competence. For such tasks, at least, infinity is small.

One reason for asking about quantity is the demand for sensible resource allocation among the various chores required. Another is that knowing the size of a problem builds courage, for even if the size is large, knowing bad news is better than suspecting even worse news.

What Exactly Is the Knowledge Needed?

Ultimately, of course, we want the knowledge. In analogy-problem analysis, we need a theory of description and matching, and in blocks-moving, we need some procedures for dealing with goals and subgoals. Much of learning a subject is collecting such knowledge. If we are to do electromagnetic theory, we want Maxwell's equations and a geometry specialist; and for genetics, we want Mendel's laws and methods for computing combinations.

SUMMARY

- Particular procedures are worth studying in detail because they demonstrate general principles or because they serve as generalized metaphors that simplify the description and understanding of new problems.

- Good representations are essential to dealing with such diverse problems as understanding geometric analogies and moving blocks. With adequate representational power, both tasks are simple; without such power, approaching either invites foolish, ad hoc thinking.

- Good representations have a number of qualities. In particular, good representations make the right things explicit and expose natural constraints.

- For solving geometric-analogy problems, relations between subfigures and subfigure movements constitute a suitable representation.

- Solving geometric-analogy problems requires description matching; description matching is required to make rules and matching is required to compare rules.

- One way to organize a problem solver is to create a collection of specialists, each of which works on one specific kind of goal.

- A goal tree is a picture of how subgoals and supergoals fit together. Goal trees are often called AND/OR trees.

- An AND/OR tree is a good representation for answering questions about how goals were achieved and why they were attempted.

- Building any intelligent system requires answering some basic questions about knowledge. Among these are: what kind of knowledge is involved; how should the knowledge be represented; how much knowledge is required; and what exactly is the knowledge needed.

REFERENCES

The ANALOGY procedure described in this chapter is based on work by Thomas Evans [1963, 1968]. For interesting work on similarity judgment, see Amos Tversky [1977].

The MOVER procedure is based on a tiny part of a system built by Terry Winograd [1971, 1972]. The main thrust of his work was natural language understanding, for the point was to show how a computer can be made to accept commands and questions expressed in English. For this early work, it was particularly important to confine the English interaction to a narrowly focused domain. Hence, the blocks world.

3

Exploiting
Natural Constraints

This chapter's primary purpose is to introduce the role of *orderly methodology* in Artificial Intelligence. You will learn that good methodology starts with the problem to be solved, stresses good representation, concentrates on constraint, emphasizes experiments, and avoids premature procedure design.

A secondary purpose of the chapter is to show that when a domain is well understood, it is often possible to describe the objects in the domain in a way that uncovers useful, interacting constraints. This is true, for example, in the domain of line-drawing analysis because *symbolic constraints* determine the *physical interpretations* of lines.

The line-drawing example provides the proper context for examining specific procedures for *constraint propagation*. Constraint-propagation procedures are popular, in part, because they achieve *global consistency* through *local computation*.

Line drawings require *symbolic constraint propagation*. Another kind of constraint propagation is *numeric constraint propagation in nets*, introduced through an example concerning the calculation of fiscal futures. The same sort of numeric constraint propagation has proved important for engineering tasks in which a change in one place can have far-reaching effects. The design of large integrated circuits is an example of such a task.

Still another kind of constraint propagation is *numeric constraint propagation in arrays*, introduced through an example in which an array of

Figure 3-1. Part of line-drawing analysis is to decide how each line in a drawing should be interpreted. Line drawings like this are easy for Waltz's procedure. Adapted from *The Psychology of Computer Vision*, edited by Patrick H. Winston, copyright 1975 by McGraw-Hill Book Company, New York. Used with permission of McGraw-Hill Book Company.

elevations is computed from scattered barometer readings. Numeric constraint propagation has established a strong presence in vision, contributing to successful procedures for stereo-based distance measurement and shading-based shape determination.

Constraint propagation is important in commonsense reasoning also, particularly in commonsense reasoning about complicated systems in which an innocuous change in one place can have far-reaching effects. In particular, with constraint propagation we can find compatible choices by *dependency-directed backtracking*. This idea is introduced through a scheduling example involving exercise, entertainment, and study time.

PROPAGATING SYMBOLIC CONSTRAINTS

We now concentrate on drawings of plane-faced objects, like the one in figure 3-1, in order to learn about symbolic constraint propagation. The main problem is to determine which lines are boundary lines that separate objects. We find that boundary, convex, concave, shadow, and crack lines come together at junctions in only a few ways. Then we see that this restriction on junction combinations determines the proper physical interpretation for each line in a drawing. Once correct line interpretations are known, it is easy to use known boundary lines to divide the drawing into objects. Along the way, we will see that some impossible drawings can be detected because there is no way to interpret all the lines consistently.

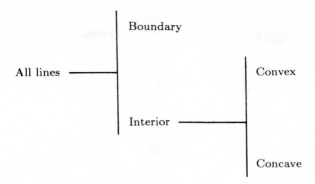

Figure 3-2. Drawings consist of boundary lines and interior lines. The interior lines may be concave or convex.

There Are Only Four Ways to Label a Line in the Three-faced-vertex World

To begin, think about crack-free polyhedra with lighting arranged to eliminate all shadows. The lines in drawings of this world represent various naturally occurring edge types. A simple partitioning of these lines is shown in figure 3-2.

First, all lines are divided into boundary lines and interior lines. *Boundary lines* are those for which one region hides the other. The two separated regions *do not* abut one another along the line. *Interior lines* are those for which the two separated regions *do abut* one another. The interior lines are those that are associated with concave edges and those that are associated with convex edges.

- For notational convenience, line interpretations are identified on drawings by *line labels*. Since these line labels will be used liberally, it is important to memorize them now:

  Convex lines have plus labels, +.

  Concave lines have minus labels, −.

  Boundary lines have arrow labels, >.

- Combinations of line labels surrounding junctions are called *junction labels*. We will see that natural constraints limit the number of junction labels that are physically realizable.

The direction of the arrow label placed on boundary lines is determined by noting which side of the line corresponds to a face of the object causing the boundary line. Imagine taking a stroll along the line keeping the boundary-line object on the right. The direction of walking is the direction of the arrow label.

It is easy to label each of the lines in figure 3-3 in a way that properly reflects our intuitions about the L-shaped solid shown. By so labeling a drawing, we exploit our understanding of the physical situation in order to arrive at interpretations for the lines. The key idea to pursue now is that of turning the process around, using knowledge about line interpretations to derive an understanding of the physical reality. To do this, we must understand the natural constraints imposed by the physical world.

The world's physical vertexes cause junctions in line drawings. These junctions can be categorized according to the number of lines coming together and the size of the angles between the lines. Figure 3-4 assigns mnemonic names to the common categories. Fortunately, the following simple assumptions shrink this list down to Forks, Arrows, Ls, and Ts:

• Limited line interpretations. There are no shadows or cracks.

• Three-faced vertexes. All vertexes are the intersection of exactly three object faces. The vertexes at the top of the Great Pyramids of Egypt are forbidden.

• General position. The choice of viewpoint is such that no junctions change type with small eye movement. The viewpoints in figure 3-5 are forbidden.

These assumptions are in force only temporarily; later, they will be relaxed. The reason these assumptions help is that they reduce the number of junction possibilities and hence the number of interpretations possible for junction-surrounding lines.

The three-faced-vertexes assumption means that all vertexes in space are places where exactly three faces meet, as on the corners of a cube. Everything in figure 3-6 involves three-faced vertexes exclusively. Note that only three types of junctions appear: Forks, Arrows, and Ls. Ts are also possible, since one object can be in front of another, but by restricting our inquiry to three-faced vertexes, we seem to avoid Peak, Psi, K, and X vertexes. Soon we shall see that this must be so.

Now, since there are four ways to label any given line, there must be $4^2 = 16$ ways to label an L. Similarly there must be $4^3 = 64$ ways to label any particular Fork, Arrow, or T. This gives an upper bound of 208 on the number of junction labels that possibly can occur in line drawings. Curiously, only 18 of these combinations occur naturally. It is not possible, for example, to find the junction labels of figure 3-7 in drawings of real polyhedral objects, given our assumptions.

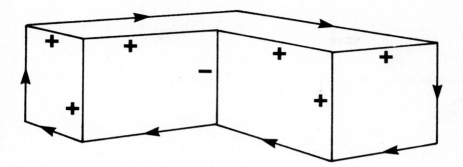

Figure 3-3. An L-shaped solid illustrates the three basic line interpretations: convex lines, marked with plus labels; concave lines, marked with minus labels; and boundary lines, marked with arrow labels.

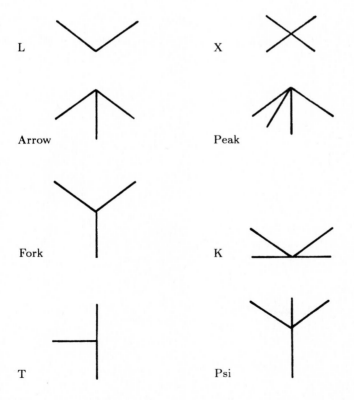

Figure 3-4. The common junctions. Most are excluded if vertexes are all three-faced vertexes and there are no shadows or cracks.

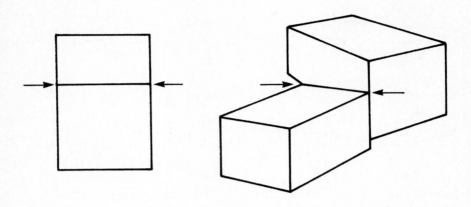

Figure 3-5. The criterion of general viewing position excludes both of these configurations because any perturbation of the viewing position changes the junctions indicated. The object on the left is a cube, seen straight on.

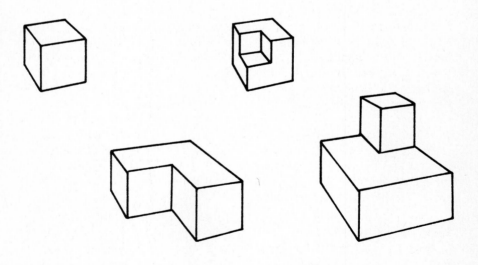

Figure 3-6. Some objects with exclusively three-faced vertexes.

Our next job is to collect the junction labels that are possible. There are only six for Ls, five for Forks, four for Ts, and three for Arrows. Having them, analyzing line drawings is like working easy jigsaw puzzles.

There Are Only 18 Ways To Label a Three-faced Junction

We proceed to look at every possible three-faced physical vertex from every possible direction in order to catalog all ways in which line labels can be placed around drawing junctions. This sounds crazy and horrifying. How could it be possible to handle all the alternatives? Forbidding all but general viewing positions provides part of the answer. Assuming that line drawings contain only three-faced vertexes provides the rest. The three faces of any three-faced vertex define three intersecting planes, and three intersecting planes divide space into eight compartments as in figure 3-8. An object forming a vertex plainly must occupy one or more of the eight compartments, or octants, so formed. The junction label says how.

Thus we can make a complete dictionary of all junction possibilities by a two-step process: consider all ways of filling up eight octants with object material, and then view each of the resulting vertexes from the unfilled octants.

Of course, if no octants are filled or if all are, then there is no vertex and consequently nothing to consider. But suppose seven of the eight are filled, as in figure 3-9a. Evidently, the seven-octant situation validates a Fork junction label in which each of the three lines involved bears a minus label. Note that the only junction of interest in the drawing is the one in the center. The surrounding drawing is only a visual aid to understanding how the seven filled octants produce a single drawing junction. Note further that since seven octants are filled, there can be only one octant from which to look at the vertex. The junction type seen is a Fork no matter what particular position is taken within the viewing octant. Fortunately, invariance within a viewing octant holds in general. The junction type does not change as the viewpoint moves within one viewing octant, even though the angles between the lines do vary considerably.

So far, the dictionary of possible junction labels has but one entry, a Fork. If only one octant is filled, there are new entries. One new entry is illustrated in figure 3-9b, again with the junction of interest surrounded by a drawing that provides a visual aid to understanding what the filled octant does to space. From one point of view, the vertex appears as a Fork junction with each line labeled with a plus. But since only one octant is filled, there must be seven from which to look, and so far we have only the junction label derived from the octant diagonally opposite the stuff of the object.

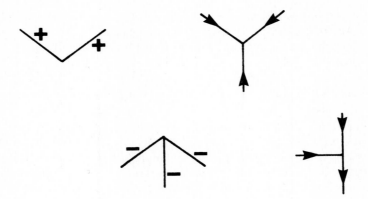

Figure 3-7. Some junction labels not found in drawings of polyhedra with three-faced vertexes.

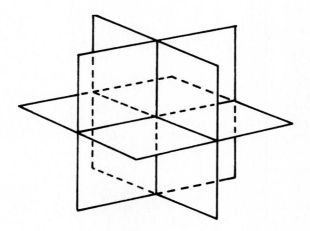

Figure 3-8. The three faces of a three-faced vertex divide space into eight octants. Here the planes meet at right angles. They need not.

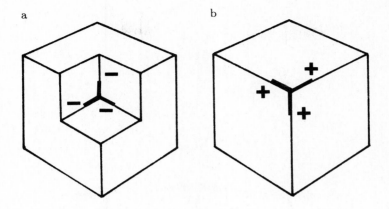

Figure 3-9. Junctions seen when seven octants are filled or when one is. In part *a*, the three concave lines are seen no matter where the viewer stands within the one available viewing octant. In *b*, the view from one octant is such that there is a Fork surrounded by convex labels. Standing in any of the six other octants gives different results.

Consequently, positions must be taken in the six other octants. Three of these are the positions occupied by the stick figures in figure 3-10. As shown in figure 3-11, for two of the three remaining octants, we put two stick figures on stilts to boost them up over the plane defined by the top of the cube. The final viewpoint is defined by the stick figure on top. All six stick-figure views provide only two new junction labels, since three of the views produce one kind of arrow label and the other three produce one kind of L. Actually, this was to be expected from the symmetry of the situation.

Now consider the situations with two, four, or six octants filled. All are excluded by the initial three-faced presumption. Suppose, for example, that two octants are to be filled. If the two are adjacent, then the edges between them would be cracks, there would be four object faces at the central vertex, and the vertex would not be three-faced. If the two filled octants are not adjacent, then they would meet either along an edge or at a common point. Either way, there would be more than three faces at the central vertex. Similar arguments exclude the four- and six-octant cases, leaving only the three- and five-octant cases to be considered.

For three octants, each of the five viewing octants provides a unique junction label shown in figure 3-12. Of course, one of the viewing octants produces the view shown, which yields an Arrow. In one of the other octants, the vertex looks like a Fork, and in each of the other three remaining, an L. Each of the L labels observed is unique.

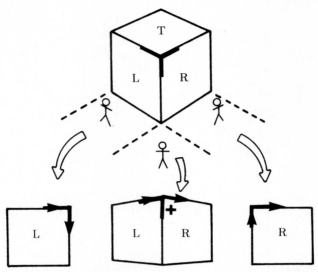

Figure 3-10. Stick figures help to show what a one-octant vertex looks like from various viewpoints. Because of symmetry, the seven viewing octants yield only three different labels. These three viewpoints yield one L and one Arrow.

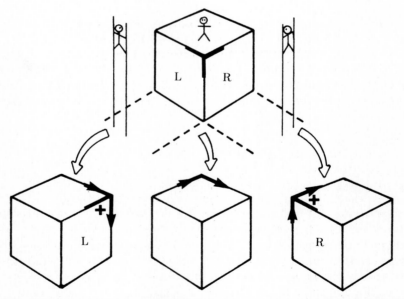

Figure 3-11. Stick figures help to show what a one-octant vertex looks like from various viewpoints. Because of symmetry, the seven viewing octants yield only three different labels. These three viewpoints yield one L, seen before in figure 3-10, and one Arrow, also seen before.

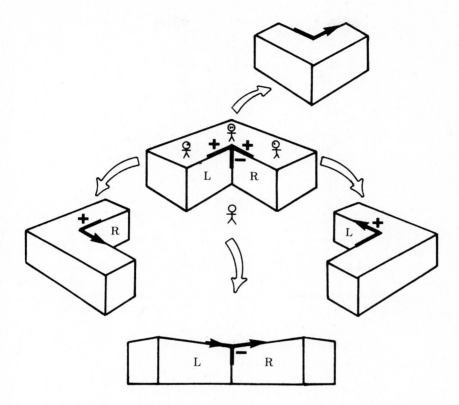

Figure 3-12. If three octants are filled, the remaining five viewing octants each supply a junction label. There are three unique Ls, one Fork, and one Arrow.

Adding the new Fork label requires some care because any of the three arms of a particular Fork may be one that should be labeled with the minus symbol. Thus the observed Fork configuration accounts for three of the 64 combinatorially possible ways to label Fork junctions.

Figure 3-13 illustrates what five filled octants do. There are three junction labels, each of which is different from the ones seen before.

Finally, since there are no cracks, there are only four ways to label Ts. All are consequences of partial occlusion. This brings the total number of ways to label a junction to 18, collected together in figure 3-14. Again, note that three of the ways to label a fork are rotationally symmetric.

We have now enumerated all possible ways in which three-faced vertexes can be formed, and we have viewed each such vertex from all possible directions. It must be that the 18 junction labels are all that there can be. Any label not on the list cannot correspond to any real three-faced vertex.

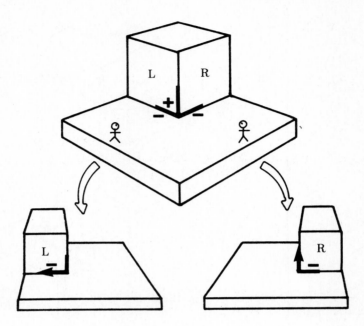

Figure 3-13. If five octants are filled, the three viewing octants supply two Ls and one Arrow.

Finding Correct Labels Is Part of Line-drawing Analysis

We now examine examples that show how to do analysis using knowledge about possible junction labels. When examining the examples, assume that each object is suspended in space. Consequently, each object's background border has only arrow labels.

Also note the following:

- There is only one kind of Arrow junction with arrow labels on its barbs. For such an Arrow, the shaft must be labeled with a plus.

- There is only one kind of Fork with any plus label. For this Fork, all the lines are forced to be labeled with plus labels.

To begin, consider a cube. Because we imagine that objects are suspended in space, the lines bordering on the background certainly can be labeled with boundary labels as in figure 3-15. Next, each of the Arrow's shafts is forced to be labeled with a plus since the barbs already have arrow labels. This leaves only the central Fork to investigate. Since all the Fork junction's lines already have plus labels assigned through previous considerations, it remains only to check that a Fork with three plus labels is in the list of natural junctions. It is.

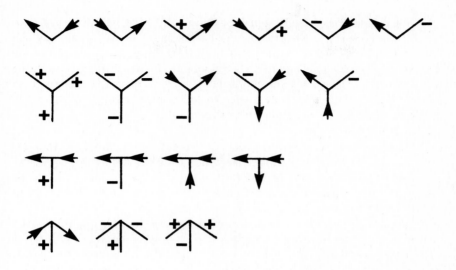

Figure 3-14. Eighteen junction configurations are possible. Were it not for natural constraints, there would be 208.

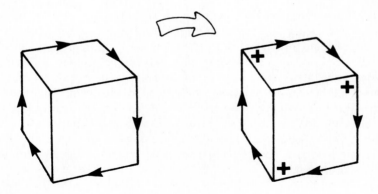

Figure 3-15. Line drawing labeling begins by placing arrow labels pointing clockwise on the border of the line drawing. Next, it is usually convenient to label the shafts of the Arrow junctions whose barbs lie on the border. In this example, a consistent labeling of all lines is possible, of course.

Now consider the slightly harder example in figure 3-16, a sort of two-tiered, double L-shaped figure. Again it is useful to begin by labeling the background boundary. Then it is easy to move toward the interior using the Arrows with arrow labels on their barbs, together with the fact that a plus on any Fork line forces two more plus labels. To move still farther requires returning to the label dictionary, using the other two Arrow junction labels. These force all of the remaining labels as shown.

Starting from interior junctions is more difficult. Unlike boundary lines, internal lines can get any label. In general, some ambiguity remains until analysis reaches a boundary, at which time the ambiguity is usually resolved. This seems true of human vision as well and may account for a class of visual reversal phenomena. Consider the example shown in figure 3-17. By covering up the sides and a little of the top, it is possible to see, for example, a series of ordinary steps, a series of steps hanging from the ceiling, or a row of thick saw blades. This may be because the interior junctions, separated by occlusion from the powerful boundary constraints, undergo reversals in which concave, minus labels, switch with convex, plus labels.

Thus symbolic constraint propagation offers a plausible explanation for one human information-processing phenomenon as well as a good way for a computer to analyze drawings. This suggests the following principle:

- For us to make a computer do something, it is often necessary to understand something about the world's constraints and regularities. These constraints and regularities make it possible for individuals to be intelligent, be they computer or human.

It is also interesting that the theory is useful not only in analyzing normal line drawings but also in identifying illegal line drawings, those that cannot correspond to real objects. The drawing in figure 3-18 is illegal, a conclusion that can be reached through a labeling argument. Proceeding as before, background lines, Arrow junctions with plus-marked barbs, and Fork junctions with plus labels can be exploited as shown. But now the indicated junction is illegally labeled. The Arrow on the end of one arm insists on a minus label for that arm, while the Fork on the other arm demands a plus label for that arm. But since there is no L with one minus arm and one plus arm, the drawing cannot be a view of a polyhedron with three-faced vertexes.

More Line and Junction Labels Are Needed
To Handle Shadows and Cracks

So far, drawings have been analyzed using an assumption that all objects are hanging suspended in front of a background. But the bottom lines of a cube represent concave edges, rather than boundaries, if the cube is resting

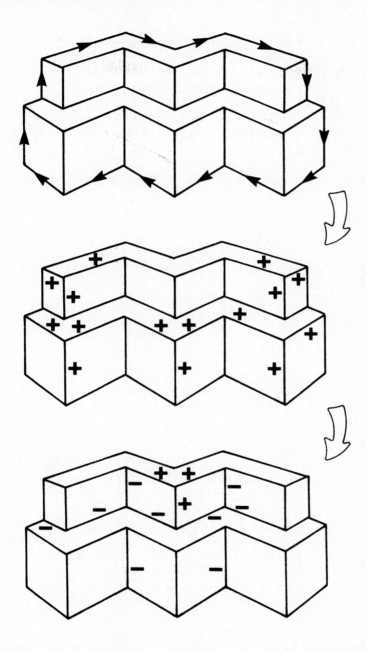

Figure 3-16. Labeling of this two-tiered figure begins with the background border. Next the shafts of the border Arrows begin a propagation of plus labels that continues through all Forks encountered. The rest of the job requires using the two other Arrow junctions.

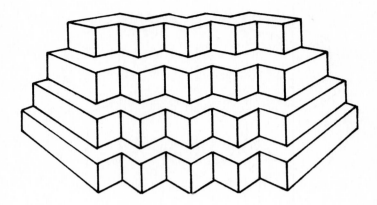

Figure 3-17. The background border contributes considerable constraint to line-drawing analysis efforts. By covering up the boundary of this object, the disconnected central portion is perceived in a variety of ways.

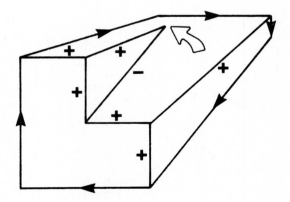

Figure 3-18. An impossible object. The indicated junction is not among the legal ones.

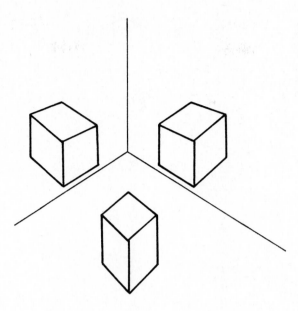

Figure 3-19. Without shadows, there are several ways to interpret a cube: it may be suspended or it may be attached to a floor or a wall by one of its hidden faces.

on a table. Such an interpretation is not unique, however, since the cube might just as well be stuck against a wall as figure 3-19 shows. Without an additional clue or assumption, several interpretations are equally plausible.

Note, however, that introducing shadows resolves the ambiguity. The block in the middle of figure 3-20 definitely seems supported by a horizontal surface while the ones to the left and right, although less familiar, seem attached vertically. Evidently, expanding labeling theory to include labels for shadows should add further constraint and simplify analysis.

Take note that the shadow labels introduced in figure 3-20 indicate a direction, just as boundary labels do: shadow labels are small arrows placed so that they point into the shadowed region.

Thus, the label dictionary, as it stands now, has six labels, two each for boundary and shadow edges, one each for concave and convex edges. It would be straightforward, but tedious, to derive the legal junction labels again for this expanded set of line labels. Having done the job, examples would illustrate that the description refinement increases the number of constraints, with consequent improvement in the speed of analysis. Rather than do this, we ask if there might be still further ways to divide up the line interpretations. There are. Two particularly good ways are described in a moment.

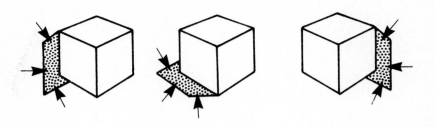

Figure 3-20. Shadows help determine where an object rests against others.

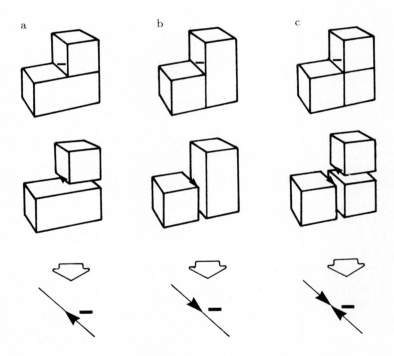

Figure 3-21. Concave edges often occur where two or three objects meet. It is useful to distinguish among the possibilities by combining the minus label with the one or two arrow labels that are seen when the objects are separated.

First, however, there is a caution about purpose. We are racing head-long toward big numbers because the set of natural junction.labels will grow considerably with the impending expansion of the set of line labels. There will be several thousand legal junction labels, not just 18 as before, and it is impossible to develop the list of them here or to attempt to simulate what a computer can do with them. Instead, we will inquire how the number of legal labels grows relative to the number of illegal labels, and we will look at experimental results to help answer questions about what improvements we get with the expanded label set and why we get those improvements.

Two line-interpretation refinements have been promised. The first recognizes that objects often come together. Consequently, the concave label can be split into subcategories indicating the number of objects involved and identifying which object is in front. Suppose a concave edge represents a place where two objects come together. Then imagine pulling the two apart slightly. The concave edge becomes a boundary edge with the label pointing in one of two possible directions, as shown in figure 3-21a and figure 3-21b. The two possibilities are indicated by compound symbols made up of the original minus label and the new arrow label. If, by chance, there are three objects, again a compound symbol is used, reflecting what is seen when the objects are pulled apart, as shown in figure 3-21c.

Cracks lying between two objects are treated analogously: each crack is labeled with a c together with an arrow label that indicates how the two objects involved fit together. With cracks between objects allowed, we have the diagram of possibilities shown in figure 3-22. There are now 11 ways any particular line may be labeled.

Illumination Increases Label Count and Tightens Constraint

Another way to refine the line descriptions incorporates single-illuminant lighting. Suppose that the state of illumination on any face falls into one of the three categories illustrated in figure 3-23: the face may be directly illuminated, it may be shadowed by another object, or it may be shadowed because it faces away from the light. The three possibilities are denoted by I, for directly illuminated, S for shadowed by another object, and SS for facing away from the light, that is, self-shadowed.

Line labels can carry knowledge about these illumination states in addition to basic information about edge type. If the illumination states and line interpretations were to combine freely, there would be $3^2 = 9$ illumination combinations for each of the 11 line interpretations, giving 99 total possibilities. But only about 50 of these are possible. There cannot be, for example, a combination in which both sides of a shadow line are illuminated. Similarly, there cannot be any change in the lighting state

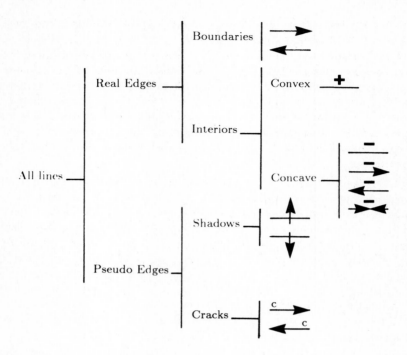

Figure 3-22. The 11 possible line interpretations and the corresponding labels.

across any sort of concave edge: such a situation would require an incredible coincidence in which a shadow line projects exactly onto the concave edge.

In summary, each of the line interpretation refinements contributes to a great expansion:

- Initially only basic lines were considered: boundary lines and interior concave and convex lines.

- These were augmented by including shadows.

- Concave lines were split up to reflect the number of objects coming together and how those objects obscure one another. Cracks between objects were introduced and handled analogously.

- Finally, line information was combined with illumination information. Just over 50 line labels emerge from this final expansion.

These changes make the set of natural junctions large, both for the original Fork, Arrow, L, and T types and for the new Peak, Psi, K, X, Multi, and Kk vertex types allowed by relaxing the three-faced-vertexes and general position constraints.[1] What is gained? What are the results of finding and using the new junction labels?

First consider how the set of natural junction possibilities compares to the unconstrained set. The following table gives the results for the original set of line labels:

Vertex Type	Number of Combinatorially Possible Junctions	Number of Physically Possible Junctions	Ratio (%)
L	16	6	37.5
Fork	64	5	7.8
T	64	4	6.2
Arrow	64	3	4.7

The percentages shown all indicate firm, but not extraordinary constraint. When the line categories are expanded, however, all numbers grow large and the constraint becomes incredible. The number of junction labels in the expanded set, known as *Waltz's set*, is large absolutely, but the number is small compared with what it might be:

Vertex Type	Approximate Number of Combinatorially Possible Junctions	Approximate Number of Physically Possible Junctions	Ratio (%)
L	2.5×10^3	80	3.2
Fork	1.2×10^5	500	4.0×10^{-1}
T	1.2×10^5	500	4.0×10^{-1}
Arrow	1.2×10^5	70	5.6×10^{-2}
Psi	6.2×10^6	300	4.8×10^{-3}
K	6.2×10^6	100	1.6×10^{-3}
X	6.2×10^6	100	1.6×10^{-3}
Multi	6.2×10^6	100	1.6×10^{-3}
Peak	6.2×10^6	10	1.6×10^{-4}
Kk	3.1×10^8	30	9.6×10^{-6}

In some cases, the legal fraction of junction labels is only about $10^{-5}\%$ of the total. To be sure, the total number of labels has increased to a size too large to use by hand, but still the constraints are so extreme that a computer using the large set can converge on a solution for a complicated drawing more quickly and less ambiguously than before.

---

[1] A Multi is a four-line junction with one angle between adjacent lines greater that 180°; a Kk is a four-line junction with one angle between adjacent lines equal to 180°.

Experiments Test Theories

One thing is sure: procedures based on Waltz's label set succeed on complicated line drawings. The line drawings in figure 3-24a, for example, are analyzed even though they exhibit holes, lighting direction coincidences, viewing-angle special cases, and vertexes that are not three-faced. The end result is a labeled line drawing, with each line interpretation indicating a particular edge type or at least restricting the edge type to a few alternatives.

From this, it is easy to divide the line drawing into objects. To see why, recall that Waltz's label set of eleven line interpretations contains seven boundary lines, of which two are ordinary boundary lines, two involve cracks, and three are concave. Boundary lines completely partition line drawings into their constituent objects. Tracing over the boundary lines in figure 3-24a brings the objects into relief, as shown in figure 3-24b.

Experiments using Waltz's label set show that the work required to do a line drawing grows in roughly linear proportion with the size of the line drawing. If the size of a line drawing is measured in terms of the number of objects in it, then this experimentally observed relation between computation and complexity suggests that the influence of particular lines and junctions tends to be confined to the locality in which they reside.

To see why, informally, suppose line drawings can be split somehow into areas of more or less fixed size in terms of the lines and junctions contained in each area. If the areas are such that constraint does not flow across their frontiers, then the total time required to analyze a line drawing is surely linearly proportional to the number of areas and hence linearly proportional to the number of junctions. There are areas and frontiers because the T junctions, common at object boundaries, have very little ability to transmit constraint: an obscuring boundary can lie in front of any kind of edge.

Waltz's Procedure Propagates Label Constraints through Junctions

Now we concentrate on *Waltz's procedure*, a powerful procedure for propagating symbolic constraints. To see how the Waltz procedure works, we first consider the drawing-labeling problem abstractly, in figure 3-25, without getting into the details of the actual labels. Think of keeping piles of label possibilities for each junction. These piles are created when a junction is visited for the first time, and they are reexamined each time an adjacent junction pile is altered.

In the illustration, Fork junction A is the first junction visited, so we pile on A all of the Fork label possibilities from the junction dictionary, as shown in figure 3-25a.

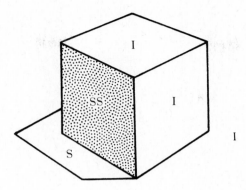

Figure 3-23. Illumination information often provides useful constraint. If there is a single light source, it is convenient to recognize three surface categories: directly illuminated, I; shadowed by intervening objects, S; and self-shadowed by virtue of facing away from the light source, SS.

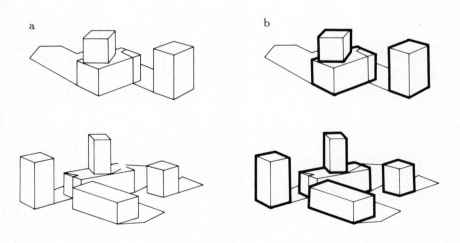

Figure 3-24. Extensions to the basic labeling scheme enable analysis of line drawings like those in part a with holes, lighting direction coincidences, vertex alignments, and vertexes with more than three faces. In b, the boundary lines have been highlighted. Adapted from *The Psychology of Computer Vision*, edited by Patrick H. Winston, copyright 1975 by McGraw-Hill Book Company, New York. Used with permission of McGraw-Hill Book Company.

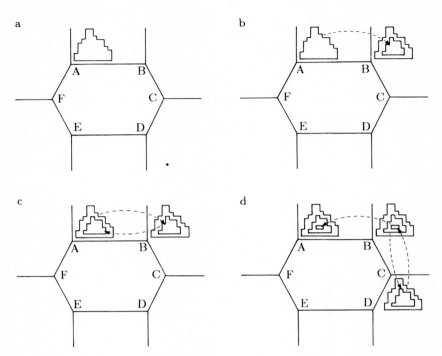

Figure 3-25. Label propagation in networks. In part *a*, an initial junction pile is placed at an arbitrary junction. In *b*, a junction pile placed at a neighboring junction is reduced so as to be compatible with something in every pile already present. In *c*, a newly placed junction pile, after reduction, influences a neighbor, reducing that neighbor. In *d*, propagation continues as long as reduction occurs at each junction pile encountered.

Suppose junction B is the next junction visited. We again pile on the Fork junction labels, but the total set is immediately reduced to those that are compatible with at least one junction in the piles of all neighboring junctions with piles. In figure 3-25b, junction A's label pile constrains what can be in junction B's pile.

Once a pile is created and reduced by neighboring piles, it is time to see if those same neighboring piles contain junction labels that are incompatible with everything at the newly installed pile. In figure 3-25c, the reduced pile at junction B constrains what can be in the pile at junction A.

Once set in motion, constraint propagation continues as long as the junction piles encountered continue to be reduced. In figure 3-25d, for example, after the junction pile at C is installed and reduced, the outward-moving part of the process starts, travels through junction pile B, and terminates at junction pile A.

If there were no change at B, the propagation initiated at C would have terminated at B. On the other hand, if there already were label piles at all junctions in the illustration, a pile reduction at C could initiate a propagation series that would travel all the way around the loop, reduce the piles at each junction, and ultimately lead to further reduction at C, the junction initiating the round-the-loop propagation. Looping cannot continue forever, however.

Now let us move from the abstract to the concrete. In figure 3-26, in which two Arrows, a Fork, and an L are buried in a drawing. Suppose, further, that these four junctions are lifted out of the drawing and analyzed using the plus, minus, and arrow line labels. The following happens:

If Arrow A is the first junction visited and none of its neighbors have been visited, then the first step is to bring in all of the possible Arrow junction labels, piling them on A.

Suppose B is the next junction investigated. There are six junction labels for Ls in the junction dictionary, but only two of these are compatible with the possibilities known for the adjacent Arrow, A. The other four are therefore rejected immediately.

Having placed labels at B, the next step is to investigate the neighboring junctions that were previously examined to see if anything can be thrown out because of the new labels at B. For this situation nothing happens since all three of the arrow labels at A are compatible with one of the two L labels at B.

Moving on to C, the dictionary supplies three entries as before, but for this Arrow, only one is compatible with the neighbors already analyzed. The other two are rejected immediately.

The last time the neighbor of a newly visited junction was revisited, nothing happened. This time, however, looking afresh at B reveals that only one of the two remaining junction labels is compatible with the adjacent Arrow, C. Having revised the list for B, the adjacent Arrow, A, must be revisited as well. Of the three original possibilities, only one survives.

Finally, looking at the Fork, D, the constraints from either of its analyzed neighbors force all but one of the five Fork entries in the junction dictionary to be rejected.

Thus the constraint is sufficient to interpret each line uniquely in this group of four junctions even though the group is lifted out of its surrounding context and separately analyzed.

The flow of constraints over a line drawing full of junctions can be dramatic when Waltz's label set is involved instead of the dwarfish set for the three-faced vertex world. Watching a film is the best way to appreciate what can happen. Lacking that, glancing at the line drawing in figure 3-27 and the trace below provides some feel for how the Waltz procedure works with Waltz's label set. It would be unbearably tedious to follow the trace in detail, but some overall points are obvious without that effort.

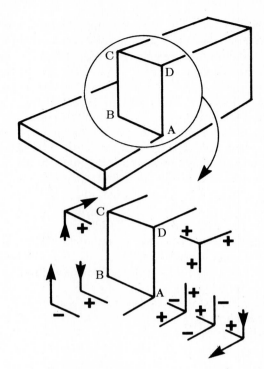

Figure 3-26. An example illustrating constraint propagation in drawings. Junction A is visited first, followed by B, C, and D. The Arrows placed at A limit the choices for Ls at B, which in turn limit the choices for Arrows at C. At C, automatic neighbor reexamination has an effect, eliminating all but one label at B and A. Finally, the C arrow label limits the Fork choices at D to the one shown.

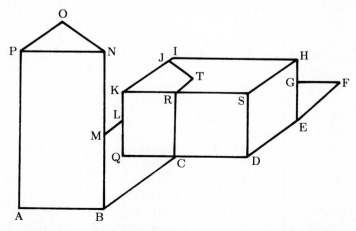

Figure 3-27. An example illustrating a labeling procedure at work.

In each of the 80 steps, the step number is followed by a letter denoting the junction involved. The letter is followed by the old number of junction labels in the pile and the new number in the pile.

Note, for example, that the junction-numbering convention indicates that boundary junctions are visited first. This exploits the extra constraint available at the boundary. Further inspection of the information shows that convergence is very rapid. After only two or three visits, most of the junctions have only one unique junction label associated with them. In step 74, for example, junction S starts with 1391 possibilities. The number is reduced to 5 by constraints coming in from one neighbor. Then constraints from another neighbor reduce the number to 1, leaving but a single interpretation.

1	A	-	→	123	31	C	20	→	2	61	P	5	→	1
2	A	123	→	76	32	B	14	→	2	62	O	2	→	1
3	B	-	→	79	33	A	20	→	2	63	Q	-	→	123
4	B	79	→	52	34	H	-	→	79	64	Q	123	→	5
5	A	76	→	32	35	H	79	→	1	65	Q	5	→	1
6	C	-	→	388	36	I	-	→	123	66	L	3	→	1
7	C	388	→	78	37	I	123	→	2	67	K	5	→	2
8	B	52	→	34	38	J	-	→	593	68	R	-	→	388
9	A	32	→	26	39	J	593	→	9	69	R	388	→	20
10	D	-	→	79	40	K	-	→	79	70	R	20	→	4
11	D	79	→	15	41	K	79	→	7	71	J	6	→	4
12	C	78	→	20	42	J	9	→	8	72	K	2	→	1
13	B	34	→	14	43	L	-	→	593	73	S	-	→	1391
14	A	26	→	20	44	L	593	→	12	74	S	1391	→	5
15	E	-	→	79	45	K	7	→	5	75	S	5	→	1
16	E	79	→	33	46	J	8	→	6	76	T	-	→	123
17	D	15	→	14	47	I	2	→	1	77	T	123	→	4
18	F	-	→	123	48	M	-	→	593	78	T	4	→	1
19	F	123	→	28	49	M	593	→	4	79	J	4	→	1
20	G	-	→	593	50	M	4	→	1	80	R	4	→	1
21	G	593	→	42	51	L	12	→	3					
22	G	42	→	18	52	B	2	→	1					
23	F	28	→	11	53	A	2	→	1					
24	E	33	→	7	54	C	2	→	1					
25	D	14	→	6	55	N	-	→	79					
26	F	11	→	2	56	N	79	→	1					
27	G	18	→	1	57	O	-	→	123					
28	E	7	→	1	58	O	123	→	2					
29	D	6	→	1	59	P	-	→	79					
30	F	2	→	1	60	P	79	→	5					

Here, in summary, is the procedure:

To find junction labels:

1   Form a queue consisting of all junctions.

2   Until the queue is empty:

   2.1   Remove the first element from the queue. Call it the current junction.

      2.1.1   If the current junction has never been visited, create a pile of junction labels for it consisting of all possible junction labels for the junction type involved. Note that a pile change has occurred.

      2.1.2   If any junction label from the current junction's pile is incompatible with all the junction labels in any neighboring junction's pile, eliminate that incompatible label from the current junction's pile. Note that a pile change has occurred.

   2.2   If a pile change has occurred, for each neighboring junction with a pile that is not on the queue, add that junction to the front of the queue.

PROPAGATING NUMERIC CONSTRAINTS

Now we turn our attention away from symbolic constraint propagation to numeric constraint propagation. There are two kinds of numeric constraint propagation to look at: propagation through nets and propagation through arrays.

Adder-multiplier Nets Propagate Constraints through Equations

Numeric constraints can be represented in a number of ways. One way, of course, is by a set of equations, like this one, which can be solved by substitution:

$$B1 = 1.1$$
$$B5 = 3000$$
$$C5 = B1 \times B5$$
$$D5 = B1 \times C5$$
$$D9 = D5 + D6 - D7$$

Alternatively, these same constraints can be represented by a net of constants, multipliers, and adders, as shown in figure 3-28.

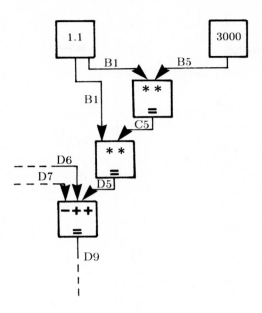

Figure 3-28. An adder-multiplier net representing a set of numeric constraints. Evidently, D5 = 3630.

Each multiplier constrains its terminals' values such that the value at the product terminal is the product of the values at the multiplicand terminals. Note that we talk of multiplicands and products, rather than inputs and outputs, because constraint can flow to any terminal. Knowing the two multiplicands of a three-terminal multiplier, we can compute the product; knowing the product and one multiplicand, we can compute the other multiplicand.

Similarly, adders constrain their terminals' values such that the value at the sum terminal is the sum of the numbers on positive addend terminals minus the sum of the numbers on negative addend terminals. As with multipliers, constraint can flow to any terminal.

To propagate numeric constraints through nets:

1 Until there are no adders or multipliers that have exactly one terminal with an unknown value:

    1.1 Select an adder or multiplier that has known values on all but one terminal.

    1.2 Find a value for that terminal.

For the example of figure 3-28, the first step is to compute a value for C5 since two of the three terminals on the top multiplier are associated with known values. Once C5 is computed, D5 can be computed too. At this point, however, we are stuck unless the values associated with D6 and D7 are already known.

Interestingly, simple nets of voltage sources, current sources, resistors, and transistors can be modeled as adder-multiplier nets. This means that our procedure for propagating numeric constraints in nets, with generalizations, can do some electronic circuit analysis. Importantly, the generalized procedure seems to work through circuits the way human engineers often do, producing a humanlike analysis.

Spreadsheets Propagate Numeric Constraints through Adder-multiplier Nets

The enormously successful electronic financial spreadsheet systems, heralded by VISICALC, are simple examples of numeric constraint propagation in nets. This is what the display of such a spreadsheet system looks like in set-up mode:

```
          A             B             C             D
1      Ratio X       1.1
2      Ratio Y       1.0
3
4                    1st year      2nd year      3rd year
5      Income X         3000       B1*B5         B1*C5
6      Income Y         5000       B2*B6         B2*C6
7      Expenses         9000       B7            C7
8                    --------      --------      --------
9                    B5+B6-B7      C5+C6-C7      D5+D6-D7
```

Each array location contains either a title, a number, or a formula. The title's purpose is to help the user understand what various things mean. The locations with numbers correspond to the constants in adder-multiplier nets. The formulas describe the constraints that tie things together and correspond to collections of adders and multipliers.

Consider the spreadsheet in *what-if* mode for a pair of pessimistic income growth predictions for two products, X and Y. The company is still losing money at the end of the third year:

	A	B	C	D
1	Ratio X	1.1		
2	Ratio Y	1.0		
3				
4		1st year	2nd year	3rd year
5	Income X	3000	3300	3630
6	Income Y	5000	5000	5000
7	Expenses	9000	9000	9000
8		--------	--------	--------
9		-1000	-700	-370

Finally, we have the same spreadsheet with more optimistic estimates for income-growth predictions. Evidently the enterprise is in trouble with more pessimistic estimates, but turns profitable with the optimistic ones:

	A	B	C	D
1	Ratio X	1.2		
2	Ratio Y	1.1		
3				
4		1st year	2nd year	3rd year
5	Income X	3000	3600	4320
6	Income Y	5000	5500	6050
7	Expenses	9000	9000	9000
8		--------	--------	--------
9		-1000	100	1370

For this example, the numeric constraint propagation procedure for adder-multiplier nets could be used. In fact, the net shown in figure 3-28 does some of the computation required by the spreadsheet in this example.

Smoothing Procedures Propagate Numeric Constraints through Data Arrays

We now turn our attention to arrays in which neighboring array elements influence each other by propagating numeric constraints. This kind of constraint propagation is particularly useful when looking at images to determine surface properties such as distance and direction.

When analyzing images, constraint propagation works because relevant surface properties change slowly almost everywhere. Surface distance and surface direction can change rapidly at edges, of course, but edge points represent only a relatively small number of the points in an image array. Properties that change slowly are said to obey a *smoothness constraint*.

In chapter 10, we look at actual applications involving smoothness constraints, but here we illustrate what is done by using an example in another, simpler domain. Suppose we want to make a digital terrain map, that is, a map giving the altitude at each intersection place on a rectangular

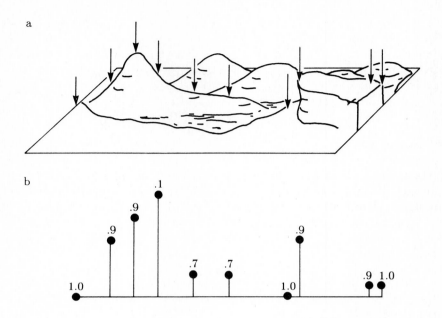

Figure 3-29. The problem in part *a* is to find good altitude estimates for each grid point, given only a few measurements taken using instruments of varying accuracy. The solution involves the propagation of numeric constraints in an array. To simplify explanation, the measurements used are along an east-west line as shown in part *b*, and the procedure described is one dimensional. Numbers beside each measured altitude indicate the degree of confidence in the measurement. Unmeasured altitudes are initially assumed to be 0 and have a confidence of 0. Absolutely certain measurements have a confidence of 1.

grid. We happen to have a collection of altitude readings obtained by sending people out with barometers to a few accessible places.

Assume the barometer readings, *b*, are sparse and noisy. Further assume that each instrument is identified with a confidence index, *c*. The confidence index ranges from 0, meaning worthless, to 1, meaning perfect.

Figure 3-29a shows some terrain for which a digital terrain map is desired, and figure 3-29b shows some measurements made along an east-west slice. Let us confine ourselves to this slice, for simplicity.

Now we can make two statements about the desired altitudes. One statement is that the estimate should be close to what the barometer says the altitude is, if measured. Another statement is that the altitude should be close to the average of the altitudes at neighboring points, a consequence of a smoothness constraint. From these two statements, it is but a small step to a formula that gives altitude, a_i, at point i, as a weighted sum of the barometer reading there, the b_i, and the average of the neighbors' altitudes. Using the confidence factor, c_i, and $1 - c_i$ as the weights, the formula slants the result toward the barometer measurement in proportion to the judged reliability of the measurement. To deal with places where there is no barometer reading, take b_i and c_i both to be 0.

$$a_i = c_i b_i + (1 - c_i) \frac{a_{i+1} + a_{i-1}}{2}$$

Since there is one equation like this for each value of the subscript i, it is time consuming to use the standard, sequential procedures for solving sets of linear equations. There is a way out, however. We can find an approximate solution by numeric constraint propagation. The procedure is simple and subject to fast, parallel computation.

The first step is to find initial altitude estimates, a_i^0, using only the b_i and c_i values (remember that both are taken to be 0 where no barometer readings exist).

$$a_i^0 = c_i b_i + (1 - c_i) \frac{b_{i+1} + b_{i-1}}{2}$$

Next, using the initial altitude estimates, we form a second, improved set of altitude estimates. We use the same formula as before, except that the neighbors' altitudes are those computed as initial estimates rather than the barometer readings. Remember that the subscript specifies place, and the superscript specifies the iteration number:

$$a_i^1 = c_i b_i + (1 - c_i) \frac{a_{i+1}^0 + a_{i-1}^0}{2}$$

In general, then, for the nth refinement, we have the following:

$$a_i^n = c_i b_i + (1 - c_i) \frac{a_{i+1}^{n-1} + a_{i-1}^{n-1}}{2}$$

This kind of numeric constraint is called a *relaxation formula*, a term inherited from mathematics. Procedures that use relaxation formulas are called *relaxation procedures*. Here is the general structure of a relaxation-based propagation procedure:

To propagate numeric constraints through arrays using relaxation:

1 Call the input array the current array.

2 Until all values are changing sufficiently slowly:

    2.1 For each element in the current array, calculate an element for a new array using the relaxation formula.

    2.2 Call the new array the current array.

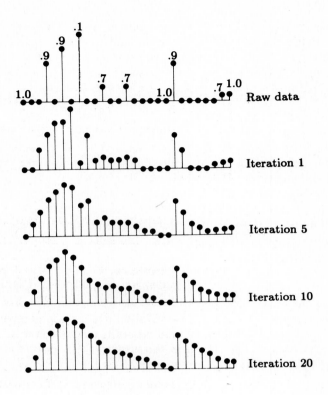

Figure 3-30. Raw altitude data and data processed by numeric constraint propagation. For each iteration, a new value is obtained for each point by computing a weighted average of the point's original raw-data value and the point's neighbors' values during the previous iteration.

Figure 3-30 shows altitude estimates at various stages. Note that the influence of the high, unreliable peak at $i = 8$ persists through the fifth iteration. By the tenth iteration, things have just about settled down. After the twentieth, changes are too small to see.

Altitude values converge to their asymptotic values slowly because our propagation procedure is too myopic. Constraint travels slowly when it travels in tiny steps. Using a larger separation between points helps, but then the result lacks fine detail. Happily, there are ways to combine the speed advantages of large separation with the fine-detail advantages of small separation.

Constraint Propagation Achieves Global Consistency through Local Computation

The overall objective of numeric constraint-propagation procedures is to find those values that are consistent everywhere with some stipulated constraints. Since propagation procedures operate independently on only a few things in small neighborhoods, propagation procedures are said to do *local computation*. When the constraints are satisfied everywhere, the consistency is said to be *global consistency*. Hence the point of numeric constraint propagation is to achieve *global consistency through local computation*.

The constraint-propagation approach to numeric problems has two major features:

- The procedure specifications are simple and transparent.

- The necessary computations can be done in parallel on fast, multiple-processor machines.

The constraint-propagation approach to symbolic problems has these features, too.

DEPENDENCY-DIRECTED BACKTRACKING

Having studied symbolic and numeric constraint propagation, we are almost prepared to study important mechanisms for decision making. To complete the preparation, an activity-planning problem is layed out, and choice boxes and limit boxes are introduced.

Imagine that each day of the week involves a particular choice. Some choices involve entertainment, others involve exercise, and still others, study. The choices are constrained by weekly objectives: there must be enough entertainment, enough exercise, enough study, and not too much money spent. To make things specific, let us assume these are options:

- Tuesday, Wednesday, and Thursday are study days. Study 2, 4, or 6 hours or not at all.

- Monday and Friday are exercise days. One choice is to take a walk, producing 5 exercise units; another is to jog 10 kilometers, producing 10 exercise units; another is to work out at a health club, producing 15 exercise units; and still another is to do nothing. The health club costs $20 in fees and taxi fares.

- Monday and Friday are also entertainment days. One choice is to go out to eat, costing $20, returning 2 pleasure units. Another is to read a library book, costing nothing, returning 1 pleasure unit. Another is to do nothing, costing nothing, returning 0 pleasure units.

- Assume that each week, to stay stimulated and healthy, there must be 6 hours of study, 2 units of pleasure, and 20 units of exercise. To keep the budget in line, expenses must be $30 or less.

All these facts can be expressed in the slightly generalized adder-multiplier net shown in figure 3-31. The daily choices are expressed in *choice boxes*. The weekly needs are expressed in *limit boxes*. If the value at the terminal of a limit box is outside the allowed range, the plan is unacceptable. Now suppose you plan the week as follows:

- On Monday, the weather is bad, so you go to the health club. This takes time, so you will not have time for entertainment.

- Study 2 hours on Tuesday.

- Study 2 more hours on Wednesday.

- Study 2 more hours on Thursday.

- On Friday, take a walk. Read.

Now, propagating these choices through the adder-multiplier net to the limit boxes, you see that you have met your study needs, for you have studied 6 hours. Exercise is also under control, for you have managed to get 20 exercise units. On the other hand, you are in trouble with entertainment. Worse yet, you cannot get enough by going out to dinner because that would leave you over your budget.

   Some choices must be altered to fix the plan. The question is, How can we find an acceptable plan quickly, preserving as much of the bad plan as possible?

Chronological Backtracking Wastes Time

One way to work on a faulty plan is to withdraw the most recently made choice, and its consequences, to select an alternative at that choice point, and to move ahead again. If all the alternatives at the last choice point have been explored already, then go farther back until an unexplored alternative is found.

   The whole process resembles what we do when working our way through a maze: we come to dead ends, we retreat, we go forward again. In chapter 4, this will be called *depth-first search*. That part of the procedure that responds to dead ends is called *chronological backtracking* to stress that everything is *undone* as we move back in *time*.

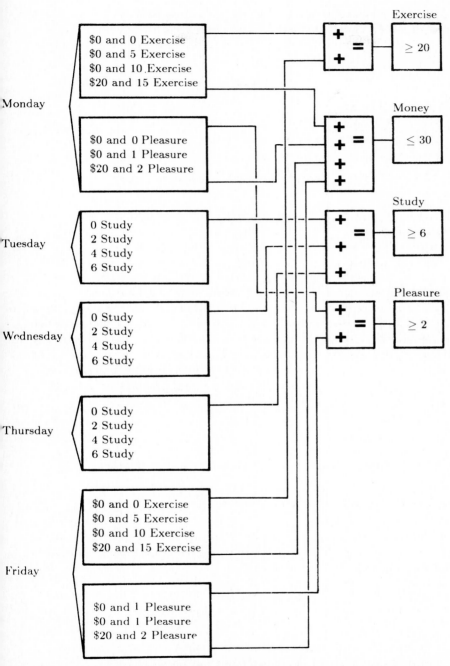

Figure 3-31. An adder-multiplier net expressing activity-planning constraints.

Chronological backtracking normally begins as soon as a dead end is detected, as stipulated in the following procedure description:

To backtrack chronologically:
1   Whenever a dead end is reached:
    1.1   Until encountering a choice point with an unexplored alternative, withdraw the most recently made choice.
    1.2   Undo all consequences of withdrawn choices.
    1.3   Move forward again, making choices.

The problem with chronological backtracking is clear: many of the withdrawn choices may have nothing whatever to do with the dead end. In the activity-planning example, chronological backtracking would begin on Friday, when the problem of meeting the entertainment objective is detected. After quickly withdrawing and trying both of the remaining entertainment choices, chronological backtracking works its way back in time, trying other exercise alternatives for Friday, and then going through all of Thursday's, Wednesday's, and Tuesday's study alternatives, none of which have anything to do with the entertainment problem that initiates the backup. Chronological backtracking must work its way through $4^3 = 64$ study combinations before reaching back to the choice point that matters.

Thus chronological backtracking can be inefficient. In real problems, the inefficiency can make a problem-solving system absurdly impractical.

Nonchronological Backtracking Exploits Dependencies

Another way to work on the faulty plan is to withdraw the choices *that matter*. To identify the choices that matter, we need only keep track of how propagation reaches from choice boxes to the dead-end announcing limit boxes. Whenever an adder or multiplier box fixes a value, we note that the value depends on the others.

Consider figure 3-32. The highlighted lines show that the entertainment-monitoring limit box complains because the choices made on Monday and Friday are incompatible. Only those choices are candidates for change.

The procedure for identifying relevant choices may be called *dependency-directed backtracking* to stress that the choices to be withdrawn are those on which the dead end *depends*.

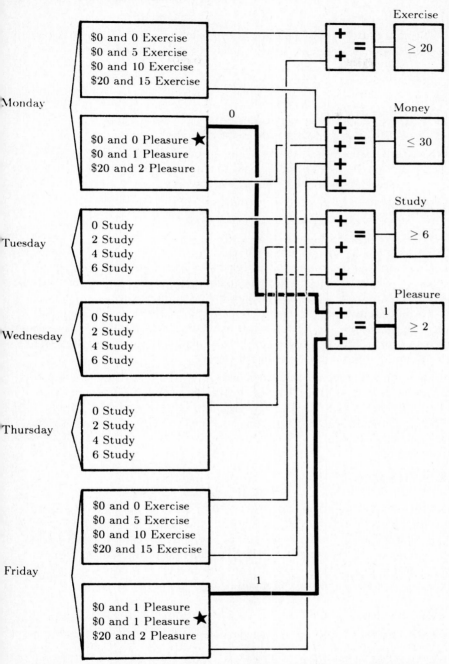

Figure 3-32. An adder-multiplier net enables nonchronological backtracking. The causes of the unmet objectives are identified by tracing back through adder boxes in this situation.

The procedure is also called *nonchronological backtracking* to stress that *time* does *not* determine which choices are to be withdrawn:

To backtrack nonchronologically:

1   Whenever a dead end is reached:

   1.1   Trace back through dependencies, identifying all those choices that contribute to the dead end.

   1.2   Until encountering a choice point with an unexplored alternative, among those that contribute to the dead end, withdraw a choice selected at random.

   1.3   Undo all consequences of withdrawn choices.

   1.4   Move forward again, making choices.

The advantage of nonchronological backtracking is clear: only the relevant choices are withdrawn. In the activity-planning example, none of the Tuesday, Wednesday, and Thursday choices are withdrawn before, during, or after the entertainment problem is fixed. Instead, Monday's entertainment choice, doing nothing, can be changed to reading, which yields 1 pleasure unit at no cost. Friday's choice can be reading again, satisfying both the pleasure and budget constraints for the week.

Thus nonchronological backtracking is an efficient way to find compatible choices as long as there is a way of tracing back over dependencies to find the relevant choice points. The idea will emerge again in chapter 7, where the constraint-propagating things are logical expressions rather than adder-multiplier boxes.

METHODOLOGY

Since this chapter describes many ideas that excite people, this is a good place for a note of caution. Experience demonstrates that many ideas in Artificial Intelligence become like sirens, seducing us toward misapplication. Consequently, we must take care to solve problems, not to look for ways of using ideas merely because they are fancy. The best way to take care is to obey the following commandments of good methodology:

- First *identify the problem.*

- Then *select or devise an appropriate representation.*

- Next *expose constraints or regularities.*

- Only now *create particular procedures.*

- Finally, *verify via experiments.*

In this chapter, we started with well-defined problems. In the first instance, it was to understand how it is possible to analyze line drawings.

Starting with the problem, we selected an appropriate representation. For line-drawing analysis, the appropriate representation involves symbols denoting the kinds of lines that appear in the blocks world.

The representation clearly exposes constraint, for we saw that the physical blocks world allows only a few line-label combinations to appear around junctions. Were there no constraint, the number of combinations would be beyond belief.

With the appropriate representation in hand, we devised a procedure for using the exposed constraint. The procedure involved propagating the label restrictions through junctions using a queue. Usually, and for this line-drawing-analysis example in particular, there are many possible procedures that can exploit the constraint.

Finally, we experimented, verifying the power of the constraints illustratively through hand simulations and elaborately through a trace of an implemented program.

Consequently, our progress mirrors the progression suggested by the commandments of good methodology. We are safe.

SUMMARY

- In drawing analysis, solid conclusions often come out of simple constraint analysis, without requiring sophisticated problem-solving and reasoning mechanisms.

- For the analysis of the three-faced vertexes world, only 18 junction labels need be remembered. For the analysis of more general line drawings, Waltz enumerated a few thousand. Although Waltz's set is large, it is still manageable.

- Waltz's procedure works by repeated reduction of the junction-label possibilities piled up at each junction. Reduction is done by eliminating junction labels that are incompatible with the junction labels of the neighbors. In principle, reduction propagation can continue through many junctions.

- Generally, the Waltz procedure produces exactly one interpretation for each line in a drawing. Only a few lines will have more than one interpretation, and then usually only two or three.

- Numbers can propagate through adder-multiplier nets just as junction-label constraints propagate through line drawings. Electronic spreadsheets provide good human interfaces for creating and exploiting such nets in financial analysis.

- Numbers also can propagate through regular arrays to enforce smoothness constraints. Relaxation is one way to do the propagation. Convergence will be slow when a small step size is used.

- Backtracking is necessary when choices lead to an impasse. Nonchronological backtracking prevents reconsideration of choices that are irrelevant with respect to the impasse.

- Good methodology demands identification of the problem first, followed by getting the representation right and exposing constraint or regularity. Only then is it right to devise particular procedures. Procedures enable verifying experiments.

REFERENCES

Early ad hoc methods for line-drawing analysis, like those developed by Adolfo Guzman [1968], stimulated much of the subsequent work on line-drawing analysis, including David Waltz's influential thesis [1972, 1975]. Waltz dealt not only with the labeling scheme explained here, but also with similar schemes involving line and surface directions. David Huffman [1971] and Maxwell Clowes [1971], working independently, devised labeling schemes directly antecedent to Waltz's. Their work was limited to the simplified domain of three-faced vertexes and no shadows. Later work by Alan K. Mackworth shows how constraints like Waltz's can be derived automatically [1973]. More recently, the work of Kokichi Sugihara has come to be regarded as a tour de force [1978].

For an interesting use of symbolic constraint propagation in quite another domain, see the work of Mark Stefik on a program that plans gene-cloning experiments in molecular genetics [1980]. For a domain-independent treatment of symbolic constraint propagation, see the work of Eugene C. Freuder [1978, 1982].

For references to how constraint propagation works in vision, see chapter 10.

Mechanisms for nonchronological backtracking were originally developed when constraint propagation was brought to the problem of understanding electronic circuits. Since the transistors in a circuit may be in any of four states, there are many combinations of choices, most of which are incompatible. To find the valid choice combinations by chronological backtracking is inconceivably tedious. This led Richard M. Stallman, in collaboration with Gerald J. Sussman, to invent nonchronological backtracking [1977].

4

Exploring
Alternatives

The purpose of this chapter is to understand how to deal with situations in which one choice leads to another, presenting us with a *search* problem. In contrast with the choices in chapter 3, the choices here are inherently ordered.

Search problems are ubiquitous, popping up everywhere Artificial Intelligence researchers and students go. In this chapter, the examples illustrate procedures used in route finding, recipe discovery, and game playing. In other chapters, there are examples involving problem reduction, rule-based problem solving, theorem proving, property inheritance, sentence analysis, obstacle avoidance, and learning.

Figure 4-1 is a roadmap for our trip through the space of possibilities. First, we study the simple, basic procedures. These are *depth-first search, hill climbing, breadth-first search, beam search,* and *best-first search.* They are used to find paths from starting positions to goal positions when the length of the discovered paths is not important.

Second, we study more complicated procedures that find shortest paths. These procedures are *the British Museum procedure, branch and bound, discrete dynamic programming,* and *A*.* They are used when the cost of traversing a path is of primary importance, as when a trip-planning system is mapping out a route for a salesman. All but the British Museum procedure aspire to do their work efficiently.

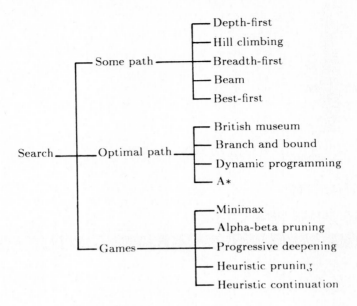

Figure 4-1. Search procedures. Many procedures address the problem of finding satisfactory paths. Others concentrate on the harder problem of finding optimal paths. Procedures for games differ from ordinary path-finding procedures, because games involve adversaries.

Third, we explore some special-case procedures that are appropriate when facing an adversary. These procedures are *minimax search, alpha-beta pruning, progressive deepening, heuristic pruning,* and *heuristic continuation.* They are common in programs that play board games, particularly checkers and chess.

In studying this chapter, you will develop a repertoire of search procedures. To use your repertoire well, you must develop skill in answering questions like the following ones:

- Which search procedures work, given the nature of the problem in hand?

- Which procedures are efficient?

- Which procedures are easy to implement?

- Is search the best thing to think about?

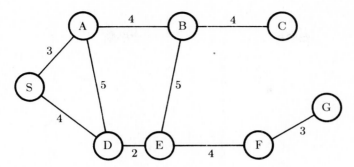

Figure 4-2. A basic search problem. A path is to be found from the start node, S, to the goal node, G. Search procedures explore nets like these, learning about connections and distances as they go.

FINDING PATHS

Suppose we want to find some path through a net of cities connected by highways, such as the net shown in figure 4-2. The path is to begin at city S, the starting point, and it is to end at city G, the final goal.

Finding a path involves two kinds of effort:

- First, there is the effort expended in *finding* either some path or the shortest path.

- And, second, there is the effort actually expended in *traversing* the path.

If it is necessary to go from S to G often, then it is worth a lot to find a really good path. On the other hand, if only *one* trip is required, and if the net is hard to force a way through, then it is proper to be content as soon as *some* path is found, even though better ones could be found with more work. For the moment we will consider only the problem of finding one path. We will return to finding optimal paths later.

The most obvious way to find a solution is to devise a bookkeeping scheme that allows orderly exploration of all possible paths. It is useful to note that the bookkeeping scheme must not allow itself to cycle in the net. It would be senseless to go through a sequence like S–A–D–S–A–D–... over and over again. With cyclic paths terminated, nets are equivalent to trees. The tree shown in figure 4-3 is made from the net in figure 4-2 by following each possible path outward from the net's starting point until it runs into a place already visited.

By convention, the places in a net or tree are called *nodes*. In nets, the connections between nodes are called *links*, and in trees, the connections are called *branches*. Also, it is common to talk about trees using terms borrowed from genealogy. Branches directly connect *parents* with *children*.

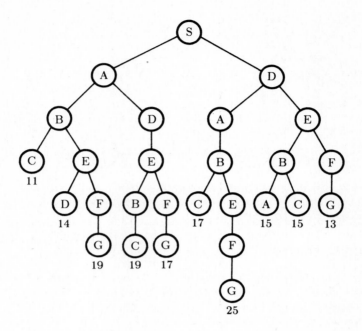

Figure 4-3. A tree made from a net. Nets are made into trees by tracing out all possible paths to the point where they reenter previously visited nodes. Node S is the root node. Node S is also a parent node, with its children being A and D, and an ancestor node, with all other nodes in the tree being descendants. The nodes with no children are the terminal nodes. The numbers beside the terminal nodes are accumulated distances.

The node at the top of a tree, the one with no parent, is called the *root node*. The nodes at the bottom, the ones with no children, are called *terminal nodes*. One node is the *ancestor* of another, a *descendant*, if there is a chain of branches between the two.

Finally, if the number of children is always the same for every node that has children, that number is said to be the *branching factor*.

Drawing in the children of a node is called *expanding* the node. Nodes are said to be *open* until they are expanded, whereupon they become *closed*.

If no node in a net is to be visited twice, there can be no more than n levels in the corresponding tree, where n is the total number of nodes, eight in the map traversal example. In the example, the goal is reached at the end of four distinct paths, each of which has a total path length given by adding up a few distances.

Depth-first Search Dives into the Search Tree

Given that one path is as good as any other, one no-fuss idea is to pick an alternative at every node visited and work forward from that alternative. Other alternatives at the same level are ignored completely as long as there is hope of reaching the destination using the original choice. This is the essence of *depth-first search.* Using a convention that the alternatives are tried in left-to-right order, the first action in working on the situation in figure 4-3 is a headlong dash to the bottom of the tree along the leftmost branches.

But since a headlong dash leads to terminal node C, without encountering G, the next step is to back up to the nearest ancestor node with an unexplored alternative. The nearest such node is B. The remaining alternative at B is better, bringing eventual success through E in spite of another dead end at D. Figure 4-4 shows the nodes encountered.

If the path through E had not worked out, then the procedure would move still further back up the tree seeking another viable decision point to move forward from. On reaching A, movement would go down again, reaching the destination through D.

Having seen an example of depth-first search, let us write out a procedure:

To conduct a depth-first search:
1 Form a one-element queue consisting of the root node.
2 Until the queue is empty or the goal has been reached, determine if the first element in the queue is the goal node.
   2a If the first element is the goal node, do nothing.
   2b If the first element is not the goal node, remove the first element from the queue and add the first element's children, if any, to the *front* of the queue.
3 If the goal node has been found, announce success; otherwise announce failure.

Be warned: depth-first search can be dangerous. Imagine a tree in which C is the gateway to a vast subnetwork instead of the end of a short dead-end path. Depth-first movement through such a tree would slip past the levels at which the goal node appears and waste incredible energy in exhaustively exploring parts of the tree lower down. For such trees, depth-first search is the worst possible approach.

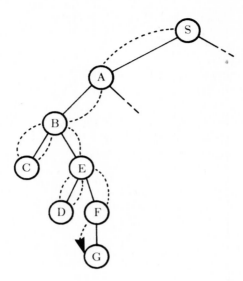

Figure 4-4. An example of depth-first search. One alternative is selected and pursued at each node until the goal is reached or a node is reached where further downward motion is impossible. When further downward motion is impossible, search is restarted at the nearest ancestor node with unexplored children.

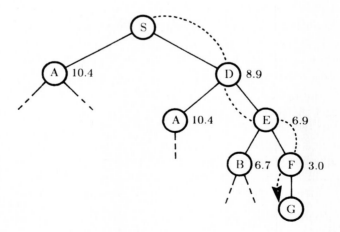

Figure 4-5. An example of hill climbing. Hill climbing is depth-first search with a heuristic measurement that orders choices as nodes are expanded. The numbers beside the nodes are straight-line distances to the goal node.

Quality Measurements Turn Depth-first Search into Hill Climbing

Search efficiency may improve spectacularly if there is some way of ordering choices so that the most promising are explored first. In many situations, simple measurements can be made to determine a reasonable ordering.

To move through a tree of paths using *hill climbing*, proceed as in depth-first search, but order the choices according to some heuristic measure of remaining distance. The better the heuristic measure is, the better hill climbing will be relative to ordinary depth-first search.

Straight-line, as-the-crow-flies distance is an example of a heuristic measure of remaining distance. Figure 4-5 shows what happens when hill climbing is used on the map-traversal problem using as-the-crow-flies distance to order choices.

From a procedural point of view, hill climbing differs from depth-first search in only one detail, the added, italicized part:

To hill climb:

1　Form a one-element queue consisting of the root node.

2　Until the queue is empty or the goal has been reached, determine if the first element in the queue is the goal node.

　2a　If the first element is the goal node, do nothing.

　2b　If the first element is not the goal node, remove the first element from the queue, *sort the first element's children, if any, by estimated remaining distance*, and add the first element's children, if any, to the front of the queue.

3　If the goal node has been found, announce success; otherwise announce failure.

A form of hill climbing is also used in parameter optimization. Here are some examples:

- On entering a room you find the temperature uncomfortable. Walking over to the thermostat, you find, to your surprise, that you cannot tell how to set it because the temperature markings have been obliterated.

- The picture on your TV set has deteriorated over a period of time. You must adjust the tuning, color, tint, and brightness controls for a better picture.

- You are halfway up a mountain when a dense fog comes in. You have no map or trail to follow but you do have a compass and a determination to get to the top.

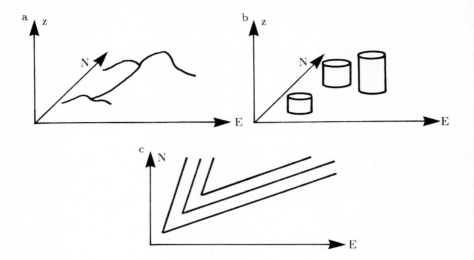

Figure 4-6. Hill climbing is a bad idea in difficult terrain. In *a*, foothills stop progress. In *b*, plains cause aimless wandering. In *c*, with the terrain described by a contour map, all ridge points look like peaks because all four east-west and north-south probe directions lead to lower quality measurements.

Each of these problems conforms to an abstraction in which there are adjustable parameters and a way of measuring the quality associated with any particular set of values for the parameters. Instead of an explicit goal, however, the procedure stops when a node is reached where all the node's children have lower quality measurements.

In the temperature example, the adjustable parameter is the thermostat setting, and the goodness is the resulting degree of comfort. In the TV example, there are various knobs, each of which interacts with the others to determine overall picture quality. And, of course, in the mountaineering example, position is adjustable, and movement is either up or down as position changes.

Thus, to move through a space of parameter values using parameter-oriented hill climbing, take one step in each of a fixed set of directions, move to the best alternative found, and repeat until reaching a point that is better than all of the surrounding points reached by one-step probes.

Although simple, parameter optimization via hill climbing suffers from various problems. The most severe of these problems are the foothill problem, the plateau problem, and the ridge problem:

- The *foothill problem* occurs whenever there are secondary peaks, as in figure 4-6a. The secondary peaks draw the hill-climbing procedure like magnets. An optimal point is found, but it is local, not global, and the user is left with a false sense of accomplishment.

- The *plateau problem* comes up when there is mostly a flat area separating the peaks. In extreme cases, the peaks may look like telephone poles sticking up in a football field, as in figure 4-6b. The local improvement operation breaks down completely. For all but a small number of positions, all standard-step probes leave the quality measurement unchanged.

- The *ridge problem* is more subtle and, consequently, more frustrating. Suppose we are standing on what seems like a knife edge running generally from northeast to southwest, as in figure 4-6c. A contour map shows that each standard step takes us down even though we are not at any sort of maximum, local or global. Increasing the number of directions used for the probing steps may help.

In general, the foothill, plateau, and ridge problems are greatly exacerbated as the number of parameter dimensions increases.

Breadth-first Search Pushes Uniformly into the Search Tree

When depth-first search and hill climbing are bad choices, *breadth-first search* may be useful. Breadth-first search looks for the goal node among all nodes at a given level before using the children of those nodes to push on. In the situation shown in figure 4-7, node D would be checked just after A. The procedure would then move on, level by level, discovering G on the fourth level down from the root level.

Like hill-climbing, a procedure for breadth-first search resembles the one for depth-first search, differing only in the place where new elements are added to the queue.

To conduct a breadth-first search:

1 Form a one-element queue consisting of the root node.

2 Until the queue is empty or the goal has been reached, determine if the first element in the queue is the goal node.

    2a If the first element is the goal node, do nothing.

    2b If the first element is not the goal node, remove the first element from the queue and add the first element's children, if any, to the *back* of the queue.

3 If the goal node has been found, announce success; otherwise announce failure.

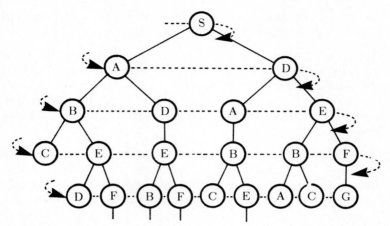

Figure 4-7. An example of breadth-first search. Downward motion proceeds level by level until the goal is reached.

Breadth-first search will work even in trees that are infinitely deep or effectively infinite. On the other hand, breadth-first search is wasteful when all paths lead to the destination node at more or less the same depth.

Beam Search Expands Several Partial Paths and Purges the Rest

Beam search is like breadth-first search because beam search progresses level by level. Unlike breadth-first search, however, beam search only moves downward from the best w nodes at each level. The other nodes are ignored.

Consequently, the number of nodes explored remains manageable, even if there is a great deal of branching and the search is deep. If beam search of width w is used in a tree with branching factor b, there will be only wb nodes under consideration at any depth, not the explosive number there would be if breadth-first search were used. Figure 4-8 illustrates how beam search would handle the map-traversal problem.

Best-first Search Expands the Best Partial Path

Recall that when forward motion is blocked, hill climbing demands forward motion from the last choice through the seemingly best child node. In *best-first search*, forward motion is from the best open node so far, no matter where it is in the partially developed tree. Best-first search works like a team of cooperating mountaineers seeking out the highest point in a mountain range: they maintain radio contact, move the highest subteam forward at all times, and divide subteams into sub-subteams at path junctions.

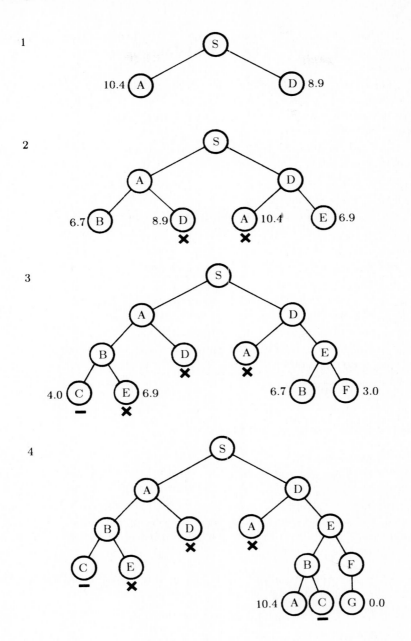

Figure 4-8. An example of beam search. Investigation spreads through the search tree level by level, but only the best w nodes are expanded, where $w = 2$ here. The numbers beside the nodes are straight-line distances to the goal node.

In the particular map-traversal problem we have been using, hill climbing and best-first search coincidentally explore the search tree in the same way.

The paths found by best-first search are more likely to be shorter than those found with other methods, because best-first search always moves forward from the node that seems closest to the goal node. Note that more likely does not mean certain, however.

Like hill climbing, the best-first search procedure requires sorting. This time, however, the entire queue must be sorted.

To conduct a best-first search:

1   Form a one-element queue consisting of the root node.
2   Until the queue is empty or the goal has been reached, determine if the first element in the queue is the goal node.
   2a   If the first element is the goal node, do nothing.
   2b   If the first element is not the goal node, remove the first element from the queue, add the first element's children, if any, to the queue, and *sort the entire queue by estimated remaining distance.*
3   If the goal node has been found, announce success; otherwise announce failure.

Search May Lead to Discovery

Finding physical paths and tuning parameters are only two applications for search ideas. More generally, the nodes in a search space may denote abstract entities, not just physical places or parameter settings.

Suppose, for example, that you are wild about cooking, particularly about creating your own omelet recipes. Deciding to be more systematic about your discovery procedure, you make a list of *recipe transformations* for varying existing recipes:

- Merge two similar recipes. That is, combine together half the amount of each of the ingredients from each recipe.

- Substitute something similar for a key ingredient.

- Double the amount of a flavoring.

- Halve the amount of a flavoring.

- Add a new flavoring.

- Eliminate a flavoring.

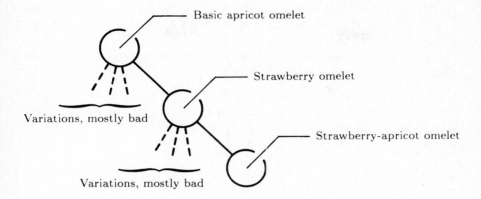

Figure 4-9. A search tree with recipe nodes. *Recipe transformations* build the tree; *interestingness heuristics* guide the best-first search to the better prospects.

Naturally, you speculate that most of the changes suggested by these recipe transformations will turn out awful, unworthy of further development. Consequently you need *interestingness heuristics* to help decide which recipes to continue to work on. Here are some interestingness heuristics:

- It tastes good.
- It looks good.
- Your friends eat a lot of it.
- Your friends ask for the recipe.

Interestingness heuristics can be used with hill climbing, with beam search, or with best-first search.

Figure 4-9 shows some of the search tree descending from a basic recipe for an apricot omelet, one similar to a particular favorite of the fictional detective and gourmand Nero Wolfe:

Apricot Omelet Recipe

1	ounce kümmel
1	cup apricot preserves
6	eggs
2	tablespoons cold water
1/2	teaspoon salt
2	teaspoons sugar
2	tablespoons unsalted butter
1	teaspoon powdered sugar

Using the substitution transformation on the apricot preserves enables the creation of many things, like apple, blueberry, cherry, orange, peach, pineapple, and strawberry omelets. Then, once we have more than one recipe, the merge transformation can be applied, producing, for example, an apricot-strawberry omelet.

Of course, to make a real recipe generator, we would have to be much better at generating plausible transformations, for we would waste too many eggs otherwise. This is consistent with the following general principles:

- More knowledge means less search.

- Search is seductive. While generally involved in many tasks, tuning a search procedure is rarely the right thing to do. More often the right thing is to improve understanding, thereby reducing the need for search.

The point of the omelet illustration, however, is that search is, nevertheless, one ingredient of the discovery procedure. The domain of discovery can be concrete, as in the world of cooking, or abstract, as in the world of mathematical concepts.

There Are Many Search Alternatives

We have seen that there are many ways for doing search, each with advantages, among them the following:

- Depth-first search is good when blind alleys do not get too deep.

- Breadth-first search is good when the number of alternatives at the choice points is not too large.

- Hill climbing is good when there is a natural measure of goal distance and a good choice is likely to be among the good-looking choices at each choice point.

- Beam search is good when there is a natural measure of goal distance and a good path is likely to be among the good-looking partial paths at all levels.

- Best-first search is good when there is a natural measure of goal distance and a good path may look bad at shallow levels.

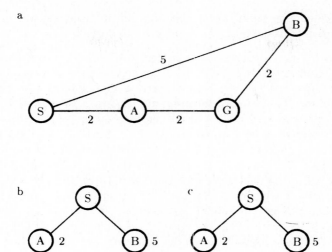

Figure 4-10. In branch-and-bound search, the node expanded is the one at the end of the shortest path leading to an open node. Expansion continues until there is a path reaching the goal that is of length equal to or shorter than all incomplete paths terminating at open nodes. A sample net is shown in *a*, along with partially developed search trees in *b* and *c*. The numbers beneath the nodes in the trees are accumulated distances. In *b*, node A might just as well be expanded, for even if a satisfactory path through B is found, there may be a shorter one through A. In *c*, however, it makes no sense to expand node B, because there is a complete path to the goal that is shorter than the path ending at B.

FINDING THE BEST PATH

In this section, we continue to explore the map-traversal problem, but now with attention to path length. In the end, we will bring together several distinct ideas to form the A* procedure.

The British Museum Procedure Looks Everywhere

One procedure for finding the shortest path through a net is to find all possible paths and to select the best from them. This plodding procedure, named in jest, is known as the *British Museum procedure*.

To find all possible paths, either a depth-first search or a breadth-first search will work, with one modification: search does not stop when the first path to the goal is found. If the breadth and depth of the tree are small, as in the map-traversal example, there are no problems.

Unfortunately, the size of search trees is often large, making any procedure for finding all possible paths extremely unpalatable. Suppose that instead of a few levels there is a moderately large number. Suppose further that the branching is completely uniform and that the number of alternative branches at each node is b. Then in the first level there will be b nodes. For each of these b nodes there will be b more nodes in the second level, or b^2. Continuing this leads to the conclusion that the number of nodes at depth d must be b^d. For even modest breadth and depth, the number of paths can be large: $b = 10$ and $d = 10$ yields $10^{10} =$ ten billion paths. Fortunately, there are strategies that enable optimal paths to be found without finding all possible paths first.

Branch-and-bound Search Expands the Least-cost Partial Path

One way to find optimal paths with less work is by using *branch-and-bound search*. The basic idea is simple. Suppose an optimal solution is desired for the net shown in figure 4-10a. Looking only at the first level, in figure 4-10b, the distance from S to node A is clearly less than the distance to B. Following A to the destination at the next level reveals that the total path length is 4, as shown in figure 4-10c. But this means there is no point in calculating the path length for the alternative path through node B since at B the incomplete path's length is already 5 and hence longer than the path for the known solution through A.

More generally, the branch-and-bound scheme works like this: During search there are many incomplete paths contending for further consideration. The shortest one is extended one level, creating as many new incomplete paths as there are branches. These new paths are then considered along with the remaining old ones, and again, the shortest is extended. This repeats until the destination is reached along some path. Since the shortest path was always chosen for extension, the path first reaching the destination is certain to be optimal.

There is a flaw in the explanation, as given. The last step in reaching the destination may be long enough to make the supposed solution longer than one or more incomplete paths. It might be that only a tiny step would extend one of the incomplete paths to the solution point. To be sure this is not so, a slightly better termination condition is needed. Instead of terminating when a path is found, terminate when the shortest incomplete path is longer than the shortest complete path.

Here, then, is the procedure with the proper terminating condition:

To conduct a branch-and-bound search:

1   Form a queue of partial paths. Let the initial queue consist
    of the zero-length, zero-step path from the root node to
    nowhere.
2   Until the queue is empty or the goal has been reached,
    determine if the first path in the queue reaches the goal
    node.

   2a   If the first path reaches the goal node, do nothing.

   2b   If the first path does not reach the goal node:

      2b1   Remove the first path from the queue.

      2b2   Form new paths from the removed path by ex-
           tending one step.

      2b3   Add the new paths to the queue.

      2b4   Sort the queue by cost accumulated so far, with
           least-cost paths in front.

3   If the goal node has been found, announce success; other-
    wise announce failure.

Now look again at the map-traversal problem and see how branch-and-bound works there. Figure 4-11 illustrates the exploration sequence. In the first step, A and D are identified as the children of the only active node, S. The partial path distance of A is 3 and that of D is 4; A therefore becomes the active node. Then B and D are generated from A with partial path distances of 7 and 8. Now the first encountered D, with a partial path distance of 4, becomes the active node, leading to the generation of partial paths to A and E. At this point, there are four partial paths, with the path S–D–E being the shortest.

After the seventh step, partial paths S–A–D–E and S–D–E–F are the shortest partial paths. Expanding S–A–D–E leads to partial paths terminating at B and F. Expanding S–D–E–F, along the right side of the tree, leads to the complete path S–D–E–F–G, with a total distance of 13. This is the shortest path, but to be absolutely sure, it is necessary to extend two partial paths, S–A–B–E, with a partial path distance of 12, and S–D–E–B, with a partial path distance of 11. There is no need to extend the partial path S–D–A–B, since its partial path distance of 13 is equal to that of the complete path. In this particular example, little work is avoided relative to exhaustive search, British Museum style.

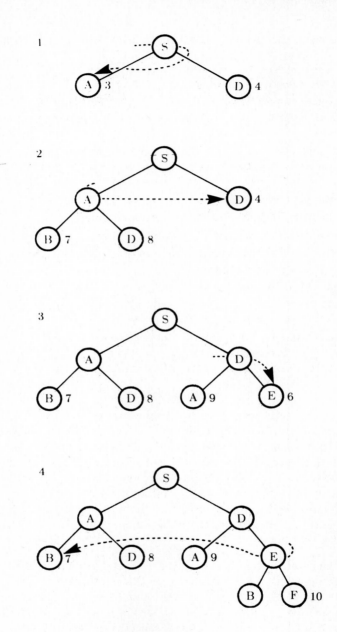

Figure 4-11. Branch-and-bound search determines that path S–D–E–F–G is optimal. The numbers beside the nodes are accumulated distances. Search stops when all partial paths to open nodes are as long as or longer than the complete path S–D–E–F–G.

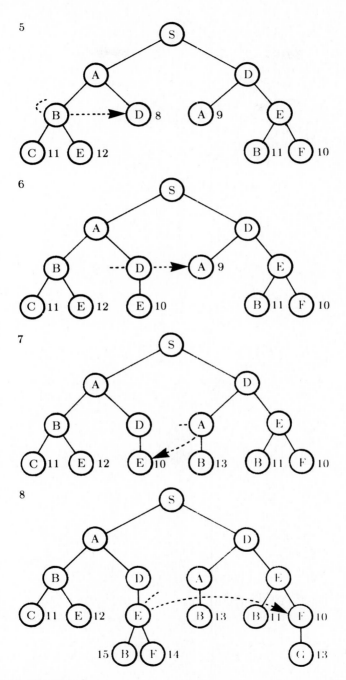

Figure 4-11. Continued.

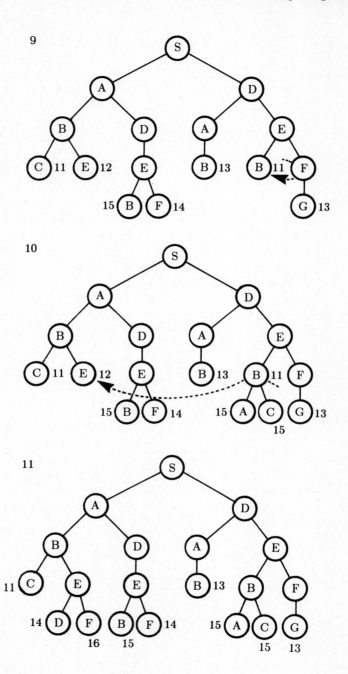

Figure 4-11. Continued.

Adding Underestimates Improves Efficiency

In some cases, branch-and-bound search can be improved greatly by using guesses about distances remaining as well as facts about distances already accumulated. After all, if a guess about distance remaining is good, then that guessed distance added to the definitely known distance already traversed should be a good estimate of total path length, e(total path length):

$$e(\text{total path length}) = d(\text{already traveled}) + e(\text{distance remaining})$$

where d(already traveled) is the known distance already traveled and where e(distance remaining) is an estimate of the distance remaining.

Surely it makes sense to work hardest on developing the path with the shortest estimated path length until the estimate changes upward enough to make some other path be the one with the shortest estimated path length. After all, if the guesses were perfect, this approach would keep us on the optimal path at all times.

In general, however, guesses are not perfect, and a bad overestimate somewhere along the true optimal path may cause us to wander off that optimal path permanently.

But note that *underestimates* cannot cause the right path to be overlooked. An underestimate of the distance remaining yields an underestimate of total path length, u(total path length):

$$u(\text{total path length}) = d(\text{already traveled}) + u(\text{distance remaining})$$

where d(already traveled) is the known distance already traveled and where u(distance remaining) is an underestimate of the distance remaining.

Now if a total path is found by extending the path with the smallest underestimate repeatedly, no further work need be done once all incomplete path distance estimates are longer than some complete path distance. This is true because the real distance along a completed path cannot be shorter than an underestimate of the distance. If all estimates of remaining distance can be guaranteed to be underestimates, there can be no bungle.

In traveling through nets of cities, the straight-line distance is guaranteed to be an underestimate. Figure 4-12 shows how straight-line distance helps. As before, A and D are generated from S. This time D is the node to search from, since D's lower-bound path distance is 12.9, which is better than that for A, 13.4.

Expanding D leads to partial path S–D–A, with a lower-bound distance estimate of 19.4, and to partial path S–D–E, with a lower-bound distance estimate of 12.9. S–D–E is therefore the partial path to extend. The result is a path to B with a distance estimate of 17.7 and one to F with 13.0.

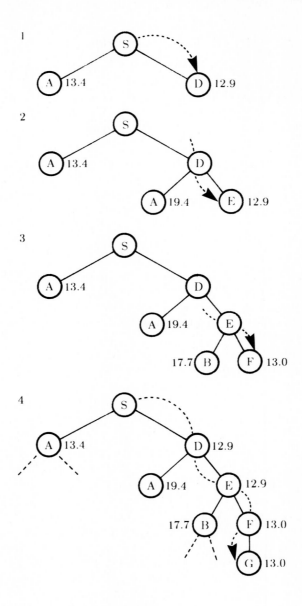

Figure 4-12. Branch-and-bound search augmented by underestimates determines that the path S–D–E–F–G is optimal. The numbers beside the nodes are accumulated distances plus underestimates of distances remaining. Underestimates quickly push up the lengths associated with bad paths. In this example, many fewer nodes are expanded than with branch-and-bound search operating without underestimates.

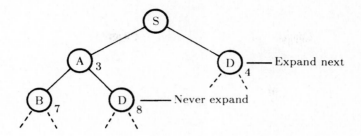

Figure 4-13. An illustration of the dynamic-programming principle. The numbers beside the nodes are accumulated distances. There is no point to expanding the instance of node D at the end of S–A–D because getting to the goal via the instance of D at the end of S–D is obviously better.

Expanding the partial path to F is the correct move since it is the partial path with the minimum lower-bound distance. This leads to a complete path, S–D–E–F–G, with a total distance of 13.0. No partial path has a lower-bound distance so low, so no further search is required.

In this particular example, a great deal of work is avoided. Here is the modified procedure:

To conduct a branch-and-bound search with underestimates:

1 Form a queue of partial paths. Let the initial queue consist of the zero-length, zero-step path from the root node to nowhere.

2 Until the queue is empty or the goal has been reached, determine if the first path in the queue reaches the goal node.

  2a   If the first path reaches the goal node, do nothing.

  2b   If the first path does not reach the goal node:

     2b1   Remove the first path from the queue.

     2b2   Form new paths from the removed path by extending one step.

     2b3   Add the new paths to the queue.

     2b4   Sort the queue by the *sum of* cost accumulated so far *and a lower-bound estimate of the cost remaining*, with least-cost paths in front.

3 If the goal node has been found, announce success; otherwise announce failure.

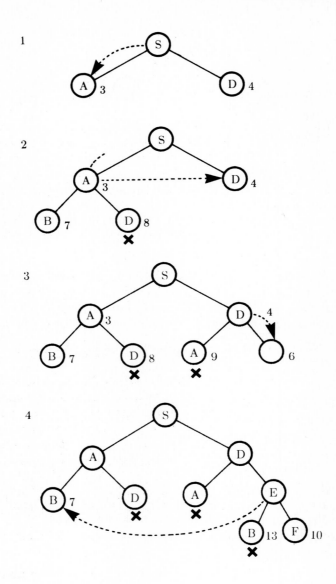

Figure 4-14. Branch-and-bound search, augmented by dynamic programming, determines that path S–D–E–F–G is optimal. The numbers beside the nodes are accumulated distances. Many nodes, those crossed out, are found to be redundant. Fewer nodes are expanded than with branch-and-bound search operating without dynamic programming.

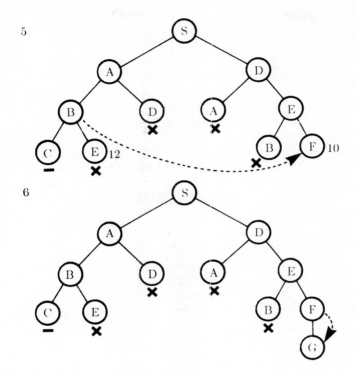

Figure 4-14. Continued.

Of course, the closer an underestimate is to the true distance, the better things will work, since if there is no difference at all, there is no chance of developing any false movement. At the other extreme, an underestimate may be so poor as to be hardly better than a guess of zero, which certainly must always be the ultimate underestimate of remaining distance. In fact, ignoring estimates of remaining distance altogether can be viewed as the special case in which the underestimate used is uniformly zero.

Discarding Redundant Paths Improves Efficiency

Now let us consider another way to improve on the basic branch-and-bound search. Look at figure 4-13. The root node, S, has been expanded, producing A and D. For the moment we use no underestimates for remaining path length. Since the path from S to A is shorter than the path from S to D, A has been expanded also, leaving three paths: S–A–B, S–A–D, and S–D.

Thus the path S–D will be the next path extended, since it is the partial path with the shortest length.

But what about the path S–A–D? Will it ever make sense to extend it? Clearly it will not. Since there is one path to D with length 4, it cannot make sense to work with another path to D with length 8. The path S–A–D should be forgotten forever; it cannot produce a winner.

This illustrates a general truth. Assume that the path from a starting point, S, to an intermediate point, I, does not influence the choice of paths for traveling from I to a goal point, G. Then the minimum distance from S to G through I is the sum of the minimum distance from S to I and the minimum distance from I to G. Consequently, the *dynamic-programming principle* holds that when looking for the best path from S to G, all paths from S to any intermediate node, I, other than the minimum-length path from S to I, can be ignored. Here is the procedure:

To conduct a branch-and-bound search with dynamic programming:

1   Form a queue of partial paths. Let the initial queue consist of the zero-length, zero-step path from the root node to nowhere.

2   Until the queue is empty or the goal has been reached, determine if the first path in the queue reaches the goal node.

   2a   If the first path reaches the goal node, do nothing.

   2b   If the first path does not reach the goal node:

      2b1   Remove the first path from the queue.

      2b2   Form new paths from the removed path by extending one step.

      2b3   Add the new paths to the queue.

      2b4   Sort the queue by cost accumulated so far, with least-cost paths in front.

      2b5   *If two or more paths reach a common node, delete all those paths except the one that reaches the common node with the minimum cost.*

3   If the goal node has been found, announce success; otherwise announce failure.

Figure 4-14 shows the effect of using the dynamic-programming principle, together with branch-and-bound search, on the map-traversal problem. Four paths are cut off quickly, leaving only the dead-end path to node C and the optimal path, S–D–E–F–G.

A* Is Improved Branch-and-bound Search

The *A* procedure* is branch-and-bound search, with an estimate of remaining distance, combined with the dynamic-programming principle. If the estimate of remaining distance is a lower bound on the actual distance, then A* produces optimal solutions. Generally, the estimate may be assumed to be a lower bound estimate, unless specifically stated otherwise, implying that A*'s solutions are normally optimal. Note the similarity between A* and branch-and-bound search with dynamic programming:

To do A* search with lower-bound estimates:

1   Form a queue of partial paths. Let the initial queue consist of the zero-length, zero-step path from the root node to nowhere.

2   Until the queue is empty or the goal has been reached, determine if the first path in the queue reaches the goal node.

   2a   If the first path reaches the goal node, do nothing.

   2b   If the first path does not reach the goal node:

      2b1   Remove the first path from the queue.

      2b2   Form new paths from the removed path by extending one step.

      2b3   Add the new paths to the queue.

      2b4   Sort the queue by the *sum of* cost accumulated so far *and a lower-bound estimate of the cost remaining*, with least-cost paths in front.

      2b5   *If two or more paths reach a common node, delete all those paths except for one that reaches the common node with the minimum cost.*

3   If the goal node has been found, announce success; otherwise announce failure.

There Are Many Optimal Search Alternatives

We have seen that there are many ways for searching for optimal paths, each with advantages, among them the following:

- The British Museum procedure is good when the search tree is small.
- Branch-and-bound search is good when the tree is big and bad paths turn distinctly bad quickly.
- Branch-and-bound search with a guess is good when there is a good lower-bound estimate of the distance remaining to the goal.
- Dynamic programming is good when many paths reach common nodes.
- The A* procedure is good when both branch-and-bound search with a guess and dynamic programming are good.

DEALING WITH ADVERSARIES

Another sort of search is done in playing games like checkers and chess. The nodes in a game tree naturally represent board configurations, and they are linked by way of branches that transform one situation into another, as figure 4-15 illustrates. Of course, there is a new twist in that the decisions are made by two people, acting as adversaries, each making a decision in turn.

The *ply* of a game tree is p if the tree has p levels, including the root level. If the depth of a tree is d, then $p = d + 1$. In the chess literature, a *move* consists of one player's single act and his opponent's single response. Here, however, we will be informal, referring to one player's single act as his *move*.

Games Require Different Search Procedures

Using the British Museum procedure to search game trees is definitely out. For chess, for example, if we take the effective branching factor to be something like 16 and the effective depth to be 100, then the number of branches in an exhaustive survey of chess possibilities would be on the order of 10^{120}, a ridiculously large number. In fact, if all the atoms in the universe had been computing chess moves at picosecond speeds since the big bang (if any), the analysis would be just getting started.

At the other end of the spectrum, if only there were some infallible way to rank the members of a set of board situations, it would be a simple matter to play by selecting the move that leads to the best situation that can be reached by one move. No search would be necessary. Unfortunately, no such situation-ranking formula exists. When board situations obviously differ, then a simple measure like piece count can be a rough guide to quality, but depending on such a measure to rank the available moves from a given situation produces poor results. Some other strategy is needed.

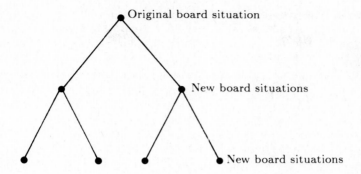

Figure 4-15. Games provide a search environment with a new twist, competition. The nodes represent game situations, and the branches represent the moves that connect them.

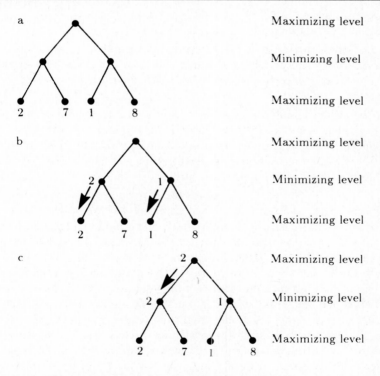

Figure 4-16. Minimaxing is a method for determining moves. Minimaxing employs a static evaluator to calculate advantage-specifying numbers for the game situations at the bottom of a partially developed game tree. One player works toward the higher numbers, seeking the advantage, while the opponent goes for the lower numbers.

The obvious generalization is to use a situation analyzer only after play has extended through several levels of move and countermove. This cannot be pursued too far since combinatorial explosion soon leads to unthinkable numbers, but if the development terminates at some reasonable depth, perhaps the terminal situations can be compared, yielding a basis for move selection. Of course, the underlying presumption of this approach is that the merit of a move clarifies as it is pursued and that the look-ahead procedure can extend far enough that even rough board-evaluation formulas may be satisfactory. This presumption is hotly debated.

The MINIMAX Procedure Is a Look-ahead Procedure

Suppose we have a situation analyzer that converts all judgments about board situations into a single, overall quality number. Further suppose that positive numbers, by convention, indicate favor to one player, and negative numbers indicate favor to the other. The degree of favor goes with the absolute value of the number.

The procedure of determining the quality number is called *static evaluation*. At the end of a limited exploration of move possibilities one finds *static evaluation scores* produced by a situation analyzer called a *static evaluator*.

The player hoping for positive numbers is called the maximizing player. His opponent is the minimizing player. If the player to move is the maximizing player, he is looking for a path leading to a large positive number, and he will assume that his opponent will try to force the play toward situations with strongly negative static evaluations.

Thus in the stylized, miniature game tree shown in figure 4-16, the maximizer might hope to get to the situation yielding a static score of 8. But the maximizer knows that the minimizer would not permit that since the minimizer can choose a move deflecting the play toward the situation with a score of 1. In general, the decision of the maximizer must take cognizance of the attitude of the minimizer at the next level down. If the search goes a step farther, then certainly the minimizer moves in accord with choices of the maximizer at the next level down. This continues until the limit of exploration is reached and the static evaluator provides a direct basis for selecting among alternatives. In the example, the static evaluations at the bottom determine that the choices available to the minimizing player yield effective scores of 2 and 1 at the level just up from the static evaluations. Knowing these effective scores, the maximizer can determine the best play at the next level up. Clearly the maximizer moves toward the node from which the minimizer can do no better than to hold the expected score to 2. Again, the scores at one level determine the action and the effective score at the next level up.

The procedure by which the scoring information passes up the game tree is called the MINIMAX *procedure* since the score at each node is either the minimum or maximum of the scores at the nodes immediately below:

To MINIMAX:

1   Determine if the limit of search has been reached, or if the level is a minimizing level, or if the level is a maximizing level:

    1a   If the limit of search has been reached, compute the static value of the current position relative to the appropriate player. Report the result.

    1b   If the level is a minimizing level, use MINIMAX on the children of the current position. Report the minimum of the results.

    1c   Otherwise, the level is a maximizing level. Use MINIMAX on the children of the current position. Report the maximum of the results.

Note that the whole idea of minimaxing rests on the translation of board goodness into a single number, the static value. But mapping goodness into a single number has a serious defect:

- A number says nothing about how it was determined. It is a poor summary, often forced on us by how little we know how to do.

Note also that minimaxing can be expensive for two reasons: first, calculating the static values; and second, generating paths can be a stumbling block. Which costs more depends on the details of the static evaluator and move generator used.

The ALPHA-BETA Procedure Prunes Game Trees

At first, it might seem that the static evaluator must be used on each situation found at the bottom of the tree. But, fortunately, this is not so. There is a procedure that reduces both the number of tree branches that must be generated and the number of static evaluations that must be done, thus cutting down on the work to be done overall. It is somewhat like the branch-and-bound idea in that some paths are demonstrated to be bad even though not followed to the limit of look-ahead.

Consider the situation in figure 4-17a, in which the static evaluator has already been used on the first two terminal situations. Performing the MINIMAX procedure on the scores of 2 and 7 determines that the minimizing player is guaranteed a score of 2 if the maximizer takes the left branch at the top node. This in turn ensures that the maximizer is

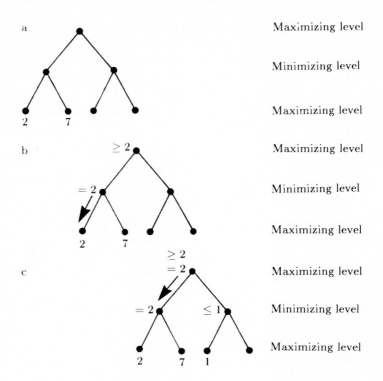

Figure 4-17. Work can be avoided by augmenting the MINIMAX procedure with the ALPHA-BETA procedure. In this illustration, there is no need to explore the right side of the tree fully, because there is no way the result could alter the move decision. Once movement to the right is shown to be worse than movement to the left, there is no need to see how much worse.

guaranteed a score at least as good as 2 at the top. This is clear even before any other static evaluations are made, since the maximizer can certainly elect the left branch if the right branch turns out worse. This is indicated at the top node in figure 4-17b.

Now suppose the static value of the next terminal node is 1. Seeing this, surely the minimizer is guaranteed a score at least as good as 1 by the same reasoning that showed that the maximizer is guaranteed a score at least as good as 2 at the top. Only the sense of *good* has changed. At the maximizer levels, *good* means toward the larger numbers, while at the minimizer levels, *good* means toward the smaller.

Look closely at the tree. Does it make sense to go on to the board situation at the final node? Can the value produced there by the static evaluator possibly matter? Strangely, the answer is no. For surely if the maximizer knows he is guaranteed a score of 2 along the left branch, he

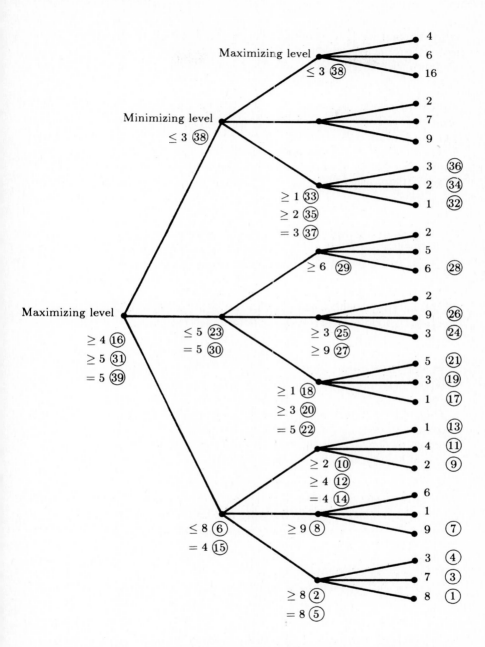

Figure 4-18. A game tree of depth 3 and branching factor 3. The circled numbers show the order in which conclusions are drawn. Note that only 16 static evaluations are made, not the 27 required without alpha-beta pruning. Evidently the best play for the maximizer is down the middle branch.

needs to know no more about the right branch other than that he can do no better than 1 there. The last node evaluated could be +100, or −100, or any number whatever, without affecting the result. The maximizer's score is 2, as shown in figure 4-17c.

On reflection, it is clear that use has been made of the following key principle: If an opponent has one response establishing that a potential move is bad, there is no need to check any other responses to the potential move. If one is gored, there is certainly no need to find out in how many ways or how badly in the worst case. This principle is the foundation of the ALPHA-BETA *procedure*. Here is how the ALPHA-BETA procedure exploits the principle:

- Whenever something is discovered about the best that can be hoped for at a given node, check what is known about ancestor nodes. It may be that no further work is sensible below the given node.

- Whenever the exact value of a node is established, check what is known about the parent. It may be that the best that can be hoped for at the parent node can be revised or determined exactly.

It is appropriate now to see how the ALPHA-BETA procedure applies to a larger example. Unfortunately, it is a bit difficult to see how static evaluations intermix with conclusions about node values on paper. We must make do with circled event numbers placed beside each conclusion showing the order in which they are determined. These are shown in the example of figure 4-18, in which we look at another stylized tree with a depth of 3 and a uniform branching factor of 3:

1–2:   Moving down the left branch at every decision point, the search penetrates to the bottom where a static value of 8 is unearthed. This 8 clearly means that the maximizer is guaranteed a score at least as good as 8 with the three choices available. A note to this effect is placed by step 2.

3–5:   To be sure nothing better than 8 can be found, the maximizer examines the two other moves available to it. Since 7 and 3 both indicate inferior moves, the maximizer concludes that the score achievable is exactly 8 and that the correct move is the first one examined.

6:     Nailing down the maximizer's score at the lowest node enables a conclusion about what the minimizer can hope for at the next level up. Since one move is now known to lead to a situation that gives the maximizer a score of 8, then the minimizer can do no worse than 8 here.

7–8:   To see if the minimizer can do better at the second level, its two
        remaining moves must be examined. The first leads to a situation
        from which the maximizer can score at least a 9. Here cutoff occurs.
        By taking the left branch, the minimizer forces a score of 8, but by
        taking the middle branch, the minimizer will do no better than 9
        and could do worse if the other maximizer choices are even bigger.
        Hence the middle branch is bad for the minimizer, there is no need
        to go on to find out how bad it is, and there is consequently no need
        for two static evaluations. There is no change in the minimizer's
        worst-case expectation; it is still 8.

9–14:   The minimizer must still investigate its last option, the one to the
        right. This in turn means seeing what the maximizer can do there.
        The next series of steps bounces between static evaluations and con-
        clusions about the maximizer's situation immediately above them.
        The conclusion is that the maximizer's score is 4.

15:     Discovering that the right branch leads to a forced score of 4, the
        minimizer would take the right branch, since 4 compares favorably
        with 8, the previous low score.

16:     Now a bound can be placed at the top level. The maximizer, sur-
        veying the situation there, sees that its left branch leads to a score
        of 4. It now knows it will get at least that. To see if it can do better,
        it must look at its middle and right branches.

17–22: Deciding how the minimizer will react at the end of the middle
        branch requires knowing what happens along the left branch de-
        scending from there. Here the maximizer is in action discovering
        that the best play is to a position with a score of 5.

23:     Until something definite was known about what the maximizer could
        do, no bounds could be placed on the minimizer's potential. Know-
        ing that the maximizer gets 5 along the left branch, however, is
        knowing something definite. The conclusion is that the minimizer
        can get a score at least as good as 5.

24–27: In working out what the maximizer can do below the minimizer's
        middle branch, it is discovered partway through the analysis that
        the maximizer can reach a score of 9. But 9 is poor relative to
        the known fact that the minimizer has one option that ensures a
        5. Cutoff occurs again. There is no point in investigating the other
        maximizer option, thus avoiding one static evaluation.

28–29: Looking at the minimizer's right branch quickly shows that it, too, gives the maximizer a chance to force the play to a worse score than the minimizer can achieve along the left branch. Cutoff saves two static evaluations here.

30:     Since there are no more branches to investigate, the minimizer's score of 5 is no longer merely a bound; 5 is the actual value achievable.

31:     The maximizer at the top, seeing a better deal through the middle branch, chooses it tentatively and knows now that it can do at least as good as 5.

32–37: Now the maximizer's right-branch choice at the top must be explored. Diving into the tree, bouncing about a bit, leads to the conclusion that the minimizer sees a left-branch choice ensuring a score of 3.

38:     The minimizer can conclude that the left-branch score is a bound on how well it can do.

39:     Knowing the minimizer can force play to a situation with a score of 3, the maximizer at the top level concludes there is no point in exploring the right branch further. After all, a score of 5 follows a middle-branch move. Note that this saves six static evaluations as well as two move generations. Both are important because the time required for each static evaluation may be more or less than the time required for each move generations.

It is not unusual to get lost in this demonstration. Even seasoned game specialists still feel magic in the ALPHA-BETA procedure. Each individual conclusion seems right, but somehow the global result is strange and hard to believe.

Note, incidentally, that in the example it was never necessary to look more than one level up in order to decide whether or not to stop exploration. This was strictly a consequence of the shallowness of the depth-3 tree used. With trees of depth 4 or more, so-called deep cutoffs can occur, forcing us to look further.

One way to keep track of all the bookkeeping is to use a procedure with parameters that record all the necessary observations. Naturally, the tradition is to call these parameters alpha and beta, as shown in the following procedure description:

To MINIMAX with ALPHA-BETA:

1   Determine if the level is the top level, or if the limit of
    search has been reached, or if the level is a minimizing
    level, or if the level is a maximizing level:

   1a   If the level is the top level, let alpha be $-\infty$ and let
        beta be $+\infty$.

   1b   If the limit of search has been reached, compute the
        static value of the current position relative to the ap-
        propriate player. Report the result.

   1c   If the level is a minimizing level:

       1c1   Until all children are examined with MINIMAX
             or alpha is bigger than beta:

            1c1.1   Set beta to the smaller of the given
                    beta values and the smallest value so
                    far reported by MINIMAX working on
                    the children.

            1c1.2   Use MINIMAX on the next child of the
                    current position, handing this new ap-
                    plication of MINIMAX the current al-
                    pha and beta.

       1c2   Report beta.

   1d   If the level is a maximizing level:

       1d1   Until all children are examined with MINIMAX
             or alpha is bigger than beta:

            1d1.1   Set alpha to the larger of the given al-
                    pha values and the biggest value so far
                    reported by MINIMAX working on the
                    children.

            1d1.2   Use MINIMAX on the next child of the
                    current position, handing this new ap-
                    plication of MINIMAX the current al-
                    pha and beta.

       1d2   Report alpha.

ALPHA-BETA May Not Help Much

It is important to understand just what the ALPHA-BETA procedure can
be expected to do. One way to understand this is to ask about the best
and worst cases.

In the worst case, for some trees, the branches can be ordered such that ALPHA-BETA does nothing. For other trees, however, there is no way to order the branches to avoid all alpha-beta cutoff.

Analyzing what can come of the best case requires some work. Suppose the tree, by great good luck, is ordered with each player's best move being the leftmost alternative at every node. Then clearly the best move of the player at the top is to the left. But how many static evaluations are needed for the topmost player to be sure that this move is optimal? To work into the question, consider the tree of depth 3 and branching factor 3 shown in figure 4-19.

Presuming that the best moves for both players are always to the left, then the value of the leftmost move for the maximizing player at the top is the static evaluation found for the board situation at the bottom left. Assuming this is correct, then the maximizer has something concrete against which the quality of the alternatives can be compared. It need not consider all of its opponent's replies to those alternatives, however.

To verify the correct move at a given node in an ordered tree, it is necessary to consider relatively few of the terminals descendant from the immediate alternatives to the move to be verified. This is true because all terminals found below nonoptimal moves by the opponent can be ignored.

Why is it necessary to deal with all the options of the moving player while ignoring all but one of his opponent's moves? This is a sticky point. The explanation requires close attention to the basic idea: if an opponent has some responses that make a move bad no matter how the moving player continues, then the move must be bad.

The key to understanding lies in the words *some*, and *no matter how*. The *some* suggests trying one of the opponent's moves wherever he has a choice and hoping that it is good enough to certify the conclusion. But to be sure that the conclusion holds no matter what the moving player might do, it is clearly necessary to check out all of the moving player's alternatives wherever he has a choice.

Thus the hope in the example is that only the leftmost branch from node 3 to node 8 will need exploration. All of the maximizer's counter-responses to that move must be checked, so static evaluations need to be made at nodes 23, 24, and 25.

These establish the maximizer's score at node 8, which in turn sets a bound on what the minimizer can do at node 3, which by comparison with the minimizer's score at node 2, should show that no further work below node 3 makes any sense. Similar logic applies to node 4, which leads to static evaluations at 32, 33, and 34.

But now how can the maximizer be sure that the score transferred up the left edge is valid? Surely it must verify that an intelligent minimizer at 2 would select the leftmost branch. This verification can be done by assuming the number coming up the left edge from 5 is correct and then rejecting

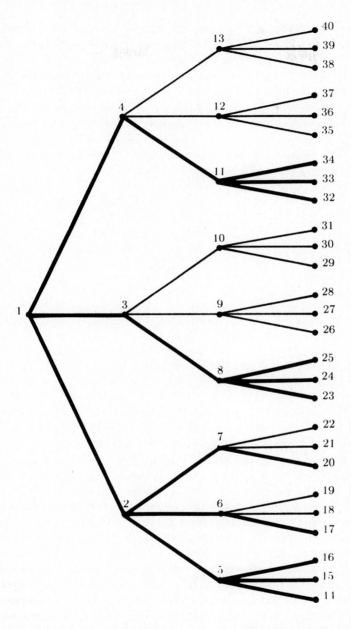

Figure 4-19. In a perfectly ordered tree, ALPHA-BETA cuts the exponent of combinatorial explosion in half. This is because all of the adversary's options need not be considered in verifying the left-branch choices. With depth 3 and branching factor 3, ALPHA-BETA can reduce the number of required static evaluations from 27 to 11.

the alternatives as efficiently as possible. But by the same arguments used at 1, it is clear that not all of the minimizer's opponent's options need be examined. Again, branching occurs only at every second level, working out from the choice to be verified along the left edge. Static evaluations must be done at 17 and 20.

Finally there is the question of the minimizer's assumption about the number coming up from 5. This requires exploring all of the maximizer's alternatives, the trivial case of the general argument, resulting in static evaluations at 15 and 16 in order to be sure that the static evaluation done at 14 yields the correct number to transfer up to 5.

Only 11 of the 27 possible static evaluations need be made in order to discover the best move when, by luck, the alternatives in the tree have been nicely ordered. In deeper trees with more branching, the saving is more dramatic. In fact, it can be demonstrated that the number of static evaluations, s, needed to discover the best move in an optimally arranged tree is given by the following formula, where b is the branching factor and d is the depth of the tree:

$$ s = \begin{cases} 2b^{d/2} - 1, & \text{for } d \text{ even} \\ b^{(d+1)/2} + b^{(d-1)/2} - 1, & \text{for } d \text{ odd} \end{cases} $$

A straightforward proof by induction verifies the formula. We need only to generalize the line of argument used in the last example, focusing on the idea that verification of a choice requires full investigation only every second level. Note that the formula is certainly correct for $d = 1$ since it then simplifies to b. For $d = 3$ and $b = 3$, the formula yields 11, which nicely verifies the conclusion reached for the example.

But *be warned:* the formula is only for the special case in which a tree is perfectly arranged. As such, the formula is an approximation to what can actually be expected, for if there were a way of arranging the tree with the best moves on the left, clearly there would be no point in using alpha-beta pruning at all. This is not to say that the exercise has been fruitless, however. It establishes the lower bound on the number of static evaluations that would be needed in a real game. It is a lower bound that may or may not be close to the real result, depending on how well the moves are in fact arranged. The real result must lie somewhere between the worst case, for which all b^d terminals must be static evaluated, and the best case, which still requires approximately $2b^{d/2}$ static evaluations. In practice, the number of static evaluations seems nearer to the best case than the worst case, an unusual accommodation of nature.

Still, the work required becomes impossibly large with increasing depth. ALPHA-BETA merely wins a temporary reprieve from the impact of the explosive, exponential growth. It does not prevent it, as figure 4-20 shows.

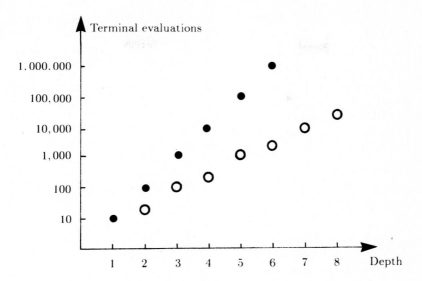

Figure 4-20. ALPHA-BETA reduces the rate of combinatorial explosion, but does not prevent it. In this illustration, the larger number of terminal evaluations is for no alpha-beta pruning; the smaller number is for the maximum possible alpha-beta pruning. In both cases, the branching factor is assumed to be 10.

Progressive Deepening Keeps Computing within Time Bounds

In tournaments, players are required to make a certain number of moves within time limits enforced by a relentless clock. This creates a problem because the time required to search to any fixed depth depends on the situation. To search to a fixed depth, independent of the evolving game, requires a conservative choice for the fixed depth. Otherwise, games will be lost by running out of time.

The way to wriggle out of this time problem is to analyze each situation to depth 1, then to depth 2, then to depth 3, and so on until the amount of time set aside for each move is reached. This way, there is always a move choice ready to go. The choice is determined by the analysis at one level less deep than the analysis in progress when time runs out. This is known as *progressive deepening*.

At first it might seem that a great deal of time would be wasted in extra analysis at shallow levels. Curiously, this is not so. To see why, suppose, for simplicity, that the dominant cost in analysis is static evaluation. The number of nodes requiring static evaluation at the bottom of a tree with depth d and effective branching factor b is b^d. With a bit of algebra, it is easy to show that the number of nodes in the rest of the tree is

$$b^0 + b^1 + \cdots + b^{d-1} = \frac{b^d - 1}{b - 1}$$

Thus the ratio of the number of nodes in the bottom level to the number of nodes up to the bottom level is

$$\frac{b^d(b - 1)}{b^d - 1} \approx b - 1$$

Thus, for $b = 16$, the number of static evaluations needed to do minimaxing at every level up to the bottom level is but a fifteenth of the static evaluation needed to do minimaxing at the bottom level. Insurance against running out of time is a good buy.

Heuristic Pruning Also Limits Search

The alpha-beta search speedup procedure guarantees as good an answer as can be found by doing complete, exhaustive minimaxing. Many other procedures have no such guarantee but are used in combination with alpha-beta pruning as additional weapons against explosive tree growth.

A brute-force way of reducing the effective branching factor in a game tree is to concentrate on the better moves. Of course, to concentrate on the better moves, there must be a method for *ordering moves plausibly* without looking ahead any further. If the static evaluator is fast enough, it can serve.

Once there is a way to order moves plausibly, one option is to arrange for the branching factor to vary with depth of penetration, possibly *tapering the search* in favor of the more plausible moves through some formula like the following:

$$r(\text{child}) = r(\text{parent}) - r(\text{rank of child among siblings})$$

where $r(\text{child})$ is the number of branches to be retained at some child node, $r(\text{parent})$ is the number of branches retained by the child node's parent, and $r(\text{rank of child among siblings})$ is the rank in plausibility of the child node among its siblings.

Thus, if a node is one of five children and ranks second most plausible among those five, then it should itself have $5 - 2 = 3$ children. A complete tree formed using this idea looks like the one shown in figure 4-21.

Another way of cutting off disasters is to stop search from going down through apparently bad moves no matter what. This makes the width of the tree sensitive to the way particular games develop. If only one line of play makes any sense at all, that line would be the only one pursued, *cutting off disasters.*

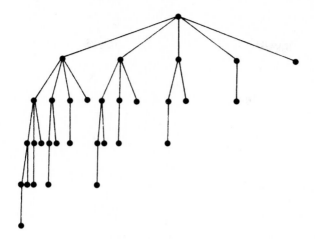

Figure 4-21. Tapering search gives more attention to the more plausible moves. Here the tapering procedure reduces the search with increases in depth and decreases in plausibility.

Needless to say, any heuristic that limits branching acts in opposition to lines of play that temporarily forfeit pieces for eventual position advantage. Because they trim off the moves that appear bad on the surface, procedures that limit branching are unlikely to discover spectacular moves that seem disastrous for a time, but then win back everything lost and more. There will be no queen sacrifices.

Heuristic Continuation Fights the Horizon Effect

Most heuristic procedures limit tree growth. Sometimes, however, it is useful to go the other way, extending the tree, to prevent certain surprises.

Surprises are often the result of delaying moves that put off but do not prevent disasters. To illustrate how this can work, suppose there is a combination that leads inevitably to queen capture. Suppose further that the side losing the queen can delay the loss by sacrificing other, lesser pieces elsewhere on the board. As long as the queen loss is inevitable, it is absurd to use delaying moves that sacrifice still more material. But delaying moves may carry play beyond depth limits established for search, pushing the bad news out of sight. In the sample of figure 4-22, the apparent choice is between losing the queen or losing a pawn. But the real choice is between losing a queen or losing the queen *and* pawn. Metaphorically speaking, when an inevitable loss is pushed beyond the field of view by a lesser sacrifice, the situation is said to be an instance of the *horizon effect*.

One way to combat the horizon effect is to continue search when an otherwise terminal situation is judged to be particularly dynamic. Such

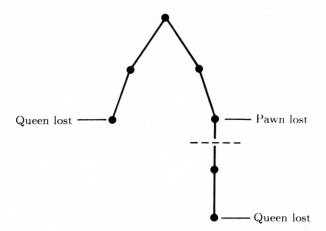

Figure 4-22. The horizon effect foils search-oriented game procedures when disasters can be delayed but not prevented. Here the left-branch move leads directly to queen loss, and the right-branch move leads to a pawn sacrifice followed by queen loss. The inferior right-branch path is followed if the delaying sacrifice pushes the disaster beyond the depth of normal investigation. Heuristic continuation helps, but more strategic play is necessary to eliminate the problem entirely.

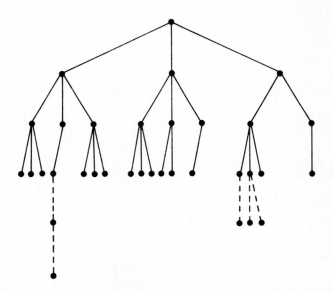

Figure 4-23. Heuristic continuation, or feedover, extends search beyond normal limits. Dotted lines are continuations of paths that ordinary search had terminated at particularly dynamic situations such as imminent piece loss.

heuristic continuation is sometimes called *feedover*. There are a number of conditions that can cause a configuration to be particularly dynamic and therefore deserving feedover:

- The king is in danger.

- Loss of a piece is imminent.

- A pawn is about to become a queen.

Figure 4-23 shows what feedover can do to the shape of a search tree.

SUMMARY

- The simplest search procedures are depth-first search and breadth-first search. Neither finds optimal paths, and both may be considerably less efficient relative to more informed procedures.

- Hill climbing is a more informed procedure that explores branches in the order of their heuristically guessed plausibility. Hill climbing shares one problem with its cousin, depth-first search, in that a wrong decision high up in the tree can lead to useless thrashing lower down.

- When used to find maxima in parameter spaces, hill climbing can be foiled by bad terrain.

- Beam search is a modification of breadth-first search in which only the best nodes at any level are retained for further search. Beam search may fail to find legitimate paths.

- Best-first searches push forward from the most promising open node yet encountered.

- Branch-and-bound search is a fundamental procedure for finding optimal paths. The basic idea is to extend the developing tree from the end of the least costly partial path. Branch-and-bound search is often improved through the use of estimates of the distances remaining to the goal and by eliminating redundant paths to intermediate places, thereby becoming A*.

- To play games, some people feel that hardly any knowledge is useful beyond whatever is needed to search through many rounds of move and countermove, imagining the likely consequences of each possible play. Others claim that brilliant strategic play is beyond the capability of approaches based solely on looking ahead—much more is required in the direction of understanding and reacting to various sorts of position patterns. At the moment, however, look-ahead operations are well understood, while pattern-directed play is a matter of continuing research and conjecture.

- The adversary nature of games makes game-tree search a special subject. The minimax idea is the foundation on which all else rests. MINIMAX is the procedure by which conclusions about what to do at the deeper nodes of the search tree percolate up to determine what should happen at the higher nodes.

- The ALPHA-BETA procedure depends on the fact that once an opponent has one way to ensure that a move is disastrous, there is no need to explore that move further. Alpha-beta pruning saves considerable work without any danger of overlooking the optimal line of play.

- Alpha-beta pruning may be augmented by a number of heuristic pruning procedures. All of these introduce some danger that the optimal play may not be selected.

- Heuristic continuation is a way to fight the horizon effect, preventing delaying moves from making disasters worse.

REFERENCES

The role of search in discovery was established by Douglas B. Lenat [1977, 1982]. His AM program, a breakthrough in learning research, discovered concepts in mathematics. AM developed new concepts from old ones using various transformations, and it identified the most interesting concepts for further development using interestingness heuristics. The discussion of omelet-recipe generation is based on these key transformation and interestingness ideas.

The basic minimax approach to games was laid out by Claude E. Shannon [1950], who anticipated most of the subsequent work to date. The classic papers on checkers are by Arthur L. Samuel [1959, 1967]. They deal extensively with tree-pruning heuristics, schemes for combining evidence, and methods for adaptive parameter improvement.

Donald E. Knuth and Ronald W. Moore [1975] probe deeply into the alpha-beta idea to understand expected performance rather than best-case or worst-case performance. Other important work has been done by the late John Gaschnig [1979].

The term *horizon effect* was coined by Hans J. Berliner [1973, 1978]. Berliner's work on chess is complemented by seminal progress on backgammon [Berliner, 1980].

Donald Michie also does important work on chess. For an insightful treatment of the key problems, see Michie's review [1980]. For other assessments, see Berliner [1978, 1981] and *Chess Skill in Man and Machine* [second edition, 1983], edited by Peter W. Frey.

5

Control
Metaphors

Studying control metaphors is a way to focus on the alternative ways procedures may interact. Many of these metaphors refer to explicit and implicit organization strategies that people use to get things done. Some of the questions addressed in selecting among control choices are as follows:

- Where is knowledge about procedures stored?
- What process decides which procedures act?
- How are computational resources allocated?
- What kind of procedures are there?
- How do procedures communicate?

The principal control metaphor to be studied in this chapter is GPS, an acronym for General Problem Solver. GPS constitutes a particular combination of control decisions.

CONTROL CHOICES

Keep in mind that the apparent complexity of a problem solution may stem more from the problem than from the structure of the system that solves it. Consider the path an ant makes on a pebbled beach. The path seems complicated. The ant probes, doubles back, circumnavigates, and zigzags. But these actions are not deep and mysterious manifestations of intellectual power. Rather, the ant is a simple problem solver operating on a complicated beach with a lot of pebbles to get around.

Thus, a simple problem solver can produce complicated behavior if the problem solver interacts with a complicated environment. It is natural, however, to suppose that complicated behavior must be the result of many procedures that interact in complicated ways. Consequently, there is a tendency to devote excessive attention to control refinement at the expense of work on representation and constraint. Avoid this tendency.

Where Is Knowledge about Procedures Stored?

We now look at some control choices with the purpose of enumerating and explaining some of the more popular options. We use the MOVER system, introduced in chapter 2, to anchor our discussion. Although MOVER uses simple, basic control ideas, it is easy to alter parts of MOVER to illustrate grander, more advanced control ideas. Here is what we will do:

- MOVE-HAND and FIND-SPACE will be more powerful because we will introduce new procedures, MOVE-SLOW, MOVE-FAST-1, MOVE-FAST-2, FIND-SPACE-1, and FIND-SPACE-2.

- PUT-ON will be more reliable because we will introduce CANNOT-PUT-ON, a procedure that prevents MOVER from putting objects onto pyramids.

The point, however, is not to add procedures, but to add them in a way that illustrates different answers to the basic control questions. We begin, then, by discussing MOVE-HAND, focusing on where knowledge about procedures is stored. We consider action-centered, object-centered, and request-centered control.

To make the choices clearer, imagine that our improved MOVER has three hands: two are fast hands, but they are suited only for lightweight objects; the third is a slow hand, but it is able to handle heavy objects as well as light ones. Each hand is under the command of its own specialist, MOVE-FAST-1, MOVE-FAST-2, or MOVE-SLOW.

The basic MOVER system uses the simplest possible method for deciding which procedures act; each procedure knows the names of the other procedures that can help it. If our new version of MOVE-HAND were to work this way, it would be MOVE-HAND's job to determine which hand, hence which specialist, is appropriate for each object movement. MOVE-HAND would include a test to check object weight, and it would select a specialist according to the test result. Obviously, the names of all potential specialists must be recorded somewhere inside MOVE-HAND.

This common way of storing knowledge about procedures makes a collection of procedures resemble an *army*: as suggested by figure 5-1, each

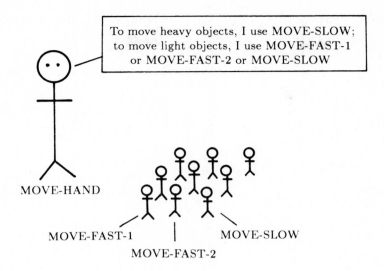

To move heavy objects, I use MOVE-SLOW;
to move light objects, I use MOVE-FAST-1
or MOVE-FAST-2 or MOVE-SLOW

MOVE-HAND

MOVE-FAST-1   MOVE-SLOW

MOVE-FAST-2

Figure 5-1. In action-centered control, each procedure knows who to order to get things done.

procedure knows the names of the subordinate procedures under its control; each procedure causes other procedures to act by issuing commands directly to those procedures; each subordinate procedure reports to its superordinate procedure when finished.

- A system exhibits *action-centered control* when the system's procedures know what subprocedures to use to perform actions.

There are, however, alternative places to put knowledge about which procedures to use. Suppose, for example, that the description of each object includes information about the classes to which the object belongs. A particular object, A, might belong to the Brick class, the Heavy-object class, and the Made-of-wood class. Further suppose that the description of each class may include information about how to perform various operations on members of that class. The description of the Heavy-object class, for example, contains a statement that MOVE-SLOW is the right procedure for moving objects that belong to the Heavy-object class. As suggested by figure 5-2, the job of our new version of MOVE-HAND is to find the name of the correct movement procedure by searching the class descriptions associated with the object to be moved. The names of the possible procedures are not recorded in MOVE-HAND itself.

- A system exhibits *object-centered control* when the system's class descriptions specify how to deal with objects in their own class.

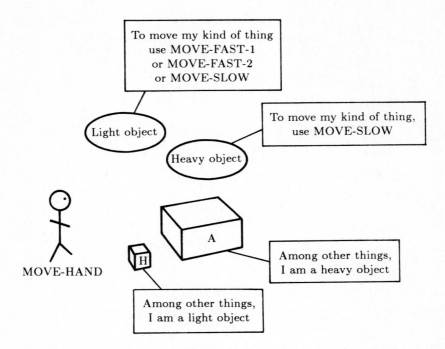

Figure 5-2. In object-centered control, each object class description includes knowledge about how to get various things done.

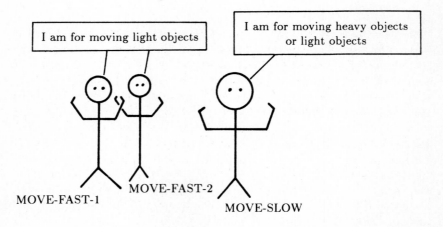

Figure 5-3. In one form of request-centered control, each procedure knows what it itself is good for but has no direct knowledge of what the others are good at.

So far, there are two choices. In action-centered control, procedures contain the names of other procedures that are good for certain jobs. In object-centered control, the object's class descriptions contain the names of the useful procedures.

There is still a third choice, however. Imagine that whenever it is time for MOVE-HAND to move an object, MOVE-HAND writes a description of what is needed on a sort of blackboard. For example, if the goal is to move brick H, MOVE-HAND would write something like this on the blackboard:

MOVE-HAND's announcement: Hand procedure needed to move object H.

Just as MOVE-HAND can write, MOVE-FAST-1, MOVE-FAST-2, and MOVE-SLOW can all read, and all know they are good for putting objects at particular places. When they see the announcement message on the blackboard, they immediately respond to MOVE-HAND that they wish to be considered candidates for achieving the announced goal by writing something like this on the blackboard:

MOVE-FAST-1's reply to MOVE-HAND: I am available.
MOVE-FAST-2's reply to MOVE-HAND: I am available.
MOVE-SLOW's reply to MOVE-HAND: I am available.

This kind of interaction makes a collection of procedures resemble an *egalitarian committee of strangers*: as suggested by figure 5-3, all procedures have equal status; no procedure knows what the others are good at; procedures interact by saying what they want done and by knowing what they are good for; and nothing gets done without a lot of cooperation.

- A system exhibits *request-centered control* when the system's procedures know their own purpose so that they may respond to requests.

Note that request-centered control raises another issue: given that knowledge exists somewhere, who uses it? In action-centered systems, the procedure that wants something done decides what to do. In object-centered systems, the procedure that wants something done again decides, using information attached to objects and classes. In request-centered control, however, there are other alternatives, discussed next.

What Process Decides Which Procedures Act?

With any form of request-centered control, when more than one work-doing procedure appears right for a goal, some decision must be made about how to select from the work-doing procedures sensibly. The simplest solution is to arrange the candidate work-doing procedures randomly, with no attempt to use any knowledge of cost or likelihood of success.

A more sophisticated solution is to put more expertise in the candidate procedures. This expertise enables each procedure to look more carefully

at the goal on the blackboard. If a procedure knows it cannot succeed, it
will not volunteer as a candidate. Otherwise, it reports interest.

A still more sophisticated solution is to have the work-requesting procedure examine all the candidates that appear, picking the one that seems
best. This additional sophistication requires more expertise in the work-
requesting procedure.

To illustrate these choices, let us suppose, for a moment, that MOVE-
HAND is to use request-centered control to decide what specialist should
be used in any given movement problem. Suppose further that candidate
procedures are tried at random and that all three object-moving procedures
respond to all hand requests.

With this choice, bad luck may lead to failure or inefficiency. If the
object is light and MOVE-SLOW is first in line, the movement will be needlessly slow. If the object is heavy and one of the fast-hand procedures is
tried first, there will be a failure at some point, requiring MOVE-HAND to
note the failure and to try the next thing in the list of candidate procedures.

Such inefficiency and failure can be avoided by permitting the candidate procedures to think a bit about the goal before volunteering. Each
should check the object to be moved. MOVE-SLOW should keep quiet if
the object is light; MOVE-FAST-1 and MOVE-FAST-2 should keep quiet if
the object is heavy.

Thus the work-doing procedures can help decide what to do. Still
more can be done, however, for the work-requesting procedure can help
too. Given that a fast hand is suitable, a good heuristic is to use the fast
hand closer to the block to be moved. Consequently, whenever MOVE-
HAND sees more than one hand-moving procedure respond to its request
for moving a light object, it makes sense for MOVE-HAND to order those
procedures according to the distances of their hands from the lightweight
object to be moved. The distances may be computed by MOVE-HAND,
or the distances may be reported by the hand-moving procedures at the
time they volunteer for the motion. Thus the following might constitute
the replies:

MOVE-FAST-1's reply to MOVE-HAND: I am available; distance is .3 m.

MOVE-FAST-2's reply to MOVE-HAND: I am available; distance is .8 m.

Thus, the work-requesting procedure, the work-doing procedures, or both,
or neither may participate in candidate selection and ordering. If both
are involved, the candidate-ordering activity resembles the negotiation we
see when managers and contractors come together to get some building
constructed:

- Usually, the first step is an *announcement* by a manager of something that is to be done.

- Next, potential contractors evaluate the announcement, and some decide to make a *bid*.

- With all the bids in hand, the manager makes a *selection*. We speak of the announcement-bid-selection cycle.

The manager-contractor metaphor forces us to address the issue of how computational resources should be allocated among parallel-running procedures. Of course, action-centered and object-centered systems, as well as request-centered systems, can have parallelism, so the issue of computational resources, treated next, is a general issue.

How Are Computational Resources Allocated?

Procedure selection is complicated if the candidate procedures are tried in parallel, by using multiple computers, or in pseudo-parallel, by slicing up and parceling out the time of one computer. For one thing, we must attend to the possibility that one procedure may interfere with another, causing a disaster. Imagine, for example, unleashing two hands simultaneously to move a single object. How to deal with potentially interfering, parallel-running procedures is not well understood, leaving it out of place to discuss such procedures here.

Still, there is room in MOVER for some safe parallel activity, with more than one procedure competing for the available computing power. Suppose, for example, that there are two procedures that find space for one object on top of another, FIND-SPACE-1 and FIND-SPACE-2. One of these, FIND-SPACE-1, finds space by trying random places, giving up if it cannot find space in the first ten tries. The other, FIND-SPACE-2, plods along, working left-to-right, back-to-front, looking at an array of positions methodically.

Clearly, which procedure is better depends on the situation. The one that looks randomly is better if the space at the back of the target object is filled; the methodical-look one is better if the target object's top is badly cluttered, making ten random looks unlikely to find any free space at all.

Consequently, it makes some sense for FIND-SPACE to try both FIND-SPACE-1 and FIND-SPACE-2 simultaneously whenever there is a need for space. The first result reported is the one used. As usual, however, this introduces some decisions. In particular, there must be a decision about how much computing power to hand over to the simultaneously-running procedures.

- In the absence of a better idea, computing power can be divided *equally* among all candidate procedures.

- Alternatively, if there is a measure of the expected quality of the result, it makes sense to put effort into the procedures *in proportion to expected quality*. For example, FIND-SPACE-1 should get more computing resources if it is better to distribute blocks uniformly over the surface of a support rather than preferentially at the back.

- Alternatively, if there is a measure of likely cost, it makes sense to distribute resources *in inverse proportion to expected cost* so as to get done quickly.

- Alternatively, if there is a measure of both expected quality and likely cost, it makes sense to distribute resources in proportion to expected *return on investment*, the ratio of expected quality to expected cost.

Not much is known about the fine points of using these choices, and what is known requires a taste for heavy doses of probability theory. Consequently, we leave off here. Usually, system designers are content with intuition-driven decisions anyway.

What Kind of Procedures Are There?

Most procedures *do something*. Not all procedures do something directly, however. Some procedures *find a way to do something*. Our revised version of MOVE-HAND, for example, moves objects by finding procedures for moving them.

Our list of procedure kinds is still incomplete, however. Not all procedures do something or find a way to do something. Some procedures *show that there is no way to do something or to find a way to do something*.

We know, for example, that there is no way to put a block on top of a pyramid, and MOVER should know this too. Otherwise, MOVER would blunder when asked to put A on top of D in figure 5-4, happily clearing off A and moving it, only to have an accident when A is let go.

MOVER can avoid the work and the accident through the introduction of CANNOT-PUT-ON, a procedure that checks to be sure that the intended action leaves the world in a stable state. All CANNOT-PUT-ON need do is recognize nonbricks.

Evidently, CANNOT-PUT-ON is an example of a procedure that shows there is no way to do something. Such procedures sometimes are called *skeptics*. Systems that use skeptics liberally are said to be *pluralistic*. Used appropriately, pluralistic systems conserve effort because provably fruitless work is avoided.

Of course it is possible to have many ordinary procedures and many skeptics active at the same time. Such a system becomes similar to a *scientific community*: there are proponents who try to do something; there are

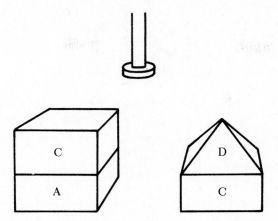

Figure 5-4. A blunder-evoking situation. Brick A cannot be placed on D, for it would fall.

skeptics who try to show that the thing cannot be done, and there are sponsors who have to decide how to allocate resources among the proponents and skeptics.

How Do Procedures Communicate?

Conceptually, to communicate, procedures must send messages to one another, just as people must. We have already seen two prominent ways that messages can be sent. According to the one way, illustrated in figure 5-5, procedures talk to others by handing them some values and receiving some values in return. One reasonable name for this method of communication is the *private-line method*, since only the calling procedure and the called procedure see the communication.

This private-line method is the natural method for action-centered and object-centered systems. Consequently, the private-line method is used by most of the procedures in our generalized MOVER. Usually the value returned simply signifies that the requested mission has been accomplished. In other instances, the value returned is used, as when FIND-SPACE comes up with the coordinates of a suitable location for a block.

Alternatively, as illustrated in figure 5-6, procedures may talk to others by way of generally accessible messages. This could be called the *party-line method*, but it is more conventional to refer to it as the *blackboard method*. Some of the new procedures in MOVER use the blackboard method.

In contrast to putting messages on a generally accessible blackboard, procedures may communicate by placing messages for each other in the same, agreed on place every time, possibly in a reserved part of physical

Figure 5-5. The private-line communication method. Each procedure hands instructions directly to the ones it needs.

memory, as illustrated in figure 5-7. Some people believe this is how our own brainware works. Let us call this the *reserved-spot method*.

Note that there is a spectrum between the blackboard method and the reserved-spot method. At one end, we have the pure blackboard, where every procedure can see all the messages. In the middle, the blackboard is partitioned into conceptual regions, allowing the formation of *interest groups* of procedures that can pay special attention to the messages of their associated region, avoiding the overhead of looking at everything. Moving from the pure blackboard, through interest groups, to the other end of the spectrum, we have the reserved-spot method, which can be viewed as taking the blackboard partition idea to the extreme where each possible interaction between procedures has a special, tiny region reserved for it.

Consider, for example, HEARSAY II, a well-known speech understanding system. HEARSAY II uses interest groups associated with particular phases of language understanding. As shown in figure 5-8, HEARSAY II's interest groups are oriented toward analysis, with those on the bottom of the horizontally layered blackboard concentrating on phoneme and sylla-

Figure 5-6. The party-line or blackboard communication method. Each procedure issues instructions and receives results via a blackboard.

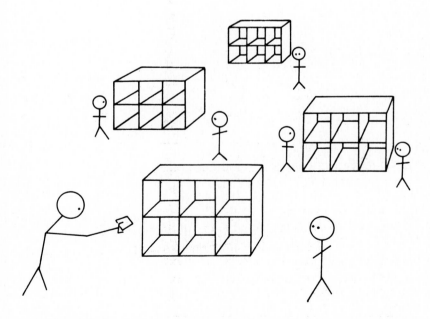

Figure 5-7. The reserved-spot communication method. Each procedure knows
about the special places where it transmits and retrieves messages.

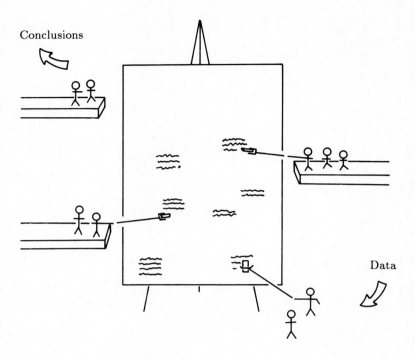

Figure 5-8. HEARSAY II is a speech understanding system with interest groups dedicated to understanding speech at various levels from phonemes and syllables at the data input end to phrases and sentences at the conclusion output end.

ble analysis, those in the middle on word analysis, and those at the top on phrase and sentence analysis.

Now let us turn our attention away from the means of communicating messages and toward the language in the messages.

In principle, procedures could communicate using a natural human language. In fact, procedures generally communicate using lists of values, with sender-receiver conventions determining the role of each value in the list. For example, PUT-AT needs two values from PUT-ON: the first is the name of the object to be moved and the second specifies the coordinates of the target position. PUT-AT would be in big trouble if these values were somehow scrambled, but as long as both PUT-ON and PUT-AT stick to the ordering convention, there is no problem. PUT-ON passes PUT-AT something like this:

A, (.77, .28, .55).

An alternative is to hand over name-value pairs rather than just values. If communication were done this way, PUT-ON would supply PUT-AT with a list like this:

Object-to-move: A, target-vector: (.77, .28, .55)

But since the values are attended by their names, PUT-ON can supply a reversed list as well:

Target-vector: (.77, .28, .55), object-to-move: A

This choice complicates some things and simplifies others.

    The language interpreter must be more complicated, but the messages themselves are more transparent.

MOVER Generalizations Illustrate Fancy Control Options

A set of control options is said to constitute a *control structure*. The control structure of our generalized MOVER is summarized in figure 5-9. Here are some things to note:

- Where is knowledge about procedures stored?

MOVER remains mostly action-centered, but there are conspicuous request-centered exceptions.

- What process decides which procedures act?

As we left the discussion, the request-centered parts of MOVER reached decisions based on negotiation between the work-requesting procedures and work-doing procedures. The decision-making process is distributed.

- How are computational resources allocated?

    As we left the discussion, the request-centered parts of MOVER shared resources in proportion to their expected return on investment.

- What kind of procedures are there?

Most of the procedures are procedures that do things. Some of the procedures are finders and others are skeptics.

- How do procedures communicate?

Most of the procedures communicate by the private-line method. Some communicate by writing on a blackboard.

    Now, to get more experience with the basic control questions, we proceed in the next section to another extended example, which introduces the General Problem Solver metaphor.

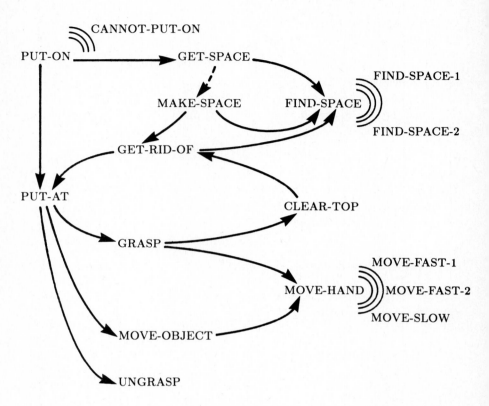

Figure 5-9. The control structure of MOVER. Several new functions have been added, all of which involve request-centered interaction, as indicated by broadcast symbols.

MEANS-ENDS ANALYSIS AND GPS

Sometimes particular control-decision combinations can become established metaphors for explaining other systems. We now take up one of the best known of these metaphoric combinations, GPS, an acronym for General Problem Solver. GPS illustrates how various control choices can be assembled into an overall metaphor.

For the moment, however, let us concentrate on how GPS works. Near the end of the section, we will discuss GPS's strengths and weaknesses as a control metaphor, once the basic ideas are understood.

For some problems, it is natural to think in terms of current situation and desired situation. We speak of the collection of facts that specify the problem and where we are on it as the *current state*. Similarly, where we want to be is the *goal state*.

Here are some examples:

- In a travel problem, the current state and the goal state are defined by physical locations.
- In a robot-assembly problem, the current state and the goal state are defined by the raw materials and the thing to be assembled.
- In a geometry problem the current state is all that is known, both general and specific. The goal state is all that is known, as before, but also including the fact to be shown.

Consider an approach to these problems in which *procedures* are selected according to their ability to reduce the observed *difference* between the *current state* and the *goal state*. This approach is known as *means-ends analysis*. GPS is a metaphor denoting a particular control strategy built on top of the means-ends-analysis idea.

The Key Idea in GPS Is Operating To Reduce Differences

In a travel situation, the difference between the current state and the goal state is the distance between the current physical place and the desired physical place. Consider a sequence of procedures P1...P5 causing movement through a series of places as in figure 5-10. Each of the procedures was selected because it was believed relevant to reducing the difference between the state in which it was applied and the goal state. Procedure P3 actually takes the problem solver farther away from the goal: there is no built-in mechanism preventing this in our version of GPS. Fortunately, P4 and P5 get the movement going back in a good direction again.

Note also that nothing prevents getting into a state whose apparent distance to the goal is short but whose actual distance is extreme. This happens when the difference measure is too crude and ignores too many factors involved in getting from one state to another. To see how this can happen, consider a hiker walking toward the mountain shown in figure 5-11. If he looks only at position differences and moves in the direction that minimizes that difference, he will needlessly climb over the intervening ridge.

Procedure Preconditions Force Recursion

Sometimes some small aspect of the current state forbids the use of a procedure relevant to reducing the difference between the current state and the goal state. If the procedure could be applied in a state near the current state, it is sensible to try to get to that nearby state. In the diagram in figure 5-12, all this is reflected in the current state, CS, the goal state, GS, the difference between them $d(CS, GS)$, and the adjacent state, AS. State AS is close to CS, but unlike CS, AS is a state that allows the

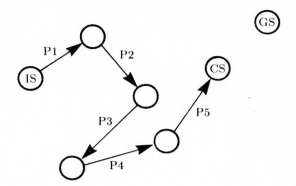

Figure 5-10. The General Problem Solver metaphor involves states and procedures for reducing differences between states. IS is the initial state; GS, the goal state; and CS, the current state. Difference descriptions determine which procedures to try. The Pi denote procedures.

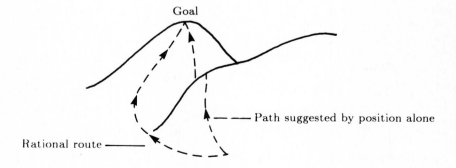

Figure 5-11. The General Problem Solver may become committed to difficult solution paths if difference descriptions fail to include some relevant aspects of a problem. There is poor performance in this example if height is ignored.

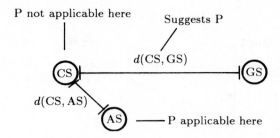

Figure 5-12. The General Problem Solver creates a subproblem when a selected procedure cannot be applied in the current state, CS, but can be applied in a nearby adjacent state, AS.

procedure suggested by $d(\text{CS}, \text{GS})$ to be applied. We say that the adjacent state satisfies the *prerequisite conditions* for the procedure.

Clearly, getting to AS is a problem that is just like any other initial-state to goal-state problem. It makes sense to work on that new problem knowing that its solution helps address the original problem of getting to GS. The new problem is solved using GPS, of course. A new GPS takes the current state as its initial state and the adjacent state as its goal state.

It is usually unreasonable to work toward an adjacent state that is actually farther away than the goal state. Consequently, our version of GPS is to reject a procedure if the distance to the associated adjacent state is such that $d(\text{CS}, \text{AS}) > d(\text{CS}, \text{GS})$.

Finally, there may be situations for which no procedure can be found that seems relevant to forward motion, and a dead end is reached. Whenever this occurs, the last operation is withdrawn, and a new path is sought from the previous state. This means that GPS does a depth-first search of state space.

An example will make everything clearer. Suppose Aunt Agatha lives in Los Angeles and has invited Robbie, a robot, from Boston to spend a few days by her pool. There are a number of different ways to travel, so Robbie needs a way to select the proper one at any given point in the trip.

Robbie decides to make the necessary decisions using a GPS-based problem solver, so he must have a procedure that relates state differences to difference-reducing procedures. He elects to think of state differences in terms of geographical distance, and he notes that possible procedures are flying, taking a train, driving, taking a taxi, and walking. He also decides to relate the differences to the procedures using a *difference-procedure table*, as shown in figure 5-13. He need not have used such a table: he could have treated the conversion of differences another way, but using a difference-procedure table is usually the method associated with GPS.

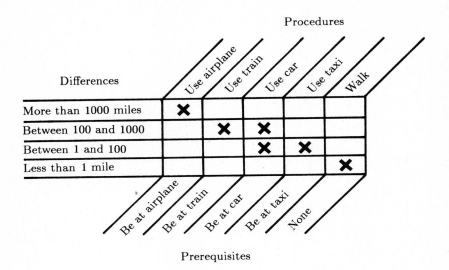

Figure 5-13. Difference-procedure tables are one way to relate differences to procedures. In this example, transportation alternatives are related to distance possibilities and prerequisite conditions are specified.

In figure 5-14a, we see how Robbie decides what to do first. In getting to Los Angeles from Boston, the initial distance is clearly greater than 1000 miles so the difference-procedure table dictates flying. But being at the airplane is prerequisite to using an airplane, and therefore being at the airplane defines an adjacent state. Thus getting to the airplane becomes the goal of a second GPS procedure. The distance is less than 100 miles but more than 1 mile, so driving is appropriate. This introduces still another prerequisite condition, namely being at the car. To satisfy this condition requires walking.

At this point something can be done: Robbie walks to the car and drives to the airport. He then faces the problem of getting to the airplane once again, as shown in figure 5-14b, but progress has been made. The distance remaining is now less than a mile, and once again, walking is appropriate.

Since walking has no prerequisite, Robbie walks again. The walk gets him to the airplane, he flies to the Los Angeles airport, and faces the situation shown in figure 5-14c. There is an apparent snag at this point. Driving, the first procedure found in the difference-procedure table, requires being

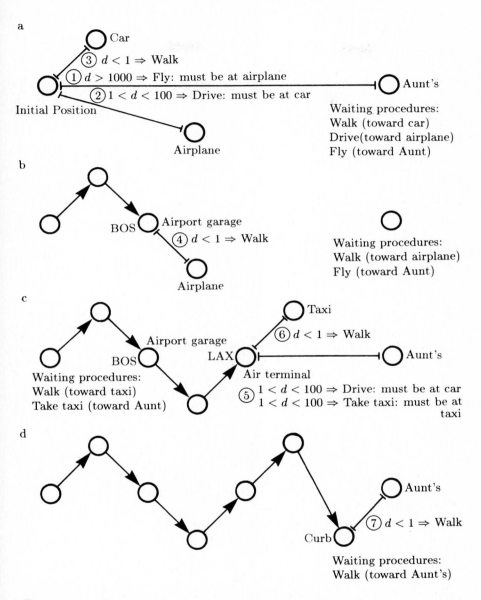

a

Car

③ $d < 1 \Rightarrow$ Walk

① $d > 1000 \Rightarrow$ Fly: must be at airplane

② $1 < d < 100 \Rightarrow$ Drive: must be at car

Initial Position

Aunt's

Waiting procedures:
Walk (toward car)
Drive(toward airplane)
Fly (toward Aunt)

Airplane

b

BOS   Airport garage

④ $d < 1 \Rightarrow$ Walk

Airplane

Waiting procedures:
Walk (toward airplane)
Fly (toward Aunt)

c

Taxi

Airport garage

⑥ $d < 1 \Rightarrow$ Walk

BOS   LAX   Aunt's

Air terminal

Waiting procedures:
Walk (toward taxi)
Take taxi (toward Aunt)

⑤ $1 < d < 100 \Rightarrow$ Drive: must be at car
$1 < d < 100 \Rightarrow$ Take taxi: must be at taxi

d

Aunt's

⑦ $d < 1 \Rightarrow$ Walk

Curb

Waiting procedures:
Walk (toward Aunt's)

Figure 5-14. The steps in using GPS to go from a place in Boston to a place in Los Angeles. Numbers beside the observed differences indicate the order of observation. In *a*, the problem requires flying, which in turn requires driving, which in turn requires walking. In *b*, the problem is to get to the car from the airport parking garage. In *c*, the problem is to get from the arrival gate in Los Angeles to Aunt Agatha's house. And in *d*, the problem is to get from the curb to her door.

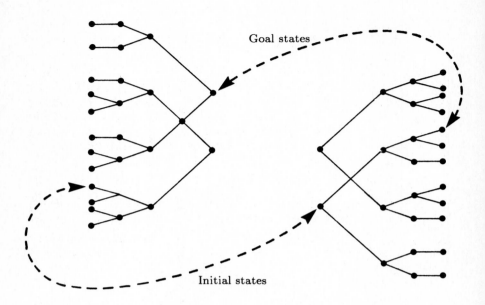

Figure 5-15. The shape of the state space determines whether forward chaining or backward chaining is better. Fan-in situations call for forward chaining; fan-out situations, for backward. The wrong choice can commit the problem solver to chasing too many dead ends.

at the car. But to be at the car would require a silly flight back to Boston. Fortunately, this is prevented because GPS automatically rejects movement to an adjacent state that is more distant than the goal state. Since the car in Boston is more distant than Aunt Agatha's when Robbie is at the Los Angeles airport, the alternative, taking a taxi, is selected. To take a taxi, Robbie must walk to the taxi stand.

Now Robbie walks, takes a taxi, and finds himself on the curb outside Aunt Agatha's house, as shown in figure 5-14d. He walks a fourth time, finishing his trip.

Normally GPS Does Forward Chaining, Not Backward Chaining

Since GPS works *from* the current state *toward* the goal state, GPS is said to do forward chaining. A long chain of procedures may develop as GPS works forward from the end of the established connections.

With only small changes, it is possible to work backward from the goal state instead of forward from the initial state. Deciding whether forward chaining or backward chaining is better depends in part on the shape of the problem space. Figure 5-15 illustrates by way of two symmetric situations. All possible states are represented along with links showing the possible movement from one state to another. In the first situation, forward chaining is better because all possible motion toward the desired goal state eventually leads to the goal state without backup. In the second situation, forward chaining can lead to *cul de sacs*, forcing backup. The first situation is an example of *fan in*; the second of *fan out*. Of course, in the second situation, the shape favors backward chaining because reversing the direction of chaining changes fan-out situations into fan-in situations.

GPS Involves Depth-first Search

Note that ordinary, forward-chaining GPS involves a commitment to one kind of search, namely depth-first search. This is illuminated by the following procedure description, with its outer, depth-first wrapper:

To reach a goal state from a current state using GPS:

1 Form a one-state queue consisting of the current state.
2 Until the queue is empty or the goal state has been reached, call the first state in the queue the current state:

    2a   If there is no untried procedure for reducing the difference between the current state and the goal state, remove the first state from the queue.

    2b   Otherwise select a procedure for reducing the difference:

        2b1   If the procedure's preconditions are not satisfied, attempt to satisfy them using GPS with the preconditions defining a new goal state.

        2b2   If the preconditions are satisfied, use the procedure and put the new state at the front of the queue.

3 If the goal state has been found, announce success; otherwise, announce failure.

Note that step 2b.1 is the one that distinguishes GPS from depth-first search.

Deferring Recursion Gives GPS Some Planning Ability

Sometimes solving a problem can involve deep recursion and considerable effort in satisfying various prerequisite conditions. To avoid wasteful diversions, care must be taken to avoid working on any of the prerequisites for a step if it is clear that the step is bad.

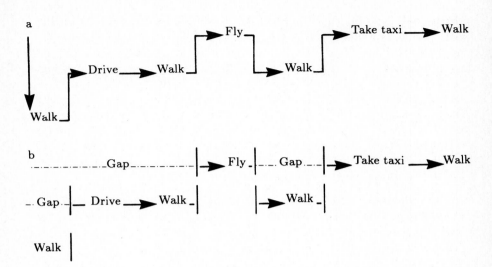

Figure 5-16. The General Problem Solver may dive deeply in order to prepare for procedures relevant to the overall goal. In part *a* for example, two second-level procedures and one third-level procedure prepare for the first-level procedure, Fly. Deferring effort on subproblems avoids wasted effort when the first-level procedure does no good. In part *b*, the first thing is to be sure that the first-level procedures reach the goal. Then the second-level prerequisite problems are investigated, again with details deferred. Finally, gaps are filled on the third level.

One way to avoid wasteful diversions is to plan a problem's solution in broad outline before working on details. One way to plan is to drop concern for prerequisite conditions temporarily.

In the travel example, prerequisites for the very first step, getting on an airplane, require some recursive problem-solving activity. We can see the scope of the recursion in the diagram in figure 5-16a.

In figure 5-16b, work at each level is viewed as a planning exercise, with details to be filled in by work at the next level down. The problem is solved first on the top level of main steps only—there would be no concern about getting to the airplane until the consequences of getting there are explored. Gaps are filled in later after overall success.

But in filling the gaps on the second level, again no attention is paid to prerequisites. The problem of getting to the car is deferred until a third pass.

Why go to this trouble? There is no particular advantage in the example used since each procedure selected proved useful and correct. But if there is a choice between several procedures, all with a good but not certain chance of being useful, then surely the problem solver should avoid wasting effort satisfying the prerequisites of one procedure if it will only prove to be a disappointing performer.

GPS Incorporates Powerful Problem-Solving and Control Ideas

Our description of GPS has made several important control decisions explicit and has stood mute on others:

- GPS applies itself to subproblems. One aspect of GPS therefore involves recursive, hierarchical, action-centered control.

- GPS achieves goals by finding procedures using differences. Since GPS finds procedures using differences, which may be thought of as constituting an object class, another aspect of GPS involves object-centered control.

- GPS itself is a procedure that finds procedures for doing things. Any use of GPS also must involve procedures that do things, namely reduce differences. There are no procedures for showing something cannot be done.

- GPS involves no statement about resource allocation among procedures. There is no parallelism, nor is a procedure stopped before it succeeds or gives up. Similarly, GPS involves no statement about communication among procedures.

Thus GPS is a name for a collection of control decisions. Note, however, that control choices blur into problem-solving paradigms.

In particular, GPS involves the following ideas, each of which can be thought of as a problem-solving paradigm:

- GPS has the goal of reducing the difference between a current state and a goal state. GPS therefore involves means-ends analysis.

- GPS moves forward iteratively, searching for a goal. GPS therefore involves search, the particular kind being depth-first search with backup.

- GPS creates subgoals. GPS therefore involves problem reduction.

- GPS, in one version, defers action on details until after the overall solution path is established. GPS therefore can involve a kind of planning.

GPS Is Not a Modern Control Structure

GPS has been described in detail because it nicely illustrates a number of important control ideas and because it embodies the important means-ends-analysis problem-solving paradigm.   It is not, however, the latest word in control structures, and therefore fails to introduce some contemporary issues like the following:

- How is it possible to maintain coherence and consensus among parallel procedures? GPS can say nothing about this since GPS involves no parallelism.
- How is it possible for a problem solver to spawn new procedures as problem solving proceeds? GPS can say nothing about this since GPS's collection of procedures is fixed.

There are many interesting proposals for dealing with these questions, but as yet the dust is still unsettled.

Control Ideas Are Seductive

Sophisticated control ideas are dangerous because they can deflect people away from fundamental questions about representation and constraint. Perhaps control ideas are seductive because complicated results seem to imply complicated means. But recall that the zigs and zags of an ant on a pebbled beach are explained by the complicated environment, not by the control mechanisms at work in the ant's brain. Keep this motto in mind:

- A sophisticated control strategy can make smart procedures smarter, but they cannot make stupid procedures smart.

SUMMARY

- Control schemes can be classified according to the choices embodied in them. These include choices about where knowledge about procedures is stored, how procedures are selected for use, how computational resources are allocated, what procedures do, and the means by which procedures communicate.
- Procedure knowledge may be stored in action-centered, object-centered, or request-centered fashion.
- The procedure to be used, if more than one applies, may be selected by the work-requesting procedure, the work-doing procedures, jointly, or at random.
- Procedures may share computational power in various ways: equally, by quality of result, by cost, or by return on investment.
- Procedures may do something, find a way to do something, or show that something cannot be done.
- Procedures may speak to each other over private lines, through blackboards, or by a variety of other means. The language spoken will lie somewhere on a spectrum from value lists, through name-value lists, to freewheeling, humanlike language.

- GPS embodies a set of control decisions and problem-solving paradigms, concentrating on difference reduction, sometimes called means-ends analysis.

- GPS exhibits both recursive, hierarchical, action-centered control and object-centered control.

- GPS is a procedure, in part, that finds procedures. GPS uses the procedures it finds to chain forward from an initial state to a goal state.

- Variations on GPS have planning ability by virtue of deferring recursion.

REFERENCES

The source of the metaphor of the wandering ant is Herbert A. Simon's book, *The Sciences of the Artificial* [1969]. This classic little book also contains a discussion of what Simon calls nearly decomposable systems and why science depends on them.

The negotiation metaphor is from the work of Randall Davis and Reid G. Smith [1983]; the scientific-community metaphor is from the work of Carl E. Hewitt and his colleagues [William A. Kornfeld and Hewitt 1981; Hewitt and Peter de Jong 1982].

Other ideas are from the work of Marvin Minsky, particularly work on what Minsky calls the society-of-minds theory [1977, 1979]. The theory concentrates on how intelligent behavior arises from communicating agents, each of which is minimally talented, each of which communicates by using reserved spots. There is emphasis on how intelligence develops in children and on anatomical implications.

HEARSAY II was developed by a team that included Raj Reddy, Victor R. Lesser, and Lee D. Erman [Lesser and Erman 1977]. The lessons to be learned from HEARSAY II remain argued. Some say powerful control ideas were demonstrated. Others retort that the particular control decisions in HEARSAY II were unimportant, insisting instead that the key to success was the involvement of powerful constraints down at the phoneme and syllable level.

GPS was developed primarily by Allen Newell, John C. Shaw, and Herbert A. Simon [1957]. For an exhaustive treatment of GPS, see *GPS: a Case Study in Generality and Problem Solving* [1969], by George Ernst and Allen Newell. The book describes a dozen or so problem domains like integral calculus and plane geometry, cast in GPS terms.

6

Problem-Solving
Paradigms

Much of Artificial Intelligence is about problem solving. Consequently, competence in Artificial Intelligence requires access to an armamentarium of problem-solving paradigms. We already have several: chapter 2 introduced the describe-and-match paradigm and the goal-reduction paradigm; chapter 3 examined constraint propagation; chapter 4 explored search; and chapter 5 looked at means-ends analysis. In chapter 7, we look at still another paradigm, that of formal logic.[1]

In this chapter, we concentrate on two other, particularly popular problem-solving paradigms, *generate-and-test systems* and *rule-based systems*. We work with generate-and-test systems first. Variations on the generate-and-test problem-solving paradigm appear in a wide variety of practical systems: one system finds airplanes in airport pictures using a kind of controlled hallucination; another identifies organic-chemical structures from their mass spectrograms.

Second, we study *rule-based systems*, also known as *production systems*. The rule-based-system paradigm is the one that is most popular in *knowledge engineering*, the part of Artificial Intelligence specialized for building

---

[1] Many problem-solving paradigms require only a weak understanding of the domains to which they are applied. Consequently, some people call such problem-solving paradigms *weak methods*. I do not use *weak* because it can be confused with *low power*.

expert systems. Some rule-based expert systems do *synthesis.* XCON configures computers, for example. Other rule-based expert systems do *analysis.* MYCIN diagnoses infectious diseases, and PROSPECTOR interprets oil-well logs. Both synthesis- and analysis-oriented rule-based systems can explain how and why they do things, and they can estimate the quality of their results.

In chapter 12, you will see a procedure that generates and learns the rules in rule-based systems.

In studying this chapter, you learn that the problem-solving paradigms explained are strong enough to make important, economically exciting problem solvers. On the other side, you must realize that these paradigms, by themselves, are too weak to support many of the characteristics of human experts (hence we will avoid the common designation *expert system*).

GENERATE AND TEST

Problem solvers adhering to the *generate-and-test paradigm* use two basic modules. One module, the *generator*, enumerates possible solutions. The second, the *tester*, evaluates each proposed solution, either accepting it or rejecting it.

Depending on the purpose and the nature of the problem, the generator may generate all possible solutions before the tester takes over, or alternatively, generation and testing may be interdigitated. Action may stop when one acceptable solution is found, or action may continue until some satisfactory number of solutions is found, or action may continue until all possible solutions are generated and tested.

Generate-and-test Systems Often Do Identification

The generate-and-test paradigm is used most frequently to solve identification problems involving no more than a few hundred possible answers. In identification problems, the generator is said to produce hypotheses.

To use the generate-and-test paradigm to identify, say, a tree, you can reach for a tree book, thumb through it page by page, stopping when you find a picture that looks like the tree to be identified. Thumbing through the book is the generation procedure; matching the pictures to the tree is the testing procedure.

To use generate and test to burgle a three-number, two-digit safe, you can start with the combination 00-00-00, move to 00-00-01, and continue on through all possible combinations until the door opens. Of course, the counting is the generation procedure, and the twist of the safe handle is the testing procedure.

The burglar in figure 6-1 may take some time with this approach, however, for there are $100^3 = 1$ million combinations. At three a minute,

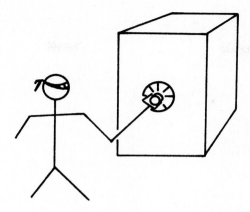

Figure 6-1. An example illustrating the generate-and-test paradigm. The generator is the procedure the safecracker uses to select and dial combinations. The tester is the burglar working with the handle. Careful safecrackers make sure they try all possibilities, without any repeats, until the handle works.

figuring he will have to go through half, on the average, to succeed, the job will take about 16 weeks, if he works 24 hours a day.

Generators Should Be Complete, Nonredundant, and Informed

It is obvious that good generators have three properties:

- Good generators are complete. They eventually produce all possible solutions.

- Good generators are nonredundant. They never damage efficiency by proposing the same solution twice.

- Good generators are informed. They use possibility-limiting information, restricting the solutions they propose accordingly.

Informability is important because there are often too many solutions to go through otherwise. Consider the tree-identification example. If it is winter and a tree we are trying to identify is bare, we do not bother going through a tree book's conifer section.

Similarly, if a burglar knows, somehow, that all of the numbers in a safe combination are prime numbers in the range from 0 to 99, then he can confine himself to $25^3 = 15,625$ numbers, getting the safe open in less than 2 days, on the average, instead of 16 weeks.

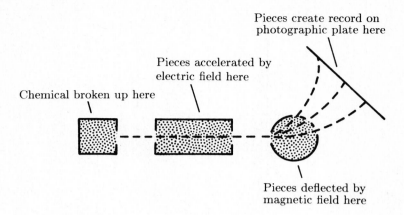

Figure 6-2. A mass spectrometer. An organic chemical under study is broken up, the fragments are separated according to their mass-to-charge ratio, and the results are recorded, making a mass spectrogram.

Analyzing Mass Spectrograms Illustrates Generate-and-test

Suppose an organic chemist wants to know the chemical nature of something newly created in the test tube. The first step, not the one of concern here, is to determine the number of atoms of various kinds in one molecule of the stuff. This is given by a chemical formula, such as $C_8H_{16}O$, which is the example used throughout this discussion. The notation indicates that each molecule has eight atoms of carbon, sixteen of hydrogen, and one of oxygen.

Once a sample's chemical formula is known, the chemist uses the sample's mass spectrogram to work out the way the atoms are arranged in the chemical's structure, thus identifying the isomer of the chemical that constitutes the sample.

The mass spectrogram is produced as indicated in figure 6-2. The spectrogram machine bombards a sample with high energy electrons, causing the molecules to break up into charged chunks of various sizes. Then the chunks are sorted by sending them through a magnetic field that deflects the high-charge, low-weight ones more than the low-charge, high-weight ones. The deflected chunks are collected, forming the spectrogram.

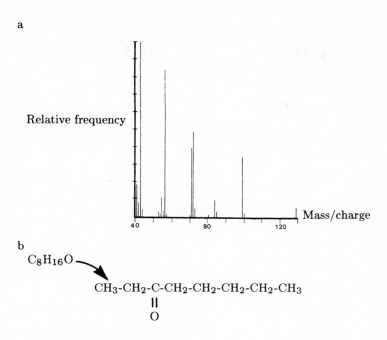

Figure 6-3. Part *a* shows a mass spectrogram. Organic chemists use such mass spectrograms, together with chemical formulas to deduce chemical structures. Part *b* shows a chemical formula and a structure consistent with the formula, with general knowledge of chemical structure, and with the given mass spectrogram. Adapted from *Machine Intelligence 4*, copyright 1969 by American Elsevier Publishing Company, New York. Used with permission of Donald Michie, editor in chief, Machine Intelligence Series.

Figure 6-3a shows a typical spectrogram. The purpose of the DENDRAL system is to work, like a knowledgeable chemist, from a chemical formula and spectrogram to a deduced structure. Such a chemical formula and deduced chemical structure are shown in figure 6-3b.

As indicated in figure 6-4, the DENDRAL system works out structures from chemical formulas and mass spectrograms using generate and test:

- The chemical formula is fed to a structure enumerator capable of generating all possible structures. The structure enumerator limits its output to things consistent with the given chemical formula.

- The structure enumerator receives information to the effect that certain substructures must be present and others must not be present. The substructure lists come primarily from a preliminary analysis of the spectrogram. (This preliminary analysis is described in a later section.)

- A mass spectrogram is synthesized for each structure generated. The combination of the structure enumerator and the mass-spectrogram synthesizer constitutes the generator required by the generate-and-test paradigm. It is complete and nonredundant because it uses a provably complete and nonredundant structure-enumeration procedure. It is informed because the structure-enumeration procedure uses the chemical formula and knowledge about necessary and forbidden substructures.

- The synthetic mass spectrograms are all compared with the real experimental spectrogram. The possible structures are those whose synthetic spectrograms match the real one adequately. The structure judged correct is the one whose synthetic spectrogram matches the real one best. The matcher constitutes the tester of the generate-and-test paradigm.

The matcher could work by forming a sum of the squares of the differences in spectrogram-peak heights, the sort of standard engineering measure of signal difference. The actual DENDRAL matcher is more involved because it is necessary to recognize that some peaks are more significant than others. The procedure used does this by way of the following:

- Certain break-up rules mark their products as especially significant.

- If any so-marked significant peak is not in the experimental spectrogram, then the structure that predicted that significant peak is rejected outright.

- The remaining spectrograms are then ranked according to how many of the experimental peaks each accounts for. The remaining spectrograms rarely tie.

This matcher usually eliminates all but a few structures, which then are reported in the order of their likelihood. In the $C_8H_{16}O$ example, with the given spectrogram, only one structure survives.

ACRONYM Finds Objects

Computer vision is another area in which the generate-and-test procedure can be used. Figure 6-5 gives a simple example having to do with line verification. The bulk of a cube has been found, conditioning a line proposer to suggest a hard look in the dotted region for one additional line. The line proposer is a generator, one heavily informed by the lines already found.

On another level, three-dimensional models can be used to predict what objects to look for, where they are, and what size they are. Figure 6-6 illustrates in a domain hybridized from blocks on one side and real structures of occasional interest on the other. Figure 6-6a defines the domain, indicating that there may be toy trains, toy grain-storage units, and toy oil tanks, made of bricks, cylinders, and spheres. In figure 6-6b, the scene evidently is viewed from above, since only a toy engine, seen from above, can look

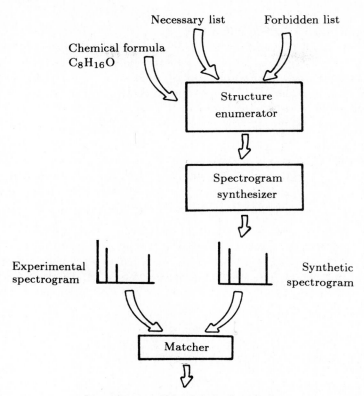

Figure 6-4. DENDRAL uses the generate-and-test paradigm to find chemical structures. The structure enumerator is influenced by lists of necessary and forbidden fragments. A spectrogram synthesizer produces a synthetic spectrogram for each proposed chemical structure. The enumeration of possible structures is complete, nonredundant, and informed. A proposed chemical structure is accepted if its synthetic spectrogram yields a good match with the experimental spectrogram.

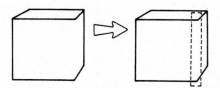

Figure 6-5. An example illustrating the generate-and-test paradigm applied to vision. Existing lines are consistent with the presence of a brick, enabling a generator to propose the missing internal vertical line, activating a line tester that looks in the dotted region.

like figure 6-6b. Knowing this enables the generator to propose additional cars in the dotted areas shown. On the other hand, seeing the rectangle in figure 6-6c, and knowing somehow that the view is from the side, enables the generator to propose additional rectangles and spheres, inasmuch as the ones already viewed suggest the presence of a toy grain elevator and a toy oil depot.

The generator must embody considerable geometric knowledge, making the creation of such generators difficult. ACRONYM, a powerful object-modeling and vision-supporting system, has such a knowledge-rich generator. Figure 6-7 illustrates how ACRONYM uses three-dimensional models to make predictions once it has a partial analysis. In this situation, expecting to see an airplane in an aerial photograph is the key to progress.

In summary, you have seen that much problem-solving knowledge can reside in generating procedures and in testing procedures, but there is no systematic way of representing that particular kind of knowledge. In the next section, you will see that much problem-solving knowledge can be packaged up in the form of rules that do embody knowledge in a systematic way.

RULE-BASED SYSTEMS FOR SYNTHESIS

So far, most successful synthesis systems and analysis systems embody the rule-based problem-solving paradigm. Rule-based problem-solving systems are built around rules like the following one, which consists of an *if* part and a *then* part:

Rn If   condition 1
            condition 2
            .
            .
            .

    then   action 1
            action 2
            .
            .
            .

To work forward with such rules, moving from condition-specifying *if* parts to action-specifying *then* parts, we use *forward-chaining*, and we speak of a *forward-chaining condition-action system* containing *condition-action rules*.

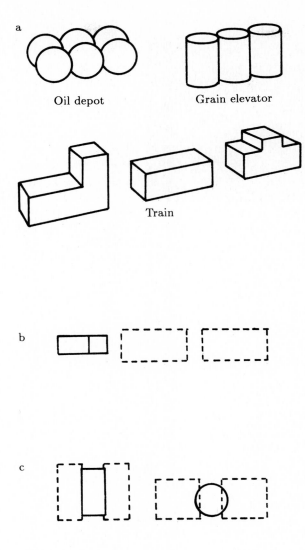

Figure 6-6. Another example of the generate-and-test paradigm applied to vision, this time at the object level rather than at the line level. Having a three-dimensional description, together with a partially analyzed picture, a talented generator can make many predictions. Part *a* defines the world. The scenes in part *b* and part *c* provide enough constraint to enable a generator to make predictions about what must lie in the dotted areas.

a

b

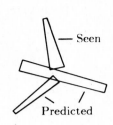

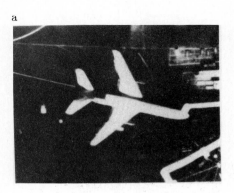

Figure 6-7. ACRONYM makes predictions using models. Once the left wing in the blurry photograph is seen in part *a*, ACRONYM uses a model to generate expectations about where the rest of the airplane must be. ACRONYM then tests the appropriate places, verifying that predictions about the body and right wing, shown in part *b*, are compatible with the image.

Here is the procedure for forward chaining:

To forward chain using if-then rules:
1 Until a problem is solved or no rule's *if* parts are satisfied by the current situation:
   1.1 Collect rules whose *if* parts are satisfied. If more than one rule's *if* parts are satisfied, use a conflict-resolution strategy to eliminate all but one.
   1.2 Do what the rule's *then* parts say to do.

When all the conditions in a rule are satisfied by the current situation, the rule is said to *be triggered*. When the actions are performed, the rule is said to *be fired*. Triggering does not always mean firing, because the conditions of several rules may be satisfied simultaneously, triggering them all, making it necessary for a conflict-resolution procedure to decide which rule actually fires. Several conflict-resolution procedures will be discussed presently, while some examples are developed.

The first example involves a synthesis-oriented, forward-chaining, rule-based toy system for bagging groceries. The next example involves a practical system for laying out computer systems. The layout system, XCON, is one of the harbingers of Artificial Intelligence's penetration into engineering design.

A Toy Synthesis System Bags Groceries

Suppose we want Robbie, our robot, to bag groceries in the manner of a grocery-store checkout clerk. We are not interested in optimal packing, but we do want Robbie to know some of the fundamentals of grocery bagging: big bottles of Pepsi go in the bottom, with not too many in any one bag; ice cream is protected with freezer bags; and little things are stuffed here and there when everything else is in place.

We will have Robbie approach the job using BAGGER, a rule-based synthesis system. BAGGER involves four steps, as shown by the following procedure description:

BAGGER:

1   Check what the customer has selected, looking over the groceries to see if something may be missing, with a view toward suggesting additions to the customer.
2   Bag the large items, with special attention to putting big bottles in first.
3   Bag the medium items, taking care to put frozen things in freezer bags.
4   Bag the small items, putting them wherever there is room.

And, of course, whenever necessary, BAGGER commands Robbie to start a fresh bag.

Now let us see how this knowledge can be captured in if-then rules. First, we need a database for the rules to look at. The database certainly must contain information about the items in each bag, the items yet to be bagged, and the current step. Here is a suitable database for illustrating what is involved:

Step: Check-order
Bag1:
Unbagged: Bread
                 Glop
                 Granola (2)
                 Ice cream
                 Potato chips

In addition, the rules need access to information about the size and other properties of various items:

Item	Container Type	Size	Frozen?
Bread	Plastic bag	Medium	No
Glop	Jar	Small	No
Granola	Cardboard box	Large	No
Ice cream	Cardboard carton	Medium	Yes
Pepsi	Bottle	Large	No
Potato chips	Plastic bag	Medium	No

Note that the database contains a step name. Each of the rules in BAGGER's rule base tests the step name. The effect is a partitioning of the rules into packets suited to each bagging step. For example, activation of the following rule is limited to the check-order step by a check-order condition:

B1   If   the step is check-order
             there is a bag of potato chips
             there is no soft-drink bottle
      then   add one bottle of Pepsi to the order

The purpose of the rule is to be sure the customer has something to drink to go along with potato chips, since potato chips are dry and salty.

Since we are interested only in illustrating some points, not in capturing all of bagging knowledge, let us move on immediately to a rule to get us out of order checking and into the next step. The following rule does this, getting us into the bag-large-items step:

B2   If   the step is check-order
      then   discontinue the check-order step
             start the bag-large-items step

At first, this rule may seem dangerous, for it looks as though it could trigger at any time in the check-order step, preventing the other rule from doing its legitimate and necessary work. No problem; we simply adopt a suitable conflict-resolution strategy. Here are some possibilities:

- *Specificity ordering.* Suppose the conditions of one triggering rule are a superset of the conditions of another triggering rule. Use the rule with the superset on the ground that it is more specialized to the current situation.

- *Rule ordering.* Arrange all rules in one long priority list. The triggering rule appearing earliest in the list has the highest priority. The others are ignored.

- *Data ordering.* Arrange all possible aspects of the situation in one long priority list. The triggering rule having the highest priority condition has the highest priority.

- *Size ordering.* Assign the highest priority to the triggering rule with the toughest requirements, where toughest means the longest list of constraining conditions.

- *Recency ordering.* Consider the most recently used rule to have the highest priority, or consider the least recent to have the highest priority, at the designer's whim.

- *Context limiting.* Reduce the likelihood of conflict by separating the rules into groups, only some of which are active at any time. Have a procedure that activates and deactivates groups.

Of course, having a set of possibilities to choose among does not mean we have a science of conflict resolution. Selection of a strategy is done ad hoc, for the most part.

Note that BAGGER uses the context-limiting strategy because, by convention, the first condition clause of each rule limits the rule to a particular step.

Assume BAGGER also uses the specificity-ordering conflict-resolution strategy. This means that the B2 check-order rule never can fire as long as any other check-order rule triggers. Each step has a rule just like B2 to switch into the next step when nothing else can be done.

Using specificity-ordering conflict resolution helps out in other ways as well. Consider, for example, the first two rules for bagging large items:

B3 If   the step is bag-large-items
            there is a large item to be bagged
            there is a large bottle to be bagged
            there is a bag with < 6 large items
     then   put the bottle in the bag
B4 If   the step is bag-large-items
            there is a large item to be bagged
            there is a bag with < 6 large items
     then   put the large item in the bag

Big items go into bags that do not have too many items already, but the bottles, being heavy, go in first. The extra condition in B3 ensures this ordering. When there is a large bottle, both rules' conditions will match, but B3's conditions are a superset of B4's, so B3 takes precedence.

Of course, we need a way of handling large bottles and other large items if there is no room in any bag. This is done by B5:

B5   If   the step is bag-large-items
             there is a large item to be bagged
      then   start a fresh bag

And finally, another step-changing rule moves us on to the next step:

B6   If   the step is bag-large-items
      then   discontinue the bag-large-items step
             start the bag-medium-items step

With the database given, simulating the rules given so far, we have one bag containing Pepsi and granola, as shown here:

Step: Bag-medium-items
Bag1:   Pepsi
               Granola (2)
Unbagged: Bread
               Glop
               Ice cream
               Potato chips

Now it is time to look at some rules for bagging medium items:

B7   If   the step is bag-medium-items
             there is a medium item to be bagged
             there is an empty bag or a bag with medium items
             the bag is not yet full
             the medium item is frozen
             the medium item is not in an insulated freezer bag
      then   put the medium item in an insulated freezer bag
B8   If   the step is bag-medium-items
             there is a medium item to be bagged
             there is an empty bag or a bag with medium items
             the bag is not yet full
      then   put the medium item in the bag

Again, the specificity-ordering conflict-resolution strategy works. If both B7 and B8 are matched, B7 wins, ensuring that frozen things are placed in insulated freezer bags before bagging.

The bag-medium-items step also needs these rules, one to get new bags going and one to get into the next and final step:

B9   If   the step is bag-medium-items
             there is a medium item to be bagged
      then   start a fresh bag

B10 If   the step is bag-medium-items
      then   discontinue the bag-medium-items step
             start the bag-small-items step

At this point, after execution of all appropriate bag-medium-item rules, we have the following database:

Step: Bag-small-items
Bag1:   Pepsi
             Granola (2)
Bag2:   Bread
             Ice cream (in freezer bag)
             Potato chips
Unbagged: Glop

Note that, according to the rules, medium items do not go into bags with large items. This is not true for small items, for the next rules can put them anywhere, but not in a bottle-holding bag, if others are available:

B11 If   the step is bag-small-items
             there is a small item
             there is a bag that is not yet full
             the bag does not contain bottles
      then   put the small item in the bag

B12 If   the step is bag-small-items
             there is a small item
             there is a bag that is not yet full
      then   put the small item in the bag

We still need a rule to get a new bag:

B13 If   the step is bag-small-items
             there is a small item
      then   start a fresh bag

And we need a rule to terminate action when done:

B14 If   the step is bag-small-items
      then   discontinue the bag-small-items step
             stop

Here is the final result for our illustration. after all rules have been used:

Step: Stop
Bag1:   Pepsi
               Granola (2)
Bag2:   Bread
               Ice cream (in freezer bag)
               Potato chips
               Glop
Unbagged:

XCON Configures Computer Systems

Now it is time to consider an example of a real rule-based synthesis system resembling BAGGER. The XCON system is appropriate, for it is famous, yet simple. Like BAGGER, XCON is a forward-chaining system.

XCON's domain concerns computer-system components. When a company buys a big computer, it buys a central processor, memory, terminals, disk drives, tape drives, various peripheral controllers, and other paraphernalia. All this must be arranged sensibly along input/output busses. Moreover, all the electronic modules must be placed in the proper kind of cabinet in a suitable slot of a suitable backplane.

Getting things arranged and placed is a task called *configuration*. Doing configuration is tedious because a typical computer component family has hundreds of possible options that can come together in an unthinkable number of combinations.

Like BAGGER, XCON does its job in stages:

XCON:
1 Check the order, looking for mismatched items and missing components.
2 Lay out the processor in cabinets.
3 Put boxes in the input/output cabinets, and put components in those boxes.
4 Put panels in the input/output cabinets.
5 Lay out the floor plan.
6 Do the cabling.

To handle these steps, XCON uses rules like this representative pair:

X1   If   the context is layout and assigning a power supply
            an sbi module of any type has been put in a cabinet
            the position it occupies in the cabinet is known
            there is space available in the cabinet for a power supply
            there is no available power supply
            the voltage and frequency of the components is known
     then   add an appropriate power supply

X2   If   the context is layout and assigning a power supply
            an sbi module of any type has been put in a cabinet
            the position it occupies in the cabinet is known
            there is space available in the cabinet for a power supply
            there is an available power supply
     then   put the power supply in the cabinet in the available space

The first rule acts rather like the one in BAGGER that adds Pepsi if the order contains potato chips but no beverage. The second is a typical insertion rule. The context mentioned in both rules is a combination of the top-level step and a substep.

Like BAGGER, XCON uses the context-limiting and the specificity-ordering conflict-resolution strategies. Context limiting is done by making the first clause in each rule conditional on what is going on. Specificity ordering enables XCON to use rules like the following one for switching contexts:

X3   If   the current context is x
     then   deactivate the x context
            activate the y context

This has the effect of deleting one item from the context designation and adding another. It fires only if no other rule associated with the context triggers, for any other triggering rule would have conditions that are a superset of unaccompanied context checking.

Curiously, XCON hardly ever backs up. For the most part, it forges ahead like BAGGER. Evidently, the domain is such that the rules embody enough constraint to prevent going into blind alleys, generally.

At the moment, XCON is a 2500-rule system and growing. XCON knows the properties of several hundred component types for VAX computers, made by Digital Equipment Corporation. XCON routinely handles orders involving one- or two-hundred components. It is representative of many similar systems for marketing and manufacturing.

Soon people will forget how to configure well, but that does not matter: people wanting to learn can study a rule-based configuration system. XCON, after all, demonstrates that a rule-based system can embody all the configuration knowledge needed to do configuration well.

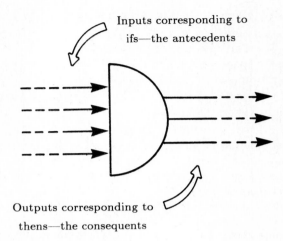

Figure 6-8. A convenient graphical notation for antecedent-consequent rules. The symbol, appropriately, is the same as the one used in digital electronics for AND gates.

Rule-based Systems Can Be Idiot Savants

Rule-based systems do some things so well, they can be said to be *savants* with respect to those things:

- They can answer simple questions about how they reach their conclusions and why they ask questions.

Still, basic rule-based systems lack many of the characteristics of human experts, qualifying them to be *idiot savants*:

- Basic rule-based systems do not learn.
- They do not reason on multiple levels.
- They do not use constraint-exposing models.
- They do not look at problems from different perspectives.
- They do not know how and when to break their own rules.
- They do not have access to the reasoning behind their rules.

In principle, there is nothing to prevent building more humanlike systems, using rules for bricks and mortar, but on the other hand, the *basic* rule-based-system paradigm takes us only partway toward those systems, at best.

RULE-BASED SYSTEMS FOR ANALYSIS

So far, we have focused exclusively on synthesis-oriented rule-based systems. We now turn away from synthesis, looking at analysis, using a toy system that does animal identification. Applications for analysis ideas are illustrated by systems for medical diagnosis and oil-well log interpretation. Such systems include procedures for answering questions and for calculating answer reliability.

Many Rule-based Systems Are Deduction Systems

Suppose that the *if* parts of some if-then rules specify combinations of known facts. Also suppose that the *then* parts specify new facts to be deduced directly from the triggering combination. So constrained, a rule-based system becomes a type of *deduction system*: the *if* parts of the rules may be called *antecedents*, and the *then* parts, *consequences*. Figure 6-8 shows a graphical notation for deduction-oriented *antecedent-consequent rules*.

The restrictions that make rule-based systems into deduction systems are satisfied by the examples in this section. Nevertheless, in discussing the examples, we will stick to the more general term, *rule-based system.*

A Toy Analysis System Identifies Animals

Suppose that Robbie, our robot, wants to spend a day at the zoo. Plainly Robbie will enjoy the visit more if he can recognize various animals. Assume Robbie can see basic features like color and size, but he does not know how to combine such facts into conclusions like, say, this is a zebra, or that is a tiger.

We will have Robbie approach the analysis job using IDENTIFIER, a rule-based system that takes collections of known facts and makes new conclusions.

Having one if-then rule for each animal in the zoo is possible, albeit dull. The consequent side of each rule would be a simple statement of animal name, and the antecedent side would be a bulbous enumeration of characteristics large enough to reject all incorrect identifications. In operation, the user would first gather up all facts available and then scan the antecedent-consequent rule list for an antecedent-consequent rule that has a matching antecedent part.

A better idea is to generate intermediate facts, making the reasoning procedure more interesting. The advantage is that the antecedent-consequent rules involved can be small, easily understood, easily used, and easily created. Using this approach, the IDENTIFIER procedure produces chains of conclusions leading to the name of the animal Robbie is examining.

Suppose Robbie concentrates on an antechamber of the zoo that contains only seven popular animals. This simplifies IDENTIFIER because only a small number of identification antecedent-consequent rules are needed.

Four of them are simple ones that determine the biological class, mammal or bird:

I1 If   the animal has hair
    then it is a mammal

I2 If   the animal gives milk
    then it is a mammal

I3 If   the animal has feathers
    then it is a bird

I4 If   the animal flies
          it lays eggs
    then it is a bird

The last of these, I4, has two elements in the antecedent collection. Although it does not really matter for our small collection of animals, some mammals fly and some reptiles lay eggs, but only birds do both.

Once it is known that an animal is a mammal, two antecedent-consequent rules determine whether it is carnivorous. The simpler has to do with catching the animal in the act:

I5 If   the animal is a mammal
          it eats meat
    then it is a carnivore

If it is not feeding time, a variety of other factors, taken together, are conclusive:

I6 If   the animal is a mammal
          it has pointed teeth
          it has claws
          its eyes point forward
    then it is a carnivore

The other animals in the zoo that are mammals all happen to be ungulates:

I7 If   the animal is a mammal
          it has hoofs
    then it is an ungulate

If Robbie has a hard time looking at the feet, IDENTIFIER may still have a chance, since any animal that chews its cud is certainly an ungulate, too:

I8   If   the animal is a mammal
             it chews cud
     then   it is an ungulate
             it is even-toed

The business about the toes is there just to show an example of an antecedent-consequent rule with multiple consequents.

Now that we have rules that divide mammals into carnivores and ungulates, it is time to look at rules that identify specific animals. For carnivores,
two possibilities exist:

I9   If   the animal is a carnivore
             it has a tawny color
             it has dark spots
     then   it is a cheetah
I10 If   the animal is a carnivore
             it has a tawny color
             it has black strips
     then   it is a tiger

Strictly speaking, the basic color is not useful since both of the carnivores are tawny. However, there is no law saying that the information in
antecedent-consequent rules must be minimal. Often it is better to focus on
the individual antecedent-consequent rule, putting in what seems natural,
accepting some superfluous antecedents.

For the ungulates, other antecedent-consequent rules separate the total
group into two possibilities:

I11 If   the animal is an ungulate
             it has long legs
             it has a long neck
             it has a tawny color
             it has dark spots
     then   it is a giraffe
I12 If   the animal is an ungulate
             it has a white color
             it has black stripes
     then   it is a zebra

Having worked through the four available mammals, the same can be done
for the three birds:

I13 If   the animal is a bird
             it does not fly
             it has long legs
             it has a long neck
             it is black and white
     then   it is an ostrich.

I14 If   the animal is a bird
             it does not fly
             it swims
             it is black and white
     then   it is a penguin

I15 If   the animal is a bird
             it is a good flyer
     then   it is an albatross

With all of the animals on the table, so to speak, note that the animals share many features. Zebras and tigers have black stripes; tigers, cheetahs, and giraffes have a tawny color; giraffes and ostriches have long legs and a long neck; and ostriches and penguins are black and white.

Now for a case study, suppose Robbie is at the zoo and proceeds to analyze an unknown animal using IDENTIFIER:

- The observed animal has a tawny color and dark spots. Antecedent-consequent rule I9 and antecedent-consequent rule I11 are suggested since both have the tawny color and dark spots antecedents. Neither is triggered yet, however, since both have additional antecedent conditions to be met.

- While nursing a baby, the animal chews its cud. Evidently the animal gives milk, a fact that fires antecedent-consequent rule I2, establishing that the animal is a mammal. Since the animal is a mammal and since the animal chews its cud, antecedent-consequent rule I8 establishes that the animal is an ungulate and has two or four toes per foot. The antecedents for antecedent-consequent rule I11 are nearly all satisfied.

- The animal has long legs and a long neck. Antecedent-consequent rule I11 fires. The animal is a giraffe.

Thus the facts flow through a series of antecedent-consequent rules from facts on the left to a conclusion on the right, as shown in figure 6-9.

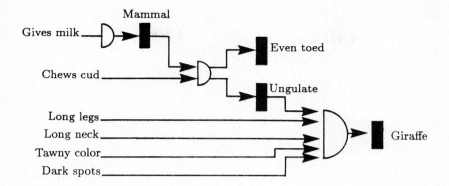

Figure 6-9. Knowing some facts about an unknown animal enables identification. Here, the facts on the left lead to the conclusion that the unknown animal is a giraffe.

Deductions Systems May Run Either Forward or Backward

So far, the deduction-oriented rule-based system is assumed to work from known facts to new, deduced facts. Running this way, a system exhibits forward chaining. But *backward chaining* is also possible, for a rule-based-system can hypothesize a conclusion and use the antecedent-consequent rules to work backward toward the hypothesis-supporting facts.

For example, IDENTIFIER might hypothesize that a given animal is a cheetah and then reason about whether the hypothesis is viable. Here is a scenario showing how things work out according to such a backward-chaining approach:

- It is hypothesized that the animal is a cheetah. To verify the hypothesis, rule I9 requires that the animal is a carnivore, that it has a tawny color, and that it has dark spots.

- We must check if the animal is a carnivore. Two rules may qualify, namely rule I5 and rule I6. Assume that rule I5 is tried first. It requires that the animal be a mammal.

- We must check if the animal is a mammal. Again there are two possibilities, rule I1 and rule I2. Let us try rule I1.

- We must check if the animal has hair. Checking this is a sensory system job again. Assume it has hair. This means it must be a mammal and IDENTIFIER can go back to working on rule I5.

- We must check if the animal eats meat. Assume there is no evidence at the moment. IDENTIFIER must abandon rule I5 and try to use rule I6 to establish that the animal is a carnivore.

- We must check if the animal is a mammal. It is, since this was already established when trying to satisfy the conditions for rule I5.

- We must check if the animal has pointed teeth, if it has claws, and if its eyes point forward. Assume the sensory system shows all are true. Evidently the animal is a carnivore, and IDENTIFIER can return to rule I9, which started everything done so far.

- It is hypothesized that the animal has a tawny color; and it is hypothesized that the animal has dark spots. Assume both are true. Rule I9 supports the hypothesis that the animal is a cheetah. Evidently it is.

Thus IDENTIFIER is able to work backward through the antecedent-consequent rules, using desired conclusions to decide what facts to look for. A backward-moving chain develops. The chaining ends successfully, verifying the hypothesis. The chaining ends unsuccessfully if some required antecedent facts are left dangling, corresponding to something that is known to be false or that cannot be established.

A deduction-oriented antecedent-consequent rule system can run forward or backward, but which is better? The question is decided by the purpose of the reasoning and by the shape of the search space. Certainly if the goal is to discover all that can be deduced from a given set of facts, then the antecedent-consequent rule system should run forward.

On the other hand, if the purpose is to verify or deny one particular conclusion, then the antecedent-consequent rule system should run backward, because many, many conclusions irrelevant to the target conclusion can usually come out of an initial, given set of facts. If these facts are fed to a forward-chaining antecedent-consequent rule system, then much work may be wasted in developing a combinatorial nightmare.

Rule-based Deduction Systems Create AND/OR Trees

One way to show what a set of antecedent-consequent rules can do is to draw a network showing how the facts that are the consequents of one rule serve as antecedents to the next. Figure 6-10, for example, shows how some of the antecedent-consequent rules in the animal-identification system, denoted by AND-gate symbols, fit together with the facts they use and produce. Vertical boxes denote raw facts, and vertical bars denote deduced facts. So displayed, the antecedent-consequent rules constitute what is called an *inference net.*

An equivalent way to show what a set of antecedent-consequent rules can do is to use an AND/OR tree. Figure 6-11 shows an AND/OR tree that reaches from base facts at the bottom, through antecedent-consequent rules, to two possible conclusions at the top. Any collection of antecedent-consequent rules defines such a tree. The collection used to define this

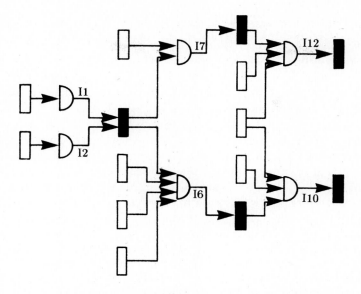

Figure 6-10. An example illustrating how antecedent-consequent rules tie facts together into an inference net. Open rectangles represent raw facts; solid rectangles represent deducible facts. The rules are those of the animal-identification system.

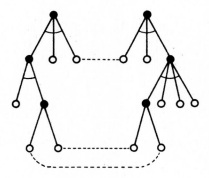

Figure 6-11. An inference net drawn to make explicit the AND/OR tree implied by collections of antecedent-consequent rules. Each AND collection of branches corresponds to an antecedent-consequent rule. Open circles represent raw facts; solid circles represent deducible facts. Raw facts used to reach more than one conclusion are represented by separate instances (here indicated by dotted lines joining the separate instances). This tree was made from the inference net in the last figure, figure 6-10.

double-rooted tree is equivalent to the set used to produce the inference net in figure 6-10.

As with ordinary AND/OR trees, conclusions are verified when it is possible to connect them to basic facts through a satisfied AND/OR tree.

Sometimes it is useful to look at the implied inference net or AND/OR tree to get a better feel for the search space, noting whether the reasoning is likely to be broad and shallow or narrow and deep or broad and deep. Caution is in order, however. When used prominently in discussing problem solving, inference nets and AND/OR trees tend to make problem solving look like just a matter of search. One bad feature of this search-oriented position is that it leads to fooling with search-procedure improvements rather than to making better problem representations.

In any event, because rule-based deduction systems generate AND/OR trees, we have the following procedure for backward chaining:

To backward chain using antecedent-consequent rules:

1   Use the AND/OR procedure from chapter 2, starting with the hypothesis. Use the antecedent-consequent rules to build the tree as the AND and the OR subprocedures work through the tree's nodes.

Some Rule-based Deduction Systems Can Explain Their Reasoning

By looking into a historical record of the antecedent-consequent rules used, rule-based systems can answer questions about *why* a fact was used or about *how* a fact was established. Much of this ability stands on the simple, highly constrained format that the rule-based-system paradigm imposes on rules. To decide how a given fact was concluded, a rule-based system need reflect only on the antecedent-consequent rules it has used, looking for those that contain the given fact as a consequent. The required answer is just an enumeration of those antecedent-consequent rules, perhaps accompanied by information about the facts in their antecedent sets.

Suppose, for example, that rule I6 has been used as shown in figure 6-12. If the question is "How did you show that the animal is a carnivore?" then the answer is determined by moving to the left, saying, "By using rule I6 and by knowing that the animal is a mammal, has pointed teeth, claws, and forward-pointing eyes." If the question is "Why did you show that the animal is a mammal?" then the answer is determined by moving to the right, saying, "Because I wanted to use rule I6 to show that the animal is a carnivore."

Other questions, such as "Did you use rule I6?" and "When did you use rule I6?" are also easy to answer.

Rule-based Deduction Systems Simplify Knowledge Transfer

When we confine our knowledge representation to condition-action rules, we lose because our flexibility and power are limited, but we gain because we can add interesting things to the basic problem-solving apparatus. To add a question-answering superprocedure, for example, we need to deal only with rules and rule histories.

Another relatively easy thing to add is a rule-transfer superprocedure that helps knowledge engineers to make new rules. Suppose, for example, that a knowledge engineer has asked enough *why* and *how* questions to determine that another rule is needed, one that captures the idea that an animal is a carnivore if it is seen stalking another.

The knowledge engineer therefore proposes the following new rule:

I16a If   the animal stalks a different kind of animal
      then it is a carnivore

There is evidence that something is missing, however. When compared with the other rules that conclude that an animal is a carnivore, this proposed one lacks a condition requiring that the animal is a mammal. Noting this, it makes sense for a knowledge-acquisition superprocedure to ask the knowledge engineer if the omission is intended. This would lead to a refined rule:

I16b If   the animal is a mammal
              the animal stalks a different kind of animal
      then it is a carnivore

With this understood, we can be a little more general, creating PRO-CRUSTES, a knowledge-acquisition procedure that encourages rule makers to have new rules look like old ones.

PROCRUSTES makes heavy use of natural rule groups. These natural rule groups are formed by filtering all existing rules down the tree shown in figure 6-13.

For each rule group, a typical member is formed by combining together all conditions and all actions that occur in, say, 30% of the group's rules. For the group of rules that conclude that an animal is a carnivore, there is one such condition, that the animal is a mammal, and, one such action, that the animal is a carnivore:

Typical-carnivore If   the animal is a mammal
                         then it is a carnivore

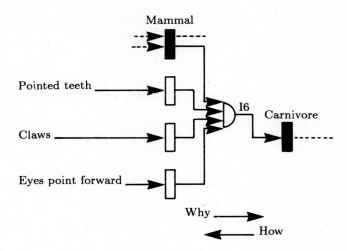

Figure 6-12. Rule-based systems retain a history of how they have tied facts together, enabling a kind of introspection. *How did you show ... ?* questions are answered by moving one step backward, mentioning rules and antecedents; *Why did you show ... ?* questions are answered by moving one step forward.

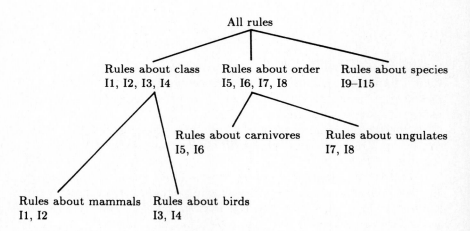

Figure 6-13. The rules in a rule-based system form natural groups according to the conclusions expressed in their action parts.

All PROCRUSTES needs to do, then, is to compare proposed rules with the typical rules of the applicable rule groups, asking the knowledge engineer for a decision whenever something in a typical rule is not in a proposed rule. In the example, the taxonomic order and carnivore rule groups are applicable, but only the carnivore group has a nontrivial typical member. Since the only condition of the typical member is missing from the proposed rule, I16a, PROCRUSTES would suggest that condition, leading to the better rule, I16b.

Thus procedures like PROCRUSTES can do a lot by *helping to transfer* rulelike knowledge from knowledge engineers to rule-based systems. In chapter 12, we discuss another procedure that can do even more by *directly producing* rulelike knowledge from precedents and exercises.

Certainty Factors Help Determine Answer Reliability

Rule-based systems used for identification usually work in domains where conclusions are rarely certain. Thus rule-based system developers often build some sort of certainty-computing procedure on top of the basic antecedent-consequent apparatus. Generally, certainty-computing procedures associate a number between 0 and 1 with each fact. This number, called a *certainty factor*, is intended to reflect how certain the fact is, with 0 indicating a fact is definitely false and 1 indicating a fact is definitely true.

Since the calculation of certainty factors is of practical importance, let us divert ourselves to look at the existing procedures. Understand, however, that none of these procedures is completely satisfactory. We are looking at what you can do now, not at what you want to do.

Note that any procedure for computing certainty factors must embody answers to three questions. First, how are the certainties associated with a rule's antecedents to be combined into the rule's overall *input certainty*? Second, how does the rule itself translate input certainty into *output certainty*? And third, how is a fact's certainty determined when the consequents of several antecedent-consequent rules argue for it, requiring the computation of a *multiply argued certainty*?

A simple, ad hoc procedure answers the questions this way:

- The minimum certainty associated with each rule's antecedents becomes the certainty of the rule's overall input as shown in figure 6-14a. This is analogous to the idea that a chain is only as strong as its weakest link.

- Each rule description includes what amounts to an attenuation factor, which, like the certainty factors, ranges from 0 to 1. To compute a rule's output certainty, the input certainty is multiplied by the attenuation factor, as shown in figure 6-14b.

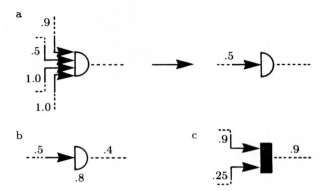

Figure 6-14. Some rule-based systems have procedures that estimate the certainty of each deduced fact. One simple procedure uses the computations illustrated here for certainty combination. In part *a*, the certainty of the combined antecedents is the certainty of the weakest one. In *b*, the certainty of a rule's consequent is the certainty of the combined antecedents multiplied by an attenuation factor. In *c*, the certainty of a deduced fact is the certainty of the strongest argument supporting it. Many consider these computations inappropriate in view of the violence they do to elementary probability theory.

- With several rules supporting some particular fact, the overall certainty attributed to that fact is the maximum certainty proposed by the supporting rules, as shown in figure 6-14c. Thus, the strength of a fact is affected only by the strongest of the supporting rules.

In figure 6-15, these computations are shown in action, passing certainties through a bit of inference net. Evidently, the tiger hypothesis is better than the zebra hypothesis.

Some familiarity with probability theory is required to understand another, *probability-based* way to pass certainties through an inference net.

Consequently, let us be content with a summary of what is done, followed by a brief explanation:

- The certainty of a rule's overall input is the product of the certainties associated with the rule's antecedents.

- The certainty of a rule's output is given by a single-valued function having input certainty on one axis and output certainty on the other.

- The certainty of a fact supported by several rules is determined by transforming certainties into related measurements called *certainty ratios*, then pumping the certainty ratios through a simple formula, and finally transforming the result back into a certainty.

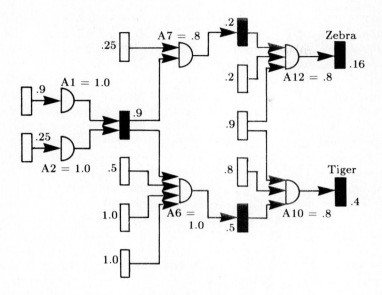

Figure 6-15. In this example, the zebra hypothesis is judged unlikely because it has a low certainty of .16, whereas the tiger hypothesis is ascribed a higher certainty of .4. The analysis presumes some fact certainties, some attenuation factors, and the combination rules shown in the last figure, figure 6-14.

The simplest of these ideas is that of using the product of antecedent certainties to get the overall certainty of input. The idea is derived directly from the notion that the probability of a joint event is the product of the probabilities of the participating events, as long as those participating events have no influence on one another. In a coin toss, for example, the probability of turning up two heads in a row is the square of the probability of turning up one head on one toss. Similarly, the probability of having a boy child followed by a girl, is the probability of having a boy multiplied by the probability of having a girl.

To summarize, the computation is expressed in algebraic notation as a formula involving the certainties of the antecedents, c_i:

$$c_1 \times \cdots \times c_n$$

One little problem with this idea has to do with the prerequisite of independence among the contributing events. In the coin toss and parenting examples, the events are said to be independent because they do not exert influence on one another. The antecedents of a rule often are dependent events, and consequently, combination by multiplication is not an operation that computes a probability from probabilities. What we are computing is analogous to a probability, but the combination formula is not justified by probability theory.

Once an input certainty is in hand, the next thing is to compute the output certainty from that input certainty. To do this, a human expert is asked to construct a function relating input to output, such as the function shown in figure 6-16a. As drawn, the function indicates that the output certainty is .8 when the input certainty is absolutely certain; the output certainty is 0 when the input certainty is 0; and in between, the output certainty lies on a straight line between the points $(0,0)$ and $(1.0, .8)$.

In fact, using this particular function is completely equivalent to using the attenuation-factor method with an attenuation equal to .8. Using the function of figure 6-16b is not equivalent to using an attenuation factor, however, because the line does not go through the origin. Evidently, the output probability goes to .2 when the input probability goes to 0. This means that the antecedents need not be true for the consequent to be true.

Unlike the examples of figure 6-16a and 6-16b, most functions have two straight-line segments, rather than one. The reason is that the relation between input and output should reflect not only end-point considerations, but also before-analysis estimates. A before-analysis estimate, called an *a priori value*, is a statement about what the certainty is in the absence of any knowledge about the particular case in hand. If we give certainties for an animal having hair or for being a mammal before we look at the animal, then we are giving the a priori certainties.

The use of a priori values is illustrated in figure 6-16c in which the input-output line jogs through the a priori certainty of the input, .5, and the a priori certainty of the output, also .5, coincidentally. Using a two-segment function to relate input and output certainties is a capitulation to necessity. Strictly speaking, according to classical probability theory, all the points evoked from a human should lie on a straight line. Evidently people are not always well-modeled by elegant mathematics.

Finally, to calculate multiply argued certainties, certainty ratios are used. Certainty, c, and a certainty ratio, r, are related like this:

$$r = \frac{c}{1 - c} \qquad c = \frac{r}{r + 1}$$

Note that a certainty of .5 corresponds to a neutral certainty ratio of 1.

After certainties are transformed into certainty ratios, the certainty ratio of a multiply argued consequent is given by the following formula:

$$r_0 \times \frac{r_1}{r_0} \times \cdots \times \frac{r_n}{r_0}$$

where r_0 is the certainty ratio corresponding to the a priori certainty of the consequent, and the r_i are the certainty ratios corresponding to the

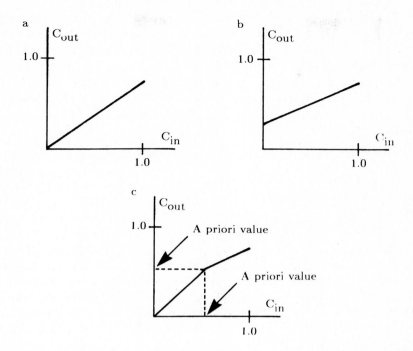

Figure 6-16. Three functions relating input certainty to output certainty. In part
a, the line relating input certainty c_{in}, to output certainty, c_{out}, is equivalent to
using an attenuation factor. In *b*, there is some certainty of output even when
the certainty of the input is 0. In *c*, the line is adjusted to go through the point
judged to reflect a priori values for both the input and output certainties.

certainties read from the input-output functions of the contributing rules.
Note that the formula reduces to the product of certainty ratios in the special case where the a priori certainty of the consequent is .5, corresponding
to an a priori certainty ratio of 1.

To justify the formula would presume too much background in probability theory and would overemphasize the idea of certainty factor computation. It must suffice to note that the formula is an illegitimate adaptation
of a legitimate probability formula, as was the formula for combining antecedent certainties into input certainties.

Transforming certainties into certainty ratios to compute the certainty
of multiply argued consequents illustrates a powerful idea: if a problem is
hard when expressed in one representation, try to transform the problem
into another representation that makes the problem easy. Going to certainty ratios is like going to logarithms to do multiplication or to Fourier
transforms to do convolution.

Finally, consider the examples in figure 6-17. In figure 6-17a, the rule combining antecedent certainty factors into an input certainty factor produces .45 rather than .5. In general, the new rule will produce a number that is equal to or lower than the old rule.

In figure 6-17b, the rule relating input certainty to output certainty uses the function shown. Since the function used in this illustration is equivalent to using an attenuation factor, the result, .4, is the same as before.

And finally, in figure 6-17c, the rule dealing with multiply argued consequents produces a final certainty of .75, rather than .9. The presumed a priori certainty of the consequent is .5, simplifying the computation required. The combination rule says to multiply certainty ratios. The two certainty factors, .9 and .25, transform into certainty ratios of 9 and .33. Multiplying yields 3; tranforming back into a certainty factor yields .75.

The certainty obtained, .75, is lower than the .9 produced by the old combination rule, because the antecedent-consequent rule contributing the certainty of .25 actually argues against the conclusion, as all antecedent-consequent rules do when the certainty they yield is lower than the a priori certainty value. If the .25 were a number greater than the presumed a priori certainty, .5, then the result would have been greater than the .9 produced by the old combination rule.

MYCIN Diagnoses Blood Infections

Now it is time to look at an example of a real rule-based analysis system resembling IDENTIFIER. The MYCIN system is appropriate, for like XCON, it is famous, yet simple.

MYCIN's expertise is in the domain of bacterial infections. It is usually necessary to begin antibiotic treatment for such bacterial infections without knowing exactly which organism is the culprit. The reason is that definitive laboratory culture evidence accumulates too slowly. For the desperately sick, therapy must begin at once, not two days from at once. This leaves two choices: the physician can prescribe broad-spectrum drugs to cover all possibilities; or the physician can prescribe better, disease-specific drugs if he or she has the special training required to exploit the available evidence.

MYCIN informs itself about particular cases by requesting information about a patient's symptoms, general condition, history, and the easy, quickly obtained laboratory tests. At each point, the question MYCIN asks is determined by MYCIN's current hypothesis and the answers to all previous questions. Thus the questions start as if taken from a checklist, but they vary as evidence builds. Here is an excerpt from a sample session:

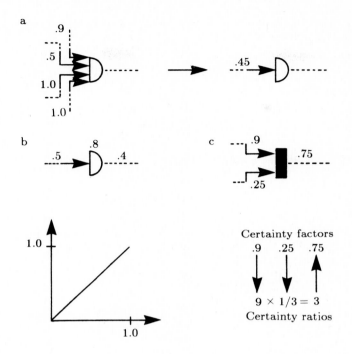

Figure 6-17. The inference-net procedure for combining certainty factors. In part *a*, certainty factors of antecedents are multiplied together to produce the certainty associated with the rule's input. In *b*, output certainty is determined by reading from an input-output function. In *c*, the certainty of a multiply argued consequent is determined by transforming to certainty ratios, multiplying, and transforming back to certainty factors.

● What is the patient's name?

John Doe

● Male or female?

Male.

● Age?

He is 55.

● Have you obtained positive cultures indicating general type?

Yes.

● What type of infection is it?

Primary Bacteremia.

● When did symptoms first appear?

May 5.

- Let's call the most recent positive culture CULTURE-1. From what site was CULTURE-1 taken?

From the blood.

- When?

May 9.

- Let's call the first significant organism from this culture ORGANISM-1. Do you know the identity of ORGANISM-1?

No.

- Is ORGANISM-1 a rod or a coccus or something else?

Rod.

- What is the gram stain of ORGANISM-1?

Gram-negative.

- Have there been positive cultures from sites that are not associated with infections about which you are seeking advice?

No.

- Did ORGANISM-1 grow aerobically?

Yes.

- Did ORGANISM-1 grow anaerobically?

Yes.

- What is the suspected portal of entry of ORGANISM-1?

The gastrointestinal tract.

$$\vdots$$

When satisfied that it has a reasonably good grasp of the situation, MYCIN starts a short line of questions in preparation for recommending a course of treatment:

- My recommendation will be based on the opinion that the identity of ORGANISM-1 may be 1. Pseudomonas-aeruginosa 2. Klebsiella-pneumoniae 3. E. Coli 4. Bacteroides-fragilis 5. Enterobacter or 6. Proteus-non-mirabilis.

- On a scale of 0 to 4, where higher numbers indicate greater severity, how would you rate the patient's degree of sickness?

3.

- Does the patient have a clinically significant allergic reaction to any antimicrobial agent?

No.

- How much does the patient weigh?

70 kilograms.

- My first recommendation is as follows: In order to cover for items 1, 2, 3, 5, and 6, give gentamycin using a dose of 119 mg (1.7 mg/kg) q8h IV [or IM] for 10 days. Modify dose in renal failure. And in order to cover for item 4, give clindamycin using a dose of 595 mg (8.5 mg/kg) q6h IV [or IM] for 14 days. If diarrhea or other gastrointestinal symptoms develop, check for pseudomembranous colitis.

With this kind of help, busy physicians could consider more factors and provide more tailored treatment.

Approximately 500 antecedent-consequent rules constitute MYCIN's pool of knowledge about approximately 100 causes of bacterial infections. The following is typical:

88 If   the infection type is primary-bacteremia
            the suspected entry point is the gastrointestinal tract
            the site of the culture is one of the sterile sites
    then   there is evidence that the organism is bacteroides

MYCIN is a backward-chaining system, because users like focused questions. By sticking with the questions that fan out in the implied AND/OR tree beneath a particular hypothesized conclusion, the questioning is guaranteed to stick to that hypothesis. A forward-running system can jump around, working first toward one conclusion and then toward another, seemingly at random. Such behavior irritates.

Another reason MYCIN was designed to be a backward-chaining system is that backward chaining simplifies the creation of an English-language interface. The interface need deal only with answers to specific questions, not free, imaginative text.

DENDRAL Analyzes Mass Spectrograms

DENDRAL was used earlier as an example of the generate-and-test paradigm at work. DENDRAL also is a good example of the rule-based-system paradigm, because it employs two rule-based subsystems.

One of these subsystems helps create necessary and forbidden substructure lists for DENDRAL's structure enumerator, as shown in figure 6-18. Usually the list of necessary substructures is constructed solely from analysis of the mass spectrogram. The forbidden substructure list, however, comes partly from the mass spectrogram and partly from general chemical knowledge about unstable configurations. The peroxides, for example, contain the unstable O–O oxygen substructure, and they therefore constitute part of the forbidden substructure list.

Altogether the initial forbidden substructure list has about two dozen such items. This initial list provides considerable constraint by itself. There would be many thousand acyclic, valence-satisfying structures with the formula $C_8H_{16}O$, but of these, only 698 emerge from the structure generator when guided by the initial list of unstable, forbidden substructures.

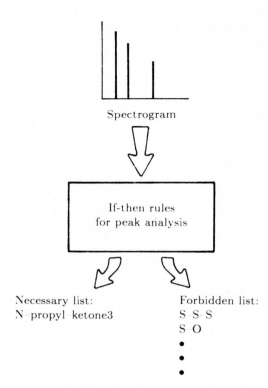

Figure 6-18. DENDRAL's spectrogram analyzer uses condition-action rules to produce a list of fragments that must be in the unknown structure and a list that must not be.

Even fewer structures are produced when the lists of required and forbidden structures are augmented by using the spectrogram. The additions recommended by the mass spectrogram reduce the number of structure possibilities for $C_8H_{16}O$ from 698 to a more manageable list of about 40 ketone structures. Thus, the information lurking in the mass spectrogram, combined with a priori knowledge about chemical stability, reduces the number of plausible structures for the example from thousands to tens.

Analysis of the particular spectrogram we have been using for an example puts N-PROPYL-KETONE3 on the required list because the antecedents for the following antecedent-consequent rule are found:

75 If there is a high peak at 71 atomic mass units
     there is a high peak at 43 atomic mass units
     there is a high peak at 86 atomic mass units
     there is any peak at 58 atomic mass units
 then there must be an N-PROPYL-KETONE3 substructure

For any given category of organic chemicals, the ketones or estrogens for example, there are about six to ten such rules. Some make insertions into the list of required substructures, and others add to the forbidden list using the absence of peaks.

Of course, in the end, the answer must be selected from the tens of possibilities, since the theory of mass spectrogram inspection is not constraining enough to do the whole job. You already have seen how this is done by generate and test.

Interestingly, the spectrogram synthesizer, buried inside the tester, also contains knowledge in rule-based-system form. The condition part of each condition-action rule recognizes the chunk that the condition-action rule knows about, and the action part specifies the type and quantity of each possible decomposition product. In a sense, the condition-action rules function like the mass spectrogram's molecular destruction chamber. Altogether there are about 100 condition-action rules for this purpose. Clearly a considerable amount of chemical knowledge is involved.

THE DIPMETER ADVISOR Analyzes Subsurface Tilt

A *dipmeter* is an instrument dropped into oil-well holes to determine the subsurface tilt. Consider figure 6-19. Beneath the oil rig, the dipmeter encounters rock tilting in various directions to varying degrees. In figure 6-19a, the rock changes from tilting down to the west to tilting down to the east. At the same time, the severity of the tilt increases greatly.

In dipmeter logs, direction of tilt and degree of tilt are encoded in so-called tadpoles like those shown in figure 6-19b. The tail of the tadpole indicates direction of tilt, while the placement of the tadpole along the horizontal axis indicates degree of tilt. Placement along the vertical axis indicates depth. The tadpoles in the log shown in figure 6-19b reflect the changes shown in the rock diagram in figure 6-19a.

Analyzing dipmeter logs is an acquired skill, with expertise continuing to grow with experience. Some people acquire the skill better, becoming better dipmeter interpreters than others. The advice of the better people often can make the difference between profitable drilling and disastrous dry holes. Consequently a good computer-based system for dipmeter analysis is worth a great deal.

Figure 6-20 shows the structure of THE DIPMETER ADVISOR, a rule-based system for dipmeter analysis. The first part creates a description of the dipmeter log by finding characteristic tadpole patterns. The second part, the one of interest to us here, analyzes the description using a rule-based system.

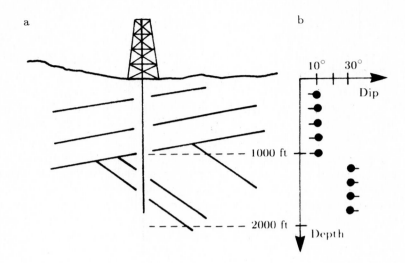

Figure 6-19. An oil well and the corresponding dipmeter log. Part *a* shows a test hole dug for oil prospecting. Part *b* shows the resulting dipmeter log. Depth is shown on the vertical axis, and degree of dip, on the horizontal. Steepest-descent direction is indicated by the direction of the lines coming out of the dots. In this example, the dipmeter log indicates a sudden increase in dip from 10 degrees to 30 degrees, at about 1000 feet, accompanied by a change in steepest-descent direction from west to east.

A sample rule taken from THE DIPMETER ADVISOR looks like this:

DA39   If   there is a red pattern over a fault
               the direction is perpendicular to the fault
               the length is greater than 200 feet
       then   the fault is a growth fault

In action, THE DIPMETER ADVISOR produces an analysis that is transparent only to petrogeologists, if anyone:

- Structural dip: from 13140 to 13770, dip is 3.9° at azimuth of 327; from 13780 to 14444, dip is 5.7° at azimuth of 213; from 14444 to 15500, dip is 25.9° at azimuth of 243.

- Faults and missing sections: from 13762 to 13790 there is a growth fault oriented along the line from 63° to 243°, with a downthrown block at 153°; from 14352 to 14444 there is an unconformity or middle age fault.

- Stratigraphy: from 15114 to 15168 there is a distributary-front with an associated channel; the channel axis is oriented at 163°; flow was oriented at 75°.

Dipmeter log

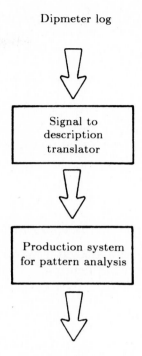

Description of geology

Figure 6-20. The structure of THE DIPMETER ADVISOR. The first part creates a description of the information in the log. The second part uses the description to make geological conjectures.

TEIRESIAS Helps Transfer Knowledge from People to Programs

Creating commercially useful rule-based systems takes years of collaboration between knowledge engineers and domain experts. TEIRESIAS is a prototype system for reducing the required time. TEIRESIAS strongly resembles PROCRUSTES in that a key idea is to compare proposed rules with typical rules from existing natural rule groups. The descriptive power of TEIRESIAS is much greater, however. For example, TEIRESIAS notes and uses statistics on the frequency with which various conditions appear together, as well as the frequency of individual conditions. Similarly, action co-occurrence frequencies are noted as well as action frequencies. Moreover, TEIRESIAS works with condition types, not specific conditions. Consequently, TEIRESIAS, working on top of MYCIN, makes observations like this: "Compared with the typical rule affirming a category, your proposed rule does not say anything about the disease's portal of entry, even though some statement about the portal is common when a category rule says something about a culture site, as yours does."

The Features and Flaws of Rule-based Systems Blur Together

Rule-based systems have the following advantages:

- Rule-based systems, as a foundation, enable much to be done because there is an enforced, homogeneous representation of knowledge.
- Rule-based systems allow incremental knowledge growth through the addition of individual if-then rules.
- Rule-based systems allow unplanned but useful interactions. A piece of knowledge can be applied whenever appropriate, not just whenever a programmer predicts it can be appropriate.

It would seem that rule-based systems allow knowledge to be tossed into systems homogeneously and incrementally without concern for relating new knowledge to old. Evidently rule-based systems should permit knowledge engineers to focus attention on well-constrained condition-action or antecedent-consequent combinations, letting interactions occur how they may, without explicit control.

There are things to worry about, however. One particular thing is that the *advantage* of not having interactions among antecedent-consequent rules can become the *disadvantage* of not being able to influence the interactions. As King Lear failed to note, bequeathing control generally means losing control.

RULE-BASED SYSTEMS FOR MODELING
HUMAN THINKING

Do computational theories of problem solving have promise as psychological models of human reasoning? The answer is yes, at least to some psychologists who try to understand ordinary human activity using metaphors shared with researchers who concentrate on making smarter computers. Rule-based systems, for example, can be a way of producing computer-based problem solvers or a way of explaining certain results in experimental psychology.

One group of experimenters addresses questions about the structure and limitations of the human information processor, assuming that some form of the rule-based-system model is valid. They probe and prod, often trying to invent unfamiliar tasks that block out the knowledge that normally interacts with the processor and obscures its nature. This intent explains why experiments with cryptarithmetic and nonsense syllables may be a valid no-nonsense approach to basic questions.

Rule-based Systems Can Model Some Human Problem Solving

In the human-modeling world, condition-action rules generally are called *productions* and rule-based systems are called *production systems*. Hard-core rule-based-system enthusiasts believe that humans have productions that are triggered by items in *short-term memory*. Short-term memory is inhabited by only a few simple symbolic *chunks*, while *long-term memory* holds all the productions. Specific combinations of the short-term memory items trigger the long-term memory's productions.

Thus the short-term memory is the key to which procedures are called, what they are given to work with, and how they return results. Each chunk in short-term memory may be a single symbol, like *Headache*, or a small constellation of symbols like *Problem: Smokes cigarettes*. Experimentally, the short-term memory seems to contain between five and nine such chunks. One often hears of the *seven-plus-or-minus-two* phenomenon.

In an *elementary* production system, only five primitive operations are allowed. To be specific, a production can write, note, mark, send, or receive, but nothing else:

- A production can *write* a new item into short-term memory. A new item goes in at the front and dislodges an item from the back end. Hence items that have spent some time in short-term memory tend to be forgotten.

- A production can *note* items in short-term memory by moving them from their existing place to the front. This tends to protect noted items from being shoved out of short-term memory by new entries.

- A production can *mark* an item in short-term memory. Since productions rarely look for marked items, those marked items tend to migrate toward the end of short-term memory and drop off, thus being forgotten permanently. Marking is often used to prevent a goal description from reactivating the same production over and over, a problem that could be a plague otherwise.

- A production can communicate with the environment in two ways: a production can *send* a message, thus requesting new information; similarly a production can *receive* a message, placing it at the front of short-term memory. In humans, most communication is through the attention and analysis procedures involved in vision and language. For computer-based simulations, both sending and receiving generally goes through terminals.

Protocol Analysis Produces Production-System Conjectures

To learn how people solve problems using built-in production systems, information-processing psychologists pore over transcripts of subjects talking their way through problems. These transcripts are called protocols. The psychologists who use them generally think in terms of two important concepts:

- The *state of knowledge* is what the subject knows. Each time the subject deduces something, forgets something, or acquires something through its senses, the state of knowledge changes.

- The *problem-behavior graph* is a trace of a problem solver moving through states of knowledge as he or she solves a problem.

Typically the problem-behavior graph is important because it helps unravel facts about the subject that produces it. By analyzing the way one state of knowledge becomes another, inferences can be made about the productions that produce the changes. Consider, for example, the following protocol fragment:

A Protocol for Robbie

> Let's see, I want to identify this animal, I wonder if it's a cheetah— I have nothing to go on yet, so I think I'll start by looking into the possibility that it is a carnivore—I had better check to see if it is a mammal first—yes, that is ok—hair—it doesn't seem to be eating anything so I can't tell if it is a carnivore—but oh, yes, it has pointed teeth, claws, and forward-pointing eyes, so it is a carnivore all right—now where was I—it's a carnivore, and I also see that it has a tawny color and dark spots—surely it must be a cheetah!

It would seem that the facts accumulate in the following order: hair, mammal, pointed teeth, claws, forward-pointing eyes, carnivore, tawny color, dark spots, and cheetah. From observations like these, the psychological cryptographer would probably deduce that Robbie's production system is a backward-chaining one with rules much like those used in the IDENTI-FIER examples. But there is not enough information to determine how the facts mentioned are assembled, and a longer protocol with more animal identifications is needed.

SUMMARY

- The generate-and-test procedure is a ubiquitous problem-solving paradigm. The generate-and-test procedure is used, for example, to understand images and to analyze mass spectrograms. Instances of generate and test often involve other problem-solving paradigms in the generator module or tester module.

- Good generators are complete, nonredundant, and informed.

- Rule-based systems use collections of rules to solve problems. The rules consist of condition and action parts or antecedent and consequent parts.

- Rule-based systems are used in synthesis, for example to configure computer systems.

- Rule-based systems are used in analysis, for example to diagnose disease and to interpret oil-well logs.

- Forward chaining means working forward from the current situation toward a conclusion. Backward chaining goes the other way, working toward the known facts from an hypothesis.

- Rule-based systems facilitate answering questions about their own behavior. *How* and *why* questions, for example, are handled by reference to the history constructed while a deduction-type rule-based system works.

- Rule-based deduction systems can be fused to procedures that compute numbers associated with the certainty of the deductions. These certainty factors can be computed in a number of ways ranging from awful to questionable.

- Rule-based systems, also known as production systems, have been used extensively to model human problem solving by information-processing psychologists.

- You should think of problem-solving paradigms as possible ingredients, not as complete solutions. In creating particular problem-solving systems, you may never use any paradigm by itself. Instead, you will mix them together, developing your own blends tailored to the problem domains you face.

REFERENCES

DENDRAL was developed primarily by Edward A. Feigenbaum, Bruce Buchanan, and Joshua Lederberg. See *Applications of Artificial Intelligence for Chemical Inference: The* DENDRAL *Project* [1980], by Robert Lindsay, Bruce G. Buchanan, Edward A. Feigenbaum, and Joshua Lederberg. ACRONYM is largely the work of Thomas O. Binford and Rodney

A. Brooks [Brooks 1981]. The generalized-cylinder representation used in ACRONYM was developed earlier by Binford [1971].

XCON was developed to configure the Digital Equipment Corporation's VAX computers by John McDermott and others working at Carnegie-Mellon University and by Arnold Kraft, Dennis O'Connor, and others at the Digital Equipment Corporation [McDermott 1982].

MYCIN was developed by Edward Shortliffe, who became a medical doctor along the way. For details, see his book, *MYCIN: Computer-Based Medical Consultations* [1976]. TEIRESIAS, the knowledge-acquisition system built on top of MYCIN, was done by Randall Davis [1976, 1982]. For the most complete treatment of MYCIN, see *Rule-Based Expert Programs: the MYCIN Experiments of the Stanford Heuristic Programming Project* [1984], by Buchanan and Shortliffe.

The most powerful diagnosis system so far is INTERNIST developed by Harry E. Pople, Jr. and Jack D. Myers, M. D., for internal medicine [Pople 1973]. INTERNIST evolved into a new system called CADUCEUS [Pople 1982]. Another well-known system, for dealing with glaucoma, is CASNET, developed by Casimir A. Kulikowski and Sholom M. Weiss [1982].

There is now a great deal of literature about Artificial Intelligence and medicine. An excellect collection is *Artificial Intelligence and Medicine* [1982], edited by Peter Szolovits.

The material on THE DIPMETER ADVISOR is from work by Randall Davis, Howard Austin, Al Gilreath, and others at the Schlumberger-Doll Research Center [Davis et al. 1981].

The first techniques for computing certainty factors were described by Shortliffe and Buchanan [1975]. The probability-based method for computing certainty factors was introduced by Richard O. Duda, Peter E. Hart, and Nils J. Nilsson [Duda et al. 1976, 1978]. Subsequent work was done by E. P. D. Pednault, Steven W. Zucker, and L. V. Muresan [1981].

Allen Newell and Herbert A. Simon are famous for their inquiries into psychological issues using computational tools. Their book, *Human Problem Solving* [1972], deals with production-system models of human problem solving and with protocol analysis. The tradition is continued in *The Psychology of Human-Computer Interaction* [1983], by Stuart Card, Thomas P. Moran, and Newell.

7

Logic And
Theorem Proving

Logic is a powerful addition to our collection of problem-solving paradigms. Like the other paradigms, logic has both seductive advantages and bothersome disadvantages.

On the positive side, the ideas of logic, having matured for centuries, are concise and universally understood, like Latin. Moreover, until recently, logicians have focused on *proving things about* what we can do with knowledge. Consequently, when a problem domain is successfully attacked by logic, as is some of mathematics, we are in luck, for we can know the limits of what we can do with what we are allowed.

On the negative side, logic can be a procrustean bed, for concentrating on logic can lead to concentrating on the mathematics of logic, deflecting attention away from valuable problem-solving techniques that resist mathematical analysis.

To understand these issues better, this chapter introduces notation, the idea of proof, and rules of inference, such as *modus ponens*, *modus tolens*, and *resolution*, that make it possible to create new expressions from existing ones. Then, using resolution, we go on to explore *proof by refutation* and *resolution theorem proving*.

Next, introducing *operators* into logic makes logic-based planning possible, but creates difficulties. For example, there must be a way to identify those expressions that persist as various operations are applied. This is called the *frame problem.*

Finally, while resolution theorem proving is powerful, *proof using constraint propagation* sometimes is a better way to go. For one thing, constraint propagation makes it easy to keep track of *justifications*, making it possible to withdraw assumptions simply, without danger to still-true expressions. This brings us back to dependency-directed, nonchronological backtracking, first seen in chapter 3.

Note that logic is difficult for beginners because there is a blizzard of new concepts. This is why expressing things in the vocabulary of logic is avoided in other chapters, even though a few things could be said, using logic, with greater precision. Compounding difficult concepts inhibits understanding.

For the same concept-blizzard reason, the key points in this chapter are illustrated with ridiculously simple examples designed to keep our human intuition fully engaged. These examples stick to the blocks world, showing how some relations can be deduced from others and showing how operation sequences can be derived for achieving goals.

RULES OF INFERENCE

We know that something is a bird if it has feathers or if it flies and lays eggs. These facts were expressed before, in chapter 6, in the form of antecedent-consequent rules:

I3 If   the animal has feathers
   then   it is a bird
I4 If   the animal flies
          it lays eggs
   then   it is a bird

We shall see that using such antecedent-consequent rules is just a special case of using logic.

Logic Has a Traditional Notation

In logic, to express the sense of the antecedent-consequent rule concerning feathers and birds, we must have a way to capture the idea that something has feathers and that something is a bird. This is done by using *predicates*, for predicates are *functions* that map object *arguments* into TRUE or FALSE values.

For example, with the normal way of interpreting the object Albatross and the predicates Feathers and Bird, we can say, informally, that the following are TRUE expressions:

Feathers(Albatross)

Bird(Albatross)

Now consider what we mean when we say this is also a TRUE expression:

Feathers(Squigs)

Evidently, Squigs is a symbol that denotes something that has feathers, for it satisfies the Feathers predicate. Thus we have a constraint on what Squigs can possibly name. We can express other constraints with other predicates like Flies and Lays-eggs. In fact, we can limit the things that Squigs can name to those things that satisfy both predicates together by saying that both of the following expressions are TRUE:

Flies(Squigs)

Lays-eggs(Squigs)

There is a more traditional way to express the idea, however. We simply combine the first expression and the second expression and say that the combination is TRUE:

Flies(Squigs) and Lays-eggs(Squigs)

Of course, we can also say that we must interpret Squigs to be the name of something that satisfies either of the two predicates. This is done using this combination:

Flies(Squigs) or Lays-eggs(Squigs)

Logicians definitely prefer a different notation, however. They like to write *and* as & and *or* as ∨.[1]

Now we can write the same things we wrote before as a logician would:

Flies(Squigs) & Lays-eggs(Squigs)

Flies(Squigs) ∨ Lays-eggs(Squigs)

When expressions are joined by &, they form a *conjunction*, and each part is called a *conjunct*. Similarly, when expressions are joined by ∨, they form a *disjunction*, and each part is called a *disjunct*.

---

[1] Actually, most logicians write *and* as ∧, instead of as &. We will stick with & because it is easier to distinguish & from ∨ for beginners.

Note that & and ∨ are called *logical connectives* because they map combinations of TRUE and FALSE to TRUE and FALSE.

In addition to & and ∨, there are two additional essential connectives: one is *not*, written as ¬, and the other is *implies*, written as ⇒. Consider this:

$$¬Feathers(Suzie)$$

For this to be TRUE, Suzie must denote something for which Feathers(Suzie) is not TRUE. That is, Suzie must be something for which the predicate Feathers is *not satisfied*.

Moving on, using ⇒, we can write down an expression that resembles one of the antecedent-consequent rules we started with:

$$Feathers(Suzie) ⇒ Bird(Suzie)$$

Saying the value of this expression is TRUE constrains what Suzie can denote. One allowed possibility is that Suzie is something for which both Feathers(Suzie) and Bird(Suzie) are TRUE. Naturally, the definition of ⇒ also allows both Feathers(Suzie) and Bird(Suzie) to be FALSE. Curiously, another possibility, allowed by the definition of ⇒, is that Feathers(Suzie) is FALSE but Bird(Suzie) is TRUE. If Feathers(Suzie) is TRUE and Bird(Suzie) is FALSE, however, then the expression Feathers(Suzie) ⇒ Bird(Suzie) is FALSE.

Perhaps it is time to be more precise about the ⇒, &, ∨, and ¬ connectives, before it is too late. Thinking of them as functions, it is easy to define them by listing the approved value for each possible combination of arguments. This is done in figure 7-1 using diagrams that are called *truth tables*.

Note that the connectives have an accepted *precedence*. In ordinary arithmetic, a unary minus sign has higher precedence than a plus sign, we can write $-a+b$, meaning $(-a)+b$, not $-(a+b)$. Similarly, because ¬ has higher precedence than ∨, we can write $¬E_1 ∨ E_2$, meaning $(¬E_1) ∨ E_2$, without any possibility of confusion with $¬(E_1 ∨ E_2)$.

The accepted precedence is ¬ first, followed by & and ∨, with ⇒ bringing up the rear. A good habit is to use parentheses liberally to keep things clear.

Note that the truth-table definition for ⇒ indicates that the values of $E_1 ⇒ E_2$ are the same as the values of $¬E_1 ∨ E_2$ for all combinations of values for E_1 and E_2. Consequently, and importantly, $¬E_1 ∨ E_2$ can be substituted for $E_1 ⇒ E_2$, and vice versa, at any time. Rules for reversible substitution are expressed using a double arrow, ⇔:

$$E_1 ⇒ E_2 ⇔ ¬E_1 ∨ E_2$$

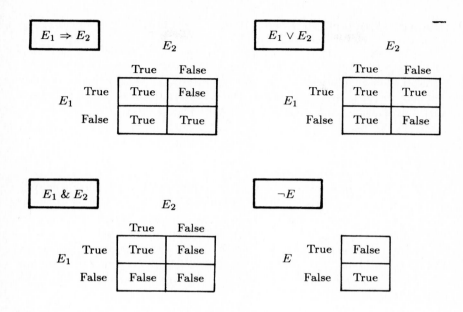

Figure 7-1. Truth tables for some basic connectives.

Truth tables also demonstrate other useful properties of logical connectives, which are listed here, partly for the sake of completeness and partly because we will use a few. First, the & and ∨ connectives are *commutative*:

$$E_1 \,\&\, E_2 \Leftrightarrow E_2 \,\&\, E_1$$
$$E_1 \lor E_2 \Leftrightarrow E_2 \lor E_1$$

Next, they are *distributive*:

$$E_1 \,\&\, (E_2 \lor E_3) \Leftrightarrow (E_1 \,\&\, E_2) \lor (E_1 \,\&\, E_3)$$
$$E_1 \lor (E_2 \,\&\, E_3) \Leftrightarrow (E_1 \lor E_2) \,\&\, (E_1 \lor E_3)$$

In addition, they are *associative*:

$$E_1 \,\&\, (E_2 \,\&\, E_3) \Leftrightarrow (E_1 \,\&\, E_2) \,\&\, E_3$$
$$E_1 \lor (E_2 \lor E_3) \Leftrightarrow (E_1 \lor E_2) \lor E_3$$

They obey *de Morgan's laws*:

$$\neg(E_1 \,\&\, E_2) \Leftrightarrow (\neg E_1) \lor (\neg E_2)$$
$$\neg(E_1 \lor E_2) \Leftrightarrow (\neg E_1) \,\&\, (\neg E_2)$$

And finally, two ¬s annihilate each other:

$$\neg(\neg E_1) \Leftrightarrow E_1$$

Quantifiers Determine When Things Are True

The antecedent-consequent rules we started with are supposed to be TRUE for all possible things. To signal that an expression is universally TRUE, we need to use a symbol meaning *for all*, written as ∀, as well as a variable standing in for possible things. In the following example, the expression, when TRUE, says that anything having feathers is a bird:

$$\forall x[\text{Feathers}(x) \Rightarrow \text{Bird}(x)]$$

Like other expressions, $\forall x[\text{Feathers}(x) \Rightarrow \text{Bird}(x)]$ can be TRUE or FALSE. If TRUE, a ∀ expression means that we get a TRUE expression when we substitute any object for x inside the square brackets. For example, if $\forall x[\text{Feathers}(x) \Rightarrow \text{Bird}(x)]$ is TRUE, then certainly Feathers(Squigs) ⇒ Bird(Squigs) is TRUE and Feathers(Suzie) ⇒ Bird(Suzie) is TRUE.

When an expression is surrounded by the square brackets associated with a quantifier, the expression is said to lie within the *scope* of that quantifier. The expression Feathers(x) ⇒ Bird(x) therefore lies within the scope of the $\forall x[\ldots]$ quantifier.

Since TRUE expressions starting with ∀ say something about all possible object-for-variable substitutions within their scope, they are said to be *universally quantified*. Consequently, ∀ is called the *universal quantifier*.

Some expressions, while not always TRUE, are TRUE at least for something. Logic embraces these too. They are written using a symbol meaning *there exists*, written as ∃, used like this:

$$\exists x[\text{Bird}(x)]$$

When TRUE, this means there is at least one possible object, which when substituted for x, makes the expression inside the square brackets TRUE. Perhaps Bird(Squigs) is TRUE; in any case, something like Bird(Squigs) is TRUE.

Expressions with ∃ are said to be *existentially quantified*. The symbol ∃ is called the *existential quantifier*.

Logic Has a Rich Vocabulary

One problem with logic is that there is a lot of vocabulary to keep straight. For reference, let us gather together and complete the common elements of that vocabulary now by way of figure 7-2 and the following definitions:

- A domain's *objects* are terms.
- *Variables* ranging over a domain's objects are terms.
- *Functions* are terms. The arguments to functions and the values returned are objects.

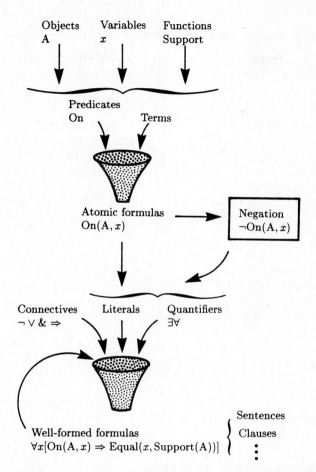

Figure 7-2. The vocabulary of logic. Informally, the sample well-formed formula says this: stating that the specific object A and the unspecified object x satisfy the predicate On implies that x is the value returned by the function Support when applied to the object A.

Terms are the only things that appear as arguments to predicates.

- *Atomic formulas* are individual predicates together with arguments.

- *Literals* are atomic formulas and negated atomic formulas.

- *Well-formed formulas*, generally referred to, regrettably, by the abbreviation WFFS, are defined recursively: literals are WFFS; WFFS connected together by, ¬, &, ∨, and ⇒ are WFFS; and WFFS surrounded by quantifiers are also WFFS.

For WFFS, there are some special cases:

- A WFF in which all the variables, if any, are inside the scope of corresponding quantifiers is a *sentence*. These are sentences:

$$\forall x[\text{Feathers}(x) \Rightarrow \text{Bird}(x)]$$

$$\text{Feathers}(\text{Albatross}) \Rightarrow \text{Bird}(\text{Albatross})$$

Variables like x, appearing within the scope of corresponding quantifiers, are said to be *bound*. Variables that are not bound are *free*. The following expression is not a sentence, because it contains a free variable, y:

$$\forall x[\text{Feathers}(x) \vee \neg\text{Feathers}(y)]$$

Note carefully that we allow variables to represent objects only. We specifically forbid variables that represent predicates. Consequently we are dealing with a kind of logic called *first-order predicate calculus*. A more advanced topic, *second-order predicate calculus* permits variables representing predicates. A less advanced topic, *propositional calculus*, permits no variables of any kind.

- A WFF consisting of a disjunction of literals is a *clause*.

Generally, we will use the word *expression* interchangeably with WFF, for using a lot of WFFS makes it hard to think about logic, rather than about kennels.

Interpretations Tie Logic Symbols to Worlds

Ultimately, the point of logic is to say something about some imaginable world. Consequently, we must associate object, predicate, and function symbols with more tangible things. As figure 7-3 illustrates, the three symbol categories correspond to three world categories:

- Objects in some domain correspond to object symbols in logic. In the example shown in figure 7-3, the object symbols A and B on the left correspond to two things in the imaginable world shown on the right.

- Relations in some domain correspond to predicates in logic. Whenever a relation holds with respect to some objects, the corresponding predicate is TRUE when applied to the corresponding object symbols. In the example, the logic-world predicate, On, applied to object symbols B and A is TRUE because the imaginable-world relation, On-relation, holds between the two imaginable-world objects.

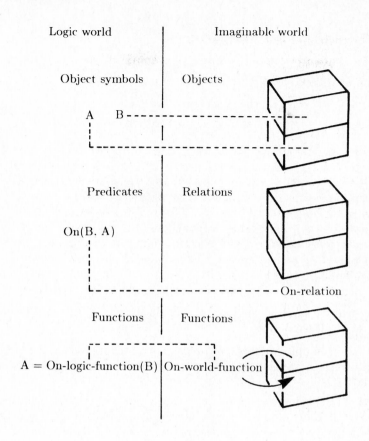

Figure 7-3. An interpretation is an accounting for how objects, relations, and functions map to object symbols, predicates, and functions.

- Functions in some domain correspond to functions in logic. The functions in the domain return domain objects when supplied with domain objects. The corresponding functions in logic return corresponding logic symbols when supplied with corresponding logic symbols. In the example, the logic-world function, On-logic-function, maps object symbol B to object symbol A because the imaginable-world function, On-world-function, does the corresponding mapping between imaginable-world objects.

An *interpretation* is a full accounting of the correspondence between objects and object-symbols, between relations and predicates, and between object functions and object-symbol functions.

Proofs Tie Axioms to Consequences

Now we are ready to explore the notion of proof. Suppose we are told that both of the following expressions are TRUE:

$$\text{Feathers(Squigs)}$$
$$\forall x[\text{Feathers}(x) \Rightarrow \text{Bird}(x)]$$

Now that we understand the notion of interpretation, we understand what it means to say that such expressions are TRUE: it means that we are restricting the interpretations for the object-symbols, predicates, and functions to those for which the implied imaginable-world relations hold. Any such interpretation is said to be a *model* for the expressions.

Since we are told that Feathers(Squigs) and $\forall x[\text{Feathers}(x) \Rightarrow \text{Bird}(x)]$ are TRUE, they are called *axioms*. Now suppose that we are asked to show that all interpretations that make the axioms TRUE also make the following expression TRUE:

$$\text{Bird(Squigs)}$$

If we succeed, we say that we have *proved* that Bird(Squigs) is a *theorem* with respect to the axioms:

- Said in the simplest terms, we prove that an expression is a theorem when we *show* that the theorem must be TRUE, *given* that the axioms are TRUE.

- Said in the fanciest terms, we prove an expression is a theorem when we show that any model for the axioms is also a model for the theorem. We say that the theorem *logically follows* from the axioms.

The way to prove a theorem is to use a *proof procedure*. Proof procedures use manipulations called *sound rules of inference* that produce new expressions from old expressions such that models that make the old expressions TRUE are guaranteed to make the new ones TRUE too. Thus, the most straightforward proof procedure is to apply sound rules of inference to the axioms, and to the results of applying sound rules of inference, until the desired theorem appears.

Generally, we will think informally in terms of using proof procedures to show that one expression, the theorem, is TRUE, given that others are, and we will drop the model-based way of saying things.

Note that proving a theorem is not the same as showing that an expression is *valid*, meaning the expression is true for all possible interpretations of the symbols. Similarly, proving a theorem is not the same as showing that an expression is *satisfiable*, meaning that it is true for some possible interpretation of the symbols.

The most straightforward sound rule of inference used in proof procedures is *modus ponens*. *Modus ponens* says this: if there is an axiom of the form $E_1 \Rightarrow E_2$, and there is another axiom of the form E_1, then E_2 logically follows.

If E_2 is the theorem to be proved, we are done. If not, we might as well add E_2 to the axioms, for it will always be TRUE when all of the rest of the axioms are TRUE. Continuing with *modus ponens* on an ever increasing list of axioms may eventually show that the desired theorem is TRUE, thus proving the theorem.

For our feathers-and-bird example, the axioms are just about right for the application of *modus ponens*. First, however, we must specialize the second expression. We have $\forall x[\text{Feathers}(x) \Rightarrow \text{Bird}(x)]$. Since we dealing with interpretations for which $\text{Feathers}(x) \Rightarrow \text{Bird}(x)$ is TRUE for all x, it must be TRUE for the special case where x is Squigs. Consequently, $\text{Feathers}(\text{Squigs}) \Rightarrow \text{Bird}(\text{Squigs})$ must be TRUE.

Now the first expression, $\text{Feathers}(\text{Squigs})$, and the specialization of the second, $\text{Feathers}(\text{Squigs}) \Rightarrow \text{Bird}(\text{Squigs})$, together fit *modus ponens* exactly, substituting $\text{Feathers}(\text{Squigs})$ for E_1 and $\text{Bird}(\text{Squigs})$ for E_2. We conclude that $\text{Bird}(\text{Squigs})$ must be TRUE. The theorem is proved.

Perhaps now is a good time to harp on something. The use of proof procedures to produce theorems is a syntactic activity, divorced from the meaning of the expressions involved, if any. We are talking of imaginable worlds, possibly silly ones, not our world. Axioms may clash with our sense of truth. In our world, Squigs may not have feathers; and there are things with feathers that are not birds. Do not be disturbed by this. The point is to show that theorems logically follow from axioms, not that the axioms correspond to what we believe.

Resolution Is a Sound Rule of Inference

One of the most important rules of inference is *resolution*. Resolution says this: If there is an axiom of the form $E_1 \vee E_2$, and there is another axiom of the form $\neg E_2 \vee E_3$, then $E_1 \vee E_3$ logically follows. The expression $E_1 \vee E_3$ is called the *resolvent* of $E_1 \vee E_2$ and $\neg E_2 \vee E_3$.

Let us look at the various possibilities to see if resolution is believable. First, suppose E_2 is TRUE; then $\neg E_2$ must be FALSE. But if $\neg E_2$ is FALSE, from the second expression, E_3 must be TRUE. But if E_3 is TRUE, surely $E_1 \vee E_3$ is TRUE. Second, suppose that E_2 is FALSE. Then from the first expression, E_1 must be TRUE. But if E_1 is TRUE, surely $E_1 \vee E_3$ is TRUE. We conclude that the resolvent, $E_1 \vee E_3$, must be TRUE as long as both $E_1 \vee E_2$ and $\neg E_2 \vee E_3$ are TRUE.

It is easy to generalize resolution such that there can be any number of disjuncts, including just one, in either of the two resolving expressions. The only demand is that one resolving expression must have a disjunct that is the negation of a disjunct in the other resolving expression. Once generalized, we can use resolution to reach the same conclusion about Squigs reached before with *modus ponens*.

The first step again is to specialize the quantified expression to Squigs. The next step is to rewrite it, eliminating ⇒, producing these:

$$\text{Feathers(Squigs)}$$
$$\neg\text{Feathers(Squigs)} \lor \text{Bird(Squigs)}$$

So written, resolution obviously applies, dropping out Feathers(Squigs) and ¬Feathers(Squigs), producing Bird(Squigs).

As a matter of fact, this example suggests a general truth: *modus ponens* can be viewed as a special case of resolution because anything concluded with *modus ponens* can be concluded with resolution as well. To see why, let one expression be E_1, and let the other be $E_1 \Rightarrow E_2$. According to *modus ponens*, E_2 must be TRUE. But we know that $E_1 \Rightarrow E_2$ can be rewritten as $\neg E_1 \lor E_2$. So rewritten, resolution can be applied, dropping out the E_1 and the $\neg E_1$, producing E_2, which is the same result obtained using *modus ponens*.

Similarly, resolution obviously subsumes another rule of inference called *modus tolens*. *Modus tolens* says this: If there is an axiom of the form $E_1 \Rightarrow E_2$, and there is another axiom of the form $\neg E_2$, then $\neg E_1$ logically follows.

RESOLUTION PROOFS

To prove a theorem, the obvious strategy is to search forward from the axioms using sound rules of inference, hoping to stumble across the theorem eventually. Another strategy, the one used in resolution theorem proving, is to show that the negation of a theorem cannot be TRUE:

• Assume that the negation of the theorem is TRUE.

• Show that the axioms and the assumed negation of the theorem together determine something to be TRUE that cannot be TRUE.

• Conclude that the assumed negation of the theorem cannot be TRUE since it leads to a contradiction.

• Conclude that the theorem must be TRUE since the assumed negation of the theorem cannot be TRUE.

Proving a theorem by showing its negation cannot be TRUE is called *proof by refutation*.

Resolution Proves Theorems by Refutation

Consider the Squigs example again. Recall that we know from the axioms the following:

¬Feathers(Squigs) ∨ Bird(Squigs)

Feathers(Squigs)

Adding the negation of the thing to be proved, we have this list:

¬Feathers(Squigs) ∨ Bird(Squigs)

Feathers(Squigs)

¬Bird(Squigs)

Resolving the first and second axiom, as before, permits us to add a new expression to the list:

¬Feathers(Squigs) ∨ Bird(Squigs)

Feathers(Squigs)

¬Bird(Squigs)

Bird(Squigs)

But now we have our contradiction. All of the things in the list are supposed to be TRUE. But it cannot be that Bird(Squigs) and ¬Bird(Squigs) are both TRUE. Consequently, the assumption that led to this contradiction must be FALSE; that is, the negation of the theorem, ¬Bird(Squigs) must be FALSE; hence the theorem, Bird(Squigs), must be TRUE, as was to be shown.

The traditional way to recognize that the theorem is proved is to wait until resolution happens upon a literal and its contradicting negation. The result is an empty expression, one with nothing in it, which by convention is written *Nil*. When resolution produces Nil, we are guaranteed that resolution has already produced manifestly contradictory expressions. Consequently, producing Nil is the signal that resolution has proved the theorem.

Usually, it is illuminating to use a treelike diagram to record how things get resolved together on the way to producing an empty expression. Figure 7-4 is the tree for the simple proof we have just done.

Using Resolution Requires Axioms To Be in Clause Form

Now that we have the general flavor of how proof by resolution works, it is time to understand a lot of manipulations that make harder proofs possible. Basically, the point of these manipulations is to transform arbitrary logic expressions into a form that enables resolution. Specifically, we want ways to transform the given axioms into equivalent, new axioms that are all

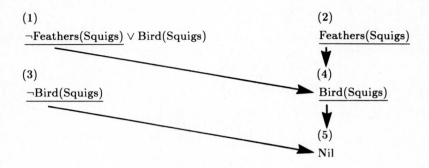

Figure 7-4. A tree recording the resolutions needed to prove Bird(Squigs).

disjunctions of literals. Said another way, we want the new axioms to be in *clause form*.

Now we begin. To illustrate the manipulations, we use an axiom involving blocks. While the axiom is a bit artificial, so as to exercise all the transformation steps, the axiom's message is simple. Evidently being a brick implies three things: first, that the brick is on something that is not a pyramid; second, that there is nothing that the brick is on and that is on the brick as well; and third that there is nothing that is not a brick and the same thing as the brick:

$$\forall x[\text{Brick}(x) \Rightarrow (\exists y[\text{On}(x,y) \, \& \, \neg\text{Pyramid}(y)]$$
$$\& \, \neg\exists y[\text{On}(x,y) \, \& \, \text{On}(y,x)]$$
$$\& \, \forall y[\neg\text{Brick}(y) \Rightarrow \neg\text{Equal}(x,y)])]$$

But as given, the axiom cannot be used to produce resolvents because it is not in clause form. These equivalent axioms, however, are in clause form:

$$\neg\text{Brick}(x) \lor \text{On}(x, \text{Support}(x))$$
$$\neg\text{Brick}(w) \lor \neg\text{Pyramid}(\text{Support}(w))$$
$$\neg\text{Brick}(u) \lor \neg\text{On}(u,y) \lor \neg\text{On}(y,u)$$
$$\neg\text{Brick}(v) \lor \text{Brick}(z) \lor \neg\text{Equal}(v,z)$$

Next we shall consider the steps needed to transform arbitrary logical expressions into clause form. Once explained, the steps will be summarized in a procedure.

- Eliminate implications.

The first thing to do is to get rid of all the implications. This is easy, for all we need to do is to substitute $\neg E_1 \vee E_2$ for $E_1 \Rightarrow E_2$. For our example, we have to make two such substitutions, leaving us with this:

$$\forall x[\neg\text{Brick}(x) \vee (\exists y[\text{On}(x,y) \text{ \& } \neg\text{Pyramid}(y)]$$
$$\text{\& } \neg\exists y[\text{On}(x,y) \text{ \& } \text{On}(y,x)]$$
$$\text{\& } \forall y[\neg(\neg\text{Brick}(y)) \vee \neg\text{Equal}(x,y)])]$$

- Move negations down to the atomic formulas.

Doing this requires a number of identities, one for dealing with the negation of & expressions, one for $\vee$ expressions, one for $\neg$ expressions, and one each for $\forall$ and $\exists$:

$$\neg(E_1 \text{ \& } E_2) \rightarrow (\neg E_1) \vee (\neg E_2)$$
$$\neg(E_1 \vee E_2) \rightarrow (\neg E_1) \text{ \& } (\neg E_2)$$
$$\neg(\neg E_1) \rightarrow E_1$$
$$\neg\forall x[E_1(x)] \rightarrow \exists x[\neg E_1(x)]$$
$$\neg\exists x[E_1(x)] \rightarrow \forall x[\neg E_1(x)]$$

For our example, we need the third identity, which eliminates the doubled $\neg$s, and we need the last identity, which eliminates an $\exists$ and introduces another $\forall$, leaving us with this:

$$\forall x[\neg\text{Brick}(x) \vee (\exists y[\text{On}(x,y) \text{ \& } \neg\text{Pyramid}(y)]$$
$$\text{\& } \forall y[\neg\text{On}(x,y) \vee \neg\text{On}(y,x)]$$
$$\text{\& } \forall y[\text{Brick}(y) \vee \neg\text{Equal}(x,y)])]$$

- Purge existential quantifiers.

Unfortunately, the procedure for eliminating existential quantifiers is a little obscure, and we must work longer to understand everything. Let us begin by looking closely at the part of our axiom involving $\exists$:

$$\exists y[\text{On}(x,y) \text{ \& } \neg\text{Pyramid}(y)]$$

Now reflect, for a moment, on what this means. Evidently, if someone gives you some particular object x, you will always be able to name an object for y that makes the expression TRUE. Said another way, there is a function that takes argument x and returns a proper y. We do not necessarily know how the function works or what it looks like, but such a function must exist. Let us call it, for the moment, Magic(x).

Now using our new function, we no longer need to say that y exists, for we have a way of producing the proper y in any circumstance. Consequently, we can rewrite our expression as follows:

$$\text{On}(x, \text{Magic}(x)) \ \& \ \neg\text{Pyramid}(\text{Magic}(x))$$

Functions that eliminate the need for existential quantifiers are called *Skolem functions*. Note carefully that our Skolem function, $\text{Magic}(x)$, must depend on x, for otherwise it could not produce a y that depends on a particular x. The general rule is that the universal quantifiers determine Skolem function arguments. There must be one argument for each universally quantified variable whose scope contains the existentially quantified variable that the Skolem function replaces.

Here then is our evolving axiom, after eliminating the $\exists$ and introducing the Skolem function, which we now call the Support function:

$$\forall x[\neg\text{Brick}(x) \vee ((\text{On}(x, \text{Support}(x)) \ \& \ \neg\text{Pyramid}(\text{Support}(x)))$$
$$\& \ \forall y[\neg\text{On}(x, y) \vee \neg\text{On}(y, x)]$$
$$\& \ \forall y[\text{Brick}(y) \vee \neg\text{Equal}(x, y)])]$$

- Rename variables, as necessary, so that no two variables are the same.

The quantifiers do not care what their variable names are. Rename any duplicates within each expression so that each quantifier has a unique name.

We do this because we want to move all the universal quantifiers together at the left of each expression in the next step, without confounding them. In our example, the substitutions leave us with this:

$$\forall x[\neg\text{Brick}(x) \vee ((\text{On}(x, \text{Support}(x)) \ \& \ \neg\text{Pyramid}(\text{Support}(x)))$$
$$\& \ \forall y[\neg\text{On}(x, y) \vee \neg\text{On}(y, x)]$$
$$\& \ \forall z[\text{Brick}(z) \vee \neg\text{Equal}(x, z)])]$$

- Move the universal quantifiers to the left.

This works because by now each quantifier uses a unique variable name—no confusion results from leftward movement.

In our example, the result is as follows:

$$\forall x \forall y \forall z [\neg \text{Brick}(x) \lor ((\text{On}(x, \text{Support}(x)) \,\&\, \neg \text{Pyramid}(\text{Support}(x)))$$
$$\&\, \neg \text{On}(x, y) \lor \neg \text{On}(y, x)$$
$$\&\, \text{Brick}(z) \lor \neg \text{Equal}(x, z))]$$

- Move the disjunctions down to the literals.

Since all this requires is to move the ∨s inside the &s, we need only use one of the distributive laws:

$$E_1 \lor (E_2 \,\&\, E_3) \Rightarrow (E_1 \lor E_2) \,\&\, (E_1 \lor E_3)$$

For the example, let us do the work in two steps:

$$\forall x \forall y \forall z [(\neg \text{Brick}(x) \lor (\text{On}(x, \text{Support}(x)) \,\&\, \neg \text{Pyramid}(\text{Support}(x))))$$
$$\&\, (\neg \text{Brick}(x) \lor \neg \text{On}(x, y) \lor \neg \text{On}(y, x))$$
$$\&\, (\neg \text{Brick}(x) \lor \text{Brick}(z) \lor \neg \text{Equal}(x, z))]$$

$$\forall x \forall y \forall z [(\neg \text{Brick}(x) \lor \text{On}(x, \text{Support}(x)))$$
$$\&\, (\neg \text{Brick}(x) \lor \neg \text{Pyramid}(\text{Support}(x)))$$
$$\&\, (\neg \text{Brick}(x) \lor \neg \text{On}(x, y) \lor \neg \text{On}(y, x))$$
$$\&\, (\neg \text{Brick}(x) \lor \text{Brick}(z) \lor \neg \text{Equal}(x, z))]$$

- Eliminate the conjunctions.

Actually, we do not really eliminate them. Instead, we simply write each part of a conjunction as if it were a separate axiom. This makes sense because each part of a conjunction must be TRUE if the whole conjunction is TRUE. Here is the result:

$$\forall x [\neg \text{Brick}(x) \lor \text{On}(x, \text{Support}(x))]$$
$$\forall x [\neg \text{Brick}(x) \lor \neg \text{Pyramid}(\text{Support}(x))]$$
$$\forall x \forall y [\neg \text{Brick}(x) \lor \neg \text{On}(x, y) \lor \neg \text{On}(y, x)]$$
$$\forall x \forall z [\neg \text{Brick}(x) \lor \text{Brick}(z) \lor \neg \text{Equal}(x, z)]$$

- Rename all the variables, as necessary, so that no two variables are the same.

There is no problem with renaming variables at this step, for we are merely renaming the universally quantified variables in each part of a conjunction. Since each of the conjoined parts must be TRUE for any variable values, it does not matter if the variables have different names for each part. Here is the result for our example:

$$\forall x[\neg\text{Brick}(x) \lor \text{On}(x, \text{Support}(x))]$$
$$\forall w[\neg\text{Brick}(w) \lor \neg\text{Pyramid}(\text{Support}(w))]$$
$$\forall u\forall y[\neg\text{Brick}(u) \lor \neg\text{On}(u, y) \lor \neg\text{On}(y, u)]$$
$$\forall v\forall z[\neg\text{Brick}(v) \lor \text{Brick}(z) \lor \neg\text{Equal}(v, z)]$$

- Purge the universal quantifiers.

Actually, we do not really eliminate them. We just adopt a convention whereby all variables at this point are presumed to be universally quantified. Now our example looks like this:

$$\neg\text{Brick}(x) \lor \text{On}(x, \text{Support}(x))$$
$$\neg\text{Brick}(w) \lor \neg\text{Pyramid}(\text{Support}(w))$$
$$\neg\text{Brick}(u) \lor \neg\text{On}(u, y) \lor \neg\text{On}(y, u)$$
$$\neg\text{Brick}(v) \lor \text{Brick}(z) \lor \neg\text{Equal}(v, z)$$

The result is now in clause form, as required to use resolution. Each clause consists of a disjunction of literals. Taking the whole set of clauses together, we have an implied & on the top level, literals on the bottom level, and ∨s in between. Each clause's variables are different and all variables are implicitly universally quantified. To summarize, let us write down what we do:

To put axioms into clause form:
1 Eliminate implications.
2 Move negations down to the atomic formulas.
3 Purge existential quantifiers.
4 Rename variables, if necessary.
5 Move the universal quantifiers to the left.
6 Move the disjunctions down to the literals.
7 Eliminate the conjunctions.
8 Rename variables, if necessary.
9 Purge the universal quantifiers.

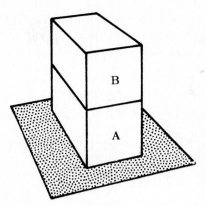

Figure 7-5. Some fodder for a proof.

With a procedure for converting into clause form, we can go on to write down a procedure for doing resolution proof:

To prove a theorem using resolution:
1 Negate the theorem to be proved and add the result to the list of axioms.
2 Put the list of axioms into clause form.
3 Until the empty clause, Nil, is produced or there is no resolvable pair of clauses, find resolvable clauses, resolve them, and add the result to the list of clauses.
4 If the empty clause is produced, report that the theorem is TRUE. If there are no resolvable clauses, report that the theorem is FALSE.

As stated, the procedure says nothing about which of many possible clause pairs to resolve at any given point. Ways of specifying just how the search is to proceed will be discussed soon.

First, however, it is time to work out an example. The following axioms account for the observed block relations in figure 7-5.

$$On(B, A)$$
$$On(A, Table)$$

These, of course, are already in clause form. Let us use them to show that B is above the table:

$$Above(B, Table)$$

To show this, we require the clause form of two universally quantified expressions. The first says that being on an object implies being above that object. The second says that one object is above another if there is an object in between:

$$\forall x \forall y [\text{On}(x, y) \Rightarrow \text{Above}(x, y)]$$
$$\forall x \forall y \forall z [\text{Above}(x, y) \ \& \ \text{Above}(y, z) \Rightarrow \text{Above}(x, z)]$$

After going through the procedure for reducing to clause form, these axioms look like this:

$$\neg\text{On}(u, v) \lor \text{Above}(u, v)$$
$$\neg\text{Above}(x, y) \lor \neg\text{Above}(y, z) \lor \text{Above}(x, z)$$

Recall that the thing to be shown is Above(B, Table). No conversion is needed after negation:
$$\neg\text{Above}(B, \text{Table})$$

Next we need some numbers for all of our clauses to keep things straight:

$$\neg\text{On}(u, v) \lor \text{Above}(u, v) \tag{1}$$

$$\neg\text{Above}(x, y) \lor \neg\text{Above}(y, z) \lor \text{Above}(x, z) \tag{2}$$

$$\text{On}(B, A) \tag{3}$$

$$\text{On}(A, \text{Table}) \tag{4}$$

$$\neg\text{Above}(B, \text{Table}) \tag{5}$$

Now we can start. Our strategy is to replace the Above relations with On relations that enable us to resolve against the axioms that specify the actual arrangement of the blocks. First, we resolve (2) and (5) by specializing x to B and z to Table so that the final part of (2) looks exactly like the thing negated in (5):

$$\neg\text{Above}(B, y) \lor \neg\text{Above}(y, \text{Table}) \lor \underline{\text{Above}(B, \text{Table})} \tag{2}$$

$$\underline{\neg\text{Above}(B, \text{Table})} \tag{5}$$

$$\neg\text{Above}(B, y) \lor \neg\text{Above}(y, \text{Table}) \tag{6}$$

Now we can resolve (1) with (6) by replacing u with y and specializing v to Table:

$$\neg\text{On}(y, \text{Table}) \lor \underline{\text{Above}(y, \text{Table})} \tag{1}$$

$$\neg\text{Above}(B, y) \lor \underline{\neg\text{Above}(y, \text{Table})} \tag{6}$$

$$\neg\text{On}(y, \text{Table}) \lor \neg\text{Above}(B, y) \tag{7}$$

Curiously, it pays to use (1) again with (7), with u specialized to B and v replaced by y:

$$\neg\text{On}(\text{B}, y) \vee \underline{\text{Above}(\text{B}, y)} \tag{1}$$

$$\neg\text{On}(y, \text{Table}) \vee \underline{\neg\text{Above}(\text{B}, y)} \tag{7}$$

$$\neg\text{On}(\text{B}, y) \vee \neg\text{On}(y, \text{Table}) \tag{8}$$

Now let us use (3) and (8), specializing y to A:

$$\underline{\text{On}(\text{B}, \text{A})} \tag{3}$$

$$\underline{\neg\text{On}(\text{B}, \text{A})} \vee \neg\text{On}(\text{A}, \text{Table}) \tag{8}$$

$$\neg\text{On}(\text{A}, \text{Table}) \tag{9}$$

Now (4) and (9) resolve to Nil, the empty clause.

$$\underline{\text{On}(\text{A}, \text{Table})} \tag{4}$$

$$\underline{\neg\text{On}(\text{A}, \text{Table})} \tag{9}$$

$$\text{Nil} \tag{10}$$

We must be finished. We have arrived at a contradiction, so the negation of the theorem, ¬Above(B, Table), must be FALSE. Hence the theorem, Above(B, Table), must be TRUE.

Proof Is Exponential

One big question is How were we so shrewd as to pick just the right clauses to resolve? The answer is that we were not so shrewd at all, for we took advantage of two things:

- First, we confined ourselves to resolving against only the negated theorem or new clauses derived, directly or indirectly, using the negated theorem.

- Second, we knew where we were, we know where we were going, we noted the difference, and we used our intuition. Having already found a solution to the problem in our head, trivially, we knew that we needed to get the above-but-not-on clause into the proof, using it to tie B to the table with A in the middle. Once that was done, we noted that we had expressions involving Above linking objects that actually satisfied On. It was clear, then, that we needed to get the above-because-on clause into action.

Unfortunately, there are limits to what we can express if we restrict ourselves to the mathematically attractive concepts in pure logic. For example, pure logic does not allow us to express things like differences, as required by means-ends analysis, or heuristic distances, as required by best-first search. Theorem provers can use such concepts, but then a large fraction of the problem-solving burden rests on knowledge lying outside the statement, in logical notation, of what is known and what is to be done.

But while some search strategies require us to separate ourselves considerably from pure logic, others do not. One such strategy, the *unit-preference strategy*, gives preference to resolutions involving the clauses with the smallest number of literals. The *set-of-support strategy* allows only resolutions involving the negated theorem or new clauses derived, directly or indirectly, using the negated theorem. The *breadth-first strategy* first resolves all possible pairs of the initial clauses, then resolves all possible pairs of the resulting set together with the initial set, level by level. All these strategies are said to be *complete* because they are guaranteed to find a proof if the theorem logically follows from the axioms. Unfortunately, there is another side:

- All resolution search strategies are subject to *the combinatorial-explosion problem*, for the search trees involved can grow wildly, preventing success for proofs that require long chains of inference.

- All resolution search strategies are subject to a version of *the halting problem*, for search is not guaranteed to terminate unless there actually is a proof.

In fact, all complete proof procedures for the first-order predicate calculus are subject to the halting problem. Complete proof procedures are said to be *semidecidable* because they are guaranteed to tell us whether an expression is a theorem only if the expression is indeed a theorem.

Resolution Requires Unification

To resolve two clauses, two literals must match exactly, except that one is negated. Sometimes literals match exactly as they stand; sometimes literals can be made to match by an appropriate substitution.

In the examples so far, the matching part of resolution was easy: the same constant appeared in the same place, obviously matching; or a constant appeared in the place occupied by a universally quantified variable, matching because the variable could be the observed constant as well as any other. In other words, we either matched identical constants or specialized a variable.

For examples later on, we need a better way to keep track of substitutions, and we need the rules by which substitutions can be made. First, let us agree to denote substitutions as follows:

$$\{v_1 \rightarrow C; v_2 \rightarrow v_3; v_4 \rightarrow f(\ldots)\}$$

By this, we mean that the variable v_1 is replaced by the constant C, the variable v_2 is replaced by the variable v_3, and the variable v_4 is replaced by a function, f, together with the function's arguments.[2] The rules for such substitutions say that we can replace a variable by any term that does not contain the same variable:

- A variable may be replaced by a constant. That is, we can have the substitution $\{v_1 \rightarrow C\}$.

- A variable may be replaced by a variable. That is, we can have the substitution $\{v_2 \rightarrow v_3\}$.

- A variable may be replaced by a function expression as long as the function expression does not contain the variable. That is, we can have the substitution $\{v_4 \rightarrow f(\ldots)\}$.

A substitution that makes two clauses resolvable is called a *unifier*, and the process of finding such substitutions is called *unification*. There are many procedures for unification. But for our examples, inspection will do.

Traditional Logic Is Monotonic

Suppose an expression is a theorem with respect to a certain set of axioms. Is the expression still a theorem after adding some new axioms? Surely it must be, for the proof can be done using the old axioms exclusively, ignoring the new ones.

Since new axioms only add to the list of provable theorems and never cause any to be withdrawn, traditional logic is said to be *monotonic*.

The monotonicity property is incompatible with some natural ways of thinking, however. Suppose you are told all birds fly, from which you conclude that some particular bird flies, a perfectly reasonable conclusion, given what you know. Then someone points out that penguins do not fly, nor do dead birds. Adding these new facts can block your already made conclusion, but cannot stop a theorem prover; only amending the initial axioms can.

Dealing with this sort of problem requires new ways of doing logic, leading to logics that are said to be *nonmonotonic*. Discussing these logics

---

[2] Other authors denote the same substitution by $\{C/v_1, v_3/v_2, f(\ldots)/v_4\}$, which is easier to write but harder to keep straight.

would be out of place here because they remain surrounded with speculation and turbulence. There is, however, some additional discussion of non-
monotonicity in chapter 12 with the introduction of antecedent-consequent
rules that block other antecedent-consequent rules.

Theorem Proving Is Suitable for Some Problems, but Not All

Logic is terrific for some jobs and not so good at others. But since logic is
unbeatable for what it was developed to do, logic is seductive. People try
to use logic for all hard problems, not just those for which logic is suited.
But this is like using a hammer to drive screws, just because hammers are
good at dealing with one kind of fastener.

Consequently, when using logic and a theorem prover seems unambiguously right, review these caveats:

- Theorem provers may take too long.

Complete theorem provers require search, and the search is inherently exponential. Methods for speeding search, like set-of-support resolution, reduce
the size of the exponent associated with the search, but do not change the
exponential character.

- Theorem provers may not help much, even if instantaneous.

Some knowledge resists embodiment in axioms. Getting some problem
formulated as logic may require enormous effort, while solving the problem
formulated in another way may be simple.

- Logic is weak as a representation for certain kinds of knowledge.

The notation of pure logic does not allow us to express such things as
heuristic distances, or state differences, or the idea that one particular
approach is particularly fast, or the idea that some manipulation works
well, but only if done fewer than three times. Theorem provers can use
such knowledge, but that knowledge must be represented by using concepts
other than those of pure logic.

PLANNING OPERATOR SEQUENCES

Logic shows what is TRUE as a consequence of what is given, but curiously,
logic can also show how to achieve truth by using operators to change
things.

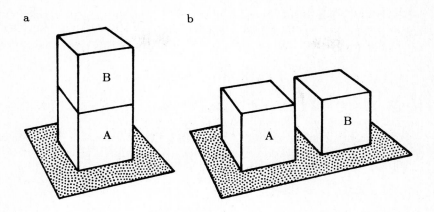

Figure 7-6. A simple initial situation and final situation involving blocks. The problem is to find a sequence of operators that transforms the initial situation into the final situation.

Finding Operator Sequences Requires Situation Variables

Suppose that we have a blocks-world situation in which block B is on top of A and A is on top of a table as suggested in figure 7-6a. Further suppose the problem is to find a way to get B onto the table, as in figure 7-6b. Using logical notation, the problem is to arrange for the following to be TRUE:

$$On(B, Table)$$

Clearly, the expression to be arranged is not TRUE in the initial situation of the problem world, but it could be TRUE in other situations with different block arrangements. Consequently, it is incomplete to say that some expression is TRUE; to be complete, we must specify the situation in which it is TRUE.

The necessary bookkeeping can be done by indicating the expressions that are known to be TRUE in various situations like the following:

Initial situation: *Final situation:*

On(B, A) & On(A, Table)   On(B, Table) & On(A, Table)

For our purposes, however, a better alternative is to add a situation argument to the predicates. To say that B is on A in situation S, the initial situation, and A is on the table, we insert S as the value of an extra argument:

$$On(B, A, S) \ \& \ On(A, Table, S)$$

Note that S is a known, constant situation, not an unknown, variable situation. Hence we use an uppercase character.

What we want is a final situation, s_f, such that B is on the table.

$$\exists s_f[\text{On}(\text{B}, \text{Table}, s_f)]$$

Note that s_f is an unknown, variable situation, not a known, constant situation. Hence we use a lowercase character.

Now imagine an operation, Putontable, that changes the situation by putting an object on the table. Roughly, this is what Putontable(x, s) is to do:

- Putontable finds block x in some situation s.

- Putontable creates a new situation for which x is on top of the table.

Viewed from the inside, Putontable must be quite complicated, if it is to deal with interfering objects, but viewed from the outside, Putontable is a black box that hands back a situation as its value. Given object x and situation s, Putontable's value is a new situation in which On(x, Table) is TRUE. Note that Putontable is definitely not a predicate, since Putontable's value is a situation, rather than TRUE or FALSE.

Realizing now that Putontable's value is a situation, Putontable can appear as an argument of On where we expect a situation to be. In fact, Putontable can be defined this way:

$$\forall s \forall x[\neg \text{On}(x, \text{Table}, s) \Rightarrow \text{On}(x, \text{Table}, \text{Putontable}(x, s))]$$

To use this, we need a way to know when something is not on the table. Clearly something is not on the table if it is on something that is not the table. This says the same thing:

$$\forall s \forall y \forall z[\text{On}(y, z, s) \,\&\, \neg \text{Equal}(z, \text{Table}) \Rightarrow \neg \text{On}(y, \text{Table}, s)]$$

Now we can use what we know to show that there is a way to have block B on the table. We simply put the definition of Putontable and the not-on-table expression on the list of axioms and turn the resolution crank. The initial axioms are

$\text{On}(\text{B}, \text{A}, \text{S}) \,\&\, \text{On}(\text{A}, \text{Table}, \text{S})$

$\forall s \forall x[\neg \text{On}(x, \text{Table}, s) \Rightarrow \text{On}(x, \text{Table}, \text{Putontable}(x, s))]$

$\forall s \forall y \forall z[\text{On}(y, z, s) \,\&\, \neg \text{Equal}(z, \text{Table}) \Rightarrow \neg \text{On}(y, \text{Table}, s)]$

The desired expression, the theorem, is

$$\exists s_f[\text{On}(\text{B}, \text{Table}, s_f)]$$

Now, negating the desired expression, we have

$$\neg\exists s_f[\text{On}(\text{B}, \text{Table}, s_f)]$$

Moving the $\neg$ down to the atomic formula, we have

$$\forall s_f[\neg\text{On}(\text{B}, \text{Table}, s_f)]$$

Adding this to the list of axioms, larding with some expressions about object-object equality, putting everything in clause form, and taking care to use unique variables in each clause, we have

$$\text{On}(\text{B}, \text{A}, \text{S}) \tag{1}$$

$$\text{On}(\text{A}, \text{Table}, \text{S}) \tag{2}$$

$$\text{On}(x, \text{Table}, s_3) \lor \text{On}(x, \text{Table}, \text{Putontable}(x, s_3)) \tag{3}$$

$$\neg\text{On}(y, z, s_4) \lor \text{Equal}(z, \text{Table}) \lor \neg\text{On}(y, \text{Table}, s_4) \tag{4}$$

$$\neg\text{Equal}(\text{B}, \text{A}) \tag{5}$$

$$\neg\text{Equal}(\text{B}, \text{Table}) \tag{6}$$

$$\neg\text{Equal}(\text{A}, \text{Table}) \tag{7}$$

$$\neg\text{On}(\text{B}, \text{Table}, s_f) \tag{8}$$

Note that we have used subscripted variables, like s_3, rather than dragging in new letters. We do this because we want to remember that these variables all represent situations. To avoid repeating a subscript by accident, the subscripts correspond to the clause number.

From here, proof is easy. Examine figure 7-7. We can resolve (3) and (8), using $\{x \rightarrow \text{B}; s_f \rightarrow \text{Putontable}(x, s_3)\}$, producing this, after renaming the variable:

$$\text{On}(\text{B}, \text{Table}, s_9) \tag{9}$$

Now we work with (9) and (4), using $\{y \rightarrow \text{B}; s_4 \rightarrow s_9\}$ and renaming the variables:

$$\neg\text{On}(\text{B}, w, s_{10}) \lor \text{Equal}(w, \text{Table}) \tag{10}$$

Resolving (10) with (7), using $\{w \rightarrow \text{A}\}$ and renaming, we get the following:

$$\neg\text{On}(\text{B}, \text{A}, s_{11}) \tag{11}$$

Finishing by resolving (11) with (1), using $\{s_{11} \rightarrow \text{S}\}$, we have Nil, the empty clause:

$$\text{Nil} \tag{12}$$

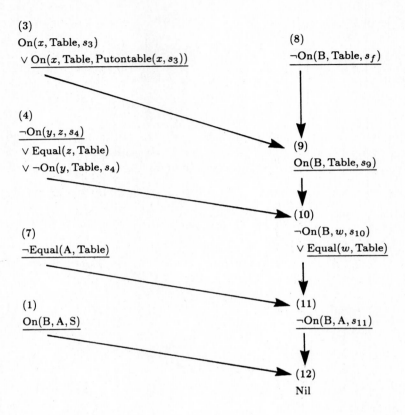

Figure 7-7. A proof involving an operator, Putontable.

But we have concluded only that it is possible to have a situation where B is on the table. We do not know how to reach that situation. Knowledge about how to get where we want to be is implicitly locked into all the unifications, however. Looking back over what we have done, we see this sequence of substitutions:

$$s_f \rightarrow \text{Putontable}(B, s_3)$$
$$s_3 \rightarrow s_9$$
$$s_9 \rightarrow s_{10}$$
$$s_{10} \rightarrow s_{11}$$
$$s_{11} \rightarrow S$$

Plugging through all the substitutions, evidently the desired situation, s_f, is the situation we get to by using the Putontable operation on B in the initial situation, S.

Tracing the situation history is a tedious, error-provoking chore for problems involving many operations. Consequently, the usual practice is to use something called *Green's trick*. The basic idea is to add an extra term to the expression of the desired result. This extra term, called the *answer term* exploits the ordinary unification apparatus to keep track of situation information. Instead of $\neg\text{On}(\text{B}, \text{Table}, s_f)$, we write $\neg\text{On}(\text{B}, \text{Table}, s_f) \lor \text{Answer}(s_f)$. Let us then repeat the steps in the proof:

$$\neg\text{On}(\text{B}, \text{Table}, s_f) \lor \text{Answer}(s_f) \tag{8}$$

$$\text{On}(\text{B}, \text{Table}, s_9) \lor \text{Answer}(\text{Putontable}(\text{B}, s_9)) \tag{9}$$

$$\neg\text{On}(\text{B}, w, s_{10}) \lor \text{Equal}(w, \text{Table}) \lor \text{Answer}(\text{Putontable}(\text{B}, s_{10})) \tag{10}$$

$$\neg\text{On}(\text{B}, \text{A}, s_{11}) \lor \text{Answer}(\text{Putontable}(\text{B}, s_{11})) \tag{11}$$

$$\text{Answer}(\text{Putontable}(\text{B}, \text{S})) \tag{12}$$

Note that since Answer is inserted only once into the axioms, it can never appear both with and without a $\neg$. Consequently, Answer can never be the basis of a resolution. On the other hand, it is carried along with every clause that can be traced back to the desired situation through a series of resolutions. Moreover, Answer's argument is always a record of the situation changes involved in the series of resolutions endured.

Of course, instead of terminating when we have Nil, we now terminate when we have a clause containing only Answer. The resolution steps are shown in figure 7-8. The revised resolution procedure is as follows:

To prove a single-literal existentially-quantified theorem using resolution with Green's trick:

1 Negate the theorem, convert it to clause form, and add the Answer term.

2 Put the list of axioms into clause form. Add the clause derived from the theorem and the Answer term.

3 Until a clause with only the Answer term is produced or there is no resolvable pair of clauses, find resolvable clauses, resolve them, and add the result to the list of clauses.

4 If a clause with only the Answer term is produced, report that the sequence of operations in the Answer term is the required answer. If there are no resolvable clauses, report that the required action cannot be done.

This procedure can be generalized to handle proofs for theorems with multiple literals and universal quantification. We shall be content with the procedure as it stands, however.

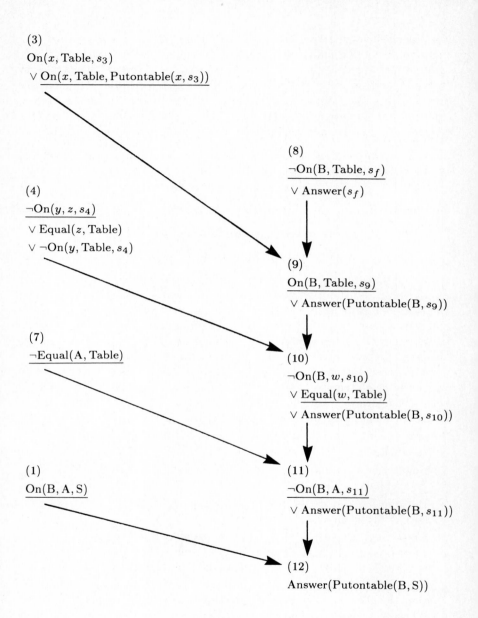

(3)
On$(x, $ Table$, s_3)$
$\lor$ On$(x, $ Table$, $ Putontable$(x, s_3))$

(4)
$\neg$On(y, z, s_4)
$\lor$ Equal$(z, $ Table$)$
$\lor \neg$On$(y, $ Table$, s_4)$

(7)
$\neg$Equal$($A$, $ Table$)$

(1)
On$($B$, $ A$, $ S$)$

(8)
$\neg$On$($B$, $ Table$, s_f)$
$\lor$ Answer(s_f)

(9)
On$($B$, $ Table$, s_9)$
$\lor$ Answer$($Putontable$($B$, s_9))$

(10)
$\neg$On$($B$, w, s_{10})$
$\lor$ Equal$(w, $ Table$)$
$\lor$ Answer$($Putontable$($B$, s_{10}))$

(11)
$\neg$On$($B$, $ A$, s_{11})$
$\lor$ Answer$($Putontable$($B$, s_{11}))$

(12)
Answer$($Putontable$($B$, $ S$))$

Figure 7-8. Appending Answer(s_f) to the goal expression is done to keep track of the situation-change operations using the standard unification apparatus. Here the proof of figure 7-7 is repeated using Answer(s_f). The result indicates that only one operation is needed to put block B on the table.

Frame Axioms Address the Frame Problem

Now suppose we try a problem similar to the last one, but requiring both B and A to be on the table in the final situation. That is, our goal is

$$\exists s_f[\text{On}(\text{B}, \text{Table}, s_f) \;\&\; \text{On}(\text{A}, \text{Table}, s_f)]$$

We know that the same operation, putting B on the table, suffices. After all, A is already on the table. Let us see. First, we negate and transform to clause form, as shown in the following step:

$$\neg \exists s_f[\text{On}(\text{B}, \text{Table}, s_f) \;\&\; \text{On}(\text{A}, \text{Table}, s_f)]$$
$$\forall s_f[\neg(\text{On}(\text{B}, \text{Table}, s_f) \;\&\; \text{On}(\text{A}, \text{Table}, s_f))]$$
$$\forall s_f[\neg\text{On}(\text{B}, \text{Table}, s_f) \lor \neg\text{On}(\text{A}, \text{Table}, s_f)]$$
$$\neg\text{On}(\text{B}, \text{Table}, s_f) \lor \neg\text{On}(\text{A}, \text{Table}, s_f)$$

The last expression is the one to number and to add to the axioms:

$$\neg\text{On}(\text{B}, \text{Table}, s_f) \lor \neg\text{On}(\text{A}, \text{Table}, s_f) \tag{8}$$

Using $\{x \to \text{B}; s_f \to \text{Putontable}(x, s_3)\}$ and renaming, as in the previous proof, we can resolve (3) and (8), producing (9).

$$\text{On}(\text{B}, \text{Table}, s_9) \lor \neg\text{On}(\text{A}, \text{Table}, \text{Putontable}(\text{B}, s_9)) \tag{9}$$

Using (9) and (4), with the substitution $\{y \to \text{B}; s_4 \to s_9\}$ and renaming:

$$\neg\text{On}(\text{B}, w, s_{10}) \lor \text{Equal}(w, \text{Table}) \lor \neg\text{On}(\text{A}, \text{Table}, \text{Putontable}(\text{B}, s_{10})) \tag{10}$$

Resolving (10) with (7), using $\{w \to \text{A}\}$ and renaming, as usual, we get

$$\neg\text{On}(\text{B}, \text{A}, s_{11}) \lor \neg\text{On}(\text{A}, \text{Table}, \text{Putontable}(\text{B}, s_{11})) \tag{11}$$

Finishing by resolving (11) with (1), using $\{s_{11} \to \text{S}\}$, we have:

$$\neg\text{On}(\text{A}, \text{Table}, \text{Putontable}(\text{B}, \text{S})) \tag{12}$$

At this point, it is tempting to resolve (12) with (2), $\text{On}(\text{A}, \text{Table}, \text{S})$. This would be a terrible blunder, however, for resolving these two would require the substitution $\{\text{S} \to \text{Putontable}(\text{B}, \text{S})\}$. But S is a situation, not a variable, so no such substitution is possible.

At first this may seem strange, for if A is on the table in the initial situation, surely it remains on the table after B is put on the table too. We know A stays put, but our knowledge is not in the logic. The Putontable axiom says what happens to the object being moved, but it does not say what happens to other objects. Without knowing more, there is no way for a logic-based engine to deduce which predicate's values are unchanged in going from one situation to another. After all, some do change. This dilemma is known as the *frame problem*.

Consequently, to get both B and A on the table, we need to inform our resolution theorem prover about preserved relations. One popular way to do this is to introduce *frame axioms*. A frame axiom is a statement about how predicates survive operations. Here is one explaining how On survives Putontable:

$$\forall s \forall x \forall y \forall z [\text{On}(x, y, s) \ \& \ \neg\text{Equal}(x, z) \Rightarrow \text{On}(x, y, \text{Putontable}(z, s))]$$

In English, this says that if x is on y before a Putontable operation, then x remains on y afterward as long as x was not the object put on the table.

Now converting our frame axiom to clause form, changing the variable names as required, we have this frame axiom:

$$\neg\text{On}(p, q, s_0) \vee \text{Equal}(p, r) \vee \text{On}(p, q, \text{Putontable}(r, s_0)) \tag{0}$$

Remember that we were stuck in our proof at the point where we had

$$\neg\text{On}(\text{A}, \text{Table}, \text{Putontable}(\text{B}, \text{S})) \tag{12}$$

But now we are no longer stuck, for our new frame axiom comes to the rescue. Resolving (12) with (0), substituting with $\{p \rightarrow \text{A}; q \rightarrow \text{Table}; r \rightarrow \text{B}; s_0 \rightarrow \text{S}\}$, we have

$$\neg\text{On}(\text{A}, \text{Table}, \text{S}) \vee \text{Equal}(\text{A}, \text{B}) \tag{13}$$

Quickly resolving (13) with (5) and the result, (14), with (2), we obtain Nil, completing the proof:

$$\neg\text{On}(\text{A}, \text{Table}, \text{S}) \tag{14}$$

$$\text{Nil} \tag{15}$$

If we desired, we could repeat using Green's trick, producing the required operator sequence.

At this point, we have managed to get two blocks on the table, but it took quite a bit of doing. In general, the approach illustrated requires a baggage of not-equal axioms and frame axioms. We need one not-equal axiom for each pair of distinct objects, and we need one frame axiom for most predicate-operator pairs. Fortunately, there are other ways to attack the frame problem, but it would be out of place to discuss them, for we have too many other directions to go.

PROOF BY CONSTRAINT PROPAGATION

So far, we have been thinking of the logical connectives, &, ∨, ¬, and ⇒, as if they were functions, accepting arguments and returning TRUE or FALSE. Now it is time to divert ourselves in another way, using logical expressions to build a net of nodes through which constraints propagate. We do this for several reasons.

First, a logic-oriented constraint net highlights the fact that theorem proving can be viewed as a way of exploiting constraints. Second, constraint nets make it easy to keep track of what is TRUE and FALSE as assumptions are made or withdrawn. This is why constraint nets are associated with the notion of *truth maintenance*. Third, constraint nets make it easy to see how dependency-directed, nonchronological backtracking can help correct the contradictions that occur when assumptions are incompatible. Note, however, that dependency-directed backtracking works with any proof procedure, not just those that involve constraint nets.

Note also that the constraint-propagation procedure to be described has limitations. One is that the procedure is not a complete proof procedure because there are TRUE expressions that the procedure cannot prove are TRUE. Another limitation is that either there must be no quantified expressions or there must be a way of preprocessing expressions with quantifiers, transforming them into a finite number of quantifier-free axioms. Thus the procedure deals with propositional calculus only.

Truth Can Be Propagated

Let us think of logical expressions as nodes in a network. If the expression associated with one node is part of an expression associated with another node, then the two nodes are linked. Consider this expression, for example:

$$\text{Happy}(A) \Rightarrow \text{Happy}(B)$$

Now, as shown in figure 7-9a, we create nodes for this expression and both of the subexpressions, Happy(A) and Happy(B). Further, assuming the big expression is TRUE, we label the associated node TRUE. We make no assumptions about the other two nodes, however, so we label them UNKNOWN.

But plainly, if we further assume that A is happy, then Happy(A) is TRUE, and Happy(B) is TRUE too. Thinking in terms of constraint propagation, introduced in chapter 3, we want the TRUE value assumed for the node associated with Happy(A), together with the TRUE value for the node associated with Happy(A) $\Rightarrow$ Happy(B), to force the node for Happy(A) to have a TRUE value too, as in figure 7-9b.

Evidently, we need some rules to enable propagation through various sorts of nodes so that a value determined for one expression can help determine values for others.

Now in a moment, we will see that the definition of $E_1 \Rightarrow E_2$ has the following logical consequences:

$$\neg E_1 \vee E_2 \vee \neg(E_1 \Rightarrow E_2)$$
$$E_1 \vee (E_1 \Rightarrow E_2)$$
$$\neg E_2 \vee (E_1 \Rightarrow E_2)$$

Note that the value of at least one of the literals on each line must be TRUE. For emphasis, let us rewrite the expressions in a *syntactically sugared* format as follows:

Require E_1 is FALSE   *or* E_2 is TRUE   *or* $(E_1 \Rightarrow E_2)$ is FALSE

Require E_1 is TRUE   *or* $(E_1 \Rightarrow E_2)$ is TRUE

Require E_2 is FALSE   *or* $(E_1 \Rightarrow E_2)$ is TRUE

Written this way, it is clear that at least one of the subexpressions on each line must match the stipulated TRUE or FALSE value. Hence, if all but one subexpression mismatches, the remaining subexpression is *required* to match. Each line, therefore, is a constraint on the values of expressions appearing in that line. Consequently, let us call such things *constraint expressions*. To propagate truth, then, we use the following procedure:

To propagate truth:

1   For all nodes:

    1.1   For each constraint expression:

        1.1a   If the value of all but one subexpression mismatches the given TRUE or FALSE value, set the remaining subexpression value so that it matches.

        1.1b   Otherwise do nothing.

Now, before we forget, we have to see where the constraints come from. Since the rest of this subsection is devoted to this somewhat tedious task, tired readers should skip to the next subsection immediately.

First, we must show which TRUE and FALSE combinations for E_1, E_2, and $E_1 \Rightarrow E_2$ are excluded by the definition of $\Rightarrow$. Next, we show that

a

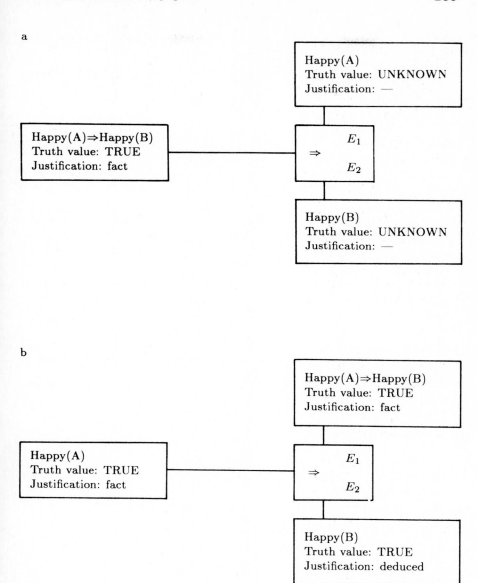

Figure 7-9. Logical expressions may be viewed as nodes in a constraint propagation network. In part *a*, a node for an ⇒ expression is shown connected to its subexpressions. In *b*, assuming one of the subexpressions is TRUE initiates a propagation through the ⇒ node to require another node to be TRUE.

using the constraint expressions associated with $\Rightarrow$ is equivalent to ensuring that the excluded combinations cannot occur.

From the truth-table definition of $\Rightarrow$, we know that $E_1 \Rightarrow E_2$ allows only the following combinations:

E_1	E_2	Forced by $E_1 \Rightarrow E_2$
TRUE	FALSE	FALSE
FALSE	FALSE	TRUE
FALSE	TRUE	TRUE
TRUE	TRUE	TRUE

But there are eight possible combinations of three TRUE-FALSE values. Consequently, these four remaining combinations must be forbidden:

E_1	E_2	Forbidden by $E_1 \Rightarrow E_2$
TRUE	FALSE	TRUE
FALSE	FALSE	FALSE
FALSE	TRUE	FALSE
TRUE	TRUE	FALSE

Saying this another way, the following must be TRUE, for each line excludes one of the four forbidden combinations:

$$\neg(E_1 \ \& \ \neg E_2 \ \& \ (E_1 \Rightarrow E_2))$$
$$\& \ \neg(\neg E_1 \ \& \ \neg E_2 \ \& \ \neg(E_1 \Rightarrow E_2))$$
$$\& \ \neg(\neg E_1 \ \& \ E_2 \ \& \ \neg(E_1 \Rightarrow E_2))$$
$$\& \ \neg(E_1 \ \& \ E_2 \ \& \ \neg(E_1 \Rightarrow E_2))$$

Taking the outside negations inside, we can rewrite the expression this way:

$$(\neg E_1 \lor E_2 \lor \neg(E_1 \Rightarrow E_2))$$
$$\& \ (E_1 \lor E_2 \lor (E_1 \Rightarrow E_2))$$
$$\& \ (E_1 \lor \neg E_2 \lor (E_1 \Rightarrow E_2))$$
$$\& \ (\neg E_1 \lor \neg E_2 \lor (E_1 \Rightarrow E_2))$$

Now combining the second and third lines and the third and fourth lines, we have the following equivalent expression:

$$(\neg E_1 \lor E_2 \lor \neg(E_1 \Rightarrow E_2))$$
$$\& \ (E_1 \lor (E_1 \Rightarrow E_2))$$
$$\& \ (\neg E_2 \lor (E_1 \Rightarrow E_2))$$

Aha! These are the consequences of $\Rightarrow$ that we assumed before. We could, tiresomely, repeat for &, $\vee$, and $\neg$. Let us be content with these summary results:

For $\Rightarrow$ nodes, we have each of the following constraint expressions:

Require E_1 is FALSE *or* E_2 is TRUE *or* $(E_1 \Rightarrow E_2)$ is FALSE
Require E_1 is TRUE *or* $(E_1 \Rightarrow E_2)$ is TRUE
Require E_2 is FALSE *or* $(E_1 \Rightarrow E_2)$ is TRUE

For & nodes, we have each of the following constraint expressions:

Require E_1 is FALSE *or* E_2 is FALSE *or* $(E_1 \& E_2)$ is TRUE
Require E_1 is TRUE *or* $(E_1 \& E_2)$ is FALSE
Require E_2 is TRUE *or* $(E_1 \& E_2)$ is FALSE

For $\vee$ nodes, we have each of the following constraint expressions:

Require E_1 is TRUE *or* E_2 is TRUE *or* $(E_1 \vee E_2)$ is FALSE
Require E_1 is FALSE *or* $(E_1 \vee E_2)$ is TRUE
Require E_2 is FALSE *or* $(E_1 \vee E_2)$ is TRUE

For $\neg$ nodes, we have the following constraint expressions:

Require E_1 is TRUE *or* $\neg E_1$ is TRUE
Require E_1 is FALSE *or* $\neg E_1$ is FALSE

Truth Propagation Can Find Justifications

Armed with these constraint expressions, we can now attack a problem. We start with four people, A, B, C, and D. A knows B, B knows C, and C knows D. Let us assume that only people who know each other can influence each other's happiness. Consequently, there are six possible expressions saying that one person's happiness causes another person's happiness. Generalizing, there are 24 possible expressions saying one person's happiness or unhappiness can cause another person's happiness or unhappiness. Of these, we assume the following expressions are the only such expressions that can be considered solid facts:

$$\text{Happy}(A) \Rightarrow \text{Happy}(B)$$
$$\text{Happy}(B) \Rightarrow \text{Happy}(C)$$

We also assume A and D are surely happy:

$$\text{Happy}(A)$$
$$\text{Happy}(D)$$

These assumed expressions correspond to the net shown in figure 7-10. There are two sets of constraint expressions. One set reflects the influence of Happy(A) on Happy(B):

Require   Happy(A) is FALSE
       or   Happy(B) is TRUE
       or   (Happy(A) $\Rightarrow$ Happy(B)) is FALSE
Require   Happy(A) is TRUE   *or*   (Happy(A) $\Rightarrow$ Happy(B)) is TRUE
Require   Happy(B) is FALSE   *or*   (Happy(A) $\Rightarrow$ Happy(B)) is TRUE

A similar set deals with the constraint between Happy(B) and Happy(C):

Require   Happy(B) is FALSE
       or   Happy(C) is TRUE
       or   (Happy(B) $\Rightarrow$ Happy(C)) is FALSE
Require   Happy(B) is TRUE   *or*   (Happy(B) $\Rightarrow$ Happy(C)) is TRUE
Require   Happy(C) is FALSE   *or*   (Happy(B) $\Rightarrow$ Happy(C)) is TRUE

Using these constraint expressions for $\Rightarrow$, together with the further fact that A is happy, it is easy to deduce that Happy(B) and Happy(C) are both TRUE.Now, however, let us assume, tentatively, that D can exert a negative influence on C's mood:

$$\text{Happy}(D) \Rightarrow \neg\text{Happy}(C)$$

This expression produces additional network structure, as shown in figure 7-11, and two sets of constraint expressions; one is for the $\Rightarrow$:

Require   Happy(D) is FALSE
       or $\neg$Happy(C) is TRUE
       or   (Happy(D) $\Rightarrow$ $\neg$Happy(C)) is FALSE
Require   Happy(D) is TRUE   *or*   (Happy(D) $\Rightarrow$ $\neg$Happy(C)) is TRUE
Require $\neg$Happy(C) is FALSE   *or*   (Happy(D) $\Rightarrow$ $\neg$Happy(C)) is TRUE

The other is for the embedded $\neg$:

Require   Happy(C) is TRUE   *or* $\neg$Happy(C) is TRUE
Require   Happy(C) is FALSE   *or* $\neg$Happy(C) is FALSE

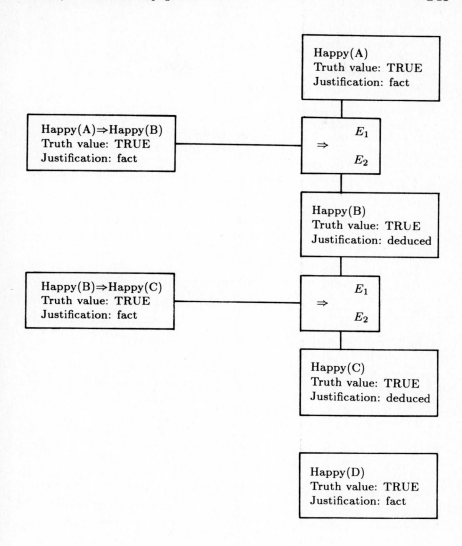

Figure 7-10. A constraint propagation network. Constraint expressions govern the propagation of truth values.

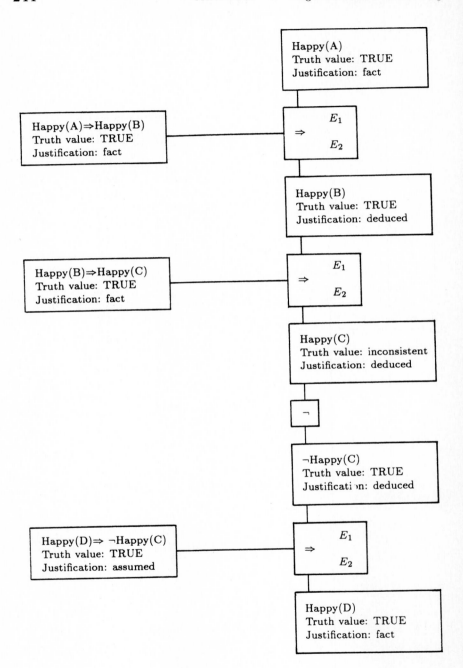

Figure 7-11. Truth values move through a truth-maintenance net from Happy(D) through ⇒ and ¬ nodes to contradict Happy(C).

These produce a contradiction. The first constraint expression of the ⇒ set forces ¬Happy(C) to be TRUE, because Happy(D) is TRUE, not FALSE, and because (Happy(D) ⇒ ¬Happy(C)) is assumed to be TRUE. But if ¬Happy(C) is TRUE, then the second constraint expression of the ¬ set forces Happy(C) to be FALSE, contradicting our previous conclusion that Happy(C) is TRUE. Something is wrong.

Justification Links Enable Change of Mind

As constraint propagation takes place, it is easy enough to keep a record of how truth values are determined. The record need only contain *justification links* that point from each deduced assertion back to the things from whence it directly came.

In the happiness example, justification links make it easy to trace back from the truth value for Happy(C) to facts and assumptions about A, D, and various happiness and unhappiness influences.

Consequently, when something goes wrong, if one line of reasoning says something is TRUE and another says it is FALSE, it is possible to track down the assumptions that lead to the contradiction. Said another way, justification links enable us to use dependency-directed backtracking, introduced in chapter 3, to find compatible assumptions.

In the example, tracing back from the TRUE value for C brings us to expressions given as solid facts:

$$Happy(A) \Rightarrow Happy(B)$$
$$Happy(B) \Rightarrow Happy(C)$$
$$Happy(A)$$

Tracing back from the FALSE value for C brings us to one expression given as a solid fact:

$$Happy(D)$$

The FALSE value also brings us to one expression given as a tentative assumption:

$$Happy(D) \Rightarrow \neg Happy(C)$$

Having traced back to all the contributions to the contradiction, it is time to consider what should be done. As described, the most obvious thing to do is to withdraw the single assumption given as tentative, leaving the solid facts alone. Thus we no longer suppose that D's happiness causes C to be unhappy.

Similarly, if an assumption happens to be withdrawn, then it is easy to track down the consequences that depend on the withdrawn assumption so that they too can be withdrawn, if necessary. Sometimes, of course, more

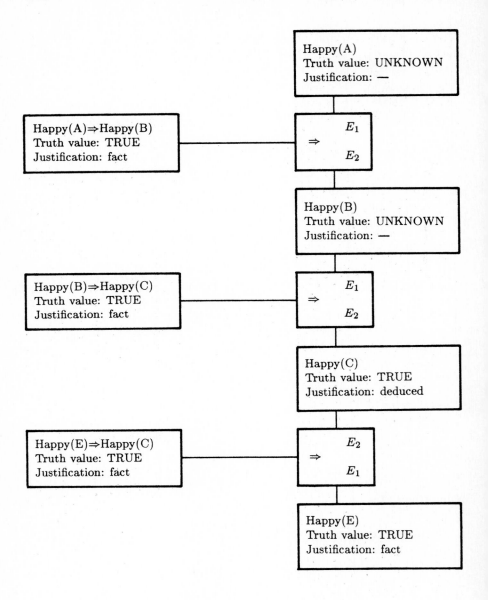

Figure 7-12. Given a second path establishing Happy(C), then Happy(C) remains TRUE after a critical assumption in the first path is withdrawn.

than one argument supports a conclusion, and withdrawing one of them leaves the conclusion intact.

For example, as things stand now, withdrawing the assumption that Happy(A) is TRUE forces us to withdraw the conclusion that Happy(C) is TRUE. However, suppose there is a fifth person, E, who is happy and whose happiness causes C to be happy, as shown by the following solid facts.

$$Happy(E)$$
$$Happy(E) \Rightarrow Happy(C)$$

Now, as shown in figure 7-12, we have a second, independent way to show that Happy(C) is TRUE, for as soon as we assume Happy(E), we can use the constraint expressions of the new $\Rightarrow$ set to conclude, again, that Happy(C) is TRUE. Withdrawing the assumption that Happy(A) is TRUE does not hurt us.

SUMMARY

- Logic is about deriving new expressions from axioms. As a subject, logic concentrates on using knowledge in a rigorous, provably correct way; other problem-solving paradigms concentrate on the knowledge itself.

- Logic has a traditional notation requiring us to become familiar with the symbols for *implies, and, or,* and *not*. These symbols are $\Rightarrow$, &, $\vee$, and $\neg$.

- When a $\forall$ is TRUE, it specifies that the expression in its scope is TRUE for all values of the quantified variable. When a $\exists$ is TRUE, the expression in its scope is TRUE for at least one value.

- A theorem logically follows from assumed axioms if there is a series of steps connecting the theorem to the axioms using sound rules of inference.

- The most obvious rule of inference is *modus ponens*. Another, more general rule of inference is resolution.

- Resolution theorem proving uses resolution as the rule of inference and refutation as the strategy. Resolution requires transforming axioms and the negated theorem to clause form. Resolution also requires a variable substitution process called unification.

- The set-of-support strategy dictates using only resolutions in which at least one resolvent descends from the negation of the theorem to be proved.

- Logic is seductive, for it often works neatly. There are caveats to obey, however, for logic is just one of many tools to have in the workshop.

- Using logic to find operator sequences requires some technique for keeping track of situations. The usual thing is to annotate predicates with situation-indicating arguments.

- Once situation-indicating arguments are introduced, there must be some technique to keep track of those predicates whose values are unchanged as operators are applied. Using frame axioms is one approach.

- Using the constraint-propagation approach to logic, truth values are propagated through nodes using constraints supplied by logical expressions.

- Using constraint propagation, it is easy to keep track of justifications for all conclusions. These justifications make it easy to deal with withdrawn assumptions.

REFERENCES

The development of the resolution method for theorem proving is generally credited to J. A. Robinson [1965, 1968], although others have made important contributions. In particular, C. Cordell Green introduced situation variables and Green's trick into logic in his influential thesis, making it possible to derive operator sequences [1969]. Green's thesis also introduced the idea of logic programming.

Robert Kowalski deserves credit for popularizing logic programming. His book, *Logic for Problem Solving* [1979], is a classic. Today, logic programming usually is done in the PROLOG programming language, developed by Alain Colmerauer and his associates [Colmerauer, H. Kanoui, R. Pasero, and P. Roussel 1973; Colmerauer 1982]. For a good collection of papers, see *Logic Programming* [1982], edited by Keith L. Clark and Sten-Åke Tärnlund. A good textbook is *Programming in* PROLOG [1981], by William F. Clocksin and Christopher S. Mellish.

In many respects, PROLOG resembles the MICROPLANNER language, developed by Gerald J. Sussman, Terry Winograd, and Eugene Charniak [1971], which was based on the PLANNER language, proposed by Carl E. Hewitt [1969]. Hewitt now marches in a different direction [William A. Kornfeld and Hewitt 1981; Hewitt and Peter de Jong 1982].

An alternative to the use of frame axioms is to endow operators with lists of expressions that they add to the axioms and lists that they delete. Such operators maintain predicate values correctly without requiring frame axioms. STRIPS is a problem solver, developed by Richard E. Fikes, Nils J. Nilsson, and Peter Hart, that combines such operators with means-ends analysis à la the General Problem Solver, GPS [Fikes and Nilsson 1971].

Truth-maintenance ideas emerged from work on electronic circuit analysis by Gerald J. Sussman and Richard M. Stallman [1975]. The formulation in this chapter is based loosely on the work of David A. McAllester [1980]. The work of Drew McDermott and Jon Doyle [1980] is also relevant.

For an excellent treatment of the role of logic in Artificial Intelligence, see Patrick J. Hayes [1977]. See also Nils Nilsson's textbook, *Principles of Artificial Intelligence* [1980]. Nilsson takes the controversial view that Artificial Intelligence should be thought of as applied logic.

8

Representing Commonsense Knowledge

Chapter 2 showed that a good representation is explicit about the right things, constraint exposing, complete, concise, transparent, computationally efficient, detail suppressing, and computable. Since chapter 2, we have flirted with the representation issue repeatedly. Now it is time to be direct, for representation is the most serious issue to be faced in Artificial Intelligence.

We begin by defining just what a representation is, distinguishing between *syntax* and *semantics*.

Next we look at a particular representation, the *semantic net*, using it as a framework for understanding popular representation tools such as *inheritance, demons, default values,* and *perspectives*. These tools lead to various procedures that make assumptions, that tell us what is relevant, and that look for information, all on the basis of class membership.

With the basic tools in hand, we will be able to talk about *frames*, a representation concept that incorporates the basic tools and adds the notion of *standard stereotypes*. To introduce frames, we consider news, observing that in news certain conventions make frame finding and instantiation particularly easy. Frames are important because they inform us about common situations, those involving commonsense knowledge, telling us about what assumptions to make, what things to look for, and what ways to look.

Going farther, we look at the possibility of *producing and recognizing paraphrases* by reducing action descriptions to canonical-form descriptions using a dozen or so *primitive-act frames*. Reduction to canonical form is important, in part because many assumptions and expectations seem to be indexed for storage and retrieval according to the *identities* of the primitive acts and the objects involved. Also, some people believe reduction to canonical form is important for language translation.

Going in the other direction, we will see that it is possible to do *summarization* of complicated descriptions by recognizing patterns called *abstraction units*. The pièce de résistance will be a diagram capturing the sense of O. Henry's intricate short story, "The Gift of the Magi." Abstraction is important, in part, because many assumptions and expectations seem to be indexed for storage and retrieval according to the *patterns* that tie acts together. Practically, abstraction also is important for conveying information rapidly.

When finished with this chapter, you will know more about what a representation is, what makes a good one, and how semantic-net and frame-type representations are used to represent commonsense knowledge. Remember, however, that semantic nets and frames are not all there is—this chapter tells you nothing about representing vision-oriented knowledge, for example.

Also remember that representation continues to be a matter of research and hot debate. Tomorrow the questions will be the same as they are today, but the answers will be different.

REPRESENTATION

Experience has shown that designing a good representation is often the key to turning hard problems into simple ones. Therefore, it is reasonable to work hard on establishing what symbols a representation is to use and how those symbols are to be arranged to produce meaningful descriptions of particular things. Before looking at the popular possibilities, however, it makes sense to agree on some terms:

- A *representation* is a set of syntactic and semantic conventions that make it possible to describe things.

- The *syntax* of a representation specifies the symbols that may be used and the ways those symbols may be arranged.

- The *semantics* of a representation specifies how meaning is embodied in the symbols and the symbol arrangements allowed by the syntax.

Programming languages, for example, are representations for procedures. Since programming languages are representations, they have syntax and semantics. The syntax often is specified in something called *Backus-Naur form*. The semantics is specified by a description of how particular syntactic constructions relate to getting something done.

In comparison with programming languages, the distinction between the syntax and the semantics of natural languages is blurred. The syntax of a natural language concerns how verbs and nouns and other parts of speech are allowed to come together to form sentences. The semantics of a natural language concerns the relationship between sentences on one side and objects, relations, acts, and events in the world on the other.

Semantics Distinguishes Semantic Nets from Ordinary Nets

All representations must provide some way to denote objects and to describe the relations that hold among them. Consequently, many representations are built around some form of *semantic net*, for semantic nets denote objects and describe relations among them.

The syntax of a semantic net is simple: there are objects, and there are relations between pairs of objects. In illustrations, the *objects* are denoted by labeled circles and the *relations* are denoted by labeled arrows. Following the standard terminology, introduced in chapter 2, the labeled circles are called *nodes*, and the labeled arrows are called *links*.

A node-and-link net is not necessarily a semantic net, however. To be a semantic net, there must be semantics. The net in figure 8-1a, for example, is not a semantic net because there is no prima facie description of an object, action, or event, nor is there an accompanying procedure that enables description.

In figure 8-1b, however, there is at least a prima facie description, for we naturally tend to ascribe meaning to links with names like IS-A and COLOR. Asked what the net means, most people would say immediately that it means there is a red toy brick. Thus there is an informal, intuition-based semantics.

There are Several Approaches to Semantics

Note that informal, intuition-based semantics repels semantics specialists, for such a semantics is imprecise in the extreme. After all, the only semantic statement made is that nets are related to objects, actions, and events by the vague, individual, ambiguous, and time-varying intuition of the beholder.

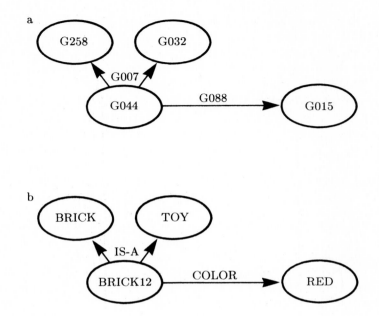

Figure 8-1. An ordinary net and a semantic net. Natural-language labels associate intuitive meanings to nodes and links, thereby producing an informal semantics. Many people regard such a semantics as slipshod or dangerous.

Consequently, it is sensible to reject intuition-based semantics in favor of one of these options:

- *Equivalence semantics.* Let there be some way of relating descriptions in the representation to descriptions in some other representation that has an accepted semantics, predicate calculus, for example.

- *Procedural semantics.* Let there be a set of programs that operate on descriptions in the representation. Say that meaning is defined by what the programs do.

- *Descriptive semantics.* Let there be precise English descriptions of just how descriptions in the representation denote objects, actions, and events in the world.

Semanticists have had long arguments over which of these is best, with fad often playing a role in determining the current favorite at any given time.

We will put semantics into semantic nets using descriptive semantics, but do not think that we are taking a position in the semantics argument. The alternatives, equivalence semantics and procedural semantics, while usually more acceptable to purists, would divert us from developing a vocabulary of links and describing their purpose. Were we to relate semantic-net descriptions to descriptions in another representation, we would have to explain the alternate representation and how *it* captures meaning. Similarly, were we to give programs for operating on semantic nets, we would have to explain the programming language, a long and potentially tedious task.

INHERITANCE, DEMONS, DEFAULTS, AND PERSPECTIVES

In this section, we examine some basic mechanisms that guide description movement from class descriptions to individual descriptions, determine descriptions in the absence of specific knowledge, specify procedures for computing descriptions, and enable descriptions to be context dependent. These mechanisms enable procedures to do the following, for example:

- To know that a particular wedge is triangular because all wedges are triangular.

- To know that a particular toy block is probably made of wood because most toy blocks are made of wood.

- To know how much a block weighs, when we need to know, by multiplying its volume times the density of the material it is made of.

- To know that a block's purpose, when viewed as a toy, is play, but that the block's purpose, when viewed as a structure, is support.

To make explanation easier, we need some words that distinguish between the node at the tail end of a link and the node at the head end. Consequently, let us agree that the links impinge on *value* nodes. Further let us agree that the *slots* of a node correspond to the different-named links. In figure 8-1, BRICK12 has three links that together constitute two slots, one slot having just one value and the other slot having two. We say that the COLOR slot is filled with RED, and the IS-A slot is filled with BRICK and TOY.

Inheritance Enables Description Movement from Classes to Instances

As soon as we know the identity of something, we generally assume a lot. Unless we know we are dealing with an exception, we assume, for example, that whales are big, birds are small, castles are old, and athletes are strong. It is as if each object class—whale, bird, castle, and athlete—is described, in part, by the description of a typical instance of the object class.

In figure 8-2, for example, WEDGE18 is identified as an instance of the wedge class by an IS-A link, and the wedge class is identified as a subclass of the block class by an AKO link, short for a-kind-of, between the WEDGE node and the BLOCK node.

No SHAPE link determines the shape of WEDGE18 directly, but by virtue of an IS-A link, WEDGE18 is known to be an instance of the wedge class and the WEDGE node has TRIANGULAR occupying SHAPE slot. Plainly, we expect this to mean that WEDGE18 has a triangular shape also.

In general, so as to obtain results corresponding to our expectations, we need a search procedure that looks for appropriate slots in appropriate nodes. One such procedure is as follows:

Value Inheritance Procedure:

Let F be the given node and S be the given slot.

1   Form a queue consisting of the node F and all the class nodes found in node F's IS-A slot. Node F is to be in front.

2   Until the queue is empty or a value has been found, determine if the first element of the queue has a value in its S slot.

    2a   If the first element has a value in its S slot, then a value has been found.

    2b   Otherwise, remove the first element from the queue and add the nodes related to the first element by AKO to the end of the queue.

3   If a value has been found, say that the value found is the value of node F's S slot; otherwise announce failure.

Since the new class nodes go to the end of the node queue, this value inheritance procedure performs a breadth-first search.

Since any node may have more than one value in a slot, more than one value may be found, in which case all are reported.

Demons Enable Access to Initiate Action

Sometimes, when we have no values, we can compute a value using existing information. We can, for example, determine a block's weight from information about volume and material.

To remember the procedures needed for such computations, we stuff the procedures into IF-NEEDED *facets* and call them *if-needed procedures.*

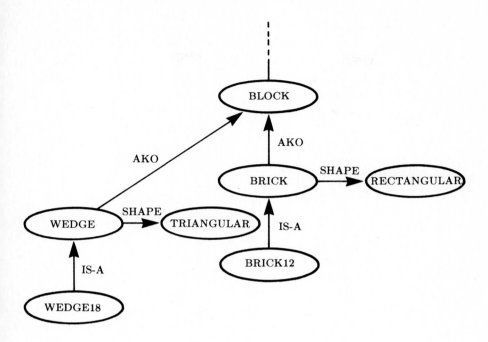

Figure 8-2. Properties of instances are obtained from classes by inheritance using IS-A links and AKO links. Asking for the shape of WEDGE18 yields TRIAN-GULAR; for the shape of BRICK12, RECTANGULAR.

If-needed procedures are also called *if-needed demons* since they lurk about in the database, ready to be used whenever needed, rather than when specifically asked to help by name. They are friendly, as demons go.

In figure 8-3a, for example, a weight-determining procedure occupies the IF-NEEDED facet of the WEIGHT slot of the BLOCK node. Here is the weight-determining procedure:

Weight-calculating if-needed procedure:
1   If there are values in the VOLUME and DENSITY slots:
   1.1   Place their product in the WEIGHT slot.
   1.2   Report their product as the value of the node's weight.

As usual, procedures in IF-NEEDED facets are inherited as are values in VALUE facets. Here is one possible inheritance procedure:

If-needed inheritance procedure for values:

Let F be the given node and S be the given slot.

1   Form a queue consisting of the node F and all the class nodes related to node F through an IS-A slot. Node F is to be in front.

2   Until the queue is empty or a successful if-needed procedure has been found, determine if the first element of the queue has a procedure in the IF-NEEDED facet of its S slot.

2a   If there is a procedure and if the procedure produces a value, then a value has been found.

2b   Otherwise, remove the first element from the queue and add the nodes related to the first element by AKO to the end of the queue.

3   If a procedure finds a value, say that the value found is the value of node F's S slot; otherwise announce failure.

Using this if-needed inheritance procedure, the procedure lying in the IF-NEEDED facet of the WEIGHT slot of BLOCK stands ready to help whenever the weight is needed for any kind of block. If enough is known when the weight is needed, as in the configuration shown in figure 8-3a, the weight-calculating procedure writes that weight into the VALUE facet of the WEIGHT slot of the BRICK12 node and reports the weight, as shown in figure 8-3b.

Defaults Enable Assumption in Lieu of Fact

Sometimes, when our assumptions are weak enough, it is good to condition our thinking with the word *probably*. We presume that judges are probably honest, but not certainly, and gems are probably expensive, but not certainly.

To capture weak assumptions, we must refine the node-slot-value idea a bit by allowing slots to have several types of values, not just one. The *ordinary* value type we have been working with, the one corresponding to certain truth, is said to be in the VALUE *facet* of a slot. The *default* value type associated with probable truth is said to be in the DEFAULT *facet*.

In figure 8-4, for example, the net expresses the idea that the probable color of a block, on the whole, is blue, but in the subclass of bricks, the

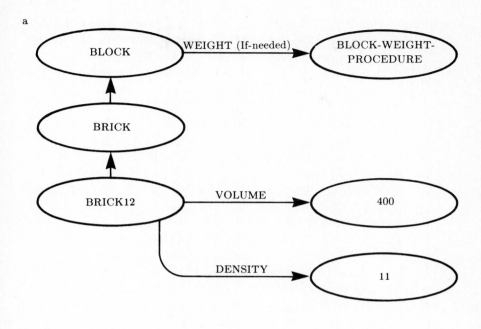

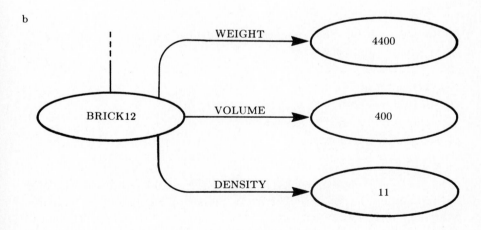

Figure 8-3. An if-needed procedure at work. We assume the node for BRICK12 is as shown in part *a*. Activated by a request for the weight of BRICK12, the procedure in the BLOCK node computes the weight from BRICK12's volume and density, reports the weight, and writes the weight into the VALUE facet of BRICK12's WEIGHT slot as shown in part *b*.

probable color is red. For both the BLOCK and BRICK nodes, the facet found in the COLOR slot is the DEFAULT facet, indicated by parentheses.

Now we need a search procedure that can exploit information in DE-FAULT facets, rather than VALUE facets. The following is one possibility:

Default Inheritance Procedure:

Let F be the given node and S be the given slot.

1 Form a queue consisting of the node F and all the class nodes related to node F through an IS-A slot. Node F is to be in front.

2 Until the queue is empty or a default has been found, determine if the first element of the queue has a value in the DEFAULT facet of its S slot.

 2a If the first element has a value in the DEFAULT facet of its S slot, then a value has been found.

 2b Otherwise, remove the first element from the queue and add the nodes related to the first element by AKO to the end of the queue.

3 If a default value has been found, say that the value found is the default value of node F's S slot; otherwise announce failure.

We now have three inheritance procedures. One way to put them together is by way of this procedure:

N inheritance procedure:

1 Use value inheritance.

2 Use if-needed inheritance.

3 Use default inheritance.

This is called *N inheritance* because the search path looks like an N, rising all the way up the IS-A-AKO structure, looking in one kind of facet, before dropping all the way down and starting over, looking in another kind of facet. N inheritance moves *up* the IS-A-AKO structure before moving *across* the various facets.

Another kind of inheritance is called *Z inheritance*, because the search path looks like a Z, looking in the VALUE, IF-NEEDED facets, and DE-FAULT of each node visited before moving on to the next node up the IS-A-AKO structure. Z inheritance moves *across* the various facets of each node before moving *up* the IS-A-AKO structure.

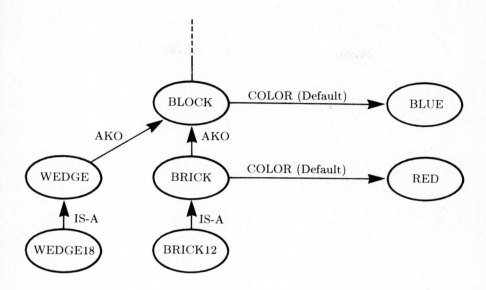

Figure 8-4. In the absence of specific information, defaults establish probable value, usually through IS-A and AKO links. Values in facets other than the VALUE facet are identified by the appearance of the facet name in parentheses. The COLOR default attached to BRICK embodies the idea that bricks are probably red, BRICK12 in particular. But since there is no default COLOR information for Wedge, WEDGE18 is probably blue, since blue is the default COLOR associated with BLOCK.

Perspectives Enable Purpose to Guide Access

Sometimes our thinking about an object is conditioned by viewing the object from some particular perspective. A racing bicycle, for example, may be considered fast for a bicycle, but slow for a means of transportation. At other times, our thinking is conditioned by the context an object is in. A particular person, for example, may be happy when operating as a mountain hiker, yet grumpy when operating as an airplane traveler.

To deal with these dependencies, we use the notion of perspectives. As shown in figure 8-5, the idea is to break nodes up into node bundles in which each bundle member specifies one named or unnamed perspective. If we ask for a value without specifying a perspective, the node bundle is treated as if it were collapsed into a single node. Answers, however, are annotated to include the name of the perspective from which they come, if any. If we ask for the SHAPE of BRICK12, we get RECTANGULAR, with no annotation, by virtue of the IS-A connection to BRICK. If we ask for the PURPOSE, we get SUPPORT, with the annotation that the perspective involved is STRUCTURE, by virtue of the STRUCTURE perspective of the

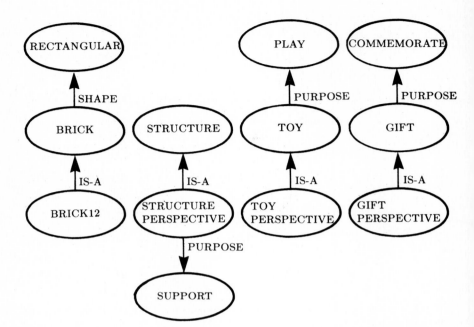

Figure 8-5. Objects may be viewed from various perspectives. Here BRICK12 is described by a node bundle in which one element is an unnamed general perspective, another corresponds to the brick viewed as a structure, another to the brick viewed as a TOY, and another to the brick viewed as a GIFT.

BRICK12 bundle. The PURPOSE slots of TOY and GIFT are not involved since there is a PURPOSE slot in one of the node-bundle perspectives, preventing search up the inheritance links.

On the other hand, if we ask for a value with respect to a certain perspective, then only that member of the node bundle corresponding to the given perspective is used. All other members of the bundle are ignored. If we ask for the PURPOSE of BRICK12 when viewed from the TOY perspective, we get PLAY, by virtue of the IS-A connection between the TOY perspective and the TOY node. Similarly, if we ask for the PURPOSE of BRICK12 when viewed as a GIFT, we get COMMEMORATE.

Note that we now have many things to specify when asking for values:

• Which facets are to be used: VALUE, IF-NEEDED, DEFAULT, or a combination of facets.

• Whether inheritance is to be used, and if so, the search strategy.

• Whether a perspective is to be used.

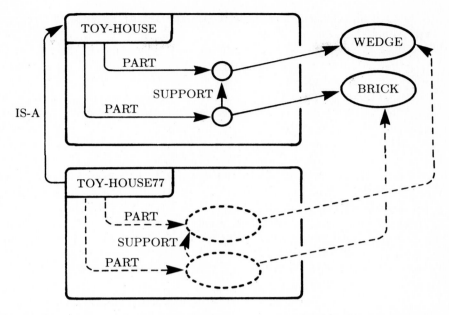

Figure 8-6. Toy houses have two parts; one is a brick and the other is a wedge. By virtue of the IS-A link to the TOY-HOUSE node, TOY-HOUSE77 is known to have two parts, a brick and a wedge, tied together with a SUPPORT link.

Similarly, the answer reported has several components:

- The number of values found and those values.

- Whether the value is an ordinary value or a default value.

- The perspective involved, if any.

Access Involving Parts Requires Matching

So far, we have described how to inherit values when dealing with things like BRICK12 and BRICK. Now we turn to a harder task, asking how inheritance might work when dealing with things that have parts, like TOY-HOUSE77 and TOY-HOUSE in figure 8-6. We must establish not only how to pass values from TOY-HOUSE to TOY-HOUSE77, but also from parts of TOY-HOUSE to parts of TOY-HOUSE77.

It is obvious, for example, that TOY-HOUSE77 must have two parts, one a brick and the other a wedge, by virtue of being a TOY-HOUSE. Moreover, the brick that is part of TOY-HOUSE77 must support the wedge. In figure 8-6, these things are indicated by dotted nodes and arrows because they are known implicitly through inheritance, not explicitly through actual nodes and links. Consequently, we say that the dotted nodes and arrows denote *virtual* nodes and links.

There is no need to copy the nodes and links from the TOY-HOUSE node into the node for TOY-HOUSE77 unless we need copies on which to hang new information that is specific to TOY-HOUSE77. To say that the brick of TOY-HOUSE77 has a red color, for example, we must create a brick node for TOY-HOUSE77 and put RED in its COLOR slot. Were we to put RED in the COLOR slot of the brick that is part of the TOY-HOUSE, that would mean that the bricks in all toy houses are red, not just the brick in the particular house described by TOY-HOUSE77.

Now consider STRUCTURE35 in figure 8-7. It is known to have two parts, a brick, BRICK12, and a wedge, WEDGE18. As soon as an IS-A link is placed between STRUCTURE35 and TOY-HOUSE, we know that BRICK12 must support WEDGE18. Hence figure 8-7 shows a dotted arrow, a virtual SUPPORT link, between BRICK12 and WEDGE18. The placement and direction of the dotted arrow is obvious because part-matching is easy. WEDGE18 surely matches the wedge that is part of the TOY-HOUSE, and BRICK12 surely matches the brick.

In figure 8-8, however, there is a problem. It is known that STRUC-TURE14 has two parts, but which is the brick and which is the wedge is not known. Consequently, there is no way to establish a correspondence between the two parts of STRUCTURE14 and the two parts of TOY-HOUSE. Matching ambiguity stalls inheritance.

Special Links Make Inheritance Opportunities Explicit

We have seen that many links have special meaning in semantic nets. These links make class-based inheritance opportunities explicit, thus facilitating the work of class-oriented inference procedures. By making the right things explicit, these links satisfy an important criterion for good representation. Here is a summary of what they do:

- IS-A and AKO links make class membership and subclass-class relations explicit, facilitating the movement of knowledge from one level to another.

- VALUE facets make values explicit.

- IF-NEEDED facets make procedures' purposes explicit, and they relate procedures to the classes those procedures are relevant to.

- DEFAULT facets make likely values explicit, without implying certainty.

- Perspectives make context sensitivity explicit, preventing confusion and ambiguity.

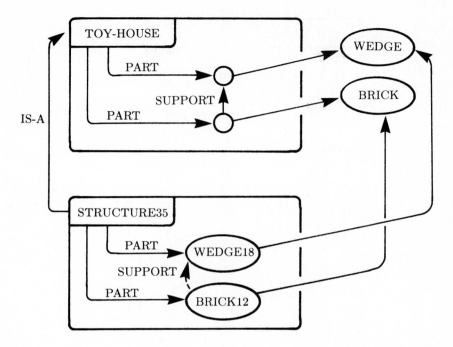

Figure 8-7. Asserting that STRUCTURE35 is a toy house enables the conclusion that BRICK12 supports WEDGE18 by inheritance from the TOY-HOUSE node. This is an easy situation because it is clear how to match the parts of STRUCTURE35 with those of TOY-HOUSE.

Let us now look at particular uses for these general links and their associated procedures.

FRAMES AND NEWS STORIES

A *frame* is a collection of semantic net nodes and slots that together describe a stereotyped object, act, or event. Frames enable procedures to do the following representative things at the sentence level and at the event level:

- To know that sentences using *go* often specify a destination.
- To know how to look for the destination in a sentence involving *go*.
- To know that earthquakes involve faults and magnitudes.
- To know how to look for the magnitude and fault in the text of earthquake news.

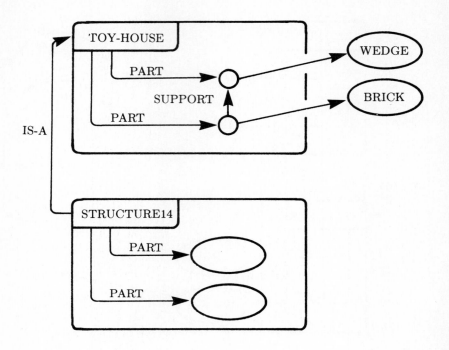

Figure 8-8. Although STRUCTURE14 is a toy house, it is not possible to know which object is which. Consequently, no inheritance is possible.

The world of news stories is a good place to start our study of *frame systems* because news is especially predictable.

Digesting News Seems to Involve Frame Retrieving and Slot Filling

Any report of an earthquake probably will supply the place, the time, the number of people killed, injured, and homeless, the amount of property damage, the magnitude on the Richter scale, and possibly the name of the geological fault that has slipped. We know information about these things is typical because of the slots that appear in the Earthquake frame, the Disaster frame, and the Event frame, as shown in the net shown in figure 8-9.

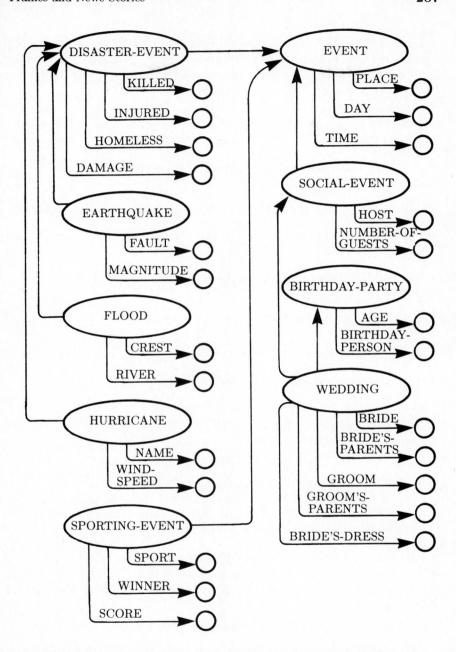

Figure 8-9. A net connecting frames for news stories. By inheritance on two levels, it is clear that earthquake stories typically have nine slots to be filled. All may have slot-filling procedures attached.

For some stories, it is easy to fill in the slots by using special-purpose procedures attached to the slots by way of, say, *text-analysis facets*. For earthquake stories, knowing that earthquakes are also disasters and events, the type of a number helps decide where it goes:

- For the magnitude slot, look for a floating-point number between 1.0 and 10.0.

- For the killed slot, look for a fixed-point number near a word with a root like *kill* or *die*.

- For the property-damage slot, look for a number next to a dollar sign.

- For the day slot, look for words like *today*, *yesterday*, *tomorrow*, and the days of the week.

- For the time slot, look for a number with a colon in it.

Other simple procedures can fill in nonnumeric slots:

- For the fault slot, look for a proper name near the word *fault*.

- For the place slot, look for a place name.

Consequently, analyzing stories like the following can be easy, given that the title evokes the proper frame:

Earthquake Hits Lower Slabovia

Today an extremely serious earthquake of magnitude 8.5 hit Lower Slabovia killing 25 people and causing $500,000,000 in damage. The President of Lower Slabovia said the hard-hit area near the Sadie Hawkins fault has been a danger zone for years.

Figure 8-10 shows the frame created for this story. Once created, the slots with values can be used to fill in a canned summary. Understand that in the following canned summary, any phrases involving missing values would be deleted.

Earthquake Summary Pattern

An earthquake occurred in *value in location slot value in day slot*. There were *value in fatalities slot* fatalities and *value in damage slot* in property damage. The magnitude was *value in magnitude slot* on the Richter scale, and the fault involved was the *value in fault slot*.

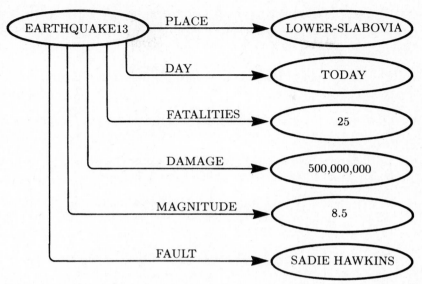

Figure 8-10. A frame produced by two news stories. One news story, correctly analyzed, is about a genuine earthquake. The other news story, muffed, is about earthquake research.

From the canned summary, with variable parts instantiated, we would get this restatement:

Instantiated Earthquake Summary Pattern

An earthquake occurred in *Lower Slabovia today*. There were *25* fatalities and $500,000,000 in property damage. The magnitude was *8.5* on the Richter scale, and the fault involved was the *Sadie Hawkins*.

On the other hand, slot filling using simple, special-purpose procedures can lead to silly results, given that the special-purpose procedures really do not understand stories. Consider this:

Earthquake Study Stopped

Today the President of Lower Slabovia killed 25 proposals totaling $500,000,000 for research in earthquake prediction. Our Lower Slabovian correspondent calculates that 8.5 research expenditures are vetoed for every one approved. There are rumors that the President's close advisor, Sadie Hawkins, is at fault.

Shudder to think: this could be summarized, naively, as if it were the story about an actual earthquake, producing the same frame shown before in figure 8-10 and the same instantiated earthquake summary pattern.

Of course, creating procedures for general news is much harder than creating procedures for specialized news. Interestingly, good news writers seem to use certain conventions that help:

- The title of a news story and perhaps the first sentence or two evoke a central frame.

- Subsequent material fills slots in the central frame. The slot-filling process evokes other frames introducing more open slots.

- CAUSE relations are given explicitly. Causes need not be deduced, because words like *because* or *since* appear frequently.

- Few pronouns, if any, are used. In political news, for example, the nation's legislature may be referred to as "Congress," or "Capitol Hill," or "Washington's lawmakers," according to fancy.

- Few new frames, if any, need be created. Creating new frames requires some thought, and a lot of thought is discouraged.

Event-describing Frames Make Stereotyped Information Explicit

We have seen that the information in frames and their slots makes certain things explicit:

- The slots in frames make explicit what we should expect to know.

- The text-analysis facets in frames make explicit how we can try to acquire what we expect to know.

By making new things explicit—what we expect to know and how to acquire it—frames satisfy an important criterion for good representation. Let us now look at how to make things explicit on a much lower level, dealing with action primitives rather than with whole events.

EXPANSION INTO PRIMITIVE ACTS

In the last section, we worked with event frames primarily, showing how they can indicate expectations. In this section, we work with act frames, showing that there are times when it is useful to expand them into combinations of implied primitive-act frames.

Here are some examples of what can be done:

- We can guess what happens when something is done. We can guess, for example, that comforting someone implies that the person goes into a happier state.

- We can guess the details of how something is done. We can know, for example, that eating probably involves moving a fork or a spoon, requiring the movement of a hand.

- We can, in principle, do simple language translation by inverting the translation of sentences into primitive acts and by using a dictionary for the target language.

Schank's Primitive Acts Describe Many Higher-level Acts

How many primitives are needed to describe the acts denoted by English verbs? The answer may be a surprisingly small number. It seems that many ordinary verbs are used as a sort of shorthand for ideas that can be expressed as well by combinations of basic primitives together with default slot fillers. The combination process, called *telescoping*, accounts for an amazing number of superficially distinct verbs.

During the 1930s, champions of Basic English as a world language argued persuasively that people can get by with a vocabulary of only a thousand words by depending heavily on *come, get, give, go, keep, let, make, put, take, have, say, see,* and *send.* The verb *eat,* for example, comes with a destination slot prefilled with something like the eater's stomach. Indeed, the eater's stomach is so firmly implied that it seems strange to have it given explicitly: one does not say, "I am eating a sandwich *into my stomach.*"

The following list of primitives is similar to the list in Basic English but better suited to our needs. The list includes acts in the physical world, the perceptual world, the mental world, and the social world:

MOVE-BODY-PART	MOVE-OBJECT
EXPEL	INGEST
PROPEL	SPEAK
SEE	HEAR
SMELL	FEEL
MOVE-POSSESSION	MOVE-CONCEPT
THINK-ABOUT	CONCLUDE

Acts Often Imply Implicit State Changes and Cause-effect Relations

Many sentences imply state changes linked to a primitive act by a CAUSE link. Consider this:

Robbie enjoyed putting the wedge on the red block.

Evidently the act caused Robbie to be in the state of being happy. Nothing is known about how he felt before he moved the block, but while he did it, he was happy. It is convenient to represent such sentences as combinations of Act frames and State-change frames. Figure 8-11, for example, pictures what happens when Robbie puts the wedge onto the red block. Note the CAUSE link. It indicates that the act causes the state change.

Of course, one act also can cause another act. This again is represented by placing a CAUSE link between the two things involved. Consider this sentence, for example:

Suzie told Robbie to put the wedge on the red block.

For this sentence, the diagram of figure 8-12 is appropriate.

Some sentences announce only state changes, leaving the acts that cause them unspecified. Suppose someone says this:

Suzie comforted Robbie.

There is a state change because Robbie is less sad than he was (using *comfort* implies original sadness). But what exactly did Suzie do? She caused Robbie to be less sad, certainly, but by what act? Did she talk with him, take him for a walk, give him a stiff drink, or just help him move the wedge? There is no way of knowing from the tiny fragment given, so all that can be done is to represent what is known as shown in figure 8-13. Note the use of the maximally nonspecific DO in the Act slot.

Let us look at one more example showing how acts and state changes can interdigitate:

Robbie was gored by the test.

This is metaphoric language. The test itself presumably did no damage to poor Robbie; it was getting a poor grade that hurt him. Moreover, no one stuck a horn in his gut; something merely made him feel bad. The real idea conveyed, when stripped of the color, is represented in figure 8-14. Note that DO is used because it is hard to guess precisely what Robbie did or perhaps failed to do. Overall, the example again demonstrates that a sentence's verb may promote a state-change image rather than an act image.

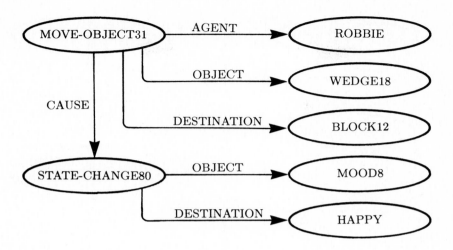

Figure 8-11. Much of the meaning of simple sentences is captured by Act frames and State-change frames tied together through CAUSE slots. Here putting a wedge on a red block makes Robbie happy.

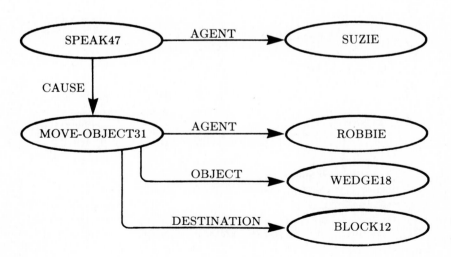

Figure 8-12. One act can cause another as when Suzie tells Robbie to do something.

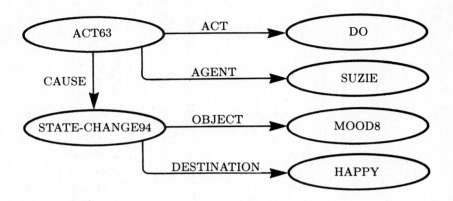

Figure 8-13. Some sentences specify only state change even though they seem to be about acts. Saying Suzie comforted Robbie gives no clue about how Robbie's improved state is achieved.

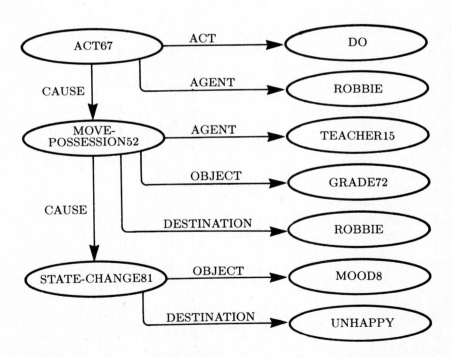

Figure 8-14. Considerable knowledge may be needed to expand some simple-sounding metaphors into an arrangement of primitive acts. The diagram here represents a statement that Robbie was gored by a test.

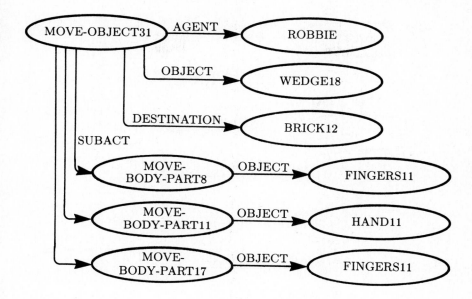

Figure 8-15. SUBACT slots offer another way of tying act frames together. This simple arrangement shows that moving a wedge is ultimately accomplished by a sequence of MOVE-BODY-PART primitives.

Acts Often Imply Subacts

The SUBACT slot is used to indicate that an act involves one or more subacts. Through SUBACT slots, acts reveal their pieces and then the pieces themselves reveal their pieces, ad nauseum.

Figure 8-15 indicates that putting a wedge on a red block involves a MOVE-OBJECT act with three MOVE-BODY-PART subacts, thereby bringing the act a bit closer to explanation in terms of the primitives that allegedly stand beneath everything else. Moving the hand employs one MOVE-BODY-PART, while grasping and ungrasping employ two others, each dealing with finger movements.

For another example, suppose that Robbie eats some ice cream. Figure 8-16 shows how the basic act, INGEST, calls to mind a MOVE-OBJECT involving a spoon. Of course there is no way of knowing that Robbie eats the ice cream with a spoon, given only "Robbie eats ice cream." He may eat an ice cream cone or drink a milk shake. Using a spoon is only a default presumption, a general image called up if explanation is wanted and nothing specific to the situation is known.

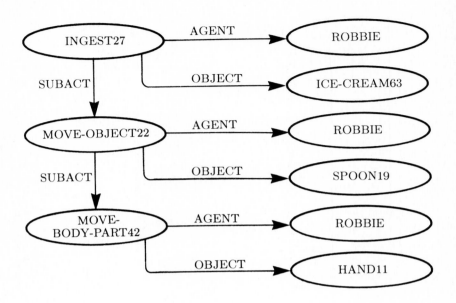

Figure 8-16. In this example, eating ice cream is done by moving a spoon to the mouth.

Primitives Facilitate Question Answering and Paraphrase Recognition

Primitive-act frames make it possible to answer certain questions just as do other kinds of frames. Here are some examples:

- How is an act done? Answer by expanding the act into primitive acts and state changes. Give more detail by working through SUBACT slots.

For example, Robbie eats ice cream by ingesting it (indicated by INGEST). He ingests it by moving a spoon (indicated by MOVE-OBJECT). He moves the spoon by moving his hand (indicated by MOVE-BODY-PART).

- What will happen if an act is done? Answer by first expanding the act into primitives and then using those primitives to find probable outcomes in memory.

For example, if Suzie hits Robbie (by MOVE-BODY-PART her fist to his body), he is likely to either hit her back (by MOVE-BODY-PART his fist to her body) or cry (by EXPEL tears). Such a sequence of tightly coupled, expectation-suggesting primitives is called a *script*.

- Does one sentence mean the same thing as another? Answer by first expanding both into primitives and then checking to see if the results are identical.

For example, "Suzie comforted Robbie" means the same thing as "Suzie did something to make Robbie happy," since both expand to an act frame with an unspecified act and a state-change frame with Robbie's happiness going up. Evidently the sentences are paraphrases of each other.

The assumption behind the paraphrase test is that sentences mean the same thing if and only if they expand into the same primitive act and state-change frames. This is a gigantic, heavily contested assumption. Some deny that primitive acts and state-change frames are really good canonical forms for describing the meanings of sentences. Others contend that even if they do qualify as a good canonical form, there is still no reason to believe that there is a procedure that will transform sentences with the same meaning into the same primitive-act and state-change descriptions. And still others do not care, arguing that paraphrase recognition is only a small, rather insignificant part of commonsense reasoning.

Primitive-act Frames Make Details Explicit

We have seen that primitive act frames make things explicit.

- The primitive acts themselves make an event's details explicit.
- The limited vocabulary of primitive acts forces implied state changes to be explicit.
- The use of CAUSE and SUBACT relations makes guessed consequences and methods explicit.

All these enable a variety of questions to be answered because the right things are made explicit. Thus primitive act frames satisfy an important criterion for good representation. Let us now look at how to make things explicit on a much higher level, moving toward abstractions and away from details.

ABSTRACTION TO SUMMARY UNITS

In the last section, we worked with primitives produced by expanding acts. In this section, we will work with abstractions produced by summarizing act combinations. From a semantic net point of view, we have presumed a process that converts a descriptive net into a larger, more detailed, lower-level one; now we presume a process that converts a descriptive net into a smaller, less detailed, higher-level one.

Our aim, in part, will be to form good summaries of stories. One ambitious target, by O. Henry, goes like this:

The Gift of the Magi

Della and her husband, Jim, were very poor. Nevertheless, since Christmas was approaching, each wanted to give something special to the other. Della cut off and sold her beautiful hair to buy an expensive watch fob for Jim's heirloom gold watch. Meanwhile, Jim sold his watch to buy some wonderful combs for Della's hair. When they found out what they had done, they were sad for a moment, but soon realized that they loved each other so much, nothing else mattered.

Lehnert's Abstraction Units Consist of Mental States Positive Events and Negative Events

To deal with abstraction, we need still another vocabulary of node types and links. Happily, we can go far with a small vocabulary of nodes consisting of just three types: mental states, denoted by MS in diagrams; positive events, denoted by +; and negative events, denoted by −.

We also need a vocabulary of links. Again, we need only a few, just three in fact. We use i, an acronym for initiates, meaning that the mental state or event at the tail of an i link leads to another at the head of the link; t, for terminates, meaning that the mental state or event at the tail turns off another at the head; and c, for corefers, meaning that the mental state or event at the tail refers to the same thing as another at the head.

In figure 8-17, each combination shown consists of two nodes and a link. Let us call such triples *base abstraction units*. The four base abstraction units shown are the only ones in which a mental state initiates an event or vice versa. As shown, if a mental state initiates an event, we have what we casually call a success or a failure depending on the sign of the event. If an event initiates a mental state, we witness enablement or motivation, again depending on the sign.

Another group of base abstraction units is shown in figure 8-18. This time, the common thing is that all have two mental states involved and no events. When one mental state initiates another, we say that *recursion* has occurred. When one terminates another, we have a *change of mind*. And if a mental state persists over a period of time, the individual involved is exhibiting *perseverance*.

Finally, the last group of base abstraction units is shown in figure 8-19. Now there are no mental states at all, only events joined by termination or coreference. The eight combinations are positive and negative trade-off, positive and negative coreference, loss and resolution, and mixed blessing and hidden blessing.

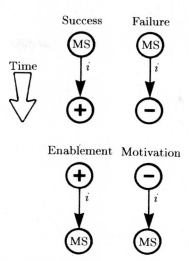

Figure 8-17. Mental states may initiate positive events or negative events and vice versa. The four possible combinations constitute instances of *success, failure, enablement,* and *motivation,* all of which are base abstraction units.

In abstract descriptions, base abstraction units often overlap, producing recognizable aggregates. Let us call these aggregates *compound abstraction units.* Figure 8-20 shows a compound abstraction unit consisting of a success base unit joined by its positive event to a loss base unit. When a success is followed by a loss, in normal language we often say that the success was fleeting, or use words to that effect. Hence this compound abstraction unit is called *fleeting success.*

Other examples of compound abstraction units are shown in figure 8-21. Note that each compound abstraction unit has a negative event, followed by a mental state, followed by a positive event. The compound abstraction units differ because they involve different links, and hence, different base abstraction units. Motivation followed by success yields *success borne of adversity*; motivation followed by a positive event that terminates the motivation-producing negative event is a matter of *fortuitous success*; and finally, motivation followed by a success involving a positive event that terminates the motivation-producing negative event is *intentional resolution.*

When more than one person is involved, more elaborate compound abstraction units are possible. In figure 8-22, for example, the situation from one person's perspective is a success borne of adversity. But in addition, the negative event from that person's perspective corefers to a positive event from the other person's perspective. Similarly, the positive event corefers to a negative event. These additions supplementing the success born of adversity constitute what we call *retaliation.*

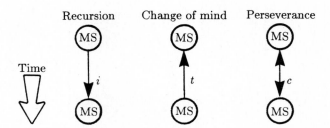

Figure 8-18. Mental states may be joined by *initiate*, *terminate*, or *corefer* links. The three possible combinations constitute instances of *recursion, change of mind*, and *perseverance* base abstraction units.

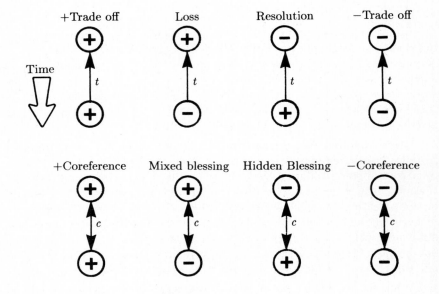

Figure 8-19. Positive events and negative events may be joined by *terminate* or *coreference* links. The possible combinations constitute instances of eight base summary units: *positive trade-off, loss, resolution, negative trade-off, positive coreference, mixed blessing, hidden blessing,* and *negative coreference*.

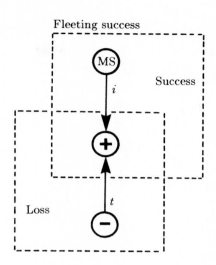

Figure 8-20. Base abstraction units join to produce larger structures. In this illustration, a success unit and a loss unit, both basic, join to produce a *fleeting success* unit, which is compound, not base.

Abstraction-unit Nets Enable Some Summarization

Now that the various abstraction units have been named and catalogued, stories can be summarized by reporting the abstraction units that are involved. Consider the following story about Thomas and Albert:

Thomas and Albert

Thomas and Albert respected each other's technical judgment and decided to form a company together. Unfortunately, Thomas learned that Albert was notoriously absentminded, whereupon he insisted that Albert have nothing to do with the proposed company's finances. This angered Albert so much that he backed out of their agreement, hoping that Thomas would be disappointed.

Figure 8-23 shows what "Thomas and Albert" looks like in terms of abstraction nodes and links. Respect is captured by the two mental states at the top. Those mental states initiate the decision to form a company, a positive event. Thomas's discovery about Albert is a negative event, which leads to a mental state in which he thinks about the company's finances, which leads to his insistence that Albert keep out of them, a positive event as far as Thomas is concerned. The insistence is a negative event from Albert's perspective, however. For Albert, the insistence leads to a mental state that leads to backing out of the agreement, which Albert views now as a positive event and Thomas views as negative.

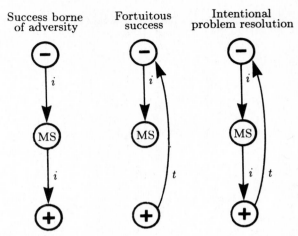

Figure 8-21. The same sequence of states and events produces different abstraction units when different base abstraction units are involved. In this illustration, a negative event is followed always by a mental state that is followed by a positive event. In the first case, a motivation base unit is followed by a success base unit producing an instance of *success borne of adversity*. In the second, the success unit disappears and a resolution unit appears, producing a *fortuitous success*. In the third, success reappears, joining the other two, producing an *intentional resolution*.

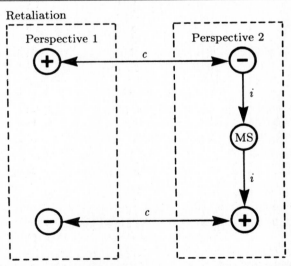

Figure 8-22. Mental states, positive events, and negative events may be linked across perspectives. In this illustration, there are two perspectives. Each perspective involves a positive event that is seen as a negative event in the other. This particular combination of perspectives, events, and a mental state is called a *retaliation*.

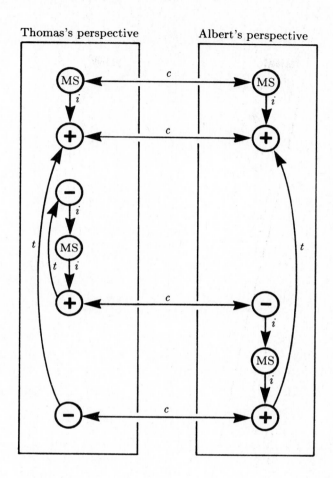

Figure 8-23. Stories may be viewed as aggregates of abstraction units, both base and nonbase. In this illustration, there are two perspectives, Thomas's and Albert's, and six top-level abstraction units, the ones that are not contained in larger abstraction units.

Now think of the diagram as a mine for abstraction units. Digging a little reveals that there are six abstraction units that are not wholly contained in some higher-level abstraction unit. These are called *top-level abstraction units*. In this particular situation, the top-level abstraction units are connected together by exactly one shared mental state or one shared event.

Figure 8-24 illustrates the resulting structure, with the six top-level units shown in the same relative positions that their pieces occupied in figure 8-23. Note that the structure diagrammed in figure 8-24 enables

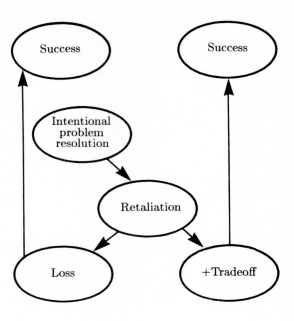

Figure 8-24. The top-level abstraction units of figure 8-23 form a net, enabling a summary description to be constructed around the most highly linked, top-level abstraction unit, the retaliation.

summary. The retaliation is mentioned first because it is obviously the central top-level abstraction unit. Then the surrounding intentional resolution, loss, positive trade-off, and success units are mentioned:

A Summary of Thomas and Albert

Albert *retaliated* against Thomas because Thomas went through an *intentional resolution* that was bad for Albert. The *retaliation* caused a *loss* for Thomas and a *positive trade-off* for Albert. The *loss* reversed Thomas's previous *success*, and the *positive trade-off* reversed Albert's previous *success*.

In addition to enabling summary, the abstraction unit diagram enables two situations to be compared usefully even if the two situations are superficially quite different. Consider the following story about John and Mary, for example. On the surface, "John and Mary" seems to have no resemblance whatever to "Thomas and Albert." More abstractly, however, both involve a central retaliation brought on by an intentional resolution leading eventually to a loss and a positive trade-off, both of which finish off previous successes:

John and Mary

John and Mary loved each other and decided to be married. A month before the wedding, John discovered that Mary's father was secretly smuggling stolen art through Venice. After struggling with his conscience for days, John reported Mary's father to the police. Mary understood John's decision, but she despised him for it nevertheless, and she broke their engagement knowing that he would suffer.

The similarities between "Thomas and Albert" and "John and Mary" are easy to see once top-level abstraction unit diagrams are constructed, for the stories' diagrams are exactly the same.

Of course, more complicated stories will have more complicated abstraction unit diagrams. Figure 8-25 shows the base abstraction units of "The Gift of the Magi," introduced at the beginning of this section. The corresponding top-level abstraction unit diagram is shown in figure 8-26.

Abstraction Units Enable Some Question Answering

Abstraction-unit frames make it possible to answer certain questions, just as other kinds of frames do. Here are some examples:

• What is the story about? Answer by naming the central top-level abstraction unit.

For example, "Thomas and Albert" is about retaliation.

• What is the result? Answer by naming the top-level abstraction units that are joined to earlier top-level abstraction units, but not later ones.

For example, the result in "Thomas and Albert" is a loss and a positive trade-off.

• Does the story involve a certain abstraction? Answer by checking for the given abstraction.

For example, "Thomas and Albert" does contain an instance of intentional resolution.

• In what way is one story like another? Answer by naming the most highly connected top-level abstraction unit appearing in both. If hard pressed, enumerate the other top-level abstraction units appearing in both.

Wants to give gift

Wants gift (chain, comb)

Wants money

Wants to sell (hair, watch)

Sells (hair, watch)

Gets money

Gets gift (chain, combs)

Gives gift

Receives gift (combs, chain)

Regrets

Appreciates

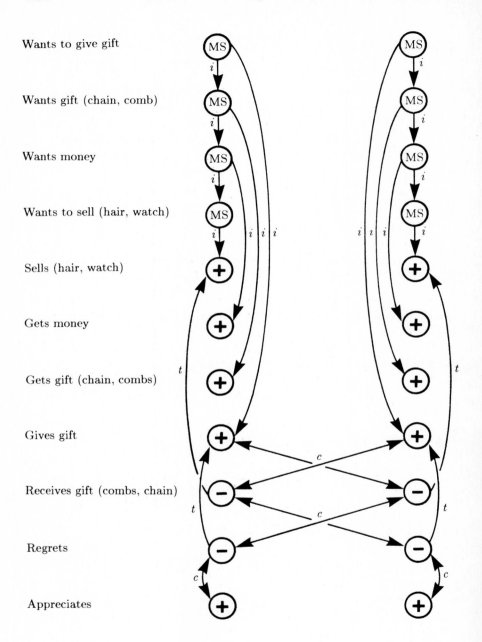

Figure 8-25. The base abstraction units of "The Gift of the Magi."

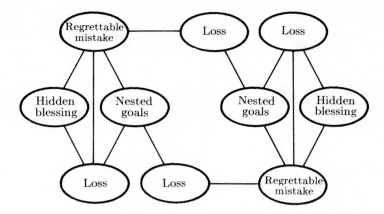

Figure 8-26. The top-level abstraction units of "The Gift of the Magi."

For example, "Thomas and Albert" is like "John and Mary" in that both involve retaliation. Moreover, both involve success, intentional resolution, loss, and positive trade-off.

In all of these examples, the answers could be made more detailed by naming the people and the events involved in the abstraction units mentioned.

Abstraction Units Make Patterns Explicit

We have seen that the information in abstraction-unit descriptions makes the occurrence of various patterns explicit, facilitating similarity analysis and rapid communication. By making something usefully explicit, abstraction-unit frames satisfy an important criterion for good representation. Some people complain, however, that abstraction-unit representation does not yet pass the computability criterion for good representation, mentioned in chapter 2, because there is no fully specified way to translate text into abstraction-unit patterns.

SUMMARY

- Syntax is about vocabulary and structure. Semantics is about the relation of vocabulary and structure to some world.

- Semantic nets consist of nodes and links and some means of relating nodes and links to objects, relations, acts, and events.

- Links are often called slots with respect to a node. The notion of slot may be refined to distinguish among a variety of facets.

- The usual semantics of IS-A and AKO links is such that information about individuals can be inherited from information about classes.

- Sometimes values are in a slot's default facet, rather than the standard value facet. A default value is something that is likely or probable, but not certain.

- Demons are procedures that are stored in slots so that they can be invoked automatically. If-needed demons compute values when values are needed.

- Sometimes nodes are split into various perspectives so that value retrieval can be conditioned by a point of view.

- When inheritance involves parts of things, matching is needed to establish how parts correspond before information flow can begin.

- News understanding seems, in part, a matter of recalling and instantiating the right frames.

- Expansion of sentence-level acts into recalled combinations of primitive acts and state changes helps carry natural language theory beyond the bog of the sentence into the mire of commonsense reasoning about everyday situations.

- Expansion into primitives can uncover implied subacts or likely consequences that, in turn, can enable question answering. In particular, expansion enables paraphrase recognition.

- Expansion to primitives makes descriptions larger, more detailed, and lower level. Contraction to abstraction units makes descriptions smaller, less detailed, and higher level.

- Abstraction units enable summarization and similarity recognition.

- Representation seems to be the key to creating computer intelligence. Many old questions remain tantalizingly open, and many new questions are emerging.

REFERENCES

Marvin Minsky is largely responsible for defining and popularizing many of the notions connected with frames [1975]. Other important contributions have been made via the various frame-oriented representation languages that have been designed and implemented, such as FRL, KRL, OWL, NETL, and KL-ONE. For example, FRL stresses demons, stereotypes, and instantiation aids [R. Bruce Roberts and Ira P. Goldstein 1977]. KRL concentrates on perspectives [Daniel G. Bobrow and Terry Winograd 1977]. OWL refines the meaning of specialization, offering several ways to relate classes [Peter Szolovits, Lowell B. Hawkinson, and William A. Martin 1977; Martin 1978]. NETL [Scott E. Fahlman 1979] and KL-ONE [Ronald J. Brachman 1979] deal with the problems of inheritance through parts. All of these languages are experimental, so it is likely that only the ideas they embody, not the languages themselves, will survive.

Generally, however, it has become clear that whatever the language, we will ultimately need special machines to deal with net search. For some intriguing ideas, see Scott E. Fahlman [1979] and W. Daniel Hillis [1981].

The use of framelike structures to summarize news was introduced by Gerald F. DeJong II [1979].

The basic book on Basic English is *Basic English: International Second Language*, by C. K. Ogden. It is a delightful book, which demonstrates that a small vocabulary can convey a lot of information. The purpose was to promote a subset of English in order to solve the international language problem.

Yorick A. Wilks contributed importantly to establishing the value of canonical primitives [1972]. Roger C. Schank's work is better known, however, and the primitives used for illustration are his. For an early presentation, see *Computer Models of Thought and Language*, edited by Schank and Kenneth Colby [1973].

For arguments against canonical primitives see William A. Woods's classic paper, "What's in a Link," [1975].

The material on abstraction units is based entirely on the work of Wendy Lehnert. The John-and-Mary story and the analysis of "The Gift of the Magi," in particular, are adapted from her highly influential paper [1981].

Causal relations are obviously important. In early work, Chuck Rieger developed a taxonomy of causes [1976]. The taxonomy recognizes three binary dimensions: the causing thing can be *continuous* or *one shot*; the causing thing can be *direct* or *gated* by some state specification; and the caused thing can be something *intended* or a *by-product*. To rely on just the CAUSE relation alone is to gloss over these important distinctions.

Subsequently, work on qualitative reasoning about causes and about quantity has advanced substantially, in large measure through the work of Kenneth D. Forbus [1981, 1982].

Language Understanding

When studying how to make computers understand human language, there are many possible questions to address:

- What domain of discourse is rich enough to be a vehicle for studying the central issues, yet simple enough to facilitate progress?

- What representations are required for sentences in the domain?

- What computations can be done? What are the constraints?

- What can it mean to say that something has been understood? Is an intelligent-sounding response enough?

- What can be done to circumnavigate roadblocks when practical language systems are needed?

Of these questions, the domain-selection question is the most critical, just as it is in many fields. In molecular biology, for example, the intestinal organism *E. coli* has been the vehicle for a great deal of progress.

The representation-selection question is also critical. The most commonly used representations in language understanding are the *parse tree*, the *thematic-role frame*, and the *world model*. Descriptions couched in parse trees and thematic-role frames are influenced heavily by the way an idea is expressed in words and sentences. Descriptions in world models, in contrast, are not supposed to be influenced by particular word and sentence choices.

Following a discussion of how the various representations might fit into the organization of a language system, we look more closely at two language procedures that work on parts of the language problem that are better understood than most. The first of these, a *parsing procedure*, creates parse trees by exploiting knowledge about word-order constraints. The second, a *thematic-role-frame procedure*, creates thematic-role frames by using knowledge about word order, prepositions, particular verbs, and context.

At this point, we turn to difficulty-avoiding, application-proven ideas. We do this by examining the *semantic grammar paradigm* for interfacing English-language queries to obscure database-interrogation commands. The idea is to simplify and to speed access to information in real-world databases.

Finally, we briefly examine the role of language in forging intellectual partnerships between people and intelligent systems.

FROM SENTENCES TO WORLD MODELS

In language understanding, good representation is the key to success. Since the gap between raw data and understanding is wide, several representations seem necessary to bridge the gap. Powerful language systems may require something like the following representations, each of which makes certain knowledge explicit:

- Facts about word arrangement are explicit in *parse trees.*

- Facts about the way acts relate to objects are explicit in *thematic-role frames.*

- Facts about meaning are explicit in *world models.*

To move from a sentence through the various representational layers requires several specialists.

The Syntactic Specialist Builds Parse Trees

The *syntactic specialist* bounces about in a sentence with only the modest goal of segmenting it into meaningful phrases and sentence constituents arrayed in a *parse tree.*

For the simplest English sentences, the syntactic specialist finds a noun phrase followed by a verb phrase. A verb phrase consists of a verb with an embedded noun phrase and possibly some embedded prepositional phrases. A prepositional phrase consists of a preposition and a noun phrase. A basic noun phrase consists of a noun, along with a determiner and perhaps one or more adjectives. To do its job, the syntactic specialist must know about things like word-order constraints.

Consider the sentence, "The silly robot moved the red pyramid to the big table." A parse tree for such a sentence records that the sentence is composed of a noun phrase and a verb phrase with an embedded noun phrase and an embedded prepositional phrase with an embedded noun phrase.

Generally, the syntactic specialist is called a *parser*. Parsers usually consist of two parts: a body of syntactic knowledge and a procedure for using the knowledge. The procedure is called an *interpreter*.

The Thematic-role Specialist Builds Thematic-role Frames

The *thematic-role specialist* determines how a sentence's noun phrases relate to the verb. For the silly-robot sentence, the thematic-role frame is shown in figure 9-1. The thematic-role frame indicates that the act involved is *move*, the agent is *the silly robot*, the thematic object is *the red pyramid*, and the destination is *the big table*.

To do its job, the thematic-role specialist must know about various constraints involving word order, prepositions, and context.

The Semantic Specialist Deals with Meaning

The *semantic specialist*, in the simplest situations, determines what the various noun phrases and pronouns refer to, building frame-style structures containing unique identifiers. Figure 9-2 illustrates.

In less simple situations, the semantic specialist must understand how sentences convey implications, evoke expectations, recall memories, establish contexts, create moods, and develop plots.

Linguists Distinguish between Performance and Competence

To linguists, *performance* and *competence* are technical terms with different meanings. *Performance* has to do with the details of how a procedure uses knowledge. *Competence* has to do with the knowledge itself. For a theory to be a good competence theory, there must be well-expressed knowledge. For a procedure to be a good performance procedure, there must be a demonstration that competence has been put to use effectively. Linguists, traditionally, have been more interested in competence than in performance. We are interested in both.

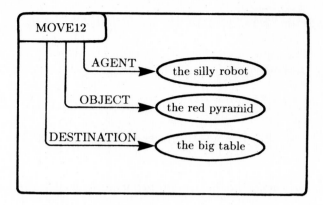

Figure 9-1. A thematic-role frame for the sentence, "The silly robot moved the red pyramid to the big table."

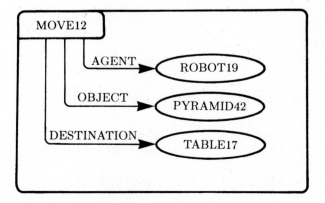

Figure 9-2. A semantic structure.

PARSING SENTENCES

To embody syntactic constraints, we need some device that shows how phrases relate to one another and to words. One such device is the *context-free grammar*. Others are the transition-net grammar and the augmented transition-net grammar. Still another is the wait-and-see grammar. We will examine each, briefly.

First, however, we need a glossary. Linguists rarely write out the full names for sentence constituents. Instead, they use mostly abbreviations:

Full Name	Abbreviation
Sentence	S
Noun phrase	NP
Determiner	DET
Adjective	ADJ
Adjectives	ADJS
Noun	NOUN
Verb phrase	VP
Verb	VERB
Preposition	PREP
Prepositional phrase	PP
Prepositional phrases	PPS

Context-free Grammars Capture Simple Syntactic Constraints

Context-free grammars consist of *context-free rules* like the following:

1	S	$\rightarrow$	NP VP-PPS
2	NP	$\rightarrow$	DET ADJS-NOUN
3	ADJS-NOUN	$\rightarrow$	ADJ ADJS-NOUN
4	ADJS-NOUN	$\rightarrow$	NOUN
5	VP-PPS	$\rightarrow$	VP-PPS PP
6	VP-PPS	$\rightarrow$	VP
7	VP	$\rightarrow$	VERB NP
8	PP	$\rightarrow$	PREP NP
9	DET	$\rightarrow$	a | the | this | that
10	ADJ	$\rightarrow$	silly | red | big
11	NOUN	$\rightarrow$	robot | pyramid | top | brick
12	VERB	$\rightarrow$	moved
13	PREP	$\rightarrow$	to | of

The first rule means that a sentence is a noun phrase followed by something denoted by the funny-looking VP-PPS symbol. The purpose of the VP-PPS symbol is revealed by the fifth and sixth rules, which show that VP-PPS is a compound symbol that can spin off any number of prepositional phrases, including none, before disappearing into a verb phrase.

The second rule says that a noun phrase is a determiner followed by whatever is denoted by ADJS-NOUN. The third and fourth rules deal with the ADJS-NOUN symbol, showing that it can spin off any number of adjectives, including none, before becoming a noun. And finally, the seventh rule says that a verb phrase is a verb followed by a noun phrase, and the eighth rule says that a prepositional phrase is a preposition followed by a noun phrase.

The first eight rules involve only upper-case *nonterminal symbols* that do not appear in completed sentences. The remaining rules determine how some of these upper-case symbols are associated with lower-case *terminal symbols* that correspond to ordinary words. A determiner, DET, may be *a*, *the*, *this*, or *that*, for example. Only such lower-case symbols actually appear in sentences.

Because of the arrows, it is normal to think of using the rules generatively. That is, starting with a one-symbol string consisting of S, the first rule can be used to rewrite S as NP VP-PPS; the second rule then can be used to rewrite NP; and so on, one step at a time, until a string is produced with only terminal symbols:

S
NP VP-PPS
DET ADJS-NOUN VP-PPS
The ADJS-NOUN VP-PPS
The ADJ ADJS-NOUN VP-PPS
The silly ADJS-NOUN VP-PPS
The silly NOUN VP-PPS
The silly robot VP-PPS
The silly robot VP-PPS PP
The silly robot VERB NP PP
The silly robot moved NP PP

⋮

The silly robot moved the red pyramid to the big table

The procedure is simple: Scan the current string from left to right until a nonterminal symbol is encountered; replace that nonterminal symbol using a rule (if there is more than one applicable rule, select one at random); and repeat until no nonterminals remain. The result of the procedure usually is shown as a *derivation tree*, like the one in figure 9-3, because it is too tedious to write out the evolving string after each step.

Such grammars are said to be *context free* because the left side of each rule consists of only the symbol to be replaced—nothing else can influence how the replacement is done. All terminal-only strings produced by the procedure with a particular grammar are *well-formed sentences* with respect to the grammar. All possible well-formed sentences constitute the *language* specified by the grammar.

But while it may be natural to associate derivation trees and language generation with context-free grammars, our purpose is to go the other way, building parse trees starting from sentences.

One way to build parse trees is to use the context-free grammar rules in reverse. Instead of starting with the single-symbol sequence S, working down toward a sentence, we start with a sentence, working up toward the S symbol. The basic procedure is simple: When the right side of a rule is observed, replace the symbols involved by the left side; if more than one rule's right side is observed, pick one at random; if an impasse occurs, back up to the most recent pick and do something else.

Consider, for example, how the procedure works on the sentence "The silly robot moved the red pyramid to the big table." Here is how it is parsed, working mostly, but not always, with the leftmost set of symbols that match a rule's right side.

The silly robot moved the red pyramid to the big table.
DET silly robot moved the red pyramid to the big table.
DET ADJ robot moved the red pyramid to the big table.
DET ADJ NOUN moved the red pyramid to the big table.
DET ADJS-NOUN moved the red pyramid to the big table.
NP moved the red pyramid to the big table.
NP VERB the red pyramid to the big table.
NP VERB DET red pyramid to the big table.
NP VERB DET ADJ pyramid to the big table.
NP VERB DET ADJ NOUN to the big table.
NP VERB DET ADJS-NOUN to the big table.
NP VERB NP to the big table.
NP VP to the big table.
NP VP-PPS to the big table.
NP VP-PPS PREP the big table.
NP VP-PPS PREP DET big table.
NP VP-PPS PREP DET ADJ table.
NP VP-PPS PREP DET ADJ NOUN.
NP VP-PPS PREP DET ADJS-NOUN.
NP VP-PPS PREP NP.
NP VP-PPS PP.
NP VP-PPS.
S.

Each time a replacement is done, we build a piece of parse tree reflecting the replacement. This kind of parsing is called bottom-up parsing because the construction of the parse tree starts down at the bottom with word replacement and moves up toward the S parse-tree node. The result is a parse tree looking exactly like the derivation tree shown in figure 9-3.

There is a lot more that can be said about building parse trees using context-free grammars. It is not said in this book, however. We travel along another path involving another kind of representation for syntactic constraint.

Transition Nets Capture Simple Syntactic Constraints

Recall that parse trees are trees in which the nodes correspond to phrases and sentence constituents. Further recall that parsers consist of a body of syntactic knowledge and an interpreter procedure for using that knowledge. Consequently, all parser interpreters must involve mechanisms for building phrase-describing nodes and for connecting those nodes together. Being more specific, all parsers must take positions on the following questions:

- When should a parser *start* work on a new node, creating it.

- When should a parser *stop* work on an existing node, completing it.

- Where should a parser *attach* a completed node to the rest of the already built tree structure.

In a traditional parser built using context-free grammar rules, a simple procedure specifies how to start and to stop nodes, and the grammar rules specify where each node is attached.

But context-free rules are just one device for expressing how phrases relate to one another and to words. Another, mathematically equivalent, device is the *transition net*. These consist of *nodes* and directed links, called *arcs*, like those shown in figure 9-4.

Think of words, phrases, and sentences as directions for how to move through the various nets. Here are the instructions for using the directions:

To parse sentences using transition nets:
1   Create a parse-tree node named S.
2   Determine if it is possible to traverse a path of arcs from the initial node to a success node, denoted by a double circle. If so, and if all the sentence's words are consumed in the process, announce success. Otherwise announce failure.

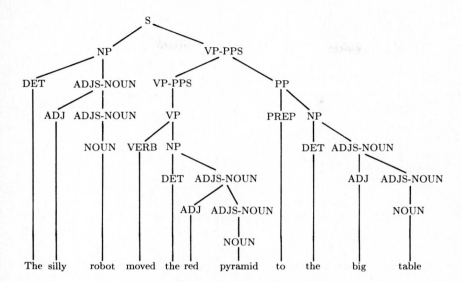

Figure 9-3. A derivation tree produced by running context-free rewrite rules forward. The tree is also a parse tree produced by running the rules backward.

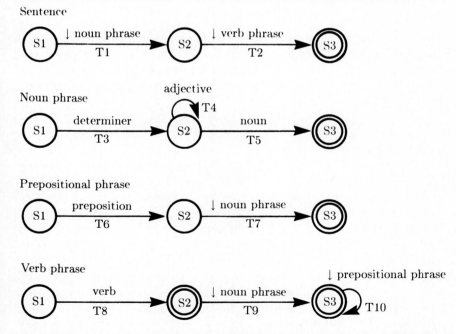

Figure 9-4. A transition-net grammar. This grammar expresses similar constraint to that expressed in the rewrite-rule, context-free grammar given in the text.

To parse phrases using transition nets:

1   Create a parse-tree node with the same name as that of the transition net.

2   Determine if it is possible to traverse a path of arcs from the initial node to a success node, denoted by a double circle. If so, announce success. Otherwise announce failure.

To traverse an arc:

   1a   If the arc has a lower-case symbol on it, the next word in the sentence must have that symbol as a feature. Otherwise fail. The word is consumed as the arc is traversed.

   1b   If the arc has a downward-pointing arrow, ↓, go off and try to traverse the subnet named just after the downward-point arrow. If the subnet is successfully traversed, attach the subnet's node to the current node. Otherwise fail.

Thus the transition-net interpreter embodies straightforward answers to the start, stop, and attach questions. A new node is started whenever a net is entered. Work on an existing node stops whenever a net is traversed or a failure occurs. And a node is attached whenever any net is traversed, other than the top-level net.

To move through the sentence net, for example, we must first traverse the noun-phrase net. To move through the noun-phrase net, the first word must be a determiner.

This procedure constitutes a form of *top-down parsing.* It is called top-down parsing because everything starts with the creation of the sentence node at the top of the parse tree and moves down toward an eventual examination of the words in the sentence.

For the sentence, "The silly robot moved the red pyramid to the big table," figure 9-5 illustrates what happens in the style of a computer program trace. Each circle corresponds to a net traversal.

As the figure shows, the first thing is to start moving through the sentence net. A sentence node is created at once for the parse tree. Just following the entry state, we encounter a noun-phrase arc, labeled T1 in figure 9-4. This causes the creation of a noun-phrase node and initiates an attempt to traverse the noun-phrase net. This in turn initiates an attempt on the determiner arc, T3, in the noun-phrase net in figure 9-4, just following the entry state.

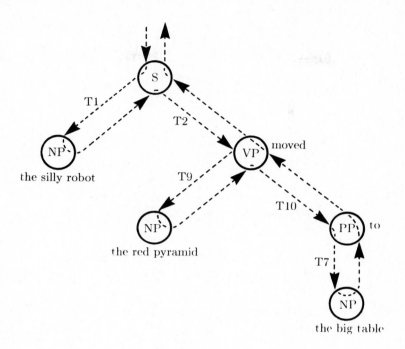

Figure 9-5. A top-down parse. The node names correspond to the net names in figure 9-4. Arrows indicate how the computation proceeds. The words beside the nodes are those involved in arc traversals in the corresponding net.

Now it is time to look at the first word in the sentence. It is *the*, one of the words associated with the *determiner* feature. Consequently, a determiner node is created and attached to the noun-phrase node. The word *the* is simultaneously attached to the determiner node.

Now we are at a place where we can take either the adjective arc, T4, or the noun arc, T5. There is an adjective, namely *silly*, so taking the adjective loop succeeds, creating and attaching an adjective parse-tree node as we go.

Since there are no further adjectives at this point in the sentence, we move on to the noun arc. Traversing it is uneventful, leading to another addition to the parse tree, this time for the word *robot*.

We are in the noun-phrase net's double-circle success node, so the noun-phrase attempt succeeds. The words written beside the noun-phrase circle in figure 9-5 are the words directly consumed in the noun-phrase net. The noun-phrase parse-tree node is connected to the sentence parse-tree node, and we return to the sentence net.

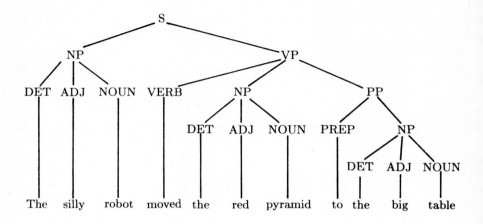

Figure 9-6. A parse tree for the sentence, "The silly robot moved the red pyramid to the big table."

The next thing to look for, determined by arc T2, is a verb phrase. After creating a verb-phrase parse-tree node and traversing arc T8 with the verb *moved*, we look for another noun phrase. This takes us back to the noun-phrase net again.

We quickly proceed through T3, T4, and T5, with the words *the red pyramid*, and return to the verb-phrase net.

There is now the possibility of going around the prepositional-phrase loop, arc T10, so we jump off to the prepositional-phrase transition net. To get anywhere in the prepositional-phrase net, the next word must be a preposition, as dictated by arc T6. The word *to* is a preposition, and *the big table* is a noun phrase, so we get through the prepositional-phrase net.

Now there are no further words in the sentence, but there is no problem, for we are in one of the verb-phrase net's double-circle success states. Having completed a verb phrase, we return to the sentence net, where we find we are also in a success state. The entire sentence is successfully analyzed, producing the parse tree shown in figure 9-6. Note that this is similar to the parse tree produced using the context-free rewrite rules given earlier, but not exactly the same.

Augmented Transition Nets Capture Additional Constraint

Context-free and transition-net grammars cannot capture all syntactic constraint. To do more requires generalization.

One popular generalization is to augment context-free grammars with *transformations*. Transformations can specify symbol rearrangement, as when the declarative sentence, "The silly robot has moved the red pyramid," becomes the interrogative sentence, "Has the silly robot moved the red pyramid?" Studying grammars that use transformations, the *transformational grammars*, takes one into territory belonging mostly to the linguists.

An alternative formalism, traditionally favored in Artificial Intelligence, is the *augmented-transition-net* grammar, where augmented transition net is invariably abbreviated to ATN. An ATN is a transition net with the power to take notes as it goes and to refer to those notes in making decisions later.

One common form of ATN notetaking is that of attaching linguistic properties called *features* to the current parse-tree node. For example, imagine traversing the noun-phrase ATN. Encountering a determiner word with the *singular* feature, such as *a* or *this*, it is reasonable to attach the *singular* feature to the entire noun phrase. When a noun-phrase's noun is encountered, that noun's features, found in a *feature dictionary*, can be inspected to see if they are consistent with any number-indicating feature already noted. This check constitutes an expression of the constraint that the determiner's features and the noun's features must be consistent.

Of course, to capture the syntactic constraints exhibited by all of English or any other natural language is a big, uncompleted job. Huge transformational grammars and wall-covering ATN grammars have been written, but none is completely satisfying.

One plausible reason for the failure to produce a satisfying grammar is that the job is too hard to have been finished yet. Another plausible reason for the failure is that the existing representations are inadequate.

Augmented Transition Nets Typically Use Depth-first Search

Our study of ATN grammars has been eased by the simple nets we used in the sample parse. Going further requires us to think about situations in which it is not clear what to do next.

Consider this slightly longer sentence: "The silly robot moved the red pyramid to the top of the big table." Parsing this with the transition nets used before leads to the parse tree shown in figure 9-7, but this is clearly discomforting. We would prefer the parse tree shown in figure 9-8, where the phrase *of the big table* is taken to describe the noun phrase *the top*, rather than to describe the verb phrase as a whole.

The obvious thing to do is to add a prepositional-phrase arc to the noun-phrase transition net. This is only part of the solution, however, for if used blindly, this modification produces the inappropriate parse tree shown in figure 9-9, where both *to the top* and *of the big table* are taken to describe the noun phrase *the red pyramid*. The modified net that produces this error is the one in figure 9-10.

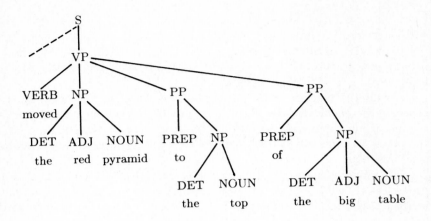

Figure 9-7. An inappropriate parse tree for the sentence, "The silly robot moved the red pyramid to the top of the big table." This is the result of a parser grammar that attaches all prepositional phrases at the verb-phrase level.

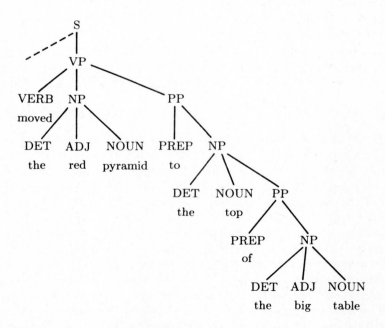

Figure 9-8. An appropriate parse tree for the sentence "The silly robot moved the red pyramid to the top of the big table."

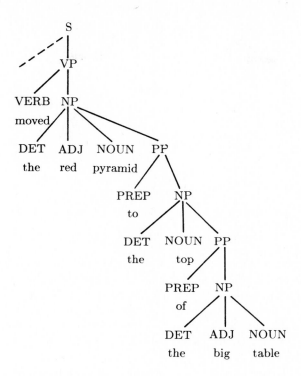

Figure 9-9. An inappropriate parse tree for the sentence, "The silly robot moved the red pyramid to the top of the big table." This is the result of a parser grammar that uses a modified noun-phrase net that consumes prepositional phrases.

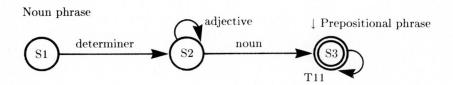

Figure 9-10. A noun-phrase transition net modified to take prepositional phrases after the noun.

Figure 9-11. Some representative meanings for the sentence, "The silly robot saw the red pyramid on the hill with the telescope."

The problem occurs because both the noun-phrase transition net and the verb-phrase transition net have prepositional-phrase loops. Faced with a prepositional phrase following a noun, sometimes a transition-net parser should go around the noun-phrase's prepositional-phrase loop; but sometimes the parser should pop out of the noun-phrase transition net, returning to a verb-phrase in progress, taking the prepositional-phrase loop in that verb phrase.

Somehow, the decision must be based on general semantic knowledge. We know, after all, that *to the top* cannot be attached to a pyramid, but *of the table* can be attached to a top.

Another problem is that proper attachment sometimes depends on specific knowledge of the world as it stands, not just knowledge of the way the world works in general. Consider this sentence: "The silly robot saw the red pyramid on the hill with the telescope." The proper attachment for both prepositional phrases depends on the situation. Some representative possibilities are shown in figure 9-11.

Another, related problem is illustrated by the pair of sentences "The silly robot saw the fire" and "The silly robot saw the fire hydrant." In one sentence, *fire* is the noun; in the other, *fire* is an adjective. When the parser encounters *fire*, it has no way to know whether the word is being used as an adjective or a noun. Whichever choice is the default choice, the parser will be wrong some of the time, getting stuck in midparse.

The typical, albeit wanting, solution to these wrong-turn problems is to search. Whenever the evolving parse tree is absurd from a specific world-model perspective or a general semantic perspective, back up to a decision point, and try something else. Similarly, whenever the parser gets stuck syntactically, with no viable branch leaving the current node, back up to a decision point, and try something else.

As a general rule, however, backup is bad. WASP parsers, introduced next, nearly eliminate the need for syntactically initiated backup.

WASP Parsers Substitute Looking Ahead for Backing Up

Parsers are embodiments of syntactic knowledge. Promising alternatives to context-free-rule parsers and ATN parsers are the WASP parsers, where WASP is an acronym for wait-and-see parser.

Take a deep breath: WASP parsers are not as simple as the others. The effort of understanding them is worth it, however, for some linguists believe they offer more insight into syntactic competence.

The typical WASP parser has the structure shown in figure 9-12. Sentences move into the WASP processor through a *noun-phrase preprocessor.* The job of the noun-phrase preprocessor is to identify noun-phrases and to replace the noun-phrase words by a noun-phrase parse-tree node. This is relatively easy since the word order in English noun phrases is constrained tightly.

Next, preprocessed sentences with words and noun-phrase nodes stream from right to left through a three-place *buffer*, ending up in a standard-looking parse tree. While under construction, parse-tree nodes stay on a *node stack*. The figure shows the node stack arranged horizontally, for such an arrangement makes an imminent simulation simpler to illustrate. The top node on the node stack, the one on the extreme right as the stack is drawn, is called the *current node.*

Flow on and off the node stack and through the buffer is controlled by *condition-action parsing rules.* The condition part of each rule is allowed to consider the contents of the buffer and the current node. Words and noun-phrases flow into the buffer automatically, whenever a place examined by a condition part of a parsing rule is empty. The action part of each rule specifies one of the following actions:

- *Create* a new node and push it onto the node stack.

- Finish the top node on the node stack and *drop* it into the first position in the three-place buffer, shifting existing items to the right.

- *Attach* the first item in the three-place buffer to the top node in the node stack, and shift other buffer items left to fill the hole left by the first item.

- *Switch* the first and the second buffer items.

Thus the key start, stop, and attach questions are answered explicitly by the condition-action parsing rules with create, drop, and attach actions.

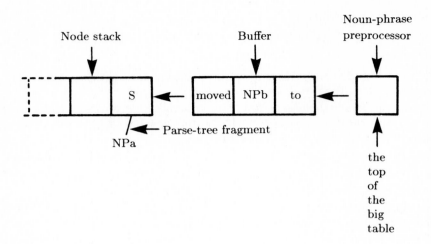

Figure 9-12. The structure of a WASP parser. Sentences first flow through a noun-phrase preparser, where noun phrases are packaged up into noun-phrase nodes. Preprocessed sentences then flow through a buffer that is the database for condition-action rules associated with the parse-tree node currently at the top of a node stack. The parse tree is built according to the actions specified in the condition-action rules.

The condition-action rules reside in a *partitioned condition-action rule memory*. Each partition corresponds to a parse-tree node type. Only those rules in the partition associated with the current parse-tree node, the one at the top of the node stack, are active. If the situation triggers more than one rule, the WASP parser applies the rule-order conflict-resolution strategy, described in chapter 6.

To begin, let us look at the parsing procedure:

To parse using a WASP parser:
1   Until the sentence is completely parsed or no active condition-action rule applies:
   1.1   Activate the condition-action rules associated with the current node.
   1.2   Use the first active rule that matches the condition of the buffer and the current node.

Thus the parsing procedure is quite simple. In contrast to the ATN parser, all the start, stop, and attach knowledge is locked up in the rules.

To see how the procedure works, we now look at some rules and parse a sentence using them. The rule set is a simple one because we want to make the example parse as easy as possible. None of the rules will use the switch action, nor will any look at more than two of the three buffer items.

Also, we will not use the official, on demand, buffer-filling procedure, for using it would add confusing detail to our example. Instead, we will simply fill empty buffer slots as they appear, remembering that this simplified buffer-filling procedure is not generally adequate. Here are the rules that are active when parsing begins and whenever the sentence node is the current node:

S1   If   first item is a noun-phrase node
     then   attach the first item
S2   If   first item is a verb-phrase node
     then   attach the first item
S3   If   first item is a verb
             current node has a noun phrase attached
     then   create a verb-phrase node
S4   If   the buffer is empty
     then   stop, reporting a successful parse

In English, certain words generally signal that it is time to start new nodes. Note, for example, that rule S3 says to start a verb-phrase node as soon as a verb is seen. Similarly, in the following rules for verb phrases, the presence of a preposition leads to the creation of a prepositional-phrase node:

VP1 If   first item is an auxiliary verb
             the second item is a verb
     then   attach the first item
VP2 If   first item is a verb
     then   attach the first item
VP3 If   first item is a noun-phrase node
     then   attach the first item
VP4 If   first item is a preposition
             second item is a noun phrase
             current node has a verb and a noun phrase attached
     then   create a prepositional-phrase node
VP5 If   first item is a prepositional-phrase node
     then   attach the first item
VP6 If   the buffer is empty
     then   drop the current node into the buffer

Rule VP1 takes care of situations involving verbs used as auxiliary verbs like *has* in *has moved* and *will* in *will move*. Rules VP2 and VP3 handle attachment of the verb and the noun phrase, if any. Rules VP4 and VP5 start prepositional phrases and attach them once finished. Rule VP6 stops the construction of the verb phrase itself, dropping it into the buffer where sentence rules can work on it.

Now let us go down another level, this time looking at rules for prepositional phrases, the rules that are active when the current node represents a prepositional phrase:

PP1   If   first item is a preposition
      then   attach the first item

PP2   If   first item is a noun phrase
      then   attach the first item

PP3   If   the buffer is empty
      then   drop the current node into the buffer

Rules PP1 and PP2 are the simple ones that attach a prepositional phrase's preposition and noun phrase to the prepositional phrase itself. Rule PP3 finishes off prepositional phrases, once complete, by dropping them into the buffer. Complete, in this situation, means that the preposition and the noun phrase have been attached.

Now we can simulate the WASP parser using the simple sentence: "The silly robot moved the red pyramid to the top of the big table." With noun phrases preparsed, the sentence reads this way: "NPa(the silly robot) moved NPb(the red pyramid) to NPc(the top of the big table)." Note that we assume a noun-phrase preparser that has enough semantic knowledge to attach embedded prepositional phrases to noun phrases only when the attachment is plausible. Hence the noun-phrase preparser knows that *of the big table* can be attached to *top* but *to the top of the big table* cannot be attached to *pyramid*.

Figure 9-13 shows the buffer, the node stack, and the evolving parse tree at all points in the analysis. In *a*, the parser is in the initial state, with a bare sentence node, S, in the stack and the first three sentence items in the buffer. In this condition, the sentence rules are active, allowing rule S1 to trigger and fire, advancing the parser to the state shown in *b*. In moving to *b*, the first noun phrase, NPa, is attached to S.

Rule S3 then takes the parser to the state shown in *c*, with a new node created to represent the verb phrase, VP. This activates the verb-phrase rules and hides the sentence rules. Verb phrase rule VP2 then takes the opportunity to attach the verb to VP, leaving the parser in the state shown in *d*. Similarly, rule VP3 attaches NPb, producing the state shown in *e*.

At this point, several rules act to create the prepositional-phrase node, PP, attach things to it, and drop it back into the buffer, moving us through the states shown in *f*, *g*, *h*, and *i*.

Then rule VP5 attaches PP to VP, giving us *j*. VP then drops into the buffer, as shown in *k*, whereupon it becomes attached to S, as shown in *l*. Nothing further can happen, but no matter, for the empty buffer and the complete sentence node signal a successful parse.

WASP Parsers Are Promising Models of Syntactic Competence

You have now seen a WASP parser in action. Now it is time to ask how WASP parsers compare with ATN parsers. Note that the comparison is along the competence dimension, not the performance, for we are interested in how well constraint-capturing knowledge is expressed, not in how efficient a certain procedure may be.

First, note that WASP parsers and ATN parsers embody different answers to the start, stop, and attach questions. For ATN parsers, the answers are bound up implicitly and rigidly in the way the ATN parsing procedure uses nets. For WASP parsers, the answers are bound up explicitly and flexibly in the rules exhibiting create, drop, and attach actions.

Next, note that our sample WASP parser has a three-item look-ahead buffer, whereas ATN parsers look at just the next item. Experiments indicate that a three-item look-ahead buffer ordinarily is enough to make decisions decisively. On ordinary sentences, the three-item WASP parse never backs up and never wastes time building doomed partial structures.

Importantly, these experiments suggest something about the nature of English. It seems that English speakers ordinarily confine themselves to sentences that a three-item WASP parser can handle without backup or wasted subtree construction.

Finally, note that in ATN grammars, syntactic knowledge is expressed in an interpreter procedure, in nodes and arcs, and in potentially obscure arc procedures; in WASP grammars, syntactic knowledge is expressed in an interpreter procedure and in relatively plain, transparent condition-action rules. While the interpreter portion of an ATN parser is simpler to explain than the interpreter portion of a WASP parser, the procedures on the arcs tend to be much more complicated than the condition-action rules in a WASP parser. Evidently, simplicity in one dimension is traded for complexity in another. Arguably, the balance is better in the WASP parsers because the linguistically motivated design choices are more accessible in WASP parsers, hence more subject to careful linguistic study and debate.

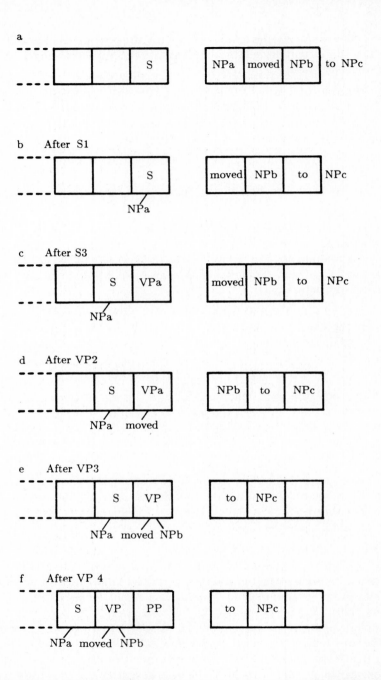

Figure 9-13. The WASP parser as it parses the sentence, "The silly robot moved the red pyramid to the top of the big table."

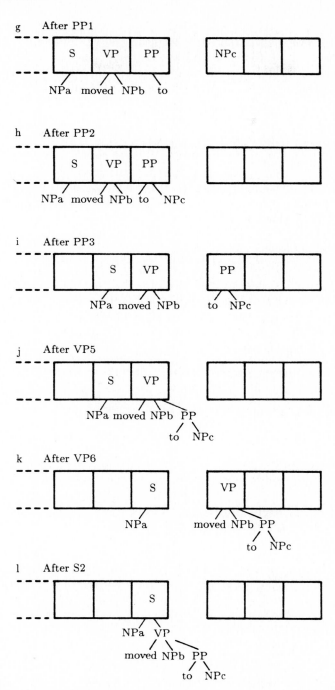

Figure 9-13. Continued.

On the whole, then, the extra complexity of WASP parsers seems worthwhile. Much more could be said about them,[1] but parsing has occupied enough of our time. Let us proceed to another important dimension of language understanding, that of describing how acts and objects fit together.

FORMING THEMATIC-ROLE FRAMES

The way an object participates in describing an act is by filling one of a small number of *thematic roles*. A noun phrase identifies *what* object participates in an act; a noun phrase's thematic role specifies *how* the object participates. One speaks, for example, of the agent, thematic object, and instrument thematic roles.[2]

The sentence, "Robbie hit a ball with a bat," for example, carries information about how Robbie, a ball, and a bat relate to the verb *hit*. A procedure that understands such a sentence must discover that Robbie is the *agent* because he performs the act of hitting, that the ball is the *thematic object* because it is the thing hit, and that the bat is the *instrument* because it is the tool with which hitting is done.

Thus sentence analysis requires, in part, the answer to these questions:

- What thematic roles are to be filled by a sentence?

- How is it possible to determine the thematic roles of a sentence's noun phrases?

An Object's Thematic Role Specifies
the Object's Relation to an Act

The number of thematic roles embraced by various theories varies considerably. Some people use a half-dozen thematic roles. Others use three or four times as many. The exact number does not matter much as long as there are enough to expose natural constraints on how verbs and thematic role instances form sentences.

---

[1] For example, we could go into a discussion showing that WASP grammars are LR(k) grammars, from the theory-of-computation perspective.

[2] Some people use the term *object* instead of *thematic object*. Using the term *thematic object* avoids confusion with the syntactic direct and indirect objects.

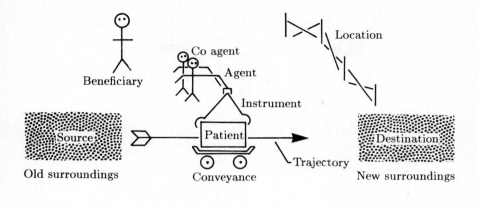

Figure 9-14. Thematic roles focus on how noun phrases relate to acts. These are some of the more common possibilities.

For illustration, we confine ourselves to a world for which the role possibilities shown schematically in figure 9-14 is adequate.

- *Thematic object*. The thematic object is the thing the sentence is really all about, typically the thing undergoing a state change. Often the thematic object is the same as the syntactic direct object as in "Robbie hit *the ball*." On the other hand the thematic object may appear as the syntactic subject as in "*The ball* was hit by Robbie."

- *Agent*. The agent is the thing that causes the act to occur. Volition is generally implied as in "*Robbie* kissed Suzie," but there are exceptions: "*The moon* eclipsed the sun." The agent is often the surface subject, but the agent also may appear in a prepositional noun phrase: "Suzie was kissed *by Robbie*."

- *Instrument*. The instrument is a tool used by the agent. The preposition *with* typically introduces instrument noun phrases: "Robbie hit a ball *with a bat*."

- *Coagent*. The word *with* also may introduce a noun phrase that serves as a slightly subordinate partner to the principal agent. They carry out the act together: "Robbie played tennis *with Suzie*."

- *Source and destination.* State changes are often simple changes in physical position. The source is the initial position and the destination is the final position: "Robbie went *from the dining room to the kitchen.*"

- *Conveyance.* The conveyance is the thing in which or on which one travels: "Robbie always goes *by train.*"

- *Beneficiary.* The beneficiary is the person for whom an act is performed: "Robbie cleaned the house *for Suzie.*"

- *Old surroundings and new surroundings.* The old surroundings is where something comes out of, and the new surroundings is where it goes into.

- *Trajectory.* Motion from source to destination takes place over a trajectory. In contrast to the other role possibilities, several prepositions can serve to introduce trajectory noun phrases: "Robbie and Suzie went in *through the front door*; he carried her *over the threshold.*"

- *Location.* The location is where an act occurs. As in the trajectory role, several prepositions are possible, each of which conveys meaning in addition to serving as a signal that a location noun phrase is coming: "Robbie and Suzie studied *in the library, at a desk, by the wall, under a picture, near the door.*"

- *Time.* Time specifies when an act occurs. Prepositions like *at, before,* and *after* introduce noun phrases serving as time role fillers.

Other roles that are common but that are not illustrated in figure 9-14 include the following:

- *Duration.* Duration specifies how long. Prepositions like *for* indicate duration.

- *Raw material.* If a substance disappears into a product, then it is an instance of the raw material role. *Out of* typically introduces the raw material: "Robbie made a computer *out of large integrated circuits.*"

A Variety of Constraints Establish Thematic Roles

As suggested by figure 9-15, many constraints help establish the thematic role of any given noun phrase:

- Each verb carries strong preferences about what thematic roles can appear and where the noun phrases that fill those thematic roles can be, relative to the verb.

- Flagging prepositions limit a noun phrase's role possibilities.

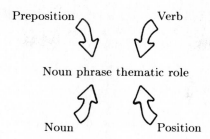

Figure 9-15. Many constraints help determine noun-phrase role.

For example, given the preposition *by*, the following table says to expect an agent, a conveyance, or a location, but not an instrument, raw material, or beneficiary.

Preposition	*Thematic Role*
from	source
to	destination
by	agent or conveyance or location
with	instrument or coagent
for	beneficiary or duration

- The noun itself may limit possible role identifications.

For example, we get a different picture from "Robbie was sent to the scrap heap by parcel post," than from "Robbie was sent to the scrap heap by Marcel Proust," because parcel post is more likely to be a conveyance, while Marcel Proust is more likely to be an agent.

- Finally, only one filler is allowed in any sentence for most thematic roles.

If, somehow, the thematic role of one noun phrase is determined, then the other noun phrases in the sentence are forced to be something else.

Note, however, that a filler may involve more than one object if the objects are joined into a sequence by *and* to make a compound filler. In "Robbie ate with a fork with a gazerkle," it is not clear if the gazerkle can be a coagent because *gazerkle* is a made-up word. It is clear, however, that the gazerkle is not an instrument because the fork has a lock on that. On the other hand, if the sentence were, "Robbie ate with a fork and a gazerkle," the fork and gazerkle would fill the instrument thematic role together.

Time, trajectory, and location are exceptions to the one-filler rule because more than one noun phrase may be involved in their description. It is perfectly reasonable to say, for example, "Robbie ate at noon on Monday."

A Variety of Constraints Establish Verb Meanings

Verbs and verb phrases in isolation exhibit meaning ambiguity just as noun phrases exhibit thematic-role ambiguity. Conveniently, meaning-selection constraints again seem to resolve the ambiguity.

The noun phrase in the thematic-object thematic role can help considerably. Consider the following examples:

He shot the rabbit.

He shot the picture.

Shooting a rifle and shooting a camera are very different kinds of shooting, even though there are similarities at a certain level of abstraction. The words *rifle* and *camera* are not specifically mentioned. Information found in the words *rabbit* and *picture* are apparently enough to pick out the verb's proper meaning. There is no other evidence, after all.

A suspicious circularity lurks here, of course. If the noun phrase in the thematic-object thematic role helps select a meaning for the verb, how is it that meaning-specific information helps to find the thematic object in the first place? Be patient. This will be sorted out when we look at a procedure for exploiting the constraints.

Another way verb meanings are selected is through a small family of selector words. By custom, selector words used in combination with verbs are called particles rather than prepositions, but the same words do both jobs. For example, see how particles select meanings for *throw* and *pick*:

He threw some food.

He threw away some food.

He threw up some food.

She picked up some candy.

She picked out a nice assortment.

One final strong influence on meaning derives from the overall context. Curiously, quite a lot can be gained from a very coarse categorization of life's subjects into a few worlds:

- *The physical world.* This is the primary one. Things change state by changing position and by losing or acquiring properties and relations. All other worlds relate strongly to the physical world through analogy.

- *The mental world.* This is the world in which the objects are facts, ideas, and concepts. We sometimes think about them with acts, properties, and relations borrowed from the physical world, just as if the abstractions were physical things. Consider these examples:

  The theory is supported by facts.

  The overall concept is solid.

  The idea was exposed in the class.

  Truth poured out of the book.

- *The ownership world.* In the ownership world the objects are abstract certificates of control, possession, or ownership, whose locations are in the hands of people or organizations. Again the happenings of this world are communicated in language strongly analogous to that of the physical world:

  Robbie took the ball away from Bozo.

  The bank took the house back.

Note that transfer of a physical thing is often, but not necessarily, implied. We assume Robbie is holding the ball he took control of, but the bank probably never sees the physical house.

Constraints Enable Sentence Analysis

Now we turn our attention to the assignment of noun phrases to thematic roles. Two kinds of procedures can do this:

- One kind of procedure exploits parse trees, using parse-tree positions, along with other constraints, to assign thematic roles.

- Another kind of procedure works directly off sentences, using sentence positions, along with other constraints, to assign thematic roles.

Regrettably, it would be out of place to work up a more powerful parsing grammar sufficient for a good demonstration of a thematic-role-filling procedure using parse trees. Consequently, we confine ourselves to a procedure that uses sentences directly, rather than parse trees, even though there are good arguments that such procedures must be the weaker ones.

Our thematic-role-filling procedure knows about the constraints shown in figure 9-16, and the procedure has access to a dictionary of stored information about nouns and verbs:

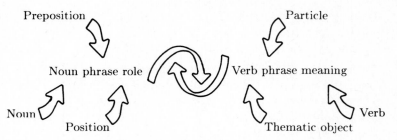

Figure 9-16. Many constraints help determine noun-phrase thematic roles and verb-phrase meanings. Among the noun phrases, the one in the thematic object role has a strong influence on verb meaning.

To determine thematic roles:

1   Obtain possible verb meanings from the dictionary. Throw away those verb meanings that are inconsistent with the verb's particle, if any.
2   Find the thematic object among the prepositionless noun phrases.
3   Throw away the verb meanings that the dictionary says are inconsistent with the thematic object.
4   For each remaining noun phrase, determine the thematic role.
5   Throw away the verb meanings that the dictionary says are inconsistent with the observed thematic roles.

We assume, for the sake of simplicity, that all noun phrases help describe the act. We forbid noun phrases that describe other noun phrases.

Note that a sentence's verb phrase may contain a verb with many possible meanings. Several steps offer opportunities to hack away successively at the collection of meanings, ultimately yielding a unique interpretation, or at worst, a small number. Noting the presence or absence of a particle helps considerably. Verb meanings inconsistent with an observed particle or inconsistent with the absence of a particle are thrown out immediately.

The next step is to locate the thematic object among the noun phrases without flagging prepositions. If the verb phrase is passive, then the thematic object, the thing the sentence is about, must occupy a spot in front of the verb. It is what you learned to call the syntactic subject in grammar school.

If the verb is active, then the thematic object follows the verb. If there is only one preposition-free noun phrase after the verb, then that noun phrase is the thematic object.

If there are two preposition-free noun phrases following the verb, then we see if the verb's dictionary entry says something about whether the first or second one is the thematic object. Otherwise, the second is the thematic object. All this is directly derailed if the verb does not require a thematic object. Assume that it does, constraining sentence construction, just so things can be kept manageable.

With the thematic object in hand, there is again an opportunity to weed out unlikely verb meanings, namely those whose stored meanings are incompatible with the thematic object.

At this point it is conceivable that more than one verb meaning remains. Although unlikely, provision must be made. The understanding process must go forward with more than one interpretation in parallel. Branching does not seem to get out of hand in human communication, however. Just as the number of interpretations seems to explode, some constraint comes in to keep things manageable.

Note, incidentally, that strength in one dimension allows flexibility in another. It is easy to imagine how a language might have a larger number of flagging prepositions than English has, with an offsetting reduction in word-order constraint. This is true, for example, of Finnish.

In any event, it is now appropriate to nail down the thematic roles for other noun phrases, starting with those without prepositions. Again the surviving verb meanings may state preferences about what is needed and where what is needed can be found. Many active verbs, for example, demand an overt agent and prefer to find it in the syntactic subject position. Such verb-carried demands are ordinarily enough to fix the role for the one or two preposition-free noun phrases that may be found in addition to the thematic object. Knowing the roles for the noun phrases without prepositions greatly simplifies further analysis because we know that only one instance of a role can appear per sentence.

Consider, for example, a sentence containing a noun phrase introduced by the word *by*. This word typically introduces either the agent role or the conveyance or the location. If the agent role is already spoken for by the syntactic subject, then only the conveyance and location possibilities remain. Generally this remaining ambiguity can then be resolved either by knowledge about the words in the noun phrase or by deference to the dictionary-stated needs of the verb.

Finally, once the thematic roles are known for all noun phrases, it may be that certain roles are present that help resolve remaining verb-meaning ambiguity.

Whew! We are done, sort of. While there are more complicated procedures, the one introduced here is powerful enough to handle the forthcoming examples.

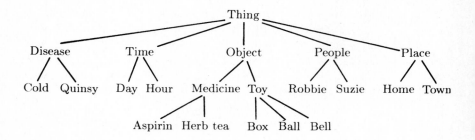

Figure 9-17. A small world used to illustrate the effect of various sentence constraints.

Examples Using *Take* **Illustrate How Constraints Interact**

Suppose Robbie and Suzie communicate using the simple, limited subset of English that includes only the things shown in figure 9-17. The verbs may have more than one meaning, but they certainly do not have all of the meanings possible in unrestricted English.

Robbie and Suzie move things, get sick, engage in business activities, and date. Consequently the verb *take* has a variety of meanings:

- *Take1* means transport. Either a source or a destination or both should appear.

- *Take2* means swindle. The source and destination roles are absent when this meaning is intended. Only people can be swindled.

- *Take3* means to swallow medicine. The available medicines include aspirin. The beneficiary is the same as the agent.

- *Take4* means to steal. People are not stolen.

- *Take5* means to initiate and execute a social event with another person. The particle *out* is always used.

- *Take6* means to remove. The particle *out* is always used. People cannot be removed.

- *Take7* means to assume control. The particle *over* signals this meaning.

- *Take8* means to remove from the body. The particle *off* is always used.

These various meanings combine with noun phrases according to the thematic-role constraints we have been studying. Assume all passive sentences have exactly one preposition-free noun phrase, the syntactic subject, and that preposition-free noun phrase appears before the verb. Also assume all active sentences have one preposition-free noun phrase before the verb and one or two following it, the syntactic indirect and direct objects.

Thematic Role	Preposition	Restriction on Fillers
thematic object	—	—
agent	by	animate
instrument	with	not animate
coagent	with	animate
source	from	—
destination	to	—
conveyance	by	not animate
beneficiary	for	animate
duration	for	a time
raw material	out of	not animate
old surroundings	out of	—
new surroundings	into	—

Now we can examine a few sentences with a view toward better understanding the way various constraints interact.

Robbie took aspirin.

The verb meanings *Take5* through *Take8* are eliminated because there is no particle. Evidently Robbie is the agent and aspirin is the thematic object by virtue of word order and the lack of alternatives. *Take1* is unlikely because there are no noun phrases that can be either the source or the destination of a transporting act. *Take2* is out because aspirin is not a subclass of people and hence cannot be swindled. Thus the sentence means that either Robbie swallowed aspirin or he stole some.

Robbie took aspirin for Suzie.

Robbie is the agent and aspirin is the thematic object by the same word-order argument used before. Again only *Take3* and *Take4* survive particle and thematic object considerations. *For* can flag either the beneficiary or duration, but since Suzie is not time, she must be the beneficiary. This in turn eliminates the *Take3* interpretation, swallowing medicine, because swallowing medicine requires the agent and beneficiary to be the same. Robbie has stolen. Of course Robbie may have swallowed aspirin because Suzie begged and pleaded him to, but that depth of analysis is not compatible with our assumptions.

Robbie took out Suzie.

The particle limits the verb meaning to *Take5* and *Take6*, to date or to remove. *Take6* requires an inanimate thematic object, so Robbie dated Suzie.

Robbie took out the box.

A box is inanimate, hence removed, not dated.

Robbie took the ball to Suzie.

The ball is the thematic object, so *Take1*, to transport, and *Take4*, to steal, are the alternatives. Since a destination is given, *Take1* is preferred.

Robbie took Suzie the ball.

Again the ball is the thematic object, but the lack of a flagging preposition makes the thematic role of Suzie unclear, and there is no ready way to decide between *Take1* and *Take4*.

Robbie took Suzie.

Suzie being the thematic object, *Take1* and *Take2*, to transport and to swindle are possible. Since there is no source or destination, Robbie has probably swindled Suzie.

Robbie took Suzie to school.

With a destination, the swindle conclusion is unlikely. Robbie has transported Suzie.

The ball was taken out of town by Robbie by car for a day for Suzie.

Since the sentence is passive, the ball is the thematic object. Since a ball is both inanimate and not a medicine, the verb meaning must be *Take1* or *Take4*. The compound preposition *out of* can flag either raw material or old surroundings. Knowing that a town is a place and places are possible old surroundings, but not raw materials, resolves the ambiguity in favor of *Take1*. *Car* is an unknown word so it could be either the agent or a conveyance. But since Robbie is animate, he must be an agent, thus filling the agent role, forcing the car to be a conveyance. Finally, a day and Suzie are easily resolved into duration and beneficiary since Suzie cannot be a time and a day cannot be a beneficiary.

Filled Thematic Roles Help Answer Questions

Once thematic roles are worked out, many questions about the indicated act are answered by simple reference to thematic roles. Consider this statement:

Robbie made coffee for Suzie with a percolator.

There are four noun phrases, each of which fits into a particular role:

Noun Phrase Thematic Role

coffee	thematic object
Robbie	agent
a percolator	instrument
Suzie	beneficiary

Four corresponding questions can be answered now:

What was made?	→	thematic object	→	coffee
Who made it?	→	agent	→	Robbie
With what was it made?	→	instrument	→	a percolator
For whom was it made?	→	beneficiary	→	Suzie

Similar results follow from another sentence:

Robbie went to the theater with Suzie by car.

Who went?	→	agent	→	Robbie
With whom did he go?	→	coagent	→	Suzie
To where did he go?	→	destination	→	the theater
By what means did they travel?	→	conveyance	→	car

Thus thematic roles roughly correspond to some of the simple questions about acts. This is not surprising. After all, the thematic roles should be an exhaustive categorization of the ways an object can help describe the act specified by the verb phrase. Consequently, the thematic roles should cover the aspects of an act that are asked about.

While such question answering is important, keep in mind that it is only one of the functions of first-line semantic analysis. Presumably the results of thematic role identification are the fodder for still deeper mechanisms that understand the relations between individual sentences, evolving contexts, and global knowledge about the world. For now we must rest content with the demonstration that understanding the interplay of constraints is a powerful way for us to approach some difficult problems.

INTERPRETING SIMPLE QUESTIONS AND COMMANDS

Limited applied language goals enable shortcuts. In some situations, it is possible to go directly from a question or command to an appropriate database query or procedure evaluation. For illustration, we look at how a toy system can deal with the following questions:

What is the height of Block1?
How many meters is Block1 from Block2?

Semantic Grammars Are Transition Trees with Semantic Labels

The most direct approach to English question answering is through a two-part system. One part identifies question patterns. The other part fills in empty slots in procedure patterns. The question-pattern identifier looks for certain kinds of questions, gathering information for the procedure-pattern filler as it goes. The act of filling is called *instantiation*.

The easiest sentence-pattern identifier to build is a procedure that uses a *transition-tree semantic grammar*. These grammars are similar to the transition-net grammars. Here are the differences:

- Some arc transitions may require seeing specific words, rather than just seeing any word of some type or making a successful traversal of a named tree. Such specific words are shown in upper case.

For example, an arc can be labeled WIDTH, as in one of the trees shown in figure 9-18, meaning that the word *width* must be next.

- Some arc transitions specify phrases semantically, rather than syntactically.

For example, downward-pointing arrows indicate that the arcs labeled with ↓attribute and ↓attributes, in figure 9-18, are semantically specified transitions. Grammars using such labels are called semantic grammars, perhaps regrettably.

- Values are attached to tree names whenever a tree is traversed successfully. The values are specified by terminal patterns.

The simplest terminal pattern is a single symbol, like those shown in the attribute tree in figure 9-19a. The word *width* makes WIDTH become the value of ATTRIBUTE. The word *breadth* has the same effect.

- Tree names are replaced by their values in terminal patterns. Each time a lower-level tree name appears prefaced by an ↑ in a terminal pattern, the tree name is replaced by the tree-name's value, previously attached.

a   Attributes

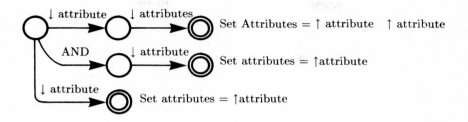

b   Attribute

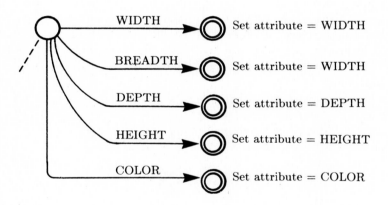

Figure 9-18. Two simple transition trees of a semantic grammar. On successful traversal, trees attach values to their names. In part *a*, the attribute tree attaches values like WIDTH, HEIGHT, and DEPTH. In part *b*, the tree for attributes combines the results produced by embedded uses of the attribute tree and the attributes tree itself.

The first terminal pattern in the attributes tree, for example, contains pattern elements ↑attribute and ↑attributes. Whenever this first pattern is instantiated, ↑attribute and ↑attributes are replaced by the values attached to ATTRIBUTE and ATTRIBUTES when the corresponding arcs are traversed.

Thus ↓ is a mnemonic preface suggesting *take processing down* into a subtree, while ↑ is a mnemonic preface suggesting *bring a value up* from a subtree.

- There are no nodes with two inputs.

This is why we are talking about trees rather than nets. Once a terminal state is reached, there is no question about how that terminal state was reached. This means there is no need to build and review a parse tree. This is convenient.

Note that going from nets to trees means that there can be no loops of the sort used previously for adjectives and prepositional phrases. Luckily, there is a way to replace loops with subprocedures. Figure 9-18 shows how. Basically, the loop is replaced with a recursive subprocedure call.

Consider the three words *width and height.* These words move the transition-tree parser along the top path in the attributes tree in figure 9-18b, with the word *width* making WIDTH the value of ATTRIBUTE. The other two words, *and height*, are handled by using the attributes tree on a lower level, working through the middle path. The lower level use of the attributes tree makes HEIGHT the value of ATTRIBUTES on the higher level. Having values for both ATTRIBUTE and ATTRIBUTES, the terminal pattern in the attributes tree is instantiated by replacing the pattern elements ↑attribute and ↑attributes. The result is the list WIDTH, HEIGHT.

Figure 9-19 shows how the trees for multiple attributes and for individual attributes work together to handle the string of words *breadth, depth, and height.* Words consumed are written beside the consuming node.

Semantic-Grammar Terminals Select Search-procedure Patterns

The value attached to the name of the top-level transition tree is more complicated than the values attached to names at lower levels. Instead of just one symbol or a list of symbols, the value attached is a complete database search-procedure specification.

The transition-tree procedure filler creates the search specification by instantiating a procedure pattern using the values attached to lower-level tree names. These values, of course, are gathered up on the way to the top-level terminal. The procedure pattern is a sort of skeleton; the lower-level values flesh it out.

Consider figure 9-20. The directions associated with the terminal node say to create a value for the interface tree by replacing the tree names with their values wherever those names appear prefaced by a ↑. The illustrating sentence is "What is the height of pyramid27?" The ↓present arc handles the words *what is*; ↓attributes does *height*; and ↓blocks does *pyramid27.* The terminal procedure pattern, specifying a search procedure, is instantiated with HEIGHT and PYRAMID27.

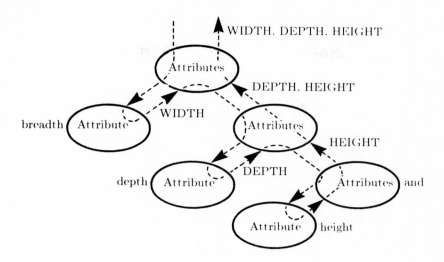

Figure 9-19. The trees for multiple attributes and for individual attributes work together to handle the string of words *breadth, depth, and height.*

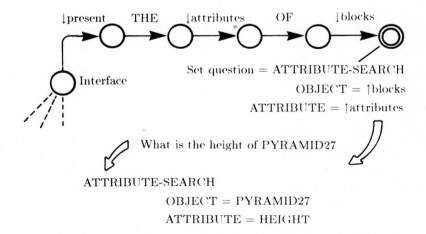

Figure 9-20. When the top-level interface transition tree is traversed, a procedure pattern is instantiated. When evaluated, the fully specified procedure searches for the items requested by the English sentence that led to the procedure pattern.

Here, in summary, is the modified traversal procedure for dealing with transition trees:

To traverse a transition tree:

1 Create a variable with the same name as that of the transition tree.

2 Determine if it is possible to traverse a path of arcs from the initial node to a success node, denoted by a double circle.

    2a If there is a path and if either the transition tree is not a sentence-level tree or the transition tree is a sentence-level tree and all the words are consumed:

        2a1 Instantiate the pattern associated with the double circle using accumulated variable values.

        2a2 Make the value of the variable created be the instantiated pattern and announce success.

    2b Otherwise announce failure.

And here is the modified traversal procedure for dealing with transition-tree arcs:

To traverse an arc:

    1a If the arc has a lower-case symbol, the next word in the sentence must have that symbol as a feature. The word is consumed as the arc is traversed.

    1b If the arc has a downward-pointing arrow, ↓, try to traverse the tree named just after the downward-pointing arrow.

    1c If the arc has an upper-case symbol on it, the next word in the sentence must be that symbol. The word is consumed as the arc is traversed.

Figure 9-21 shows more of the interface tree for a simple transition-tree semantic grammar.

Question

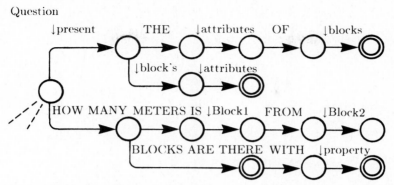

Figure 9-21. A simple interface transition tree. Sentences like "What is the height of pyramid27" make it through this tree.

INTELLECT Translates Sentences into Database Searches

The INTELLECT system is one example of a practical natural-language interface based on a semantic grammar approach. Here is an example of how INTELLECT can be used with Fortune magazine's database for the 500 largest industrial companies:

```
Count the electronics companies.
Answer:  39
```

This question is easy. "Count the electronics companies," after all, is not much different from "Count the red blocks."

```
Sales, earnings, and income/assets by company.
```

Responding, INTELLECT prints a table:

Name	Sales (000's)	Net Income (000's)	Income/Assets
Allegheny	1,907,809	81,000	.033
AMP	1,234,295	134,770	.131

Of course, INTELLECT prints information for the other 37 at this point. Note that *earnings* was taken to mean *net income* and *for the electronics companies* was assumed.

Average.

Again, INTELLECT prints a table:

```
Sales        Net Income   Income/Assets
             (000's)      (000's)
3,514,947    168,091      .060
```

Note that INTELLECT takes the context of the question into account.

Which are the top ten in terms of their income/assets?

INTELLECT produces another table at this point. Note the use of the interrogative pronoun *which*.

Show their 10 year average return.   Order by growth rate.

INTELLECT produces still another table. Note the use of the possessive pronoun *their*.

Let me see the performance of General Instrument.

INTELLECT produces a table with all sorts of business data.

INTELLECTUAL PARTNERSHIPS

Language understanding is not the only prerequisite for creating exciting intellectual partnerships with computers.

Here, for example, are some of the things we ourselves exhibit, viewed as intellectual partners to each other:

- *Understanding and explanation.* We understand, we speak, and we keep track of what is being discussed, thereby communicating smoothly and efficiently. Often we augment natural language with diagrams, drawings, and pictures.

- *Knowledge and expertise.* As human experts, we know things other humans need to know. We know about things in depth, making us capable of explanation at many levels of detail.

- *User models.* We learn how much other people know, and we tailor our explanations to suit them. We know a word or short phrase suffices for experts, particularly in crisis situations. We know long tutorials are better for knowledge-hungry students.

Computer-based intellectual partners need the same capabilities in addition to good natural-language interfaces.

SUMMARY

- Understanding natural language is an incredibly complex phenomenon. It seems that understanding several kinds of representation are necessary. Among these are the parse tree, the thematic-role frame, and the world model.

- Context-free grammars capture syntactic constraints by way of context-free rewrite rules.

- Transition nets capture syntactic constraints by way of nodes and arcs, and transition-net parsers provide a convenient, perspicuous way of employing those constraints in analysis. To cope with ambiguity, transition-net parsers generally use some form of depth-first search.

- Augmented transition nets are augmented because ATN parsers are free to take notes and to refer to those notes as transitions are made. Typically those notes attach features to parse-tree nodes.

- Wait-and-see parsers use a small look-ahead buffer to eliminate the need for search. In addition, wait-and-see parsers have a noun-phrase preprocessor and a partitioned set of condition-action rules. The structure of wait-and-see parsers is a statement about the nature of language.

- Simple sentences consist of a verb phrase and some number of noun phrases supporting the verb phrase by filling thematic roles. In any one sentence, there is at most one filler for most thematic roles.

- Some common roles are thematic object, agent, instrument, coagent, source, and destination. Except for the thematic-object thematic role, all are closely associated with one or a few flagging prepositions.

- Constraint-based sentence analysis makes use of knowledge about the thematic roles and their prepositions; the verbs, their particles, and the roles they require; the world under discussion; and some facts about standard ordering.

- A transition-tree semantic-grammar parser can assemble together the material for search procedures in the course of question or command analysis. Language interfaces based on such parsers are commercial successes.

REFERENCES

Noam Chomsky's book, *Syntactic Structures* [1957], is the classic work on transformational grammar. A more recent view is offered in his book *Lectures on Government and Binding* [1981].

Using augmented transition nets for natural language seems to have started with a paper by J. Thorne, P. Bratley, and H. Dewar [1968]. Work by Daniel G. Bobrow and Bruce Fraser [1969] and by William A. Woods [1970] developed and popularized the idea soon thereafter. Woods, especially, became a major contributor.

The work of Woods and the work of Terry Winograd [1971, 1972] were the precursors to today's commercial language interfaces, for they showed that sentence-analysis procedures can fill in search-procedure slots. Woods's work involved questions about moon rocks. Winograd's work involved questions about a simulated world of blocks.

For an excellent treatment of syntax, see *Language as a Cognitive Process, Volume I: Syntax* [1983], by Winograd. For a good exposition of transition-tree semantic grammars, see work by Gary Hendrix and his associates [Hendrix et al. 1978]. The well-known LIFER system is based on this work. For information on INTELLECT, see work by Larry R. Harris [1977]. INTELLECT is a product of the Artificial Intelligence Corporation.

Wait-and-see parsers were introduced by Mitchell P. Marcus in his landmark thesis and subsequent book [1977, 1980].

C. J. Fillmore is closely associated with thematic-role grammar, which he called case grammar [1968], although many of his original ideas are now disputed. Many of the ideas in this chapter were more directly influenced by the late William A. Martin. Most of his work has not been published, regrettably.

For the other side of language, generation, see particularly the work of David D. McDonald [1983]. Good language generation is one of the problems of discourse, a hotly pursued research area. A good book is *Computational Models of Discourse* [1983], edited by J. Michael Brady and Robert C. Berwick. Berwick's overview is a good introduction to the problems.

Programming is a good example of fertile ground for human-computer intellectual partnerships. For interesting reading on the creation of apprentices for programmers, see Charles Rich and Howard E. Schrobe [1978] and Richard C. Waters [1982].

10

Image
Understanding

Our objective in this chapter is to understand some of the problems involved in making a computer sense and manipulate its environment intelligently. The focus is on images, for the enterprise of understanding images is a major focus of Artificial Intelligence.

Three representations seem to promote the exploitation of natural constraints. Two of these three representations are the *primal sketch* and the $2\frac{1}{2}$-*D sketch*, which describe images from a *viewer-centered* perspective. The third representation is the *world model*, which describes objects from a *viewer-independent* perspective.

Following a brief discussion of how these representations fit into the organization of vision systems, we look at two particular visual processing problems that happen to be better understood than most. The first of these, the *binocular stereo problem*, is to find the distance from the viewer to surfaces using two slightly different viewpoints. The second problem, the *shape-from-shading problem*, is to determine surface-direction at each point in an image by exploiting the way surfaces in the image are shaded.

Next, we turn away from representative theories to difficulty-avoiding, proven applications. We do this by examining the *feature-space paradigm* for identification and localization.

Finally, having stressed vision, we briefly survey other parts of robotics. Along the way, some of the topics may seem to take us away from Artificial

Intelligence. Do not think so. If we define robotics to be that field concerned with the intelligent connection of perception to action, then plainly robotics and Artificial Intelligence are closely related.

FROM IMAGES TO OBJECT MODELS

There is a wide gap between raw images and an understanding of what is seen. It is too hard to bridge this wide gap with one giant leap. To identify, describe, and localize objects, we need intermediate representations that make various kinds of knowledge explicit and that expose various kinds of constraint:

• Facts about brightness values[1] are explicit in the *image.*

• Facts about brightness changes, groups of similar changes, blobs, and texture are explicit in the *primal sketch.*

• Facts about surfaces are explicit in the $2\frac{1}{2}$-*D sketch.*

• Facts about volumes are explicit in the *world model.*

Information in the primal sketch and the $2\frac{1}{2}$-D sketch makes explicit what is going on at each point in the original image. Hence the primal sketch and the $2\frac{1}{2}$-D sketch often are said to be *viewer centered.*

An *intrinsic image* consists of values for some single intrinsic characteristic at each image point, together with information about where there are discontinuities in that characteristic. Typical intrinsic characteristics, each associated with a different intrinsic image, are surface direction, distance, reflectance, and incident illumination. The $2\frac{1}{2}$-D sketch, therefore, can be viewed as an amalgam of certain intrinsic images.

Unlike the information in the primal sketch and the $2\frac{1}{2}$-D sketch image, the information in a world model often is expressed in terms of coordinate systems attached to objects. Such world models are said to be *object centered.*

The Primal Sketch Makes Brightness-change Facts Explicit

Information in the *primal sketch* is about things like brightness changes, groups of similar changes, blobs, and texture. Most of the information focuses on the rapid brightness changes associated with physical edges and edge-termination points. Figure 10-1 highlights the edge-description part of the primal sketch.

---

[1]   To be precise, *brightness* refers to image irradiance, the power per unit area falling on the image sensor.

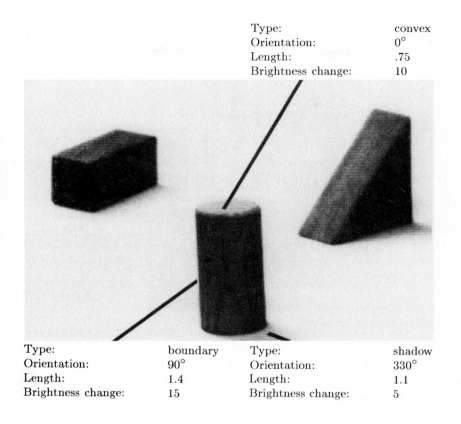

Type:	convex
Orientation:	0°
Length:	.75
Brightness change:	10

Type:	boundary	Type:	shadow
Orientation:	90°	Orientation:	330°
Length:	1.4	Length:	1.1
Brightness change:	15	Brightness change:	5

Figure 10-1. Some of the entries in the primal sketch are shown together with their reference points in the image they come from. The primal sketch makes facts about brightness changes explicit. The primal sketch is not an image; rather, the primal sketch is a description of an image.

Each edge-caused brightness change is associated with a description in the primal sketch that gives information like the following:

- The rate of brightness change and the overall change in brightness associated with the edge.

- The length, curvature, and orientation of the edge.

If the edge-finding procedure in use produces short fragments, grouping procedures must tie those short fragments together when their descriptions are compatible.

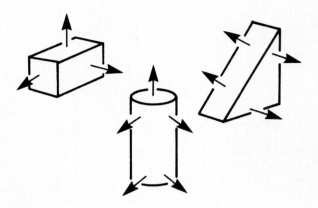

Figure 10-2. A needle diagram, an important part of the $2\frac{1}{2}$-D sketch. The arrows are vectors that are perpendicular to the surfaces they rest on; that is, they are surface normals.

The Two-and-a-half-dimensional Sketch Makes
Surface Facts Explicit

Information in the $2\frac{1}{2}$-*D sketch* is about surfaces. Figure 10-2 suggests the sort of surface direction information in the $2\frac{1}{2}$-D sketch. Surface normals stick out of the objects, making the objects look as if they were stuck full of needles. Indeed, this part of the $2\frac{1}{2}$-D sketch occasionally is called the *needle diagram*. Other information finding a natural home in the $2\frac{1}{2}$-D sketch would include the distance to the viewer from all parts of the image.

The World Model Makes Volume Facts Explicit

The next level of representation makes facts explicit about how objects fill space. One approach is to use *generalized cylinders*. Like many great ideas, the generalized-cylinder idea is simple. As shown in figure 10-3, an ordinary cylinder can be described as a circle moved along a straight line through its center. A wedge can be described as a triangle moved along a straight line through its center. More generally, a generalized cylinder is a *two-dimensional shape* moved along a line called the *axis*. The shape is kept at a constant angle with respect to the line. The shape may be any shape. The shape may vary in size as it is moved. The line need not be straight.

The idea is developed further in figure 10-4, where there are some objects with varying cross sections. For a cone, the circle shrinks linearly as it moves. For a bottle, the circle varies in a more complicated way along the axis.

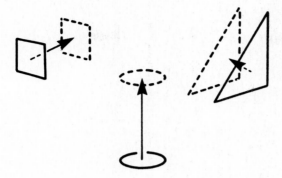

Figure 10-3. Two generalized cylinders, one describing a wedge, and another describing a cylinder. Each has a constant cross-section projected along a straight axis.

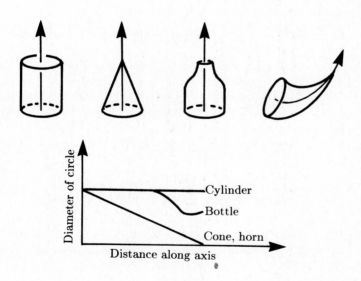

Figure 10-4. The generalized cylinder representation is good for a large class of objects. The simplest generalized cylinders are fixed, two-dimensional shapes projected along straight axes. In general, the size of the two-dimensional shape need not remain constant, and the axis need not be straight. Also, the two-dimensional shape may be arbitrarily complex.

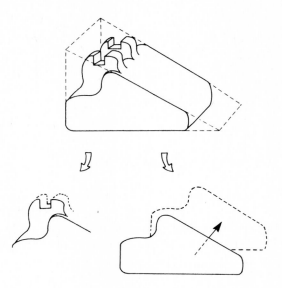

Figure 10-5. Complicated shapes can be described as combinations of simple generalized cylinders. A telephone is a vaguely wedge-shaped cylinder with U-shaped protrusions.

Complicated objects often consist of generalized cylinders stuck together. Typically, a dominant, central cylinder is modified by indentations and protrusions that themselves are cylinders. The result is like the compositions found in elementary books on drawing. In figure 10-5, for example, we have part of an old-fashioned telephone. A vaguely wedge-shaped generalized cylinder forms the body, while two U-shaped cylinders form the cradle.

Proper Vision-system Organization Is Hotly Argued

It seems likely that all powerful vision systems must use something like primal sketches, $2\frac{1}{2}$-D sketches, and world models. Unfortunately, however, it is not yet clear how information in one representation should influence the acquisition of information in another.

One possibility is that information flows *bottom up* through the various representations, with the computation at each stage depending only on the description produced at the immediately preceding stage. With bottom-up organization, the computation of the $2\frac{1}{2}$-D sketch, for example, needs information in the primal sketch, but the computation does not need information directly from the image and does not use any hints about the nature of what is to be seen. Each procedure used in the computation operates independently or nearly so.

Another possibility is that the computation of everything in the primal sketch and the $2\frac{1}{2}$-D sketch is done using *heterarchical constraint propagation*. Information from stereo processing, for example, helps improve the computation of surface direction from shading and vice versa. Information can flow in all directions.

Still another possibility is that image understanding really depends heavily on *controlled hallucination*, with information flowing *top down*, whereby early vision is guided by firm expectations about what is to be seen.

Perhaps it is best to be agnostic on the matter of vision-system organization inasmuch as controversy rages. As yet, no organization has been proved adequate, so there is not even the possibility of arguing about which is best. In this respect, image understanding is like language understanding.

One thing is clear nevertheless. Whatever organization is used, there must be a way to exploit the best information available, recognizing that the reliability of any particular aspect of the image will vary with the image being analyzed. Vision systems surely do better when they are sensitive to the quality of the information used in making decisions.

Consider *segmentation*, the problem of dividing an image into coherent regions corresponding to object faces. If one vision system always does this on the basis of just one facet of the image description, such as brightness, that vision system cannot do as well as another system that exploits the strongest of many facets, including such additional things as hue, saturation, surface orientation, and depth.

This is illustrated in figures 10-6 and 10-7. In figure 10-6, the house image is segmented on the basis of brightness alone. In figure 10-7, the segmentation is done using color measurements as well. Note the following:

- The chimney has nearly the same brightness as the sky. Segmentation was better in the color-exploiting mode.

- One of the bushes has nearly the same brightness as the grass. Segmentation was better in the color-exploiting mode.

- The sky is more or less uniformly bright, but the color varies considerably. Only the color-exploiting mode notes this.

COMPUTING EDGE DISTANCE

Having finished a rapid tour through representation land, we now attend to the localization of edges and the computation of depth from stereo information. Our purpose is to get a feel for the sort of computations needed to produce the $2\frac{1}{2}$-D sketch.

Figure 10-6. Segmentation is better if done with many parts of an image's description. In this illustration, only image brightness is used to segment. Courtesy of Keith Price.

Figure 10-7. Segmentation is better if done with many parts of an image's description. In this illustration, color is used as well as brightness to segment. Courtesy of Keith Price.

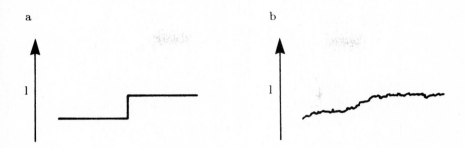

Figure 10-8. The brightness profile in *a* is that of an ideal edge between two flat faces. The one in *b* is that of a real edge.

Averaged and Differenced Images Highlight Edges

At the edge between two flat faces, brightness should change sharply from one value to another as shown in figure 10-8a. In practice, however, the steplike change generally is corrupted, as in figure 10-8b, making it hard to determine just where the edge is. One reason is that image input devices do not produce simple clean images. We must cope with variations in brightness sensitivity across the sensor, errors in image coordinate information, electronic noise, light-source hum, and inability to accept wide variations in brightness. Another reason is that images are complicated. Edges may be slightly rounded, rather than sharp, and there may be mutual-illumination effects, misleading scratches, fingerprints, and dust.

One way to cope with noisy edges involves four steps. The first step is to make an average-brightness array from the image. Local brightness averages reduce the influence of noise. The following formula illustrates the computation that needs to be done. For simplicity, the formula is a one-dimensional version of what is used in two dimensions. I_i is the image brightness at point i, and A_i is the local average of brightnesses around point i:

$$A_i = \frac{I_{i-1} + I_i + I_{i+1}}{3}$$

Next, make an average-first-difference array from the average-brightness array. To do this, we average the right-neighbor difference, $A_{i+1} - A_i$, and the left-neighbor difference, $A_i - A_{i-1}$. This is equivalent, of course, to averaging the right and left neighbors. F_i, then, is the average first difference of average brightness (and a finite difference approximation to the first derivative).

$$F_i = \frac{(A_{i+1} - A_i) + (A_i - A_{i-1})}{2} = \frac{A_{i+1} - A_{i-1}}{2}$$

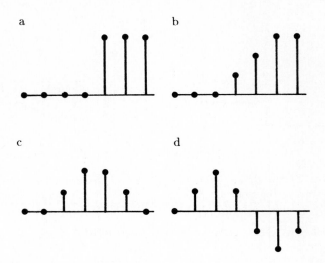

Figure 10-9. The steps in processing edge brightnesses. The brightness change that is to be analyzed is shown in *a*. Part *b* shows the same sequence after averaging. Part *c* shows the averaged differences of *b*, and *d* shows the averaged differences of *c*. The result in *d* localizes the step in *a*.

Next, make an average-second-difference array from the average-first-difference array. To do this, we average the first differences. S_i, then, is the average second difference of average brightness:

$$S_i = \frac{(F_{i+1} - F_i) + (F_i - F_{i-1})}{2} = \frac{F_{i+1} - F_{i-1}}{2}$$

Finally, work with the resulting array, taking note of peaks, steep slopes, and zero crossings, looking for edge-signaling combinations.

The averaging procedure transforms both perfect and noise-corrupted steps into smoothed steps. The first differencing procedure transforms smoothed steps into bumps. And the second differencing procedure transforms bumps into S-shaped curves that cross zero steeply between positive and negative peaks.

Figure 10-9 shows what these procedures do to a perfect step. The step shown in figure 10-9a becomes a smoothed step in 10-9b, a bump in 10-9c, and an S-shaped curve in 10-9d.

Somewhat miraculously, the effect of first averaging and then differencing can be combined into one grand averaging procedure. As shown by the following formula, the contribution of each input point, I_j, to an output point O_i varies according to the separation between the input point and

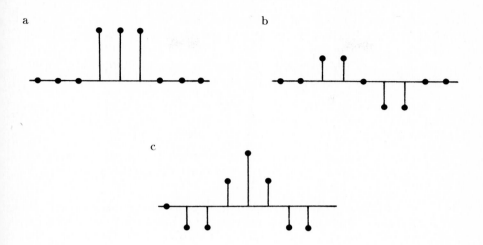

Figure 10-10. The first and second differences of an averaging point-spread function. Part *a* shows the averaging function. Part *b* shows the averaged neighboring differences of the point-spread function of *a*; it is also the point-spread function equivalent to averaging followed by the average of neighboring differences. Part *c* shows the averaged neighboring differences of the averaged first differences; using the function in *c* as the point-spread function is equivalent to averaging followed by two differencing steps.

the output point. P is the function that expresses how the contribution depends on the separation:

$$O_i = \sum_j P_{j-i} \times I_j$$

P is called a *point-spread function* because it shows how a single isolated nonzero brightness point would spread out its influence in an output image. When outputs are determined from inputs according to this formula, the output is said to be *filtered by* the point-spread function.[2]

Figure 10-10a shows the point-spread function equivalent to three-point, one-dimensional averaging. Figure 10-10b shows the point-spread function equivalent to averaging followed by averaging neighboring differences. And 10-10c shows the point-spread function equivalent to averaging followed by two rounds of averaging neighboring differences.

Of course the point-spread functions used with real images must combine the influence of many more points than those we have illustrated.

---

[2] *Convolution* is the more technical term for filtering.

Moreover, they must be two dimensional, not one dimensional. Nevertheless, there are reasonable computational arguments indicating that the peak-and-trough shape of our narrow, two-dimensional point-spread function is essentially correct and particularly convenient. Here is a synopsis of those computational arguments:

- Noise should be confronted by filtering with a point-spread function that attenuates high frequencies. The two-dimensional Gaussian function is a particularly good choice, better than averaging.

- Edges should be localized by two rounds of differencing. Importantly, the noise reduction of the Gaussian filtering cancels the noise enhancement of the differencing procedures.

- Two-dimensional Gaussian filtering followed by two rounds of two-dimensional differencing is equivalent to filtering with a single point-spread function that looks rather like a Mexican hat or sombrero. The sombrero shape is a two-dimensional analog to the peak-and-trough shape we argued for in one dimension.

- The two-dimensional Mexican-hat-shaped point-spread function is approximated closely by the difference between a narrow positive Gaussian point-spread function and a wide negative Gaussian point-spread function, as suggested by figure 10-11.

- Mathematically, filtering with two-dimensional Gaussian point-spread functions is equivalent to sequential filtering with two one-dimensional Gaussian point-spread functions, one vertical and the other horizontal. This means two-dimensional Gaussian filtering can be fast. Therefore sombrero filtering can be fast too.

The Primate Retina May Do Something Like Sombrero Filtering

The sombrero filter, attractive from the perspective of computational arguments, seems consistent with certain experiments aimed at understanding early vision processing in primates.

The key experiment is illustrated in figure 10-12. The experimental animal looks at a variety of stimuli moving across a white background. The stimuli include a thin black bar, a wide black bar, and a single white-to-black edge. Recording needles determine the response of various neurons. The neuron responses are compared with predictions based on sombrero filtering.

Figure 10-13 shows the results. Figure 10-13a shows brightness profiles for three left-to-right traveling stimuli. Figure 10-13b shows the result of filtering the given brightness profiles with a sombrero filter of appropriate width. Figure 10-13c shows the experimental data taken from what are called X ganglion cells. There are actually two kinds of X cells: the firing

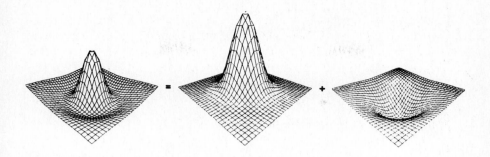

Figure 10-11. The point-spread function corresponding to Gaussian filtering followed by differencing is closely approximated by the difference of two appropriate Gaussians. Courtesy of W. Eric L. Grimson.

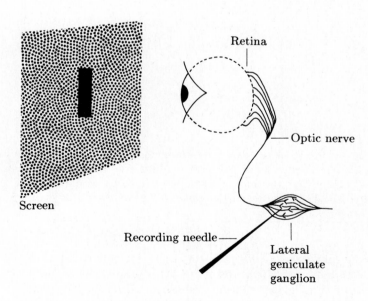

Figure 10-12. An experiment for exploring retinal input-output characteristics. The results are compared with those predicted on the basis of sombrero filtering.

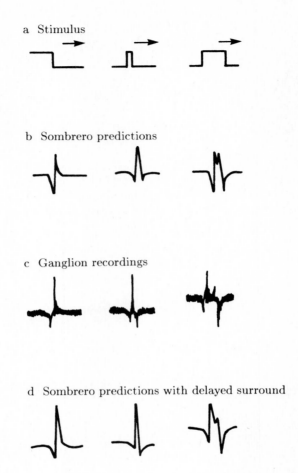

Figure 10-13. Part *a* shows some test stimuli for exploring retinal input-output characteristics. Part *b* shows the predicted response, as a function of time, at a single point in the processed image. Part *c* shows a recording made from a stimulated monkey. Part *d* shows a modified predicted response with a delay incorporated.

rate of one kind seems to resemble the positive part of the sombrero-filtered image; and the firing rate of the other seems to resemble the negative part. For ease of comparison, the data shown in figure 10-13c is actually the difference in the firing rates for the positive and negative cells. Comparison of figure 10-13b and figure 10-13c indicates encouraging similarities, suggesting that the primate retina may indeed do something like sombrero-filtering.

The similarity is improved if the sombrero filter is modified slightly. Recall that a sombrero filter is closely approximated by the difference of a narrow positive Gaussian and a wide negative Gaussian. If the response of the wide negative Gaussian is slightly delayed in time with respect to the response of the narrow positive one, then figure 10-13d shows the responses for the test stimuli. These new curves follow the primate data much better. The similarity is strong enough to lend support to the following conjectures:

- Part of the filtering done by the primate retina is computationally similar to filtering with a sombrero point-spread function.

- Since firing rate cannot be negative, there must be two populations of retinal cells. One population carries the positive part of the filtered image; the other population carries the negative part.

- For each of the two populations, the sombrero filter is implemented by a combination of excitation and inhibition. Together, the excitation and inhibition implement a filter equivalent to taking the difference of two two-dimensional Gaussian-filtered images. The surrounding inhibition effect is delayed slightly with respect to the central excitation effect.

Multiple-scale Stereo Enables Distance Determination

Stereo vision uses information from two eyes to determine distance. Stereo vision works because it is easy to find the distance to something once the thing is found in two images from eyes with known separation.

In figure 10-14, we see an image point, two lenses, and two image planes from above. The axes of the lenses are parallel. Both lenses are separated from the image planes by their focal length f, and they are separated from each other by a baseline distance b. The point P is at a distance l from the left lens axis and r from the right. Similarly, P appears on the left image at a distance α from the left lens axis and in the right image at a distance β from the right lens axis.

An easy way to find the formula relating object distance, d, to α and β is to write two equations derived from similar triangles:

$$\frac{d}{l} = \frac{d+f}{l+\alpha} \qquad \frac{d}{r} = \frac{d+f}{r+\beta}$$

These equations, with $b = l + r$, are easy to solve, giving the following expression for d:

$$d = \frac{fb}{\alpha + \beta}$$

Thus distance to a point is inversely proportional to $\alpha + \beta$, the amount of shift of the point's position in one image relative to the point's position in the other. This shift is called *disparity*.

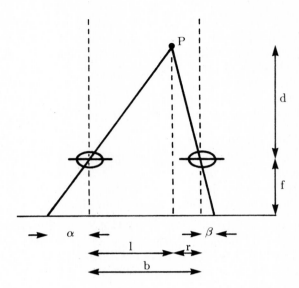

Figure 10-14. The geometry of the two eyes involved in doing stereo. The distance to the object, d, is given by $d = fb/(\alpha + \beta)$.

Of course, the real problem in stereo vision is to find corresponding things in the left and right images so that disparity can be measured. There are many different stereo-vision systems that find corresponding things with varying success. To understand them, several questions must be answered:

- What kind of visual entities does the stereo-vision system work with?

- How does the system match the visual entities in one image with the correct corresponding entities in the other?

- How does the system cope with ambiguous situations in which many equally plausible matches are possible?

To illustrate, we consider a stereo-vision procedure that focuses on the zero crossings in sombrero-filtered images. This one was selected because sombrero-filtering and zero-crossing matching are easy to understand. Understand that while sombrero-filtered images seem to be part of the biological stereo-vision story, the jury is still out on the matter of zero-crossing matching. There are many competing stereo-vision procedures.

Our zero-crossings-oriented procedure is based on three assumptions: first, that it is good to work with things that are easy to identify in both images of a stereo pair; second, that it is good to work with things that are easy to localize with good accuracy; and third, that steep zero crossings are easy to identify and to localize.

Figure 10-15. Matching with a simple stereo-matching procedure for zero crossings. The zero crossings in a slice are considered matched if they are nearest other-image neighbors.

To see how the procedure works, examine figure 10-15, which shows a narrow horizontal slice of two superimposed zero-crossing images. Zero crossings from the right image are shown solid and those from the left image are shown dashed. In the slice, we identify the closest dashed zero-crossing fragment for each solid zero-crossing fragment and vice versa. Thus, for each image, we find each zero crossing's nearest neighbor in the other image. Two zero crossings are considered matched if they are each others' nearest other-image neighbors and if they are closer than some specified distance from each other. Other zero crossings are ignored.

All this is captured in the following procedure. The width, w, involved is the width of the sombrero filter's central peak measured from zero crossing to zero crossing:

To determine initial correspondence:

1   Find zero crossings using a width w sombrero filter.

2   For each horizontal slice:

    2.1   Find the nearest neighbors for each zero-crossing fragment in the left image.

    2.2   Find the nearest neighbors for each zero-crossing fragment in the right image.

    2.3   For each pair of zero-crossing fragments that are the closest neighbors of one another, let the right fragment be separated by δ_{initial} from the left. Determine if δ_{initial} is within the matching tolerance, m. If so, consider the zero-crossing fragments matched with disparity δ_{initial}.

In the example, all pairs match, fortuitously. In general, however, there will be ambiguity and mismatch, for if the width, w, is small enough to give good resolution, there will be too much detail to match well.

Figure 10-16. Some blocks for demonstrating edge and stereo processing. The two pictures are arranged so that you can see depth yourself with the aid of a stereoscopic viewer.

To see why a large width eases matching, take off your glasses, if you wear them. All the fainter details blur out. Filtering with a wide sombrero filter has the same effect. Filtered versions of the blocks shown in figure 10-16 are shown in figure 10-17. The wider the filter is, the more the image is blurred.

As the sombrero filter gets wider, the blurring increases, and the number of zero crossings decreases, as shown in figure 10-18. With fewer zero crossings, the number of accidental mismatches is reduced.

Of course, a large sombrero width also gets rid of just the detail needed to make distance judgments precise. But we can burn this particular candle at both ends by working with more than one sombrero filter.

Figure 10-19 illustrates how. Assume that a wide sombrero filter, with width w, produces the zero crossings at the top. Pair a matches with a disparity of 11; pair b matches with a disparity of 9; and pair c matches with a disparity of 4.

Assume that a narrower sombrero filter, with width $\frac{w}{2}$, produces the zero crossings in the middle. Since the width is different, the zero crossings are in slightly different places. Note that the dotted line of pair b is equally close to two solid lines, suggesting difficulty.

Now comes the key step, however. Before matching the width $\frac{w}{2}$ zero crossings, we shift the right-eye, solid line zero crossings by the disparity obtained at width w. This gives us the zero crossings at the bottom. The initial disparity estimate, introduced by shifting, places these zero crossings close together, making matching easy. The final disparities are judged to be 10, 8, and 5.

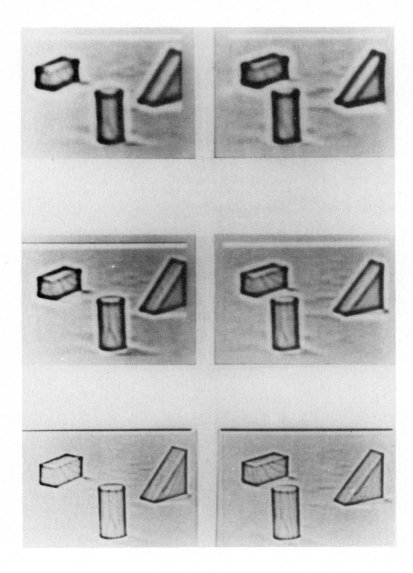

Figure 10-17. The result of sombrero filtering using sombrero filters ranging from wide to narrow. Courtesy of W. Eric L. Grimson.

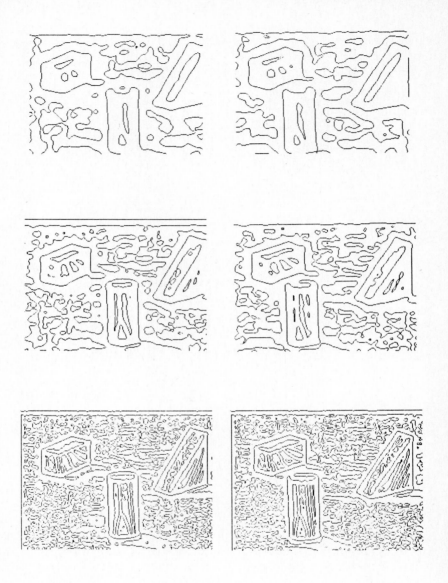

Figure 10-18. The result of sombrero filtering. Shown are the zero crossings found using sombrero filters ranging from wide to narrow. Courtesy of W. Eric L. Grimson.

In summary, here is the procedure for establishing final correspondence; it is a slightly altered version of the previously exhibited procedure for finding initial correspondence:

To determine final correspondence:

1. Find zero crossings using a sombrero filter of *reduced* width, $\frac{w}{2}$, rather than w.
2. For each horizontal slice:
   - 2.1 For each zero-crossing fragment in the left image:
       - 2.1.1 Determine the nearest zero-crossing fragment that matched when the sombrero filter width was w.
       - 2.1.2 Offset the zero-crossing fragment by a distance equal to $\delta_{initial}$, the disparity of the nearest matching zero-crossing fragment found at the lower resolution associated with filter width w.
   - 2.2 Find the nearest neighbors for each zero-crossing fragment in the left image.
   - 2.3 Find the nearest neighbors for each zero-crossing fragment in the right image.
   - 2.4 For each pair of zero-crossing fragments that are the closest neighbors of one another, let the right fragment be separated by δ_{new} from the left. Determine if δ_{new} is within the *reduced* matching tolerance, $\frac{m}{2}$. If so, consider the zero-crossing fragments matched with disparity $\delta_{final} = \delta_{new} + \delta_{initial}$.

Figure 10-19 shows how the procedure works. The zero-crossing fragments from a wide filter match, producing initial disparity estimates of 11, 9, and 4. Using these disparities, the narrow-filter, solid-line fragments are offset, bringing them into close proximity with the dashed-line fragments. Without the offset, one of the narrow-filter, dashed-line fragments would be equally close to two solid-line fragments.

If necessary, the match-offset-match cycle may be repeated many times to zero in on a precise disparity judgment. Generally, however, three or four cycles are sufficient.

Thus a key idea is to use results on intentionally blurred images to guide work on less blurred images. Sometimes the idea is called *multiple-scale image analysis*.

The sample stereo-vision procedure copes with ambiguous matches by using multiple-scale matching:

To find distance:
1   Use multiple-scale image analysis to find corresponding zero-crossing fragments.
2   Use zero-crossing-fragment disparity, δ_{final}, to find distance d.

Figure 10-20 shows what happens when a related, but more complicated stereo procedure works with the zero crossings shown in figure 10-19.

Having developed a stereo procedure, we now have one way to write information into the $2\frac{1}{2}$-D sketch, for distance information has its natural home there. Note that this information comes by way of the primal sketch, for zero crossings are part of edge description and edge description is part of the primal sketch.

In the next section, we develop another way to write into the $2\frac{1}{2}$-D sketch, this time using shading to produce surface-direction information. Since shading information is located in the raw image, we will be circumnavigating the primal sketch.

COMPUTING SURFACE DIRECTION

We now consider a procedure that computes surface-direction information from shading. Our purpose is to gain more exposure to the sort of computations needed to produce information for the $2\frac{1}{2}$-D sketch.

Reflectance Maps Embody Illumination Constraints

The amount of light we see reflected from a surface obviously depends on the material covering the surface. In addition, the amount of light we see depends on the various angles shown in figure 10-21: the *emergent* angle e between the surface normal and the viewer direction; the *incident* angle i between the surface normal and the light-source direction; and the *phase* angle g between the viewer direction and the light-source direction.

A *Lambertian surface* is a surface that looks equally bright from all possible viewpoints. The observed brightness depends only on the direction to the light source. The dependence is governed by the following formula, in which E is the observed brightness; ρ is the surface *albedo*, a constant for any particular surface material; and i is the incident angle:

$$E = \rho \cos i$$

In ordinary English, Lambertian surfaces are those that we would call matte or nonspecular. Lambertian surfaces are also called perfect diffusers.

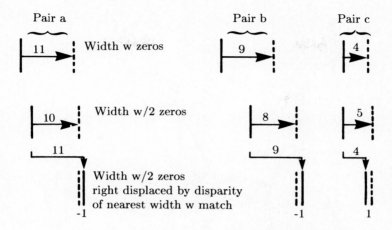

Figure 10-19. Matching with a simple stereo-matching procedure for zero crossings. Initial disparity estimates are made using a wide filter. The initial estimates are used to offset the estimates made using a narrow filter. Offset narrow-filter lines are easy to match.

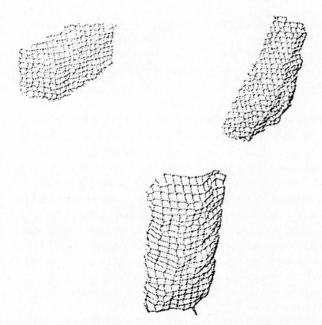

Figure 10-20. The results of stereo processing on a simple, three-block scene. Courtesy of W. Eric L. Grimson.

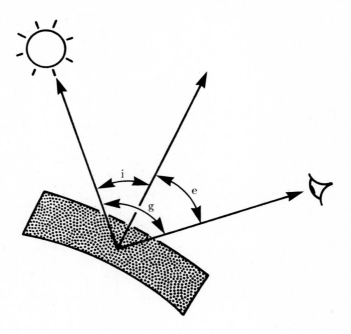

Figure 10-21. In this illustration, we have a surface-centered view of the relative positions of the viewer and the light source and the relative orientation of the surface. The angles are e between the surface normal and the viewer; i between the surface normal and the light source; and g between the viewer and the light source. For many surfaces, observed brightness is proportional to $\cos i$ and independent of e and g.

For some surfaces, our moon's in particular, the observed brightness varies not as $\cos i$, but as the ratio of $\cos i$ and $\cos e$. When the moon is full, that is, when the sun is behind us, $g = 0$ and $i = e$ for every point. Consequently $\cos i / \cos e$ is a constant, the observed brightness is constant, there is no dimming at the edges, and the moon looks flat.

Most surfaces, however, are more like Lambertian surfaces than they are like the moon. To develop a feel for how Lambertian surfaces reflect light, we could paint a sphere with Lambertian paint and observe this Lambertian sphere as a single-point light source is moved around. For each light-source position, we could keep notes on the dependence of the brightness on the direction of the surface normal. An easy way to keep these notes is to draw some *isobrightness lines*, lines along which the brightness has a constant value.

Figure 10-22 illustrates for three different light-source directions. In Figure 10-22a, the light is coming from directly behind the viewer, and the isobrightness lines are concentric circles. The brightest point, with a

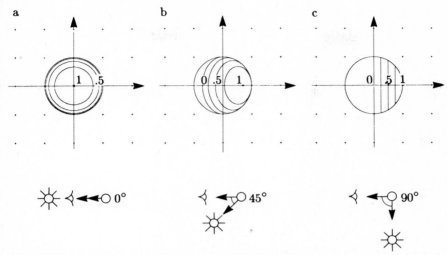

Figure 10-22. Isobrightness lines on images of Lambertian spheres illuminated from three different directions. The isobrightness lines are determined by the values of cos i. In a, the light source is directly behind the viewer, so the angle between the viewer direction and the light-source direction is 0°. In b, the light source is moved around to the right with the new angle being 45°. In c, the angle is 90°. Courtesy of Katsushi Ikeuchi.

brightness ρ, is the one for which the surface normal points directly at the viewer, since there cos $i = 1$. Brightness shades off toward the sphere's boundary, becoming 0 at the boundary, since cos $i = 0$ at the boundary.

In figure 10-22b, however, the circumstances are different because the light-source direction is different. The viewer direction and the light-source direction are now separated by 45°, not 0°. Again the brightest point has a brightness ρ, but now it is no longer the point for which the surface normal points toward the viewer. As always for Lambertian surfaces, the brightest point is the one for which the surface normal points toward the light source. Note that the line where the brightness is 0, while a circle on the sphere, is not part of a circle in our two-dimensional image of the sphere. The line where the brightness is 0 is sometimes called the *shadow line* or the *terminator*, particularly when talking about the Earth's moon.

Finally, in figure 10-22c, the light is coming in from the right, with the viewer direction and the light-source direction forming a right angle. Now the brightest point is on the edge of the sphere and the shadow line is straight as seen by the viewer.

Although illuminating, the spheres of figure 10-22 are not used in practice to keep track of the relation between surface orientation and brightness. Instead, the isobrightness lines are projected onto a flat surface, just as in

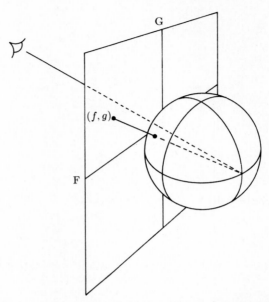

Figure 10-23. Points relating surface direction to observed brightness are projected from the surface of a sphere to the FG plane tangent to the sphere and parallel to the image plane.

making a map of the Earth. Projected isobrightness lines constitute what are called *reflectance maps.* There are many ways to make reflectance maps since there are many ways to project lines from a sphere to a plane, as we learn from cartographers, who are the custodians of this sort of knowledge.

One especially useful projection takes points on a unit sphere to points on a tangent plane where the coordinate axes are labeled F and G. The projection is done, as shown in figure 10-23, by drawing a straight line from the point on the sphere opposite the viewer, through the point to be projected, to the tangent FG plane. By convention, the FG plane is parallel to the viewer's image plane. Figure 10-24 shows what the isobrightness lines of figure 10-22 look like when projected onto the FG plane to form FG reflectance maps.

In some circumstances, it is more convenient to use a different projection called the PQ projection. Instead of projecting directions onto a tangent plane from the point on the sphere opposite the viewer, we project onto the plane from the center of the unit sphere, as shown in figure 10-25. Note that the location of the PQ plane is the same as for the FG projection; only the projecting point has changed.

Note that isobrightness lines in PQ space extend to infinity, as shown in figure 10-26.

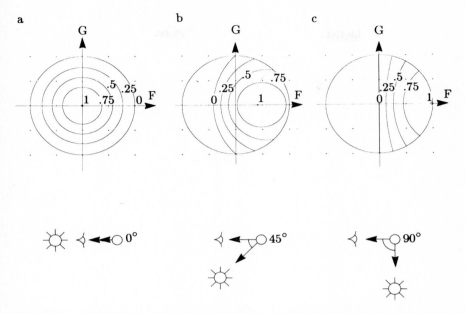

Figure 10-24. Isobrightness lines projected from a Lambertian sphere to the FG plane. Interestingly, the isobrightness lines are circles and arcs of circles because circles on the unit sphere always map into circles on the FG plane. In a, the angle between the viewer direction and the light-source direction is $0°$. In b the angle is $45°$. And in c, the angle is $90°$. Courtesy of Katsushi Ikeuchi.

Making Synthetic Images Requires a Reflectance Map

Given f and g for every point in an image, it is easy to determine the proper brightness at every point using an appropriate FG reflectance map.

Consequently, it is easy to synthesize artificial images of what the Earth looks like from satellites. All that is required is f and g for every point in the synthetic image and an FG reflectance map corresponding to the desired position for the sun. Getting f and g is straightforward, for f and g can be derived from elevation data. Getting an FG reflectance map is also straightforward, for we can start out assuming the Earth is covered with Lambertian paint. Figure 10-27 shows two synthetic images for a portion of the Rhone river valley lying in southwestern Switzerland. Note that one corresponds to morning; the other, to afternoon.

Albedo Images Picture Flattened Scenes

Recall that the observed brightness of a Lambertian surface may be written as the product of an albedo factor, ρ, and the cosine of the incident angle,

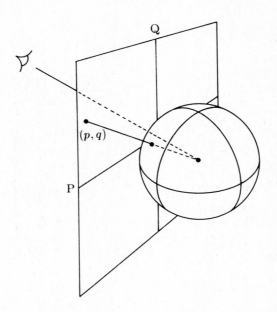

Figure 10-25. The PQ projection.

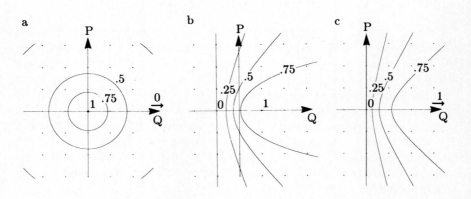

Figure 10-26. Isobrightness lines projected from a Lambertian sphere to the PQ plane. The isobrightness lines extend to infinity. In a, the angle between the viewer direction and the light-source direction is $0°$. In b the angle is $45°$. And in c, the angle is $90°$. Courtesy of Katsushi Ikeuchi.

Figure 10-27. Two synthetic images for the same terrain. One corresponds to morning; the other, to afternoon. Courtesy of Berthold K. P. Horn.

$\cos i$. This means that brightness can be written as a product of a term that depends on the material, ρ, and a term that depends on surface direction, which in turn depends on f and g:

$$E(x, y) = \rho_{\text{material}} \cos i$$

For many non-Lambertian surfaces, the dependence on incident angle will be different, but brightness still can be written as the product of an albedo factor and some reflectance function that depends on f and g:

$$E(x, y) = \rho_{\text{material}} R(f, g)$$

Many surface materials have different albedo factors while they share the same reflectance function. In satellite images, for example, most of the Earth's surface can be characterized by the same reflectance function even though the albedo function will vary according to the ground cover. Broad-leaf trees, for example, have a different albedo factor than conifers.

Knowing the albedos, then, can help determine what is on the ground. To determine the albedo at various points, (x, y), from observed brightness, we must attend to surface slope, since brightness depends not only on the albedo at (x, y), which is $\rho_{\text{material}}(x, y)$, but also on the value of the reflectance factor at (x, y), which is $R(f, g)$, where f and g are functions of x and y.

For a synthetic image, however, we can make $\rho = 1$ everywhere. Thus, for point (x, y), the real image brightness, $E_r(x, y)$, and the synthetic image brightness, $E_s(x, y)$, will differ by $\rho_{\text{material}}(x, y)$:

$$E_r(x, y) = \rho_{\text{material}}(x, y)R(f, g)$$
$$E_s(x, y) = R(f, g)$$

Obviously, then, $\rho_{\text{material}}(x, y) = E_r(x, y)/E_s(x, y)$. Said another way, the albedo at every point in an image can be determined by dividing the real image brightness by the corresponding synthetic image brightness. An *albedo image* is just the point-by-point division of a real image by the corresponding synthetic image.

Figure 10-28 shows a real image and an albedo image for the Rhone River valley shown before in figure 10-27. Note the following:

- Airglow and other atmospheric effects make the real image look hazy. To make good albedo maps, synthetic images should exhibit the same effects.

- The albedo image looks flatter than the real image since the effect of surface orientation on brightness is greatly diminished.

- There is a dark, V-shaped band in the albedo image. This band identifies the fruit orchards that dominate the lower slopes on the southern-facing sides of the valley.

The intermediate slopes are mostly pasture, with snow and rock appearing higher. The valley floor itself is mostly covered by vineyards.

Surface Shading Determines Surface Direction

So far, we have seen how to use surface direction to predict surface brightness. Now we go the other way, computing surface direction parameters f and g from perceived brightness.

At first, recovering surface direction by recovering f and g might seem impossible, for the brightness of a small piece of surface determines only a curve in FG space rather than a single point. In fact, recovery is possible, but only because surfaces vary smoothly for the most part. There are few discontinuities in depth or direction. Consequently there are two constraints to exploit, not just one:

- *Brightness.* The surface direction, pinned down by f and g, should not vary much from what the brightness of the surface demands.

- *Surface smoothness.* The surface direction at one point should not vary much from the surface direction at neighboring points.

Figure 10-28. A real image and an albedo image. The albedo image is made by dividing each brightness in the real image by the brightness in a synthetic image. The resulting ratios are determined by surface cover—snow, rock, and various kinds of vegetation—rather than by a combination of surface cover and surface slope. Courtesy of Berthold K. P. Horn.

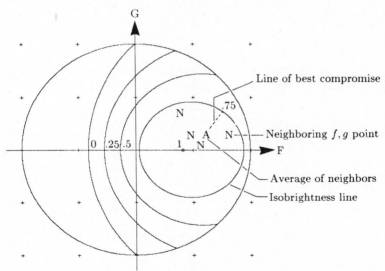

Figure 10-29. The f and g value for a point in an image can be computed by compromising between the value suggested by brightness and the value suggested by surface smoothness. In this illustration, the f and g values for neighboring image points are at points marked N. Their average is at A. The good compromises are points on the perpendicular line from the image point's isobrightness contour to A.

Each point's calculated f and g values should be some compromise between the values suggested by each of the two constraints. In figure 10-29, brightness suggests that a particular point's f and g values should lie on the isobrightness line shown. Meanwhile smoothness suggests that the f and g values should lie near the average of the values at neighboring points.

Intuitively, it makes sense to pick a point somewhere between the average point and the isobrightness line. Two questions remain, however. First, exactly where is somewhere; and second, how do we happen to know the correct values for the neighbors. Here are two reasonable answers:

- Compromise at some point on a line that passes through the average point and that is perpendicular to the isobrightness line.

- Start by assuming that all points with unknown f and g have $f = 0$ and $g = 0$. Find new values for each point by compromise between the average point of the initial values and the isobrightness line. Repeat using updated values until f and g values stop changing much.

Thus f and g can be found by relaxation, starting with some assumptions that disappear into oblivion after a few steps. We need some values for f and g to anchor the process, however. Happily, there usually are some such points. On the occluding boundaries of objects without sharp edges, surface direction is perpendicular to the viewer's line of sight. All such directions project onto a circle of radius two in FG space. The exact point on the circle is such that the circle's direction in FG space and the occluding boundary's direction in the image are the same.

Now it is clear why we use FG space instead of PQ space. On the PQ plane, boundary points are off at infinity and cannot be used to anchor our attack on f and g.

To verify that all this makes sense requires a little worthwhile, but optional, calculus, to which we now divert ourselves briefly. Consider two error measures, one capturing departures from smoothness, e_1, and the other capturing departures from predicted brightness, e_2:

$$e_1 = \sum_i \sum_j (f_{i,j} - \bar{f}_{i,j})^2 + (g_{i,j} - \bar{g}_{i,j})^2$$

$$e_2 = \sum_i \sum_j (E_{i,j} - R(f_{i,j}, g_{i,j}))^2$$

where

$$\bar{f}_{i,j} = \tfrac{1}{4}(f_{i+1,j} + f_{i,j+1} + f_{i-1,j} + f_{i,j-1})$$

$$\bar{g}_{i,j} = \tfrac{1}{4}(g_{i+1,j} + g_{i,j+1} + g_{i-1,j} + g_{i,j-1})$$

The total error is then $e = e_1 + \lambda e_2$, where λ is a constant chosen to put the two kinds of error in reasonable balance. To find values for $f_{i,j}$ and

$g_{i,j}$ that minimize the total error, we differentiate with respect to $f_{i,j}$ and $g_{i,j}$, setting the results to zero, producing the following equations:

$$f_{i,j} = \bar{f}_{i,j} + \lambda(E_{i,j} - R(f_{i,j}, g_{i,j}))\left(\frac{\partial R}{\partial f_{i,j}}\right)$$

$$g_{i,j} = \bar{g}_{i,j} + \lambda(E_{i,j} - R(f_{i,j}, g_{i,j}))\left(\frac{\partial R}{\partial g_{i,j}}\right)$$

Set up this way, these equations suggest solution by way of rules relating the values of f and g on the $(n+1)$th iteration, $f_{i,j}^{n+1}$ and $g_{i,j}^{n+1}$, to the values on the nth iteration, $f_{i,j}^n$ and $g_{i,j}^n$:

$$f_{i,j}^{n+1} = \bar{f}_{i,j}^n + \lambda(E_{i,j} - R(f_{i,j}^n, g_{i,j}^n))\left(\frac{\partial R}{\partial f_{i,j}}\right)^n$$

$$g_{i,j}^{n+1} = \bar{g}_{i,j}^n + \lambda(E_{i,j} - R(f_{i,j}^n, g_{i,j}^n))\left(\frac{\partial R}{\partial g_{i,j}}\right)^n$$

where $f_{i,j}^0 = 0$ and $g_{i,j}^0 = 0$.

These rules are called relaxation formulas. Using these relaxation formulas amounts to improving f and g estimates by taking a step from the previous estimate toward the isobrightness line along a perpendicular to that isobrightness line. The size of the step is proportional to the difference between the observed brightness and that predicted by the current f and g values. The size is also proportional to the error-balancing parameter, λ.

Procedures using such relaxation formulas are usually called *relaxation procedures*. Sometimes they are called *cooperative procedures* because they reach for compromises influenced by all the available constraints.

To calculate surface direction using relaxation:

1   Call the input array the current array. For all nonboundary points, let $f = 0$ and $g = 0$. For all boundary points, let f and g define a vector of length 2 normal to the boundary.

2   Until all values are changing sufficiently slowly:

   2.1   For each point in the current array:

   2.1a   If the point is a boundary point, do nothing.

   2.1b   If the point is a nonboundary point, compute a new value for f and g using the relaxation formulas.

   2.2   Call the new array the current array.

In some situations, not yet specifiable mathematically, f and g converge, producing consistent values. Figure 10-30 shows a sample image and result.

Figure 10-30. A vase and the surface computed from it using relaxation. The vase was designed by the Finnish architect Alvar Aalto. Courtesy of Katsushi Ikeuchi.

INTERPRETING SIMPLE BINARY IMAGES

Limited applied vision goals enable shortcuts. In some situations, it is possible to go directly from an image to object identification and location. In the simplest situations, it is even possible to use a *binary image*, one with only two levels of brightness, zero and one.

The Feature-space Paradigm Enables Binary-image Identification

The most direct approach to using simple binary images is through a two-part system consisting of a feature extractor and a feature evaluator. The feature extractor measures simple things like an object's image area. Values obtained by the feature extractor become the coordinates of a *feature point* in *feature space*, a multidimensional space in which there is one dimension for each feature measured. To identify an unknown object, we compare the distances between the unknown's feature point and those of various idealized possibilities. The most likely identity is determined by the smallest distance. Figure 10-31 shows the points determined by some electrical-box covers in a box-cover feature space.

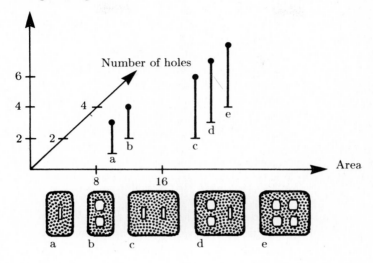

Figure 10-31. A feature space. An unknown object is identified according to the distances between the unknown and the models.

Generally, speed and discrimination considerations determine which features are used in particular situations. The following are typical of the candidates:

- Total object image area

- Hole area

- Number of holes

- Perimeter length

- Minimum distance from center of area to edge

- Maximum distance from center of area to edge

- Average distance from center of area to edge

- Length of major axis of ellipse of equal inertia moment

- Length of minor axis of ellipse of equal inertia moment

- Total area minus hole area

- Ratio of hole area to total area
- Ratio of perimeter squared to area

Sample feature combinations from images of real objects may form uniform, multidimensional Gaussian clusters around the ideal points in feature space. Often, however, all sorts of complications interfere with straightforward analysis: the feature points may not cluster equally close about each of the object centers; the features may interact with each other producing elliptical rather than symmetric distributions; or worst of all, the clusters may not look Gaussian.

Dealing analytically with such feature spaces has proved mathematically challenging, so it is there in feature-space that most of the work has been done. For some classes of problems, the results have been worthwhile. Today, the practitioner of feature-space vision does well when images satisfy two criteria:

- The values exhibited by the characteristic features do not change much over the range of circumstances likely to be encountered.
- The measurement of each characteristic feature over the entire image is dominated by the measurement of the characteristic over the object immersed in the image.

These criteria help explain why classifying a single well-framed, electrical-box cover is different from deciding if a room has a telephone in it. A telephone looks different when rotated or seen from different points of view, and from any point of view, a telephone has only minor influence on any globally measured quality.

CONSIGHT Uses Structured Light
To Simplify Image Thresholding

The obvious way to get a binary image is to compare each brightness in a gray-level image with a threshold. If the brightness is above the threshold, the binary value is taken to be one; otherwise, zero.

For many years, the utility of binary-image identification was thought to be limited because good thresholding is difficult in practice. Our purpose now is to see that there is a way to rescue binary-image identification, even though objects may be specular, transparent, or covered with paint of wildly varying albedo.

First, a system is said to use *structured light* whenever the system's operation depends critically on special light arrangements. Rather than thresholding ordinary images, the clever CONSIGHT system uses the structured-light arrangement shown in figure 10-32. CONSIGHT builds up the equivalent of a binary image as objects pass through two planar sheets of light projected onto a moving conveyor belt at 45° angles.

When there is no object in view, the planar sheets of light make a bright line across the belt. Where the planar sheets are obstructed by an object, the light is displaced, as seen from above, because the planar sheets go in at 45° angles.

The camera has a long, narrow field of view; it looks only at where the bright line usually is, ignoring any displaced light. At any instant, therefore, the camera sees a bright line interrupted by a dark gap whose length is the object's width measured across the conveyor belt. The gap grows and shrinks as the object's width increases and decreases at the camera position. A sequence of belt positions therefore produces a sort of silhouette of an object equivalent to a binary picture, as in figure 10-33.

Unfortunately, CONSIGHT cannot deal with parts lying jumbled in a bin. For applications involving simple parts lying separated on a conveyor belt, however, CONSIGHT works just fine.

Of course, simple binary vision systems are not all there is to building interesting robots. Eventually, robots should have more sophisticated vision systems, as well as the manipulation and reasoning capabilities described in the next section.

ROBOTICS

Having finished our discussion of vision, we now glance at some other parts of the field of robotics. Of course, we must be content with sniffing a few corks, for we cannot drink all of the wine. We mention some of the problems, hint at some of the solutions, but supply no details.

Robots should have many of the capabilities we have, although not necessarily achieved in the same way. Here are some of those capabilities:

- *Sensors and sensor understanding.* Vision is our primary sensing capability. Force and touch are also important. These capabilities enable us humans to find things, to make new things, and to fix broken things.

- *Manipulators and manipulator control.* We have fantastic arms capable of fast, accurate motion, together with extremely flexible, sensor encrusted hands, capable of grasping all sorts of objects dexterously. Much of this capability is derived from the liberal use of tendons and the careful arrangement of joints.

- *Object- and space-oriented problem solving.* We move around, in spite of clutter, without bumping into things. We read blueprints, study instructions, build jigs, and select tools. We visualize how parts might fit together. We plan and execute mating strategies for things that fit together tightly, avoiding binding.

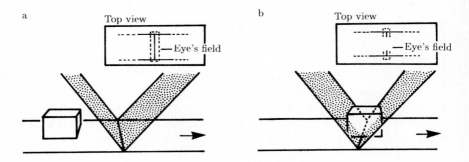

Figure 10-32. The CONSIGHT system for making binary images. In *a*, two projected planes of light produce a line across a conveyor belt. The box is not yet close enough to have an effect. In *b*, the box interrupts both planes of light: the right plane produces a displaced line across the top of the box; while the left plane strikes the side.

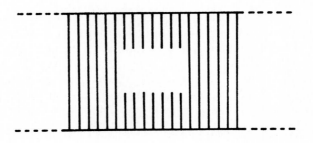

Figure 10-33. The image of a box as seen by CONSIGHT. As a box moves past the camera's narrow field of view, gaps are produced in the line seen by the camera. These gaps constitute a negative image of the light-displacing box.

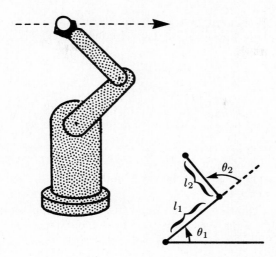

Figure 10-34. A robot arm throwing a ball. The robot must know the joint-angles that produce the straight line motion shown, and it must know how to apply torques that produce the desired joint-angles.

Of course, robots need not resemble people. After all, they are built of different materials, and they must cope with the factory, not the jungle and savanna that dominated most of our history. Consequently, intelligent robots will do things in different ways and think things through with different, nonanthropomorphic procedures. Still, at a certain level of abstraction, they must have the same capabilities: they must sense; they must move; and they must reason.

To get a better feel for the problems raised by a desire to achieve these various capabilities, as they might be exhibited by robots, we now consider some representative problems associated with manipulator control and with spatial reasoning, adding a little to the previous discussion of vision. Naturally this brief treatment is intended to illustrate the flavor of the problems involved, rather than to enable deep understanding.

Robots Need the Mathematics of Kinematics and Dynamics

Consider the problem of moving a hand along a prescribed path in space, as in figure 10-34. To succeed, we clearly need to know how joint angles dictate manipulator positions, for joint angles are the things that sensors sense.

Relating the joint angles to manipulator position and orientation is a *kinematics* problem. It is relatively easy to derive formulas that relate manipulator position and orientation to joint angles. For the two-joint, two-dimensional manipulator shown in figure 10-34, it is also relatively easy to derive the inverse formulas relating joint angles to manipulator position:

$$\theta_2 = \cos^{-1}\left(\frac{x^2 + y^2 - l_1^2 - l_2^2}{2l_1l_2}\right)$$

$$\theta_1 = \tan^{-1}\left(\frac{y}{x}\right) - \tan^{-1}\left(\frac{l_2\sin\theta_2}{l_1 + l_2\cos\theta_2}\right)$$

In general, however, it is impossibly hard to derive the inverse formulas that relate joint angles to manipulator position and orientation. To make the formula inversion practicable, it is necessary to impose constraints on how arms are designed.

We are not finished with motion, however. Given some formulas for joint angles, it might seem easy to move a manipulator: just chop the desired trajectory up into pieces, determine the necessary joint angles at the end of each piece, and tell the motors about the results. Unfortunately, the thing you tell to most motors is the torque you want them to supply, not the angles you want them to achieve in a joint.

If fast motion is not important, simple feedback loops solve the translation problem by making each motor's torque proportional to its joint-angle error. Unfortunately, fast motion is important, and simple feedback loops cannot include the necessary information in their calculations.

Relating joint motions to required motor torques is a *dynamics* problem. Like the kinematics problem, the arm-and-hand dynamics problem can be unbearably intricate mathematically, even though everything ultimately is just a matter of Newton's second law: force = mass × acceleration. Here is the complicated-looking result, ignoring gravity, assuming cylindrical links, for the mere two-joint, two-dimensional manipulator shown in figure 10-34:

$$\tau_1 = \ddot{\theta}_1\left(I_1 + I_2 + m_2l_1l_2\cos\theta_2 + \frac{m_1l_1^2 + m_2l_2^2}{4} + m_2l_1^2\right)$$
$$+ \ddot{\theta}_2\left(I_2 + \frac{m_2l_2^2}{4} + \frac{m_2l_1l_2}{2}\cos\theta_2\right)$$
$$- \dot{\theta}_2^2\frac{m_2l_1l_2}{2}\sin\theta_2$$
$$- \dot{\theta}_1\dot{\theta}_2 m_2l_1l_2\sin\theta_2$$
$$\tau_2 = \ddot{\theta}_1\left(I_2 + \frac{m_2l_1l_2}{2}\cos\theta_2 + \frac{m_2l_2^2}{4}\right)$$
$$+ \ddot{\theta}_2\left(I_2 + \frac{m_2l_2^2}{4}\right)$$
$$+ \dot{\theta}_1^2\frac{m_2l_1l_2}{2}\sin\theta_2$$

where each τ_i is a torque, each θ_i is an angular velocity, each $\ddot{\theta}_i$ is an angular acceleration, each m_i is a mass, each l_i is a length, and each I_i is a moment of inertia about a center of mass.

Needless to say, the solution for manipulators with more joints is bulkier, but necessary, since it is possible to show that six joints are required to position a manipulator at a given position in space with a given orientation. Like the solution for two joints, the real-world solutions demonstrate that the required torques depend, in general, on accelerations, on velocities squared, on velocity products, and on multipliers that depend on joint position:

- Because there are velocities squared, the torques necessarily involve *centripetal forces*.

- Because there are products of different velocities, the torques involve *Coriolis forces*.

- Because there are multipliers that are functions of several angles, the torques involve *variable, cross-coupled moments of effective inertia*.

Although the formulas are complicated, they must be used in full, for even at moderate speeds, the velocity terms can dominate the acceleration terms. Happily, there are fast ways to do the computation as arms move. But even with precisely determined torques, there still is a need for feedback, for errors introduced by friction, noise, and measurement inaccuracy must be corrected.

Robots Need Mixed Position and Force Control

Suppose, for example, that a manipulator is to write its name on the blackboard, as shown in figure 10-35. To write, the manipulator must press the chalk into the blackboard hard enough to leave a mark, but not so hard as to break the chalk. Also, the manipulator must control the position of the chalk in the plane of the blackboard.

If there were exactly one joint motor assigned to dealing with each force and position, control would be simple. But in problems like this, the natural coordinates of the problem are related to the joint angles by the complicated geometry of the manipulator. The complicated geometry couples everything together.

Moving from classroom world to workshop world, consider driving the screw shown in figure 10-36. Again there is a need for mixed force and position control. There must be position control to keep the screwdriver from slipping out of the screwhead, and there must be force control to turn the screw and to drive it home.

With well-chosen coordinate systems, many force-and-position-control problems can be viewed as problems of augmenting simple natural constraints with simple user-specified constraints. For the screw, for example,

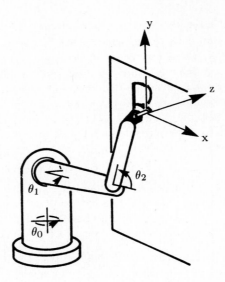

Figure 10-35. The blackboard problem. To write its name on the blackboard, the robot must control force into the blackboard and position in the plane of the blackboard. Correcting a force error will require action in all the arm's motors, introducing position errors. The interaction occurs because the natural coordinate systems of the problem and the arm have a complicated relationship.

Figure 10-36. Well-chosen coordinate systems make problem description and solution easier. The constraints involved in driving a screw are described most easily in a coordinate system attached to the end of the screwdriver blade.

the well-chosen coordinate system is one attached to the head of the screw, moving as the screw moves. Slipping is prevented by the combination of the natural constraint on y position enforced by the slot, together with a user-specified constraint on x position enforced by a manipulator. Good contact is ensured through a user-specified constraint on z force.

After getting the coordinate system right, the next problem is to relate forces and positions expressed in that coordinate system to motor torques and motor positions. This is a tractable problem in matrix and vector manipulation. But beyond knowing what forces to apply and positions to maintain, there is a need to keep those forces and positions on target, in spite of error and noise.

Of course, industrial assembly does not require robots to write their names on blackboards or to drive screws with workshop-style screwdrivers. There are many industrial analogs, however. One analog, involved in more than half of all industrial assembly procedures, is the peg-and-hole part-mating problem. This problem is encountered, for example, when fasteners go in holes, when rotors are installed in motors, and when pistons go into engine blocks. These things can be done only by a combination of force and position control, or said another way, by achieving *compliant motion*.

Robots Need Spatial Reasoning

Before a robot begins to move, it must think of a path to get to where it wants to be without bumping into things, possibly breaking something delicate. This holds for locomotion of the whole robot through a cluttered environment and for manipulator motion through a component-filled workspace.

Figure 10-37 illustrates the motion problem abstractly. In the figure, there is a triangular robot that wants to move, without turning, to the new position indicated by the dashed-line triangle. The issue is Can the robot make it through the strait between the two obstacles?

In two dimensions, a profound trick makes the problem easy. The general idea of the trick is to transform the problem into a different, simplifying representation, solve the problem in the simplifying representation, and transform the solution back into the original representation. Overall, this is like doing multiplication by moving back and forth between numbers and their logarithms, and it is like doing signal analysis by moving to and from the domain of Fourier transforms.

For obstacle avoidance, the transformation is from the space of moving objects and obstacles to the space of points and larger, virtual obstacles called *configuration-space objects*. Figure 10-38 shows how to make a configuration-space object using the object to be moved and the obstacle to be avoided.

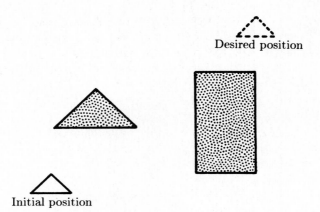

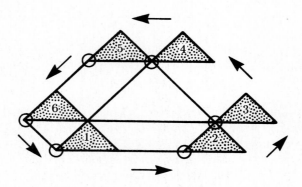

Figure 10-37. An obstacle-avoidance problem. The problem is to move the small triangular robot to a new position, shown dotted, without bumping into the large triangle or the rectangle.

Figure 10-38. The configuration-space transformation. The heavy line shows the locus of the small triangle's lower left corner as the small triangle is moved around the big one. Numbered positions are the starting points for each straight-line run. Keeping the lower left corner away from the heavy line keeps the small triangle away from the large one.

Desired configuration space position

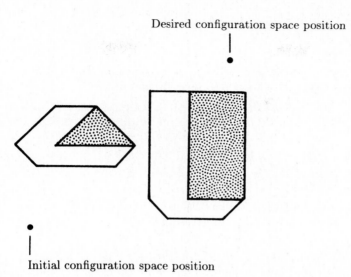

Initial configuration space position

Figure 10-39. The configuration space for the problem shown in figure 10-37. No collision occurs if the point is kept out of the shaded area. The original obstacles are shown cross hatched.

Imagine sliding the object around the obstacle, maintaining it in contact at all times. As shown in figure 10-38, we keep track of one arbitrary tracing point on the moving object as we go. As the tracing point moves around the obstacle, it builds a six-sided fence. Convince yourself that there can be no collision between object and obstacle as long as the tracing point stays outside the fence. The fence defines the configuration-space obstacle associated with the original obstacle.

Figure 10-39 supplies the configuration-space obstacles made from the original triangle and square obstacles shown in figure 10-37. The lower left vertex of the triangular robot was used. Evidently the robot can get through the gap since the configuration-space obstacles are not large enough to close up the space.

To use the configuration-space transform more generally, it is necessary to consider rotations. This quickly makes the problem attractive to complication-loving mathematicians. Conceptually, however, one approach is simple: first make several configuration spaces corresponding to various degrees of rotation for the moving object; then generalize the search to move not only through individual configuration spaces, but also from space to space.

SUMMARY

- Various representations are required to bridge the gap between an image and a description of the objects that appear. By one account, at least a primal sketch, a $2\frac{1}{2}$-D sketch, and a world model are needed.

- Facts about brightness changes go into the primal sketch; facts about surfaces go into the $2\frac{1}{2}$-D sketch; and facts about volumes go into the world model.

- Vision systems may be bottom up, top down, or somewhere in between. The matter attracts great controversy, with no organization standing as a clear winner.

- Much vision research explores the constraints the world imposes on images. Work on binocular stereo and on extracting shape from shading are representative successes.

- A difference-of-Gaussians, sombrero filter combines smoothing and differencing. A sombrero filter is one mechanism for highlighting edges.

- Stereo vision depends on matching things in one image with things in another. Multiple-scale matching of the zero crossings in sombrero-filtered images is one technique.

- Reflectance maps are representations of reflectance constraints. Reflectance maps enable the creation of albedo images in which the effect of surface orientation on brightness is eliminated.

- Surface direction can be recovered from shading by compromising between smoothness and brightness constraints.

- The feature-space identification paradigm concentrates on global feature extraction followed by feature-space gymnastics. The results often have practical value in solving applied problems, especially when structured light can be used.

- Intelligent robots must sense, move, and reason. Motion requires the mathematics of kinematics and dynamics. Dealing with contact requires mixed force and position control. Getting places requires spatial reasoning.

REFERENCES

David Marr is the person most associated with the idea of organizing vision research around the constraints imposed by nature. For a full account, including a discussion of the primal sketch and the $2\frac{1}{2}$-D sketch, see Marr's book, *Vision* [1982], published posthumously.

Marr borrowed the generalized-cylinder idea from Thomas O. Binford, who first wrote about it in an obscure paper [Binford 1971]. Representing things at the world-model level is hard, but Binford, with his notion of generalized cylinders, has opened a crack for us to widen. Happily, Binford has become more prolific, writing some excellent papers on vision in general [Binford 1981, 1982].

John M. Hollerbach used generalized cylinders, together with a representation for protrusions and indentations, to describe Greek vases [1976]. In many respects, Hollerbach's ideas resemble those involved in the PADL language, developed by H. B. Voelcker, Aristides A. Requicha, Christopher M. Brown, and others, for describing parts. For a good general introduction to PADL and similar languages, see Requicha [1980].

The work by Rodney A. Brooks is also a milestone, for it is the primary reference on ACRONYM, the generalized-cylinder-oriented vision system described in chapter 6; Brooks is particularly clear about his ideas for making image predictions from object models and a viewpoint [1981]. For more recent work on describing shape, see Takeo Kanade [1981] and J. Michael Brady [1983].

The idea of intrinsic images belongs to Harry G. Barrow and Jay M. Tenenbaum [1978, 1981]. In their paper introducing the idea, they proposed important ideas for combining relaxation within a single intrinsic image with relaxation among multiple intrinsic images.

For a discussion of segmentation using multiple cues, see work by Ronald B. Ohlander [1975], and by Ohlander, Keith Price, and D. Raj Reddy [1979]. In their work, they segment a variety of natural scenes, ranging from a living room to a house, using red, green, and blue brightness values, together with measures derived from those values, namely overall brightness, hue, saturation, and the color TV parameters Y, I, and Q.

Hans P. Morevec first brought the idea of multiple-scales analysis to stereo [1977].

The first proposal to use zero crossings in stereo was by Marr and Tomaso Poggio [1979]. Their stress on the use of zero crossings was amplified in the work of Ellen C. Hildreth on edge detection [1980]. For a review of earlier edge detection work, see *Digital Picture Processing* [1976], by Azriel Rosenfeld and Avinash C. Kak.

For a more recent study of biological stereo, with arguments that zero crossings are not enough, see John E. W. Mayhew and John P. Frisby [1981].

The stereo correspondence procedure introduced in this chapter is based on that of W. Eric L. Grimson. See Grimson's book *From Images to Surfaces* [1981] for details. Grimson's book also covers his procedure for surface reconstruction between points of known depth. Building on Grimson's results, Demetri Terzopoulos subsequently introduced an improved surface reconstruction procedure that handles discontinuities better, works faster, and allows multiple sources of depth and orientation data [1983].

The idea of zero crossings and of multiple scales is important in many aspects of vision. One example is the work of J. Michael Brady on reading printed text [1981]. Another is the work of Andy Witkin on analyzing signals such as those involved in oil-well data logging [1983].

Berthold K. P. Horn is responsible for our understanding of the relation between shape and shading. His work dates back to his thesis [1970, 1975]. Horn also introduced the needle diagram for surface representation [1982].

Katsushi Ikeuchi and Horn show how needle diagrams can be produced from shading and occluding boundaries using relaxation procedures [1981]. Robert J. Woodham shows how to use multiple light sources to produce needle diagrams [1978, 1981]. Philippe Brou shows how to use needle diagrams to determine identity and orientation [1983].

For an excellent survey of how constraint propagation works in vision, see Larry S. Davis and Azriel Rosenfeld [1981]. Also see Rosenfeld, Robert A. Hummel, and Steven W. Zucker [1976] and Robert M. Haralick, Larry S. Davis, and Rosenfeld [1978]. For a mathematical treatment, with attention to convergence, see Hummel and Zucker [1983].

For early work on unraveling the mysteries of biological vision systems see papers by Horace B. Barlow [1953], Jerome Lettvin, R. R. Maturana, W. S. McCulloch, and W. H. Pitts [1959], and David H. Hubel and Thorsten N. Wiesel [1962].

For a discussion of zero crossings and the primate retina, see Jacob Richter and Shimon Ullman [1982].

Of some historical interest is a paper by me that gives a description of the first system for copying reasonably general blocks-world structures from samples [Winston 1972].

There are now several textbooks on vision. *Robot Vision* [1984], by Horn, takes readers on several adventures in applied mathematics, explained beautifully. Also among the best are *Computer Vision*, by Dana H. Ballard and Christopher M. Brown and *Machine Perception*, by Ramakant Nevatia. The first part of *Pattern Recognition and Scene Analysis*, by Richard O. Duda and Peter E. Hart [1973], is excellent introductory material on feature-space-based recognition. The second part, concentrating on line-drawing analysis, has aged a bit, however.

CONSIGHT was developed at the General Motors Research laboratory. For details, see Stephen W. Holland, Lothar Rossol, and Mitchell R. Ward [1979].

For a discussion of issues in manipulation and manipulator control, see the textbook, *Robot Manipulators: Mathematics, Programming, and Control* [1981], by Richard P. Paul, and see the introduction to *Robot Motion: Planning and Control* [1982], edited by J. Michael Brady, John M. Hollerbach, Timothy L. Johnson, Tomás Lozano-Pérez, and Matthew T. Mason. For work on dynamics, see especially the papers by Hollerbach in *Robot Motion: Planning and Control*.

For work on reasoning about forces, see Matthew T. Mason [1979, 1981, 1982]. For work on spatial reasoning, see Tomás Lozano-Pérez [1980,

1983] and see Rodney A. Brooks [1983]. For a review of work on robot programming, see Tomás Lozano-Pérez [1982].

For insights into mechanical hands, see J. Kenneth Salisbury, Jr. [1982], Salisbury and John J. Craig [1982], and Salisbury and B. Roth [1983].

11

Learning Class Descriptions From Samples

Most people consider *the ability to learn* to be situated prominently in the definition of intelligence, for our greater human ability to learn distinguishes us sharply from other animals. Moreover, of all our various intelligence-demonstrating talents, our learning talents seem to be the hardest to explain and the hardest to capture in procedures. In this chapter, our purpose is to see that at least some kinds of learning can be explained and demonstrated.

We begin by introducing a group of *induction heuristics* that enable a procedure to learn *class descriptions* from *positive and negative samples*. With induction heuristics, procedures can learn, for example, that an arch consists of one brick that must be supported by two others that must not touch each other. Among these heuristics are the *require-link* and *forbid-link* heuristics that enable learning about classes from *near-miss* samples that miss being class members because of small number of reasons.

The induction heuristics are used by two learning procedures. The first of these learning procedures expects a cooperative teacher to present carefully chosen samples, one after another. The procedure learns whatever it can from each sample as the sample is presented and then forgets the sample forever. The second illustrative learning procedure expects to have all samples presented at once, unordered. Samples are remembered forever.

In one application, a learning procedure, similar to one discussed in this chapter, learned criteria for recognizing more than a dozen soybean

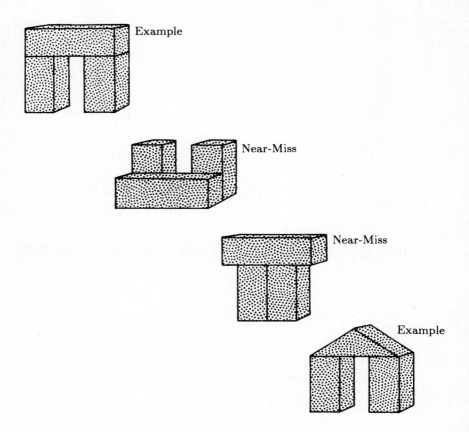

Figure 11-1. A sequence of examples and near misses for learning about arches.

diseases, producing results superior to human specialists. Since a considerable fraction of the world's population relies on soybeans for survival, to learn to recognize soybean diseases is to do something important.

INDUCTION HEURISTICS

Consider the ARCH and nonARCH sequence shown in figure 11-1.[1] Note that the series starts with a sample that is a typical arch. From this sample, we want a learning procedure to derive a very general idea of what an arch is. The procedure should learn that an arch involves two standing bricks that together support a third brick lying on its side.

---

[1] Properly speaking, the structure shown is a lintel and pair of posts, but for our purpose, that does not matter.

Each subsequent sample should drive home some particular point. In the second sample, the procedure sees the same objects as before but in a different configuration. Told that the pieces no longer form an arch, the procedure should conclude that the support links must be an important aspect of the general arch concept. Note that this correct idea can be conveyed by a single well-chosen sample rather than by extended, tedious training exercises.

In the third sample, the two standing bricks touch. Again the procedure is told that the structure is not an arch. Nothing else is significantly different from the first arch in the sample sequence. Evidently the standing bricks must not touch if there is to be an arch. Progress can be made once again by way of a good sample and the knowledge that it is not an arch.

The teacher may or may not claim the fourth sample is an arch, according to personal taste. If it is given as an arch, then the learning procedure should note that having a brick on top is not essential. At the very least, either a brick or a wedge will do; it is even reasonable to guess that any simple parallelepiped is acceptable.

Responding to Near Misses Improves Models

We now explain a learning procedure, W, showing how it learns about arches by dealing with descriptive frames produced from the line drawings in figure 11-1. To begin, W needs a typical example whose description forms the *initial description* shown in figure 11-2a. During learning, the initial description is augmented by information indicating what links are important in identification. The augmented description is called a *model.*

A *near miss* is a sample that does not qualify as an instance of the class being taught for some small number of reasons. The description shown in figure 11-2b is not a description of an arch, but since it is only a little different from the arch description in figure 11-2a, it is a near miss with respect to arches. Its purpose is to teach the importance of the SUPPORT links.

Since the SUPPORT links are missing, comparing the two descriptions leads naturally to the conclusion that the SUPPORT links are de rigueur for arches. Thus the synthesis of the two descriptions should be a new, refined description in which the SUPPORT links are replaced by the emphatic form, MUST-SUPPORT, as in figure 11-2c. Hence no group of blocks should be identified as an arch unless there are SUPPORT links. Used in this way, the near miss is said to supply information for the *require-link* heuristic.

The W procedure normally faces several differences when comparing an evolving model with a near miss. In general, then, W must have a way to identify the right differences for treatment, ignoring the others.

Generally, W uses only the single most important difference. Situations leading to two or more strongly similar differences are the only exceptions.

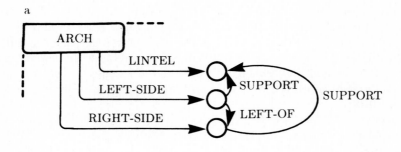

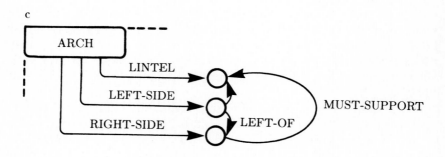

Figure 11-2. The require-link generalization rule. Compared with the ARCH frame in *a*, the near-miss frame in *b* lacks SUPPORT links. The conclusion is that SUPPORT links are essential, so the SUPPORT links in the ARCH frame are altered, indicating that they are required in all arches, as shown in *c*. The LEFT-OF link is shown to emphasize the need for evidence that is sufficient to establish the correct correspondence between the parts of the arch and the parts of the near miss. Many links have been omitted from the drawing for clarity.

Consider, for example, the two missing-SUPPORT differences associated
with the near miss to the arch in figure 11-2b. W's sensible reaction is
to suppose that the teacher intends that the two differences are to be
handled in the same way. Thus both SUPPORT links are replaced by
MUST-SUPPORT through the single sample.

The next comparison, the one between the evolving model in figure 11-3a and the near-miss in figure 11-3b, also involves two similar differences, namely two new TOUCH links relate the posts. Now, however, the
near miss fails to be an arch because links are present rather than absent.
It must be that the new links should be forbidden. This is accomplished
through the conversion of each TOUCH link to the negative emphatic link,
MUST-NOT-TOUCH, as shown in figure 11-3c. This is an example of the
forbid-link heuristic at work.

Note that the require-link and forbid-link heuristics work because there
is a representation in which the key links are explicit and because there is a
way of zeroing in on the proper links to modify. These points bear elevation
to principles:

- You cannot learn if you cannot know. Teachers can help by indicating
  the appropriate representation.

- You cannot learn if you cannot distinguish the important from the
  incidental. Teachers can help by using near misses as well as examples.

Responding to Examples Improves Models

So far, each near miss restricts what can be an arch. Positive examples
take the model the other way. Consider the situation of figure 11-4. Compared to the evolving model in figure 11-4a, the example configuration in
figure 11-4b has a wedge on top instead of a brick. If this is to be an
arch, some change in the model should reflect a loosening of constraint. At
the very least the IS-A connection between the top of the arch and BRICK
should be cut away and replaced by a MUST-BE-A link to a more general class as shown in figure 11-4c. Doing just this is known as using the
climb-tree heuristic.

Of course going for the most specific shared class is only one alternative.
In the example, going for PARALLELEPIPED represents a conservative
position with respect to how much induction to allow, for bricks and wedges
are also polyhedra, physical objects, and things. The new target for the
top's MUST-BE-A link could be anything along the chain of AKO links,
depending on how impetuous a learning procedure is to be.

Sometimes, however, there is no classification tree to climb at all. For
example, if bricks and wedges were not known to be members of any common class, the climb-tree heuristic would not be of any use. In such a case,
it would make sense to form a new class, the BRICK-OR-WEDGE class,

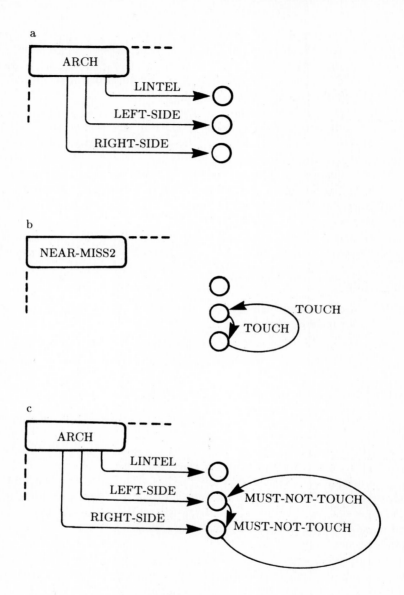

Figure 11-3. The forbid-link generalization rule. Compared with the ARCH frame in *a*, the near-miss frame in *b* adds touch links. The conclusion is that the touch links must not be present, so touch links are added to the ARCH frame, altered to indicate that they are forbidden in all arches, as shown in *c*. Many links have been omitted from the drawing for clarity.

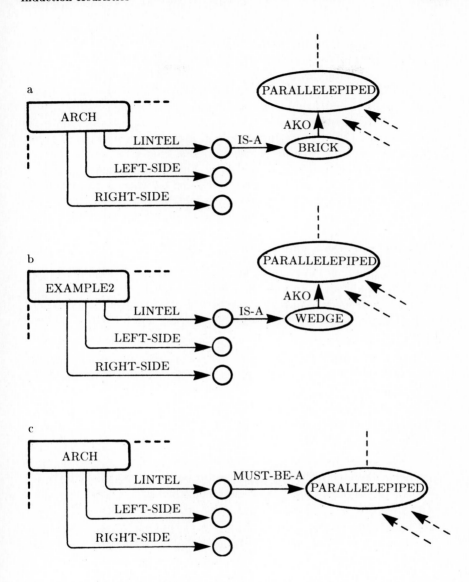

Figure 11-4. The climb-tree heuristic. The lintel in the ARCH frame in *a* is a brick, while the corresponding object in the example frame in *b* is a wedge. Evidently it does not matter. The IS-A link in the ARCH frame is changed to MUST-BE-A and redirected from BRICK to PARALLELEPIPED, as shown in *c*, which is the most specific common generalization of BRICK and WEDGE. Many links have been omitted from the drawing for clarity.

and join the top part of the arch to this new class with MUST-BE-A. This heuristic for generalization is known as the *enlarge-set* heuristic.

If there are no objects other than bricks and wedges, however, we should get rid of the IS-A link completely. This is known as the *drop-link* heuristic.

The *drop-link* heuristic is also used when a link in the evolving model is not in the example. If the initiating example has color information for some blocks and the other examples do not, it makes sense to ignore color, dropping all color references out of the evolving model.

Finally, another heuristic is used if the things involved are numbers. If one example exhibits a 10-centimeter brick and another, a 15-centimeter brick, then it makes sense to suppose any length brick between 10 centimeters and 15 centimeters will do. This is the *close-interval* heuristic.

Near-miss Heuristics Specialize; Example Heuristics Generalize

Having seen a number of induction heuristics at work, it is time to summarize the ones we have. Note that the near-miss heuristics, require link and forbid link, both work to make a more restrictive, specialized model. The positive example heuristics go the other way, producing a more permissive, generalized model.

- The *require-link* heuristic is used when an evolving model has a link in a place where a near miss does not. The model link is converted to a MUST form.

- The *forbid-link* heuristic is used when a near miss has a link in a place where an evolving model does not. A MUST-NOT form is installed in the evolving model.

- The *climb-tree* heuristic is used when something in an evolving model corresponds to a different thing in an example. MUST-BE-A links are routed to the most specific shared class in the classification tree above the model thing and the example thing.

- The *enlarge-set* heuristic is used when something in an evolving model corresponds to a different thing in an example. MUST-BE-A links are routed to a new class composed of the union of the things' classes.

- The *drop-link* heuristic is used when the things that are different in an evolving model and in an example form an exhaustive set. The *drop-link* heuristic is also used when an evolving model has a link that is not in the example. The link is dropped from the model.

- The *close-interval* heuristic is used when a number or interval in an evolving model corresponds to a number in an example. If the model uses a number, the number is replaced by an interval spanning the model's number and the example's number. If the model uses an interval, the interval is enlarged to reach the example's number.

Here then are the procedures that use these heuristics:

SPECIALIZE:

1 Match the evolving model to the sample to establish correspondences among parts.

2 Determine whether there is a single, most important difference between the evolving model and the near miss:

    2a If there is a single, most important difference, determine whether the evolving model or the near miss has a link that is not in the other:

        2aa If the evolving model has a link that is not in the near miss, use the require-link heuristic.

        2ab If the near miss has a link that is not in the model, use the forbid-link heuristic.

    2b Otherwise ignore the sample.

GENERALIZE:

1 Match the evolving model to the sample to establish correspondences among parts.

2 For each difference, determine the difference type:

    2a If the difference is that the link points to a different class in the evolving model from the class the link points to in the sample, determine if the classes are part of a classification tree:

        2aa If the classes are part of a classification tree, use the climb-tree heuristic.

        2ab If the classes form an exhaustive set, use the drop-link heuristic.

        2ac Otherwise, use the enlarge-set heuristic.

    2b If the difference is that a link is missing in either the evolving model or the example, use the drop-link heuristic.

    2c If the difference is that different numbers, or an interval and a number outside the interval, are involved, use the close-interval heuristic.

    2d Otherwise ignore the difference.

Note that SPECIALIZE does nothing if it cannot identify the most important difference. One way to identify the most important difference is to use a procedure that ranks all differences by difference type and by link type. There are other ways.

Note also that both SPECIALIZE and GENERALIZE involve matching. Detailed discussion of one particular matcher appears in chapter 12. For now, be assured that there are procedures that tie the parts in two descriptions together such that the following stipulations hold, insofar as possible:

- For every MUST link, there is a link of the same name joining the corresponding, tied-together parts.

- For every MUST-NOT link, there is no link of the same name joining the corresponding, tied-together parts.

INDUCTION PROCEDURES

Now we are ready to be more specific about the way various learning procedures work. We begin with W and finish with M. Importantly, both use the same specialization and generalization heuristics.

Procedure W Learns from Sequences

W uses teacher-supplied samples. Keep in mind that the teacher-supplied samples may be either examples or near misses in general, but the first must be an example. The teacher decides on the order. The learner analyzes each sample as it is given; the learner does not retain samples once they are analyzed.

To learn using the W procedure:
1   Let the description of the first sample, which must be an example, be the initial description.
2   For all subsequent samples:
    2a   If the sample is a near miss, use procedure SPECIAL-IZE.
    2b   If the sample is an example, use procedure GENER-ALIZE.

Learning Procedures Should Neither Guess nor Alter

As given, the W procedure never unlearns something once learned. Other, more elaborate versions of W have been devised that find and resolve inconsistencies by altering the evolving model. Such model debugging is hard, however, because it is hard to track down where a mistake may have been made, given only an inconsistency occurring long after the mistake. Consequently, it seems better to avoid mistakes in the first place by being conservative. This suggests the following:

- *The no-guessing principle.* When there is doubt about what to learn, learn nothing.

It may seem like cowardice to refuse to act because no act is absolutely safe. There is a point, however, where risk-taking heroism becomes foolhardiness. Honoring this no-guessing principle, the learner is not condemning itself to eternal stupidity; the learner is merely expecting the ignored situations to be encountered again when the learner knows more.

Note that there are places manifesting the no-guessing principle in procedure W—an entire teacher-supplied near miss is ignored if the procedure cannot determine which difference is the most important one.

One way to avoid guess-provoking situations is to arrange guess-avoiding conventions that both teachers and students obey. For example, if a teacher knows a student is using procedure W, the teacher should try to prevent more than one difference from appearing with each near miss. Knowing the teacher is doing this, the student can be assured that the single difference is important. Such learning-facilitating teacher-student conventions are called *felicity conditions.*

Still, even with felicity conditions, there may be no way to avoid all inconsistencies. Sometimes there will be situations when a model is not consistent with an example, even though the model is basically correct. Penguins, after all, can be birds, even though penguins cannot fly.

In such situations, it seems best to avoid altering the evolving model, particularly if it is evolving in accordance with the no-guessing principle. The way out is to honor another principle:

- *The no-altering principle.* When something known to be an example fails to match a general model, create a special-case exception model.

Thus the no-altering principle says to avoid all temptation to change a general model. Fixing a general model in one way is likely to break it in another.

Learning Procedures Should Learn in Small Steps

Finally, note that the W learning procedure is incremental. W works because it exploits the knowledge it has, adding to that knowledge in small steps using new examples.

Skillful teachers know that we humans learn mostly in small steps, too. If there is too much to figure out, there is too much room for confusion and error. William A. Martin put it this way:

- *Martin's Law.* You can't learn anything unless you almost know it already.

Procedure M Learns from Sets

The W procedure forces the teacher to make irrevocable decisions about the sample order, and if the sample is a near miss, W forces the learner to make irrevocable decisions about what difference to consider most important or to just ignore the near miss.

An alternative is to hand the learner all the samples at one time, permitting the learner to search for the best sample order and to search for the best difference to use. The result is procedure M. Procedure M is more powerful, but less humanlike in the way it learns, for unlike W, there is no incremental learning and no forgetting. All samples are available when learning starts and all are retained until learning stops.

M has two main steps. In step 1, M starts with an empty description that matches everything (since an empty description has no MUSTs or MUST-NOTs). Then M tries to specialize by adding MUSTs or MUST-NOTs until none of the wrong things match.

Next, in step 2, M tries to generalize its description in order to match as many class members as well as possible, while never generalizing so as to start matching any nonmembers.

To see how all this works, we use another arch-learning example, for the numbers involved are small: we work with only two members, three nonmembers, and at most a few differences between any pair. The actual differences are shown in figures 11-5 and 11-6. As figure 11-5 shows, there is one coupled pair of differences between the two arches. And as 11-6 shows, there is either one coupled pair of differences, or two ordinary differences, or two ordinary differences and one coupled pair, between any arch and any nonarch.

The first job is to select one of the arches, either the arch with a brick on top or the one with a wedge. The next job is to select one of the near-miss nonmembers, the one with the top removed, or the one with the sides pushed together, or the one with the cylinder on top. As figure 11-7 shows, there are six possible paths to consider at this level in the tree. Two of

A
B
C
A′
B′
C′
A is BRICK
A′ is WEDGE

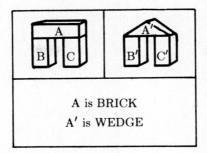

Figure 11-5. The differences between two arches.

EXAMPLE
NEAR-MISS
A
B
C
A
B
C
A′
B′
C′
B′ and C′ touch
A is WEDGE
A′ is BRICK
B′ and C′ touch
B′
C′
A′
B and C support A
A is WEDGE
A′ is BRICK
B and C support A
A′
B′
C′
A is BRICK
A′ is CYLINDER
A is WEDGE
A′ is CYLINDER

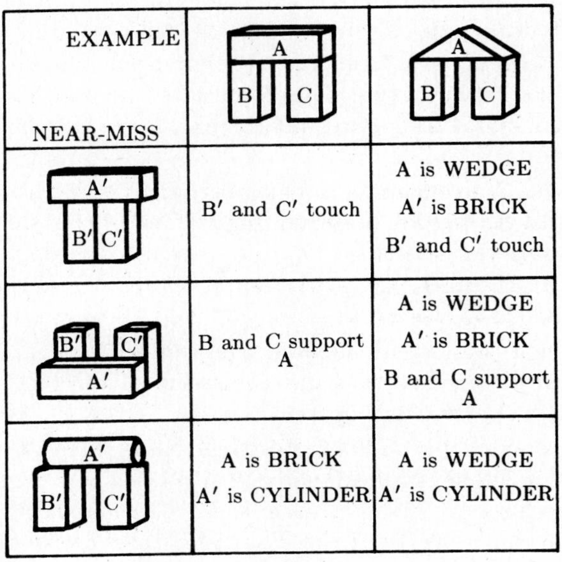

Figure 11-6. The differences between two arches and three nonarches.

these paths lead to just one difference; two lead to two differences; and two lead to three.

Specialization is done by using the specialization heuristics together with one of the observed differences. Consequently, at the level where the first specialization change is made to the description, there are twelve possibilities.

To cope with a potentially explosive tree, M uses beam search to prune away the weaker candidates among its growing class descriptions. This means M needs some measure of class-description quality to retain good prospects and discard bad ones.

To keep our simulation particularly simple, let us use a narrow beam width and a simple quality measure. Take the beam width to be four. Take the quality measure to be the number of MUST and MUST-NOT links inserted, a crude measure of degree-of-constraint.

Now if two MUST-SUPPORT or two MUST-NOT-TOUCH links are added to the naked initial model, a total of two points are awarded. If MUST-BE WEDGE, or MUST-NOT-BE BRICK, or MUST-NOT-BE CYLIN-DER link-object combinations are added, only one point is awarded. Consequently, the four paths to be continued will have a quality score of two, while the eight that are terminated have a quality score of one.

At this point, one of the two remaining nonmembers is selected for each of the four surviving paths. The one with the cylinder leads to two branches. The others lead to one or three. Thus, at the next level, we have sixteen possibilities. As before, we retain only the best four results of the specialization heuristics. This eliminates the branches involving the cylinder near miss, for they score only three points, while the winners score four.

Finally, the one remaining nonmember, the one with the cylinder is selected. It leads to eight branches, each of which tie with five points. Many of these are redundant, however, so we really have only three distinct results: the MUST-BE BRICK arch; the MUST-BE WEDGE arch; and the MUST-NOT-BE CYLINDER arch.

Step 1 is now complete because all nonmembers have been excluded by specializing the description using the require-link and forbid-link heuristics. Next, step 2, generalization, begins.

One member remains imperfectly matched along two of the three paths. In both of these two cases, the unmatched member differs from the evolving description because MUST-BE-AKO links have incompatible destinations, suggesting the climb-tree heuristic. This heuristic works out since no nonmembers start matching when the climb-tree heuristic moves the AKO link from WEDGE or BRICK to PARALLELEPIPED. No further generalization is needed, so M terminates with two successful descriptions: one is the MUST-BE PARALLELEPIPED arch; the other is the MUST-NOT-BE CYLINDER

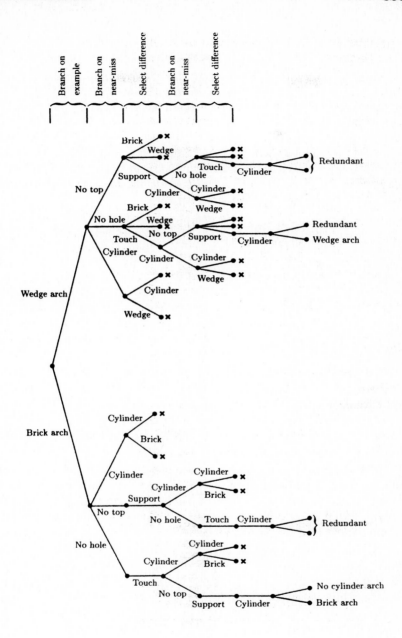

Figure 11-7. A tree generated by procedure M operating on the two arches and two nonarches of figure 11-6. Beam search is in use, with a beam width of four. The beam scoring function is the number of MUST and MUST-NOT links.

arch. For both, all members match without flaw; no nonmembers match at all because of MUST or MUST-NOT clashes. All four paths work out.

Since M is complicated, let us go over the explanation again, this time abstractly. In step 1, M first selects a class member to work with. Then it selects a nonmember to be excluded by an addition to the class description under construction. Then it selects a difference to work with, using either the require-link heuristic or the forbid-link heuristic to augment the description. Nonmember selection and description augmentation is repeated until all nonmembers are excluded. Of course, one addition to the class description may fortuitously exclude more than one nonmember and may unfortunately exclude one or more members.

All this so far is illustrated schematically in figure 11-8, where we show a sequence of specialization steps on a collection of type A objects and type B objects. In figure 11-8a, one of the A members has been selected, but no description specialization has happened, so the empty description matches everything. In figure 11-8b, one of the nonmembers has been selected, a specialization heuristic has been applied, and the augmented description now excludes several nonmembers. In 11-8c, one of the remaining, not yet excluded, nonmembers is selected, and the specialization process is repeated. Note that this time some of the members have been excluded as well, regrettably.

After the description is specialized enough to exclude all nonmembers, step 2 begins, and an attempt is made to generalize the description. The description is used with other, unmatched class members to drive the generalization heuristics, namely climb tree, enlarge set, close interval, and drop link. No generalization heuristic is allowed if it would generalize the description such that a nonmember starts matching again.

This is illustrated in figure 11-9. In 11-9a, the description so far derived fails to match all the members perfectly. In 11-9b, a second, not-covered member, is selected, and a generalization heuristic extends the description under construction, fortuitously embracing more than one member. In 11-9c, the description is generalized again.

Of course, there may be no way to make the description match all class members during step 2. When this happens, the class members that are matched are put aside, one of the remaining class members is selected, and the whole specialization-generalization process is repeated. When the process must be repeated like this, the total description specifies that a class member can match any of several individual descriptions.

Note that there are many decision points in the procedure where an object or a difference is selected. These decision points form a tree of possible paths to a satisfactory description. The tree can be extremely large. Suppose, for example, there are m members, n nonmembers, and d differences between any pair of objects. Then the size of the tree could be as large as $m! \times n! \times d \times (m-1)!$—if all the numbers are just 10, a modest number, the result is nearly 10^{20}, an immodest number.

M uses beam search because of these explosive combinatorics, as stipulated in the following procedure description:

To learn using the M procedure:

Doing all the select operations in the manner of beam search, until all class members are described, select a class member that is not yet described. Call this the current class member. Start a description consisting of only nodes for the parts, with no links. Call this description the current description.

1   Until the current description describes none of the nonmembers:

    1.1   Select a nonmember.

    1.2   Select a MUST-producing difference between the current class member and the nonmember.

    1.3   Using SPECIALIZE and the difference, add a MUST or a MUST-NOT to the current description.

2   For each class member not yet described, attempt to generalize the current description using GENERALIZE and the class member not yet described. The attempt fails if the generalization describes a nonmember.

Note that search eliminates the requirement that the nonmembers be near misses. With procedure W, the nonmembers had to be near misses because W might otherwise go forward with a bad, irrevocable choice. With procedure M, the nonmembers need not be near misses because M explores alternative choices.

IDENTIFICATION

Learning procedures prepare information for identification procedures. To see that W and M do their jobs adequately, we now examine some identification procedures to see how they work and to see what they need.

MUSTs and MUST-NOTs Dominate Matching

One way to determine if an unknown matches a model is to check the unknown to see whether it is compatible with the emphatic links found in the model. Clearly any links with names prefixed by MUST signal positions where the importance of a particular link has been established by

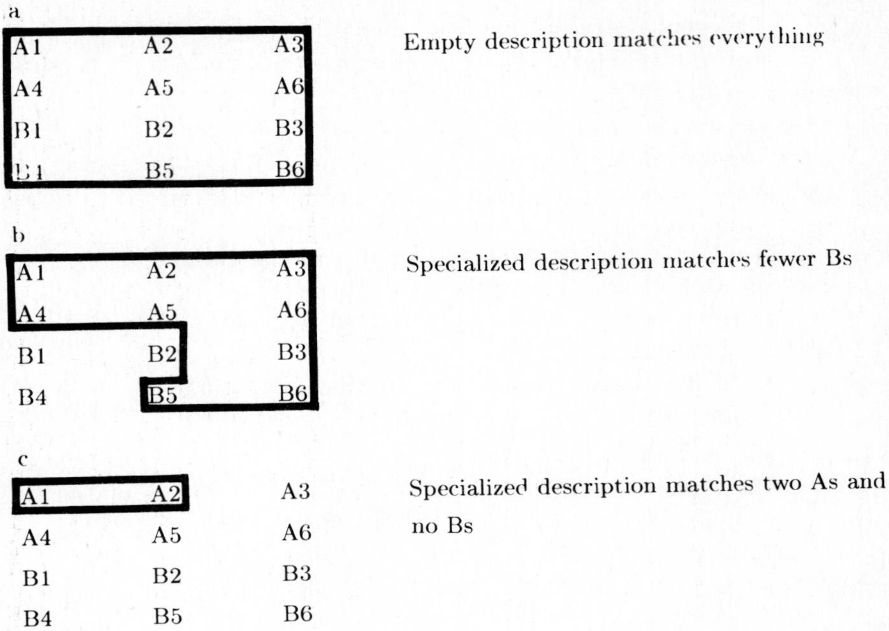

a

A1	A2	A3
A4	A5	A6
B1	B2	B3
B4	B5	B6

Empty description matches everything

b

A1	A2	A3
A4	A5	A6
B1	B2	B3
B4	B5	B6

Specialized description matches fewer Bs

c

A1	A2	A3
A4	A5	A6
B1	B2	B3
B4	B5	B6

Specialized description matches two As and no Bs

Figure 11-8. Procedure M uses specialization heuristics to augment an initially empty description. Each step shrinks the number of objects covered. In *a*, the empty class description matches everything. In *b*, an A and a B member work together using a specialization heuristic to shrink the set of things that match the class description. In *c*, the A member works with another B member to shrink still further.

some learning experience. Should a corresponding link be absent from the unknown, the match fails without further consideration. Similarly, model links prefixed by MUST-NOT cause match failure if the unknown exhibits the corresponding link.

Going beyond this to evaluate a match requires judgment of the degree of similarity between the unknown and model. It is necessary to translate the abstract notion of similarity between unknown and model, $s(U, M)$, into a concrete measurement. Simple ways of doing this were described in chapter 2 in connection with the geometric-analogy procedure.

It must be said, however, that any number-oriented weighting scheme for combining evidence is limited. For one thing, all information is compressed into a singularly inexpressive number. This is fine unless it becomes necessary to understand what happened later on. When identification through selection of a model is the top-level goal, the approach does no particular damage.

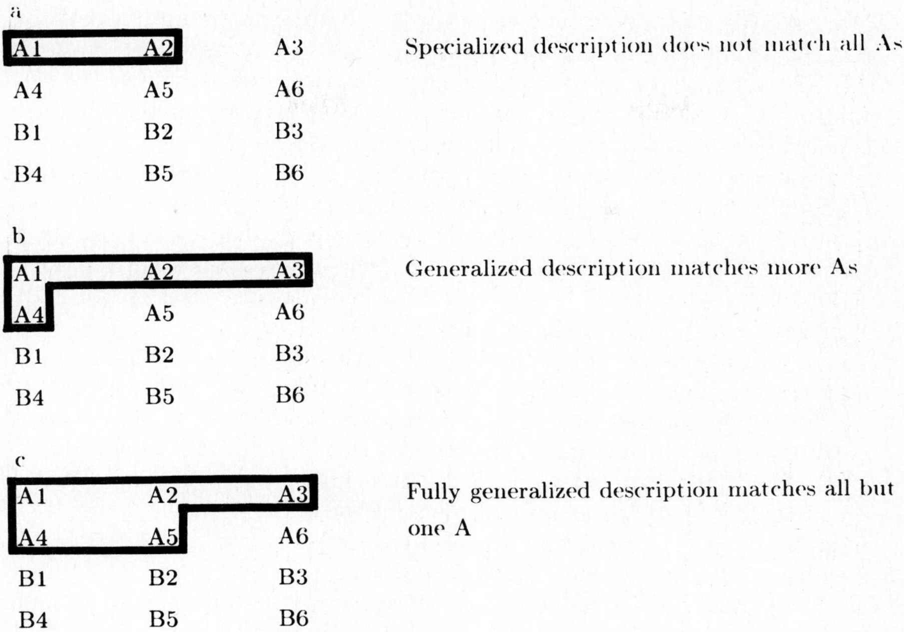

a

A1	A2	A3	Specialized description does not match all As
A4	A5	A6	
B1	B2	B3	
B4	B5	B6	

b

A1	A2	A3	Generalized description matches more As
A4	A5	A6	
B1	B2	B3	
B4	B5	B6	

c

A1	A2	A3	Fully generalized description matches all but one A
A4	A5	A6	
B1	B2	B3	
B4	B5	B6	

Figure 11-9. Procedure M uses generalization heuristics to augment descriptions once they are restrictive enough to exclude all nonmembers. Each augmentation increases the number of objects covered. In part *a*, the class description matches only two of the class members. In *b*, the set is enlarged. In part *c*, the set is enlarged again, but not enough to cover all of the As.

Models May Be in Trees, Lists, or Nets

Given a mechanism for matching an unknown with a model, the next issue is that of how to arrange the models for testing. We consider three possibilities: decision trees, model lists, and similarity nets.

One way to identify unknowns actually involves no explicit matching of the unknown with models. Instead, an implicit match is made as the unknown traverses a tree of tests, usually called a *decision tree*, as illustrated in figure 11-10. A decision tree is used rather like a pinball machine: unknowns are dropped into the tree at the top; the various tests deflect them one way or another; and they drop out at the bottom at places associated with various identification conclusions. Generating efficient decision trees from models is a big subject. We ignore it.

A second possibility, matching against the models in a model list, is reasonable if the number of models is small. The identification procedure is trivial: Try the models one after another until one is found to be satisfactory, as illustrated in figure 11-11.

The third approach to arranging models is to use a similarity net. Imagine a set of models organized into a kind of net. Similarity links connect pairs that are very similar in the near-miss sense.

Now suppose that an unknown object is to be identified. What should be done if the first comparison against some particular model in the net fails as it ordinarily will? If the match did not fail by much, if the unknown seems like the model in many respects, then surely other similar models should be tried next. These new similar models are precisely the ones connected by similarity links to the old, tested model.

In an obvious improvement, the similarity links between models not only convey similarity but also describe the difference, as shown in figure 11-12. If an unknown differs from a test model in the same way a neighbor of the test model differs from it, then that neighbor is a particularly good model to test next. The initial match is not a failure, it is a knowledge probe. This not only allows selection of the next test model from a family of likely candidates, but also ensures selection of the particular member of that family most likely to succeed.

Note that this is a kind of hill climbing because the movement through the similarity net is determined by moving to the immediate neighbor that seems most likely to yield an improved match against the unknown. Note also that the procedure for movement from one model to another is like the procedure in chapter 2 for solving geometric-analogy problems. The analogy with geometric analogy fits because the decision about which neighbor to use is determined by comparing descriptions of differences. In solving analogy problems, we were concerned with descriptions of the difference $d(A, B)$ between drawings A and B and the difference $d(C, X)$ between C and some possible answer, X. To solve a geometric-analogy problem, the rule taking A into B is compared with all the others. This comparison itself is a description that must be minimized over X.

$$\min_{X} d\big(d(A, B), d(C, X)\big)$$

For moving through a similarity net, the difference description $d(U, T)$ is between the unknown, U, and the test model, T, and the difference description $d(N, T)$ is between the various neighbors, N, and the test model. To move, these descriptions are compared, minimizing over N:

$$\min_{N} d\big(d(U, T), d(N, T)\big)$$

Similarity nets probably should not be thought of as homogeneous structures resembling huge fishing nets. Instead, they should be like road maps in which small local roads provide access to even the obscure villages while

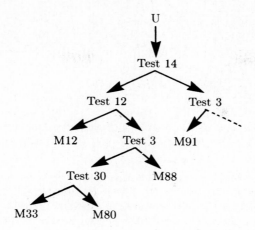

Figure 11-10. Identification using a decision tree. Each test deflects unknowns away from incorrect identifications until only one remains.

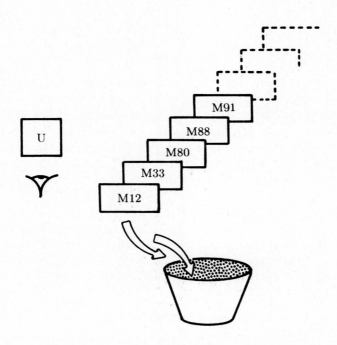

Figure 11-11. Identification using a model list. Each model is tried successively until one succeeds. Models that do not match are discarded.

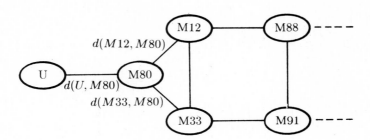

Figure 11-12. Identification using a similarity net.   Progress from hypothesis
to hypothesis is guided by comparing difference descriptions. In this illustration, M80, M12, M33, M88, and M91 are possible hypotheses, and $d(U,\ M80)$,
$d(M12,\ M80)$, and $d(M33,\ M80)$ are difference descriptions. M80 is presumed to
be the first hypothesis tried. M12 is next if difference description $d(M12,\ M80)$
is more like difference description $d(U,\ M80)$ than difference $d(M33,\ M80)$ is
like difference $d(U,\ 80)$.

larger and less dense arteries bring the local roads within reach of the
limited-access superhighways. Various cities standing outside the superhighways would be the centers through which all traffic would flow because
a given locality would be presumed to be characterized by the qualities of
the representative cities.

   With this improvement, the use of similarity nets begins to resemble
the use of sophisticated identification tools used by people. *Differential
diagnosis*, as practiced in medicine, is one example of such a sophisticated
tool.

SUMMARY

- A near miss, relative to a class, is a sample that is not a class member
  but only because of one distinguishable, most important difference.
  Near misses are vitally important in teaching through sequences of
  samples. Near misses are used to specialize models via the require-link
  heuristic and the forbid-link heuristic.

- Examples are used to generalize models. The heuristics involved are
  climb tree, enlarge set, close interval, and drop link.

- Given induction heuristics, learning can be a cooperative effort between
  a learner and a teacher. In one mode the teacher supplies examples
  and near misses in a careful sequence, leaving the learner to determine
  exactly what to do after each.

- The induction heuristics also can be used in a different mode in which the teacher supplies the examples and nonexamples all at once, leaving the learner to search for a suitable way to use them.

- In general, it is difficult to correct learning mistakes. It is best to learn from clear situations only, ignoring confusing ones. Similarly, it is better to refrain from altering concepts, once learned.

- Felicity conditions are teacher-student conventions that facilitate learning.

- Martin's Law holds that you cannot learn anything unless you almost know it already.

- For identification, models may be arranged in model lists, decision trees, or similarity nets.

REFERENCES

Procedure W is adapted from my early work [Winston 1970, 1975]. This work introduced the notion of near miss and many of the induction heuristics.

Since the use of near misses was introduced by me, several researchers have offered improved procedures for using specializing and generalizing induction heuristics. In particular, most of the induction-heuristic names and procedure M are adapted from AQ11, a predecessor of INDUCE, a much more sophisticated procedure developed by Ryszard S. Michalski [Michalski 1980, 1983; Michalski and Richard L. Chilausky 1980]. Michalski's INDUCE, among other things, includes several additional induction heuristics, many of which deal with chains of links and properties of groups. INDUCE has exhibited some extraordinary learning feats. In one example, it learned descriptions for dozens of soybean diseases from several hundred previously identified samples [Michalski and Chilausky 1980]. Michalski's procedures' soybean-disease descriptions are in no case worse than those supplied by human controls, and in some cases, better.

Tom M. Mitchell [1982] has contributed the notion of delimiting the set of possible class descriptions with maximally specific and maximally general models. The space of all possible models is called *version space*.

Steven A. Vere [1977] has taken learning in still another direction. Noting that most models are statements of what must be, together with reservations in the form of what must not be, he generalized to allow reservations on the reservations. He calls these *multilevel counterfactuals*.

Perhaps the hardest learning is the kind that is done with no teacher at all. Douglas B. Lenat is one of the few who study the problem successfully. His programs search concept spaces, such as the world of number theory, using heuristic measures of interestingness [1977, 1982]. This was discussed in chapter 4.

Michalski has introduced a procedure, CLUSTER, that also learns without a teacher. CLUSTER finds coherent classes in an undifferentiated set of object descriptions [Michalski and Robert E. Stepp 1983]. CLUSTER borrows many ideas from INDUCE.

The no-guessing principle and the no-altering principle are my names for two of Marvin Minsky's *laws of noncompromise* [*The Society of Mind*, book in preparation]. The no-guessing principle is also related to what David Marr called the *principle of least commitment* [1977].

Martin's Law is from a talk given by William A. Martin in Dubrovnik, Yugoslavia, in 1979.

For work on learning procedures, see Gerald J. Sussman [1975] and Ira P. Goldstein [1975]. For work on inferring formulas from graphlike numerical data, an important part of the scientific discovery process, see Pat Langley, Gary L. Bradshaw, and Herbert A. Simon [1983].

For a general overview, see *Machine Learning* [1983], edited by Ryszard S. Michalski, Jaime G. Carbonell, and Tom M. Mitchell.

12

Learning Rules
From Experience

In this chapter our purpose is to study two radically different procedures that learn from experience by working exercises. These procedures happen to learn rules, rather than object descriptions, and they work using *positive examples only*, rather than using both positive and negative examples.

The first procedure, META-WASP, learns grammar rules using sample sentences as exercises. META-WASP starts when a WASP parser staggers to a halt while working on a sample sentence, whereupon META-WASP uses *generate and test* to build a new WASP rule. META-WASP works because WASP rules have such a constrained, simple form.

The second procedure, MACBETH, learns rulelike principles using simple situations as exercises. MACBETH starts by *matching* an exercise situation to a precedent situation, followed by *constraint transfer* from the precedent to the exercise. The transferred constraint enables MACBETH to solve the exercise problem and to construct a *condition-action rule*. MACBETH works because constraints among relations tend to persist across analogous situations.

MACBETH learns, for example, that greedy wives of weak nobles can make their husbands want to be king: given an attention-focusing exercise, MACBETH uses a précis of *Macbeth* to solve the exercise and to construct the want-to-be-king rule. In another illustration, MACBETH learns to relate *form and function*: given a functional definition for cups, MACBETH uses prior knowledge of other objects, together with physical descriptions of particular cups, to construct a variety of possible physical descriptions, enabling cup recognition.

LEARNING GRAMMAR RULES FROM SAMPLE SENTENCES

In chapter 11, you saw that near-miss samples are useful, as distinguished from plain misses, because the number of possible conclusions that can be drawn from a near-miss sample is severely limited. In this chapter, you see that in other circumstances, the number of conclusions that can be drawn from a sample is limited because there are few conclusions no matter what.

Suppose, for example, that we are working with the WASP parser introduced in chapter 9, and we want a way to learn a new rule whenever the parser reaches an impasse for which no existing rule triggers and fires. If we assume the existing node-creating rules and node-finishing rules are correct and complete, then the only possible action for any new rule is attach or switch. Similarly, the only possible condition features are those associated with the buffer items and current node at the time when the parser fails.

We conclude that the constraining representation of the parser rules severely limits what can be concluded when parsing stops prematurely on a legitimate sentence.

The Most Instructive Sentences Are Legitimate and Nearly Parsable

To make the role of constraining representation clear, note, for example, that the WASP rules given in chapter 9 do not permit us to parse the sentence "Had the silly robot moved the red pyramid to the top of the big table?" The reason is that there is no rule in the sentence group that can handle a leading auxiliary verb. In fact, the only rule in the sentence group that works with verbs at all is S3, a rule that requires a noun phrase to be attached already:

S3 If   first item is a verb
           current node has a noun phrase attached
    then   create a verb-phrase node

Let us look at a simplified rule-learning procedure, META-WASP, that handles this impasse. First, note that the preprocessed sentence looks like this: "Had NPa(the silly robot) moved NPb(the red pyramid) to NPc(the top of the big table)?" Consequently, the first buffer item at the time the parser drops dead is the word *had* with the features *auxiliary*, *verb*, and *past*; the second item is the noun-phrase node NPa with the feature *noun-phrase*; and the third is the verb *moved* with the features *verb* and *past*.

From this, META-WASP makes the following partial rule:

NEW1   If   first item is the past auxiliary verb *had*
                   second item is a noun-phrase node
                   third item is the past verb *moved*
                   current node has nothing attached
      then   ...

Next META-WASP must add an action. META-WASP does this by way of a simple generate-and-test sequence involving attach and switch. META-WASP first generates a rule using attach. Here is how META-WASP decides if the attach succeeds:

- Verbs can be attached only to verb phrases. Nouns can be attached only to noun phrases.

- Phrases can be attached only to phrases. The phrases must be of different types.

In our example, attach fails because verbs cannot be attached directly to sentence nodes.

Switch works, however, for switching *had* and NPa around leaves the parser in a state that the existing rules handle without further incident. The new rule is this:

NEW1   If   first item is the past auxiliary verb *had*
                   second item is a noun-phrase node
                   third item is the past verb *moved*
                   current node has nothing attached
      then   switch the first and second buffer items

This is an ugly, overly specific rule, but since there is nothing in the existing sentence-level rule set that switches, META-WASP must add it in. Happily, however, it will not last long, for META-WASP can learn more by working on this sentence: "Will the happy child congratulate him?" After preprocessing, we have "Will NPa(the happy child) congratulate NPb(him)?"

As it stands, our new rule is too specific to work, so META-WASP must generate a second new rule in much the same way. The result is as follows:

NEW2   If   first item is the present auxiliary verb *will*
                   second item is a noun-phrase node
                   third item is the infinitive verb *congratulate*
                   current node has nothing attached
      then   switch the first and second buffer items

Now, however, META-WASP notes that NEW1 and NEW2 have the same action, so rather than adding NEW2, META-WASP modifies NEW1 by retaining only those features that are common to both NEW1 and NEW2.

Thus we have a new version of NEW1:

NEWNEW1   If   first item is an auxiliary verb
                  second item is a noun-phrase node
                  third item is a verb
                  current node has nothing attached
          then   switch the first and second buffer items

Here, in summary, is META-WASP:

To generate grammar rules using META-WASP:

1   When there is an impasse, with no existing rule firing, make
    a new rule as follows:

    1.1   Make conditions out of each of the buffer items and
          the state of the current node.

    1.2   Make an action out of the first alternative that works:

          1.2a   Try using attach. Fail if the first buffer item
                 cannot be attached to the current node, and fail
                 if the proposed rule does not allow a successful
                 parse of the rest of the sentence with no further
                 interruption.

          1.2b   Try using switch. Fail if the proposed rule does
                 not allow a successful parse of the rest of the
                 sentence with no further interruption.

2   If using attach or switch succeeded, merge the new rule
    into the rule set as follows:

    2a   If there is no rule in the current rule set with the same
          action, add the new rule to the front of the set.

    2b   If there is a rule in the current rule set with the same
          action, generalize the two rules by dropping the con-
          dition features that are not common to both the new
          rule and the existing one.

Experiments show that META-WASP can learn a large fraction of the rules
of English grammar, suggesting that English has the following characteristics:

• English grammar rules can be learned using grammatical sentences
  only; there is no need for nongrammatical examples.

• English grammar rules can be learned by adding a rule, whenever im-
  passes occur, to the rule set that is active at the time.

Some people argue that all natural-language grammars must exhibit such characteristics in order to be learnable.

META-WASP Illustrates Martin's Law

The META-WASP learning procedure works because it exploits the knowledge it has, adding that knowledge together in new ways dictated by its exercise-working experience. Thus META-WASP adds to what it knows in small steps, resonating with Martin's Law, the idea that you cannot learn anything unless you almost know it already.

Martin's Law and the no-guessing principle are exhibited again in the next section, as we turn from rules about parsing to rules about situations.

LEARNING RULELIKE PRINCIPLES

Teachers constantly supply precedents, give exercises, and expect students both to work the exercises and to discover principles that apply to life's situations. The students must find the correspondence between the precedents and the exercises, apply the knowledge in the precedents to work the exercises, generalize to form principles, and index the principles so that they can be retrieved when appropriate. This sort of teaching and learning by analogy pervades subjects like management, economics, law, medicine, and engineering as well as the development of commonsense knowledge about life in general.

Consider, for example, the following exercise and précis of *Macbeth*:

An Exercise

This is an exercise concerning a weak noble and a greedy lady. The noble is married to the lady. Show that the noble may want to be king.

Macbeth

This is a story about Macbeth, Lady Macbeth, Duncan, and Macduff. Macbeth is an evil noble. Lady Macbeth is a greedy, ambitious woman. Duncan is a king. Macduff is a noble. Lady Macbeth persuades Macbeth to want to be king because she is greedy. She is able to influence him because he is married to her and because he is weak. Macbeth murders Duncan with a knife. Macbeth murders Duncan because Macbeth wants to be king and because Macbeth is evil. Lady Macbeth kills herself. Macduff is angry. He kills Macbeth because Macbeth murdered Duncan and because Macduff is loyal to Duncan.

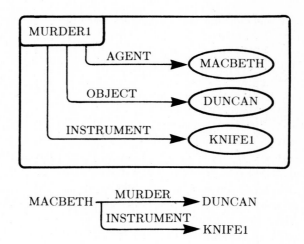

Figure 12-1. A shorthand notation for link frames. The MURDER1 frame in *a* is replaced in *b* by an instrument link tied directly to the MURDER link between Macbeth and Duncan.

Told by a teacher that *Macbeth* is to be considered a precedent, a student should establish the correspondence between the noble and Macbeth and between the lady and Lady Macbeth. Next the student should announce that the precedent suggests that the noble may want to be king. Finally the student should form some sort of rule suggesting that the weakness of a noble and the greed of his wife can cause the noble to want to be king.

Thematic-role Frames Capture Sentence-Level Meaning

The first step in doing an analogy is to prepare suitable descriptions, cast in a good representation. For the *Macbeth* story, as given, it is convenient to describe the sentences using thematic-role frames, which were introduced in chapter 9.

As shown in figure 12-1, it is also convenient to use a shorthand notation for thematic-role frames. When more than an agent and a thematic object are involved in an act, a supplementary description is tied to the act-specifying link, making the representation capable of bearing the information occupying other thematic roles. Information about properties and classes is easily conveyed by using IS links and IS-A links.

Let us assume that some simple deductions are made as English input is translated into the thematic-role-oriented semantic net, thereby reducing the need for tedious attention to details. For example, given that Macbeth marries Lady Macbeth, Lady Macbeth clearly marries Macbeth. Similarly, since Macbeth murders Duncan, it is clear that Macbeth kills Duncan, which makes it clear that Duncan is dead. Such obvious deductions are done by a few procedures that are invoked when links are added to or removed from the database. These are called IF-ADDED and IF-REMOVED procedures.

Constraint Transfer Solves New Problems Using Old Precedents

How is it possible to know if some link holds in an exercise, given that the exercise is analogous to another, well-understood precedent? The answer is that the constraint links in the precedent suggest the right questions to ask. Here we consider only constraints involving causal connections. The key assumption is that the causal structure of a precedent is likely to say something about the possible cause structure in an exercise to be analyzed. Ultimately, this rests on the assumption that if two situations are similar in some respects, then they may be similar in other respects as well.

We now examine MACBETH, a procedure that uses this key assumption. To see how MACBETH works, consider the *Macbeth* precedent and the accompanying exercise. When asked to demonstrate that the noble in the exercise may want to be king, given the *Macbeth* precedent, MACBETH proceeds as follows:

- The people in the precedent are matched with the people in the exercise. In the description of *Macbeth*, Macbeth is weak and his wife, Lady Macbeth, greedy. In the exercise, the noble is weak and his wife, greedy.

- The cause structure of the precedent is transferred to the exercise. The cause structure of *Macbeth* is shown in figure 12-2. The transferred links from *Macbeth* connect the links in the question, involving wanting to be king, to existing links, involving marriage, greed, and weakness, as shown in figure 12-3.

- It is determined that the transferred cause structure ties the link to be shown to links known to be true.

In this simple illustration, there is only one precedent involved. When a single precedent cannot supply the total cause structure needed, MACBETH attempts to chain several together. In the example, if it were not known already that the noble is weak, as required for application of the *Macbeth* precedent, weakness might be established through another precedent or already learned rule.

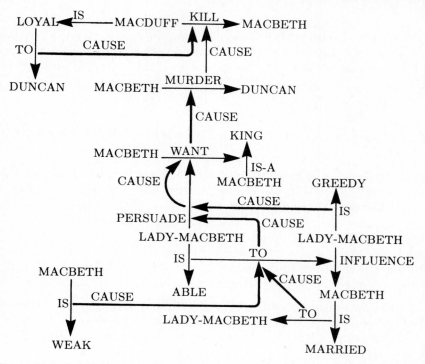

Figure 12-2. Problems are solved by transferring the existing CAUSE links of a precedent onto the problem to be solved. This figure gives the causal links in the *Macbeth* precedent. Heavy links are causal links.

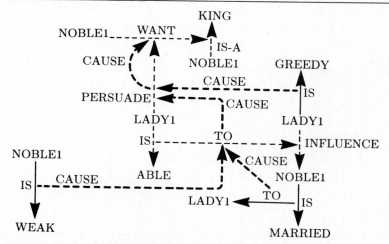

Figure 12-3. Problems are solved by transferring the existing CAUSE links of a precedent onto the problem to be solved. This figure gives an exercise, together with dotted links representing the links transferred from the *Macbeth* precedent. Heavy dotted links are transferred CAUSE links.

To be more specific, the following steps are taken when the user asks about some link in an exercise, given a precedent:

- The link in question may actually be in the exercise. If so, no further action is needed.

- The link in question may be caused by other links in the precedent. If so, try to establish the other links in the exercise.

- The link in question may be both absent from the exercise and causeless in the precedent. If so, seek another precedent that exhibits causes for the causeless link, pushing the analysis still further.

Thus the cause structures in precedents serve as templates, guiding the student to the possible causes of the link in question, the one for which justification or explanation is sought.

The next example illustrates what happens when one precedent is not enough. This time we do not know that the noble is weak, but we do know that the lady is domineering:

An Exercise

This is an exercise concerning a noble and a domineering, greedy lady. The noble is married to the lady. Show that the noble may want to be king.

Now the *Macbeth* precedent is not enough to establish the desired result, for in *Macbeth*, Macbeth wanted to be king, in part, because he was weak. However, a second precedent, the *Linda and Dick* story, can help establish that our new noble is weak, as the use of *Macbeth* requires.

Linda and Dick

This is a story about Linda and Dick. Linda is a woman, and Dick is a man. Dick is married to Linda. Dick is weak because he is drained. He is drained because Linda is domineering.

Figure 12-4 shows what *Linda and Dick* looks like. Note that there is an intermediate link standing between Dick's weakness and Linda's domineering nature.

Now *Macbeth* and *Linda and Dick* are enough to solve the problem posed in the exercise. Figure 12-5 shows how the two precedents stretch from the thing to be shown to the things that are known. *Macbeth* handles the top part; *Linda and Dick*, the bottom; and the two are joined at the place where the noble is said to be weak.

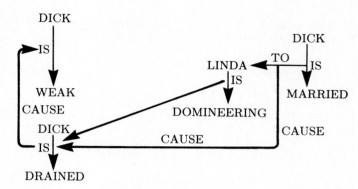

Figure 12-4. A precedent connecting one person's weakness to another person's domineering nature.

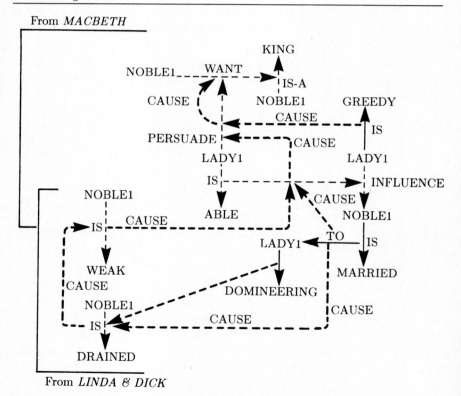

Figure 12-5. An example illustrating reasoning by analogy using two precedents. *Macbeth* establishes that the noble may want to be king, but only if it can be established that the noble is weak. *Linda and Dick* establishes that the noble may be weak by pushing the analysis further back, linking up to things that are actually known.

To summarize, here is the key procedure. Note that the MATCH procedure, used by MACBETH, is explained later.

MACBETH:

1 Match the exercise with the precedent using MATCH.

2 Transfer the causal structure from the precedent to the exercise.

3 Trace through the transferred causal structure. Determine if the desired conclusion is supported by existing links.

   3a If the desired conclusion is supported, succeed.

   3b Otherwise, if MACBETH can justify needed, but missing links, using other precedents, then succeed.

   3c Otherwise, fail.

Commonsense Reasoning Can Generate Rulelike Principles

One way to explain how the analogy-oriented reasoning process works is to note that all the precedents used to deal with an exercise determine an AND tree. The root is the link to be shown in the exercise; the tips are links that hold in the exercise; and the structure in between is supplied by the precedents.

When constructing an exercise for use with a single precedent, the teacher causes attention to be drawn to a particular fragment of the cause structure exhibited in the precedent. One reason to do this is that the fragment involved may be worthy of special notice. It may be that for broad classes of objects, the links at the AND tree tips often lead to the link at the root, not just in the precedent and the exercise.

Suppose that MACBETH forms a new description by copying structure from the CAUSE-link specified AND tree. Further suppose that the new parts in the description are created by using the climb-tree generalization heuristic on the tied-together parts of the precedent and exercise:

MAKE-RULE:

1 Find the CAUSE-specified AND tree, implied by the precedents, that is used to work the exercise.

2 Using climb-tree, generalize the objects in the AND tree.

3 Build a new description using the links involved in the AND tree and the generalized objects.

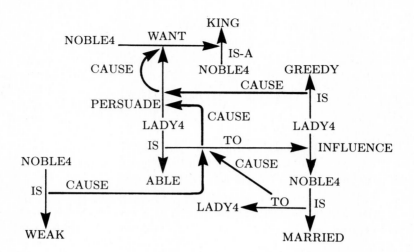

Figure 12-6. An exercise causes part of the causal structure of a precedent to be extracted, forming a new description. The new description is in the same representation used for the precedent and the exercise. Heavy links are causal links.

In the simple example using just *Macbeth* and the accompanying exercise, the new description synthesized by MAKE-RULE from the precedent and the exercise is illustrated in figure 12-6.

These new descriptions may constitute constraint-describing summaries that are worth remembering as plausibility-indicating principles. When the bottom and the top are seen in English, it becomes clear that these summaries resemble the condition-action rules used in rule-based systems:

> The Want-to-be-king Rule:
>
> If   a weak noble is married to a greedy lady
> then   the noble may want to be king

Since these plausibility-indicating rules are represented internally in the same way precedents are, they can be used by the same learning machinery that works for ordinary precedents. Thus old rules can contribute to new ones, just as precedents can.

The MACBETH Procedure Illustrates Martin's Law

The MACBETH learning procedure works because it exploits the knowledge it has, adding that knowledge together in new ways dictated by its exercise-working experience. Thus MACBETH, like META-WASP, honors Martin's Law.

MATCHING IS BEHIND ANALOGY

Matching is a fundamental part of the MACBETH procedure. Consequently, let us divert ourselves here to look at a set of procedures that do matching. There are many possible ways to get a good match, whatever *good* means, so the procedures presented here are merely to show that matching can be done; they are not held to be efficient or otherwise wonderful.

Link Configurations Aid Matching

To understand the procedures, we need to work with what we will call *link configurations*. If a link joins two objects, the link configuration for that link consists of just the link itself. If a link joins one or two other links, then the link configuration consists of the link itself plus the link configurations of the one or two other links. In the diagram for *Macbeth*, the link configuration of the MURDER link consists of only the MURDER link. The link configuration of the CAUSE link going into the MURDER link is bigger: it consists of the CAUSE link plus MURDER, WANT, and IS-A links.

The key idea behind the MATCH procedure is this: find a useful link configuration that appears in both of the stories to be matched. Then use that link configuration to tie objects together:

To match two situations using MATCH:

1. Create L1, a list of link configurations in one situation. Also create L2, a list of link configurations in the other situation.
2. Until L1 is empty or no link configurations in L1 are useful or all objects have been tied together:
  2.1 Using USEFUL?, find a useful link configuration in L1.
  2.2 Use the useful link configuration and its compatible mate in L2 to tie objects together using TIE.

A link configuration is useful, basically, if there is a corresponding configuration in the other situation such that the two can be used to tie things together unambiguously. To be useful, the two configurations must at least be compatible. That is, the link names must be the same and the various objects involved must be identical or tied together compatibly or still dangling.

COMPATIBLE? checks all this using itself recursively:

To decide if link configurations are compatible using COMPAT-
IBLE?:

1a   If the things are links, they are compatible if their
      names are the same and the things at the head and
      the tail of the links are compatible.

1b   If the things are not links:

   1ba   If the things are tied together, they are com-
          patible.

   1bb   If the things are the same node, they are com-
          patible.

   1bc   If the things both are not tied, they are com-
          patible.

Unique Link Configurations Provide Unambiguous Matches

Given COMPATIBLE?, the main event in USEFUL? is to make sure there
is no possibility of ambiguity:

To decide if a link configuration is useful using USEFUL?:

1   Let L1 be a list of all link configurations for the situation
    with the given link configuration. Let L2 be a list of all
    link configurations for the other situation.

2   Using COMPATIBLE?, determine if the given link configu-
    ration is compatible with exactly one link configuration in
    L2.

   2a   If so, using COMPATIBLE?, determine if the compati-
         ble link configuration in L2 is compatible with exactly
         one link configuration in L1.

      2aa   If so, determine if there is at least one nontied
             object involved in the link configuration.

         2aaa   If so, the link configuration is useful.

Now that we have a way to decide which link configurations are useful, we
could work out a way to order the surviving link configurations according
to some reliability criteria. However, let us be content to use an unordered
list and to move on.

The shape of the procedure for actually tying things together resembles that of COMPATIBLE?:

To use compatible things to tie things together using TIE:

   1a   If the things are links, tie things together using the things at their head and the things at their tail.

   1b   If the things are not links:

       1ba   If the things are tied together, do nothing.

       1bb   If the things are the same node, do nothing.

       1bc   Otherwise, tie them.

LEARNING FORM FROM FUNCTIONAL DEFINITIONS

Interestingly, MACBETH also can be used to learn about physical appearance from functional definitions and physical examples. We begin by showing how the appearance of a cup can be learned from a functional definition and a particular example.

The first step is to describe the cup concept in terms of functional qualities such as liftability, stability, and the ability to serve as an accessible container. This is done by way of the following English:

A Cup Definition

This is a definition concerning an object. The object is a cup because it is stable, because it is liftable, and because it is an open vessel.

Of course, other, more elaborate definitions are possible, but this one provides good illustration.

A Particular Object

This is an exercise concerning a red object. The object's body is small. The object's bottom is flat. The object has an upward-pointing concavity. The object has a handle. Show that the object is a cup.

In contrast to the definition, the qualities involved in the description of the particular cup are all physical qualities, not functional ones.

Translated into semantic nets, the functional definition and the particular object are as shown in figure 12-7.

Now it is time to demonstrate that the functional requirements are met by the physical description. The demonstration requires precedents that relate the cup's functional descriptors to physical descriptors in the description of the particular cup. Three precedents are used. One indicates a way an object can be determined to be stable; another relates liftability

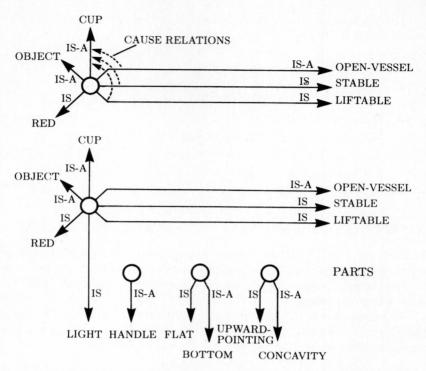

Figure 12-7. The functional definition of a cup and a physical description of a particular cup. These semantic nets are produced using English descriptions.

to weight and having a handle; and still another explains what being an open vessel means. All contain one thing that is irrelevant with respect to dealing with cups; these irrelevant things are representative of the detritus that can accompany the useful material.

Some Precedents

This is a description of a brick. The brick is stable because the brick's bottom is flat. The brick is hard.

This is a description of a suitcase. The suitcase is liftable because it is graspable and because it is light. The suitcase is graspable because it has a handle. The suitcase is useful because it is a portable container for clothes.

This is a description of a bowl. The bowl is an open vessel because it has a concavity and because the concavity is upward-pointing. The bowl contains cherry soup.

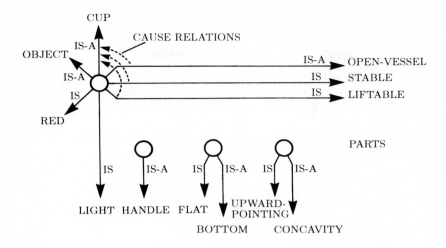

Figure 12-8. The CAUSE links of a functional description, acting as a precedent, are overlaid on the exercise, leading to other questioned links. Note that all of the exercise description is physical, albeit not all visual. Overlaid structure is dashed.

With the functional definition in hand, together with relevant precedents, the MACBETH apparatus is ready to work. First there is a search for precedents relevant to showing that the object in the exercise is a cup. The functional definition is retrieved. Next, MATCH determines the correspondence between parts of the exercise and the parts of the functional definition, a trivial task in this instance. Now MACBETH overlays the CAUSE links of the functional definition onto the exercise. Tracing through these overlaid CAUSE links raises three questions: Is the observed object stable, is it an open vessel, and is it liftable? All this is illustrated in figure 12-8.

Questioning if the object is liftable leads to a second search for a precedent, this time one that relates function to form, causing the suitcase description to be retrieved. The suitcase description, shown in figure 12-9, is matched to the exercise, its causal structure is overlaid on the exercise, and other questions are raised: Is the observed object light and does it have a handle? Since it is light and does have a handle, the suitcase description suffices to deal with the liftable issue, leaving open the stability and open vessel questions.

Thus the suitcase precedent, in effect, has a rule of inference buried in it, along with perhaps many useless things with respect to our purpose, including the statement about why the suitcase itself is useful. The job of MACBETH, then, is to find and exploit such implicit rules of inference.

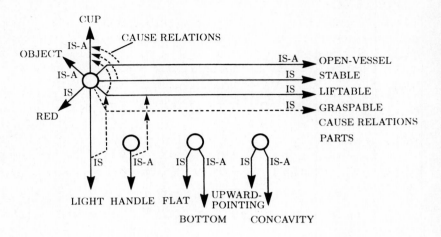

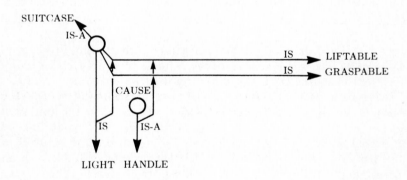

Figure 12-9. CAUSE links from the suitcase precedent are overlaid on the exercise, leading to questions about whether the object is light and whether the object has a handle. Overlaid structure is dashed. Many links of the suitcase precedent are not shown to avoid clutter on the diagram.

Checking out stability is done using the description of a brick. A brick is stable because it has a flat bottom. Similarly, to see if the object is an open vessel, a bowl is used. A bowl is an open vessel because it has an upward-pointing concavity. Figure 12-10 illustrates.

At this point, there is supporting evidence for the conclusion that the exercise object is a cup. Now we are ready for the final task, to build a rule that embodies a physical model of the functionally defined concept. This is done by constructing a rule from the links encountered in the problem-solving process: the questioned link goes to the *then* part; the links at the bottom of the transferred cause structure go to the *if* part. The result follows:

A Cup Description:

If   an object is light
         the object has an upward-pointing concavity
         the object has a flat bottom
         the object has a handle
then   the object is a cup

From this scenario, it is clear that learning form from function requires a physical example and some precedents in addition to a functional definition:

- The physical example is essential, for otherwise there would be no way to know which precedents are relevant.

- The precedents are essential, for otherwise there would be no way to know which aspects of the physical example are relevant.

IMPROVING RULES USING LEARNABLE CENSORS

Unfortunately, viewing our rulelike summaries as condition-action rules can lead to blunders. Returning to the world of *Macbeth*, consider the following exercise:

A Censor-evoking Exercise

This is an exercise concerning a weak noble and a greedy lady. The noble is married to the lady. He does not like her. Show that the noble may want to be king.

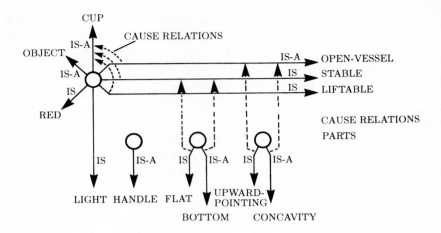

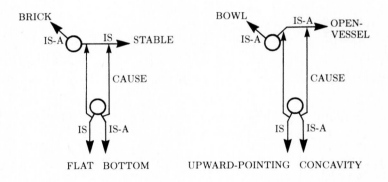

Figure 12-10. The brick precedent and the bowl precedent establish that the object is stable and that it is an open vessel. The CAUSE links of the precedents are overlaid on the exercise, leading to questioned links that are immediately resolved by the facts. Overlaid structure is dashed. Many links of the precedents are not shown to avoid clutter on the diagram.

This situation is different from the previous exercise because it is difficult for a person to influence someone who does not like her. If we look at only the tips of the want-to-be-king rule, the conclusion follows nevertheless. The rule is overly general, ready to reach conclusions when it should not. Evidently, there is a need to block rules in certain circumstances.

Censors Prevent Rule Misapplication

One way to block rules is to attend to the rules' intermediate link configurations lying between the roots and the tips. Think of negations of these intermediate link configurations as *unless conditions*. Augmenting the want-to-be-king rule with unless conditions, we have this:

> The Augmented Want-to-be-king Rule:
>
> If a weak noble is married to a greedy lady
> then the noble may want to be king
> unless the lady is not able to influence the noble
>   she is not able to persuade the noble to want to be king

Now we demand that the rule does not apply if either of the unless conditions corresponds to something that is obviously true.

Introspectively, it seems wrong to go deeply into reasoning about unless conditions because they usually describe unlikely things. Hence MACBETH adheres to the following:

- *The prima facie proscription.* If any unless condition of a triggered rule corresponds to a link configuration that is justifiable by one rule working directly from link configurations already in place, then the triggered rule is blocked.

Here is the rule-using procedure that enforces the prima facie proscription:

To use a rule:
1 Until there is a failure or all conditions are checked:
 1.1 For each condition, determine that the condition is in place or that the condition can be supported using another rule or precedent.
 1.2 For each unless condition, determine that the condition is not in place and that the condition cannot be supported using only one other rule together with links in place.
2 If there has been no failure, do what is prescribed by the action part of the rule.

Using this procedure, the augmented want-to-be-king rule is blocked if the following rule applies:

The Not-able-to-influence Censor:

If   person x does not like person y
then y may not be able to influence x

A rule becomes a *censor* when it blocks the application of another rule. Since censors look just like any other rules, censors can be learned, stored, and retrieved in the same ways.

Note that when the not-able-to-influence censor is used to block another, it works only if it is known at the time of use that there is dislike. There is no attempt to demonstrate dislike when not already known.

Note also that the viability of the prima facie proscription also depends on having all solid facts available before backward-chaining problem solving begins. This means that all solid facts are either given facts or deduced already by forward chaining from given facts using reliable rules. Reliability is ensured by forward chaining only with rules that reach unassailable conclusions.

Censors Can Block Censors

Actually, it is possible to be influenced by someone you dislike if for some reason you trust them in spite of the dislike. Perhaps the real not-able-to-influence censor should look like this:

The Augmented Able-to-influence Censor:

If   person x does not like person y
then y may not be able to influence x
unless x trusts y

Such a censor is blockable by another censor that states that you believe someone if they have the ability to convince you:

The Trust Censor:

If   person x is able to convince person y
then y may trust x

To illustrate how these can interact, consider the following situation:

A Censored Censor

This is an exercise concerning a weak noble and a greedy lady. The noble is married to the lady. He does not like her. The lady is able to convince the noble. Show that the noble may want to be king.

This produces the following scenario:

- First, the problem is posed and the want-to-be-king rule is fetched. Its condition parts are satisfied.

- Next, the unless part of the want-to-be-king rule is examined. The unless condition involving the ability to influence causes the not-able-to-influence censor to be fetched. Its condition parts are satisfied. The want-to-be-king rule is about to be blocked.

- But the not-able-to-influence censor's unless part must be examined. The unless condition involving trust causes the trust censor to be fetched. Its condition parts are satisfied. Thus the trust censor blocks the not-able-to-influence censor, preventing the able-to-influence censor from blocking the want-to-be-king rule.

- Finally, the want-to-be-king rule succeeds, establishing the link originally asked about.

Augmented Rules Are Not Ordinary Rules of Inference

It is tempting to write augmented rules in the following way:

$$A_1 \, \& \, \ldots \, \& \, A_n \, \& \, \neg(B_1 \vee \ldots \vee B_n) \Rightarrow C$$

or alternatively,

$$A_1 \, \& \, \ldots \, \& \, A_n \, \& \, \neg B_1 \, \& \, \ldots \, \& \, \neg B_n \Rightarrow C$$

where the As are the conditions of the rule and the Bs are the unless conditions.

Logical notation is deceptive, however, for in the use of augmented condition-action rules, the As and Bs get treated differently from each other, in contrast to the conventions of traditional logic. Unlimited effort is to be put into showing the As are true; but only one-step effort is put into showing that the Bs are true, with the Bs assumed false on failure.

Interestingly, from the point of view of logic, the use of augmented rules and censors introduces a form of the nonmonotonic property, described in chapter 7. Recall that a new censor can prevent the use of a rule that otherwise would work. Thus a new piece of knowledge can subtract from what can be concluded, making the reasoning nonmonotonic.

Augmented Rules Suggest an Approach to Certain Definition Problems

Consider the word *bachelor*. To be sure, a bachelor is an unmarried adult man, but such a definition causes trouble if used when someone says, "Please invite some nice bachelors to my party," for it would be strange to invite certain kinds of bachelors. For example, Catholic priests and misogamists, while satisfying the dictionary definition, are clearly not what party givers have in mind.

The augmented-rule idea offers one approach to the problem. Consider the following definition of *bachelor*, stated as an augmented condition-action rule:

The Bachelor Definition:

If   an adult man is not married
then   the man is a bachelor
unless   the man is not expected to be married
          the man is not able to be married

With this definition, the conclusion can be avoided, even though the condition part of the rule is fully satisfied, provided that the individual involved is not able to be married or is not expected to be married. This takes care of the Catholic priest and the misogamist problems, given the following censors:

The Misogamist Censor:

If   a person is a misogamist
then   the person is not expected to be married

The Catholic-priest Censor:

If   a man is a Catholic priest
then   the man is not able to be married

Evidently, it is possible to have a simple, stable definition of bachelor, while at the same time allowing for knowledge relevant to bachelors to interact with the definition, when appropriate, as that knowledge is accumulated. As more is learned, the definition is used more intelligently, and, in a sense, the definition is never closed. Think of the censors as forming a sort of fence around each rule. As the number of censors increases, the fence contracts.

SUMMARY

- META-WASP learns WASP rules. META-WASP works because WASP rules have a heavily constrained form. It may be that rules must have a heavily constrained form so that language can be learned.

- MACBETH solves problems analogically and creates rules as a by-product. The rules are useful because they are easy-to-use summaries.

- Matching is the process of tying corresponding objects together. Constrained, unusual link configurations help.

- Condition-action rules can be improved by adding unless conditions that enable censors to block them in inappropriate contexts. The effort expended in attempting to demonstrate unless conditions should be limited.

- Analogical problem solving enables physical models to be inferred using a functional definition, a particular physical example, and precedents.

REFERENCES

META-WASP is based on the work of Robert C. Berwick. Building on the WASP work of Mitchell P. Marcus [1980, 1981], Berwick demonstrated that an impressive corpus of WASP grammar rules can be built using a series of correct, but otherwise unprepared sentences [1982]. Naturally, his procedure, LPARSIFAL, is more complex than META-WASP.

James A. Moore and Allen Newell, in an early paper on analogy, addressed the process of analogy and how it can be involved in learning [1974]. Their paper gropes toward a mechanism that would permit a new piece of knowledge to be constructed by transforming an old one, rather than just by specialization or generalization. Other important work was done by P. Freeman and Newell on the role of functional reasoning in design. In their paper on the subject [1971], they proposed that available structures should be described in terms of functions provided and functions performed, and they hinted that some of this knowledge might be accumulated through experience. For other work on analogy, see Jaime G. Carbonell [1983].

The work on analogy described here, however, is my own, introduced in a series of papers [Winston 1980, 1982; Winston, Thomas O. Binford, Boris Katz, and Michael R. Lowry 1983].

The theory was shaped to a great degree by experiments that would have been extraordinarily tedious to perform without the English interface, developed by Boris Katz [1982], by means of which the experimental database was prepared, revised, and revised again. As Artificial Intelligence progresses beyond toy-world domains, it becomes obvious that databases prepared and accessed using English are necessary for research, not simply for research presentation.

The discussion of the word *bachelor* was motivated by Terry Winograd [1976] and by conversations with John C. Mallery, who pointed out that the word *bachelor* implies that the man involved is expected to be married.

For an excellent treatment on how rules might be repaired, see Frederick Hayes-Roth [1983].

There is, of course, a great deal of psychologically oriented literature on analogy. Among the best of this literature are papers by Dedre Gentner [1980, 1983].

EXERCISES

Many of the exercises introduce important contributions to the field such as Mitchell's version-space learning procedure, Morevec's reduced-images stereo procedure, and the STRIPS problem solver.

EXERCISES FOR CHAPTER 1

Exercise 1-1

Criticize the following statements:

1-1a

Artificial Intelligence is the enterprise of simulating human intelligence.

1-1b

Artificial Intelligence is part of computer science.

1-1c

A working program is prima facie evidence of successful research in Artificial Intelligence.

Exercise 1-2

Criticize the following statements:

1-2a

Computers can do only what they are told to do by a programmer.

1-2b

Computers cannot think aesthetically.

1-2c

Intelligence cannot be understood.

EXERCISES FOR CHAPTER 2

Exercise 2-1

This exercise explores the classic problem of transporting three missionaries and three cannibals across a river in a boat that can hold only two at a time. The constraint, of course, is that the cannibals cannot outnumber the missionaries anywhere, or else disaster.

This is a simple problem, once the representation is right. We will use a representation devised by Saul Amarel [1968]. He suggests using triples, (e, w, b), to denote the states, where e is the number of missionaries on the west bank, w is the number of cannibals, b is 1 when the boat is on the west bank, and b is 0 otherwise. Thus the initial state is denoted by $(3, 3, 1)$, and the goal state by $(0, 0, 0)$.

Clearly the number of possible states equals the number of possible triples, which is $4 \times 4 \times 2$. The number of safe states is smaller, however.

Note that it is useful to make a 4×4 diagram in which each point represents the number of missionaries and cannibals on the west bank, leaving the position of the boat ambiguous. West-to-east trips are indicated by arrows with closed heads, while east-to-west trips are indicated by arrows with open heads. For example, in figure E-1, the closed-head arrow indicates a trip with two cannibals from west to east; the open-head arrow indicates a trip with one cannibal from east to west.

2-1a

Identify the safe points.

2-1b

Find a path via safe points from the intial state to the desired state. Your path will take you through all the legal points.

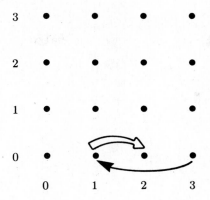

Figure E-1. A search space for the missionaries and cannibals.

Exercise 2-2

Criticize the following statements:

2-2a

Since a procedure can do analogy problems, it makes no sense to use them on human intelligence tests.

2-2b

If one is to construct answers to an analogy test according to some model of the person who designed the test, then one should pay particular attention to the designer's conventions for description, description matching, and comparison of description matches.

2-2c

The analogy procedure's intelligence, if any, is inside the description apparatus since the matching and match comparison processes can be described as straightforward rulelike behavior.

Exercise 2-3

Write out the rule descriptions in detail to show why the analogy procedure wrongly selects answer 1 in the problem given in figure E-2.

Exercise 2-4

The analogy procedure, as described, cannot do the problem in figure E-3. When matching the A-to-B rule with the C-to-1 rule, x must be associated with l and y with m. Similarly for C-to-2, the opposite pairing is forced, and we have x associated with m and y with l. But note that under the associations given, both C-to-1 and C-to-2 give exact match against A-to-B. What should be done?

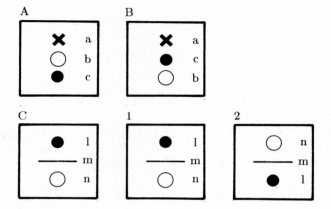

Figure E-2. An error-producing analogy problem.

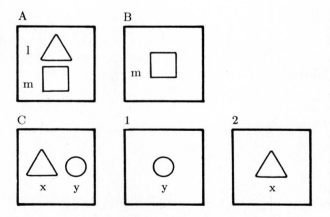

Figure E-3. An analogy problem with equally good answers.

Exercise 2-5

What parts of the analogy procedure would need replacement in order to handle the three-dimensional analogy problem in figure E-4? What is the best answer?

Exercise 2-6

Consider the three-block tower in E-5.
2-6a
Create an AND/OR tree reflecting what MOVER does when asked to put A on B.
2-6b
Use the AND/OR tree to answer the following questions:

1   *Why did you move D?*
2   *Why did you move C?*
3   *Why did you move A?*
4   *How did you clear the top of A?*
5   *How did you get rid of C?*

2-6c
How, in general, would you deal with questions involving *when*? Use your procedure to deal with the following questions:

1   *When did you move D?*
2   *When did you move C?*
3   *When did you move A?*

Exercise 2-7

Consider the situation in figure E-6.
2-7a
Create an AND/OR tree reflecting what MOVER does when asked to put A on C.
2-7b
How does MOVER blunder?
2-7c
How would you prevent MOVER's blunder?

EXERCISES FOR CHAPTER 3

Exercise 3-1

Decide which objects in figure E-7 can be labeled using the four-line-label set. Justify your answer.

440

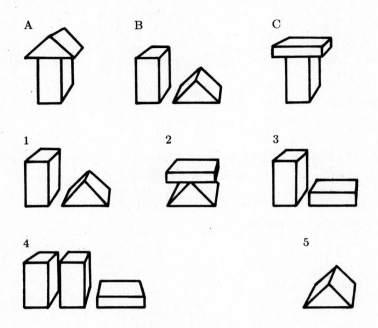

Figure E-4. A three-dimensional analogy problem.

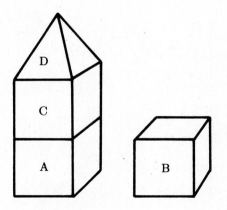

Figure E-5. Coping with three blocks.

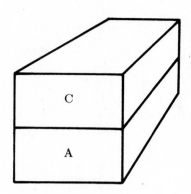

Figure E-6. A placement problem.

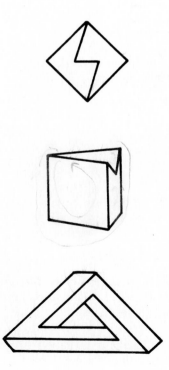

Figure E-7. Legal and illegal drawings.

Exercise 3-2

Suppose a robot lives in a world of polyhedra known to have no concave edges.

3-2a

How should the four-line-label theory be modified by this robot to detect impossible objects in its world? What are the physically realizable junctions?

3-2b

Label the objects in figure E-8 using the new junction set.

Exercise 3-3

The original purpose of labeling was to determine if an object is physically realizable by determining if any consistent labeling exists for that object. However, there may be more than one consistent labeling for some objects. Finish labeling figure E-9 indicating all possible combinations of labels that are consistent with the four-label set.

Exercise 3-4

What conclusion should be drawn when the Waltz procedure eliminates all labeling possibilities at a junction?

Exercise 3-5

How is analyzing a line drawing like solving algebraic equations?

Exercise 3-6

Why is it that the Waltz procedure cannot get stuck propagating constraints around some junction loop forever?

Exercise 3-7 (Linda J. Rosentzarat)

The number of possible labels for a line is $11 \times 3^2 = 99$, where there are 11 basic line types and 3 states of illumination on either side of each line. Hence, for an L junction, the number of combinatorially possible labels is $11^2 \times 3^4 = 9801$.

Waltz argued that only about 50 labels survive for lines when line type and illumination constraints are considered, giving about $50^2 = 2500$ possible L junction labels.

Ignoring the interaction of line types and illumination states, argue on the basis of region continuity that there can be no more than 1089.

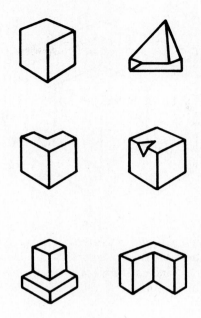

Figure E-8. Some legal and illegal convex-world objects.

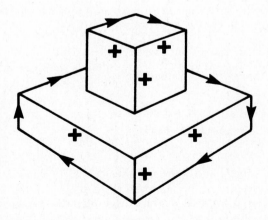

Figure E-9. An ambiguous drawing.

444

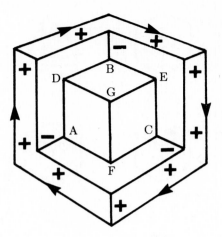

Figure E-10. A situation in which no further labeling is forced.

Exercise 3-8

Suppose that the unlabeled lines of the drawing fragment in figure E-10 are to be labeled. Note that there is no junction whose neighbors force a unique configuration choice.

Using the basic set of four line labels, treating the junctions in alphabetic order, show how Waltz's procedure labels the drawing.

Exercise 3-9 (Kenneth D. Forbus)

Suppose Peter, Paul, and Jane are musicians. One of them plays saxophone, another plays guitar, and the third plays drums. As it happens, one of them is afraid of things associated with the number 13, another of them is afraid of cats, and the third is afraid of heights. You also know that Peter and the guitarist skydive; that Paul and the saxophone player enjoy cats; and that the drummer lives in apartment 13 on the thirteenth floor.

Soon we will want to use these facts to reason about whether or not certain identity relations hold or are excluded. Assume X(Peter, Guitarist) means "the person who is Peter is not the person who plays the guitar." In this notation, the facts become:

1   X(Peter, Guitarist)

2   X(Peter, Fears heights)

3   X(Guitarist, Fears heights)

4   X(Paul, Fears cats)

5   X(Paul, Saxophonist)

6   X(Saxophonist, Fears cats)

7   X(Drummer, Fears 13)

8   X(Drummer, Fears heights)

Now we can represent the possible relations implicitly by means of entries in a table. Each row and column is labeled by the members of a particular class, an X entry in the table denotes that the identity relationship is excluded, and an I denotes that the identity relationship actually holds. Numbers in the boxes indicate the fact used to establish the entry:

	Guitarist	Saxophonist	Drummer
Peter	X,1		
Paul		X,5	
Jane			

Of course, we need two more tables, one to represent the possible identities between the people and the fears, and another to represent the possible relationships between the instrument players and the fears.

The following rules describe how new table entries can be deduced from those already there:

1   If all but one entry in a row are Xs, then the remaining one is an I.

2   If one entry in a row is an I, then all others in the row are Xs.

3   If all but one entry in a column are Xs, then the remaining one is an I.

4   If one entry in a column is an I, then all others in the column are Xs.

5   If you know I(x, y) and X(y, z), then you may conclude X(x, z).

3-9a

For rule five, write a short English sentence that describes the property of the world that it captures.

3-9b

Find which sort of instrument player Paul is by using the rules and the three tables below. Note that the facts are already filled in.

	Guitarist	Saxophonist	Drummer
Peter	X,1		
Paul		X,5	
Jane			

	Fears 13	Fears cats	Fears heights
Peter			X,2
Paul		X,4	
Jane			

	Fears 13	Fears cats	Fears heights
Guitarist			X,3
Saxophonist		X,6	
Drummer	X,7		X,8

3-9c

Using the rules and the tables is similar to line-drawing analysis. What corresponds to lines? What corresponds to labels? What corresponds to junctions?

Exercise 3-10

Constant-adder-multiplier nets can model certain electronic components. The net in figure E-11a, for example, is a model for the resistor shown in another representation in E-11b.

3-10a

Compute values for the quantities lacking values.

3-10b

Try to compute values for the quantities lacking values in figure E-12. Why do you fail? How could you generalize the numeric constraint propagation procedure to handle such situations?

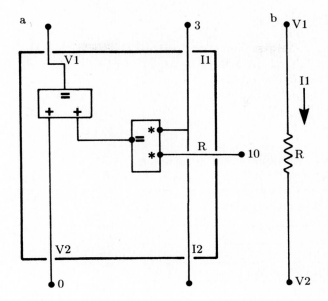

Figure E-11. A resistor.

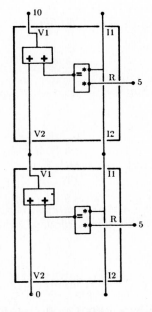

Figure E-12. A problem-causing constant-adder-multiplier net.

Exercise 3-11

The relaxation procedure for calculating heights from initial altitude estimates used initial altitude estimates of zero when there was no information. Suggest a better alternative.

Exercise 3-12

The relaxation procedure for calculating heights from initial altitude estimates converged slowly. One reason is that it takes so long to propagate information through many array points. Suggest a way to use coarse grids to speed convergence.

EXERCISES FOR CHAPTER 4

Exercise 4-1

Criticize the following statements:

4-1a

Beam search always finds optimal paths.

4-1b

More knowledge generally means more search since more alternatives must be considered.

4-1c

Depth-first search can lose completely if a tree is infinite. There is no analogous way for breadth-first search to lose.

4-1d

Dynamic programming is a useful concept when searching for optimal paths but has no useful role when doing ordinary depth-first search and breadth-first search.

Exercise 4-2

Write down the procedure for doing beam search in structured English.

Exercise 4-3 (Robert C. Berwick)

A video game company has asked you to try out their new game, SEARCHMAN. The concept is to locate and obtain a hoard of precious gold and silver, in two distinct phases. Being an expert in search techniques, you agree to the trial.

Your job is to locate where the precious metal is. The terrain consists of a flat plain stretching out along the X and Y axes.

There is a simulated metal detector that indicates the strength of the metal deposit directly below the point where you aim the detector. You also have a joystick to simulate wandering over plain with your detector in hand. You start at the point $(x, y) = (4, 5)$. Your plan is to find the strongest signal by first stepping along in just the X direction until the detector reading peaks, then to do the same in the Y direction. You take unit steps. Your first shot at this yields the following results:

X Y Reading
4 5 91
5 5 140
6 5 89
5 5 140
5 6 89
5 5 140
5 4 91
5 5 140

Evidently, the maximum reading you obtain by this method is 140. Feeling a bit unsure about the result, you try the same exercise, but starting at point $(x, y) = (4, 3)$.

X Y Reading
4 3 93
5 3 42
4 3 93
3 3 144
2 3 95
3 3 144
3 4 93
3 3 144
3 2 95
3 3 144

Your fears are confirmed: this is a better final result than before.

4-3a

What is the general name for this kind of search strategy?

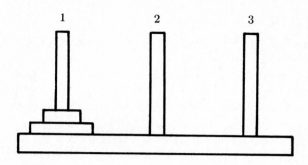

Figure E-13. The towers of Hanoi.

4-3b

Characterize the reason why this strategy does not seem to be working very well.

4-3c

How could this kind of failure be avoided in this particular case?

Exercise 4-4

Consider a game with two disks and three pins as shown in figure E-13. The objective of the game is to move both the disks from the left pin to the right pin, subject to the following constraints:

- You can move only one disk at a time.

- You cannot place the large disk on top of the small disk.

We can indicate the arrangement by a list, (x, y), where x is the pin number for the large disk and y is the pin number for the small disk. Using this notation, the nine possible arrangements are denoted:

[1] (1,1) [2] (1,2) [3] (1,3)
[4] (2,1) [5] (2,2) [6] (2,3)
[7] (3,1) [8] (3,2) [9] (3,3)

Arrangement [8], for example, is the arrangement in which the large pin is on pin 3 and the small one is on pin 2.

4-4a

Create a table indicating which transitions between arrangements are possible in one move.

4-4b

Find a solution using depth-first search, taking care to ensure that no path visits the same node twice.

4-4c

Repeat using breadth-first search, again taking care to ensure that no path visits the same node twice.

4-4d

Find a solution by expanding the highest numbered open node, again taking care to ensure that no path visits the same node twice. What sort of search is this?

Exercise 4-5

As given, the A* procedure can be made more efficient.

4-5a

Show how, by rearranging two steps.

4-5b

Show how, by refining the path-discarding step.

Exercise 4-6

You have probably seen something called a *15-puzzle*. Consider a smaller version, an *8-puzzle*, consisting of a tray with room for eight tiles and a blank space. The tiles may be slid around to produce various arrangements. This is the initial position:

2	8	3
1	6	4
7		5

And this is the desired final position:

1	2	3
8		4
7	6	5

4-6a

You are to use A* to find the shortest sequence of moves that take the initial position to the final position. Let the number of misplaced tiles be the estimate of the remaining distance, e(board position). Your answer is to be the search tree with the estimated total distances and the solution path marked.

4-6b

Suppose we were to use e(board position) = 0 as the estimate of remaining distance. What sort of search would A* become?

4-6c

Suppose we were to use the misplaced-tiles estimate alone, ignoring the number of accumulated moves. What sort of search would A* become?

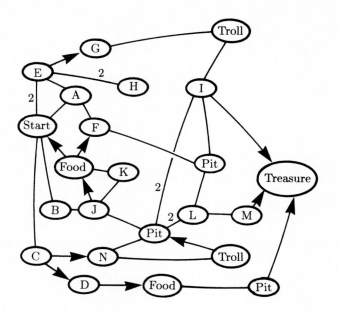

Figure E-14. Some caves.

4-6d

We say that one estimate of remaining position is *more informed* than another if the value of its e(board position) function is always strictly greater than the value of the other's e(board position) function. For example, the misplaced-tiles estimate is more informed than e(board position) $= 0$. Describe a lower bound estimate that is more informed than the misplaced-tiles estimate.

Exercise 4-7 (Robert C. Berwick)

You want to locate a hoard of precious gold and silver in a vast warren of interconnected caves, shown in figure E-14.

The hoard is in the cave marked Treasure. Caves are connected via two-way paths, unless indicated otherwise by directional links. You have a limited energy supply, measured in food quanta (fqs) and walking from one cave to another uses one fq unless indicated otherwise by a number above the link connecting two caves. There are four kinds of caves: banal, pit, troll, and food. Nothing extraordinary happens in a banal cave; they are labeled with letters. If you enter a pit, then you must climb out, and this uses 5 fqs of energy. If you enter a food cave, you gain 5 fqs of energy.

You may traverse the same cave more than once, except for troll caves, which are impassable. You begin at the Start cave with 5 fqs of energy. If you run out of energy before you find the treasure, you lose. You have a map to plan your route with.

4-7a

Would it be better to use depth-first search or breadth-first search?

4-7b

Would branch-and-bound, with energy used as the accumulated distance measurement, be a good strategy for searching for a path in the network? Why or why not?

4-7c

If your object were to get to the goal with the least energy used, what would be the best path?

4-7d

What is the maximum energy you could arrive at the goal with?

Exercise 4-8

Criticize the following statements:

4-8a

The alpha-beta theorem demonstrates that on the average no more than $2b^{d/2} - 1$ terminals need be examined in trees of even depth.

4-8b

Given a plausible move generator that always perfectly orders the moves, the alpha-beta procedure gives optimal tree pruning, and only a fool would not use it.

4-8c

The alpha-beta procedure can prevent spectacular moves such as queen sacrifices leading to checkmate in chess.

Exercise 4-9

Assume that you conspire with an opponent to fix a game. You agree to some secret signals that allow you to tell him exactly how to move. The objective is to beat him as badly as possible. How effective is the alpha-beta procedure under these conditions?

Exercise 4-10

In qualitative terms, how should a better static evaluator and a better plausible move generator affect the balance between depth and breadth of search.

Exercise 4-11

Consider the game tree in figure E-15.

4-11a

Explore the tree using the alpha-beta procedure. Assume the top level is a maximizing level. Cross out all nodes where static evaluation need not occur. Indicate the winning path or paths.

4-11b

Repeat, working from right to left through the tree, rather than from left to right.

4-11c

Are there any opportunities for deep cutoff?

Exercise 4-12

Consider the game tree in figure E-16.

4-12a

Explore the tree using the alpha-beta procedure. Assume the top level is a maximizing level. Cross out all nodes where static evaluation need not occur. Indicate the winning path or paths.

4-12b

Are there any opportunities for deep cutoff?

Exercise 4-13

Does it make sense to explore the remainder of the partially analyzed tree in figure E-17?

EXERCISES FOR CHAPTER 5

Exercise 5-1

Criticize the following statements:

5-1a

The key to intelligence is sophisticated control.

5-1b

The blackboard method for procedure communication is better than the private-line method and the reserved-spot method.

5-1c

The communication within a scientific community is reminiscent of the private-line method for procedure communication.

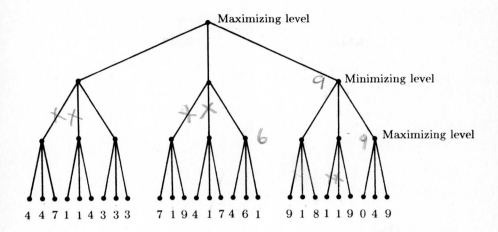

Figure E-15. A depth-three game tree.

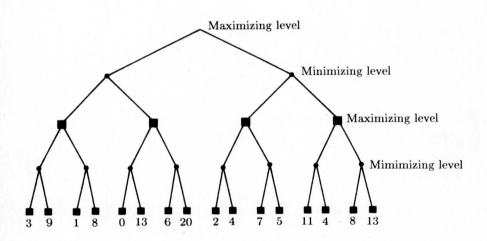

Figure E-16. A depth-four game tree.

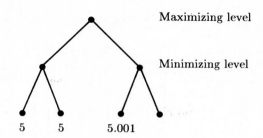

5   5   5.001

Figure E-17. A game tree with low return on investment.

5-1d

A group of strangers, at a management class, are told to build a house. To accomplish anything, they should start out using hierarchical, action-centered control.

Exercise 5-2

Suppose Robbie, growing sick of Los Angeles, wants to go home to Boston. Show the time sequence and level for each of the procedures his plan will include.

Exercise 5-3

Suppose Robbie needs to visit people in Los Angeles often. How can he simplify his problem solving?

Exercise 5-4

A procedure can answer questions about how GPS has achieved some particular goal and why GPS has used some particular procedure.

5-4a

Explain how.

5-4b

How would the procedure answer the following questions about the travel example:

1   *Why did Robbie walk to the parking garage.*

2   *How did Robbie take the airplane.*

Exercise 5-5

Three cannibals and three missionaries are standing on the west bank of the Mississippi River, seeking to go eastward. A boat is available that will hold either one or two people. Importantly, if the missionaries are ever outnumbered anywhere, the cannibals will eat the missionaries. Is GPS a good way to approach this problem? Why or why not?

Exercise 5-6

In the travel example, GPS's differences are mutually exclusive, so there is never any ambiguity about which to use. In other problems involving difference-procedure tables, the procedure selected is the one identified as relevant to reducing the highest priority difference, the one nearest the top in the difference-procedure table.

Invent a table-oriented scheme for procedure selection that does the following:

- Combines the evidence from all the differences in force.

- Considers the likelihood with which the various procedures reduce the various differences.

- Considers the priority of the differences.

EXERCISES FOR CHAPTER 6

Exercise 6-1

Explain how the generate-and-test paradigm can be viewed as a simple search.

Exercise 6-2

You are working quietly with your terminal when attacked by an army of ants. Wishing to counterattack, you run to the supermarket and look around wildly, hoping that some useful weapon will catch your eye as you randomly scan the beverages, foods, household cleaners, and other things. You are using the generate-and-test paradigm, of course, but your generator is not likely to have certain desired properties. What are those properties?

Exercise 6-3

Simulate the BAGGER procedure using the following property list and shopping list. Assume two medium items or three small items take the same room as one large item.

Item	Container Type	Size	Frozen?
Bread	Plastic bag	Medium	No
Glop	Jar	Small	No
Granola	Cardboard box	Large	No
Ice cream	Cardboard carton	Medium	Yes
Paper towels	Plastic bag	Large	No
Pepsi	Bottle	Large	No
Popsicles	Cardboard carton	Small	Yes
Potato chips	Plastic bag	Medium	No

Step: Check-order
Bag1:
Unbagged: Bread (3)
          Glop (2)
          Ice cream (2)
          Paper towels (4)
          Pepsi (4)
          Popsicles (1)

Exercise 6-4

Suppose BAGGER considers whether an item is crushable as well as its other properties. The table of item properties then looks like this:

Item	Container Type	Size	Frozen?	Crushable?
Bread	Plastic bag	Medium	No	Yes
Glop	Jar	Small	No	No
Granola	Cardboard box	Large	No	No
Ice cream	Cardboard carton	Medium	Yes	No
Pepsi	Bottle	Large	No	No
Potato chips	Plastic bag	Medium	No	Yes

Add rules to the BAGGER system so that nothing gets crushed.

Exercise 6-5 (John McDermott)

In our version of BAGGER, each step is deactivated and another activated by rules that look like this:

B2 If   the step is check-order
    then   discontinue the check-order step
            start the bag-large-items step

Show how to do all deactivation by a single rule. Similarly, show how to do all activation with rules that depend on what has been done rather than on the step.

Exercise 6-6

Assume the IDENTIFIER procedure pursues hypotheses in the following order:

- Cheetah

- Tiger

- Giraffe

- Zebra

- Ostrich

- Penguin

- Albatross

Now here are some facts to assume true, if inquiry is made:

- The animal has feathers.

- It lays eggs.

- It does not fly.

- It is black and white.

- It swims.

And here are some to assume false, if inquiry is made:

- It has hair.
- It gives milk.
- It flies.
- It eats meat.
- Its eyes point forward.
- It has pointed teeth.
- It has claws.
- It has hoofs.
- It chews its cud.
- It has a tawny color.
- It has dark spots.
- It has black stripes.
- It has long legs.
- It has a long neck.
- It has a white color.
- It is a good flier.

6-6a

Simulate IDENTIFIER's behavior on the given facts. Take care to use the hypotheses in the specified order. Indicate your answer by showing the sequence in which the rules fire and the name of the animal.

6-6b

Repeat, but assume that the animal does have long legs and a long neck. The other properties are unchanged. Why is the result peculiar?

Exercise 6-7

Add rules to the IDENTIFIER system so that it can recognize porcupines, raccoons, and eagles.

Exercise 6-8

Write out a procedure, in structured English, for backward chaining using antecedent-consequent rules.

Exercise 6-9

You wish to analyze a fruitcake you have just discovered. A friend suggests that you break it up with a hammer and pass the detritus through a series of sieves. This leads you to believe that your friend has been reading this book. Why?

Exercise 6-10 (Karen A. Prendergast)

You are just starting a quiet evening at home when an old friend calls to announce he is coming over for dinner at your place. This being a big surprise, you immediately undertake emergency dinner preparations.

Within a few minutes, you have managed to load up the BARTENDER expert system on your personal computer so that you can select a beverage.

BARTENDER is a backward-chaining production system with rules given below. Note that when more than one rule has a consequent matching the current problem, those rules are tried in the order given in the list.

B1 If   expensive wine is indicated
       it is New Year's Eve
   then   Bond's Champagne

B2 If   expensive wine is indicated
       entree is steak
   then   Chateau Earl of Bartonville Red

B3 If   cheap wine is indicated
       entree is chicken
       guest is not well liked
   then   Honest Henry's Apple Wine

B4 If   cheap wine is indicated
       entree is unknown
   then   Toe Lakes Rose

B5 If   beer is indicated
       entree is Mexican
   then   Dos Equis

B6 If   beer is indicated
   then   Coors

B7 If   guest is a health nut
   then   Glop

B8 If   guest is a health nut
       carrots are not to be served
   then   carrot juice

B9 If   wine is indicated
       guest should be impressed
   then   expensive wine is indicated

B10 If   wine is indicated
   then   cheap wine is indicated

B11 If   guest is sophisticated
   then   wine is indicated

B12 If   entree is Mexican
     then   beer is indicated

B13 If   guest is not well liked
           entree is catered by Death-wish Caterers
     then   beer is indicated

B14 If   true
     then   water

BARTENDER's hypotheses are as follows:

- Bond's Champagne
- Chateau Earl of Bartonville Red
- Toe Lakes Rose
- Honest Henry's Apple Wine
- Dos Equis
- Coors
- Glop
- Carrot juice
- Water

Now here are some facts to assume true, if inquiry is made:

- Entree is catered by Death-wish Caterers.
- Entree is Mexican.
- Guest is not well liked.
- Guest is sophisticated.
- It is New Year's Eve.
- The entree is chicken.

And here are some to assume false, if inquiry is made:

- Carrots are not to be served.
- Entree is unknown.
- Guest is a health nut.
- Guest should be impressed.
- The entree is steak.

6-10a

Simulate BARTENDER's behavior on the given facts. Take care to use the
hypotheses in the specified order. Indicate your answer by showing the
sequence in which the rules fire and the name of the drink selected.

6-10b

With some different set of facts, could BARTENDER ever recommend the
Chateau Earl of Bartonville Red with Mexican food? If not, why not?

6-10c

With some different set of facts, could BARTENDER ever recommend carrot
juice with steak? If not, why not?

6-10d

Suppose BARTENDER2 not only has many more rules than BARTENDER, but also
has certainty factors associated with them. In particular, BARTENDER2 has
a new rule similar to rule B4:

B4a If   entree is known
            cheap wine is indicated
     then   Toe Lakes Rose

Is rule B4a likely to have a higher or lower certainty factor than rule B4?
Why?

6-10e

Suppose beer is universally acknowledged to be the best thing with Death-
wish's food. You write to the software house that supplies BARTENDER suggesting simplification of rule B13. They write back defending their rule as
is. What is their defense?

EXERCISES FOR CHAPTER 7

Exercise 7-1

The most popular of the two-argument connectives are &, ∨, and ⇒. How
many two-argument connectives are there?

Exercise 7-2

Show that modus tolens is a special case of resolution.

Exercise 7-3

Show the steps required to put the following axioms into clause form:

$$\forall x \forall y [\text{On}(x, y) \Rightarrow \text{Above}(x, y)]$$
$$\forall x \forall y \forall z [\text{Above}(x, y) \,\&\, \text{Above}(y, z) \Rightarrow \text{Above}(x, z)]$$

Exercise 7-4

Put the following axiom in clause form, which merely says that if x is above y, but not directly on y, there must exist some third block, z, in between. Note that a Skolem function will be needed.

$$\forall x \forall y [\text{Above}(x, y) \ \& \ \neg \text{On}(x, y) \Rightarrow \exists z [\text{Above}(x, z) \ \& \ \text{Above}(z, y)]]$$

Exercise 7-5

Suppose you are given the following axioms:

$$\forall x [\neg \text{Equal}(x, x + 1)]$$
$$\text{Equal}(2, 3)$$

7-5a
Show that all apples are oranges.
7-5b
Why were you able to reach a silly conclusion?

Exercise 7-6

Before two clauses are resolved, they must have no variable names in common. Consequently, it might seem superfluous to prohibit replacement of a variable by a term containing that variable. Explain why the prohibition is not superfluous.

Exercise 7-7 (Tomás Lozano-Pérez)

Here are some logical expressions for solving blocks world problems:

$$\forall x \forall y \forall s [\text{Clear}(x, s) \ \& \ \text{Clear}(y, s) \Rightarrow \text{On}(x, y, \text{Puton}(x, y, s))]$$

$$\forall x \forall y \forall s [\text{On}(x, y, s) \Rightarrow \neg \text{Clear}(y, s)]$$

$$\forall x \forall y \forall s [\text{On}(x, y, s) \ \& \ \text{Clear}(x, s) \Rightarrow \text{On}(x, \text{Table}, \text{Puton}(x, \text{Table}, s))]$$

$$\forall x \forall y \forall s [\text{On}(x, y, s) \ \& \ \text{Clear}(x, s) \Rightarrow \text{Clear}(y, \text{Puton}(x, \text{Table}, s))]$$

These are the same expressions in clause form:

$$\neg \text{Clear}(x_1, s_1) \lor \neg \text{Clear}(y_1, s_1) \lor \text{On}(x_1, y_1, \text{Puton}(x_1, y_1, s_1)) \quad (1)$$

$$\neg \text{On}(x_2, y_2, s_2) \lor \neg \text{Clear}(y_2, s_2) \quad (2)$$

$$\neg \text{On}(x_3, y_3, s_3) \lor \neg \text{Clear}(y_3, s_3) \lor \text{On}(x_3, \text{Table}, \text{Puton}(x_3, \text{Table}, s_3)) \quad (3)$$

$$\neg \text{On}(x_4, y_4, s_4) \lor \neg \text{Clear}(x_4, s_4) \lor \text{Clear}(y_4, \text{Puton}(x_4, \text{Table}, s_4)) \quad (4)$$

The initial state of the world is as follows:

$$On(A, B, S) \tag{5}$$

$$On(B, C, S) \tag{6}$$

$$Clear(A, S) \tag{7}$$

The following frame axioms will prove useful in your proofs:

$$\forall u \forall x \forall y \forall s[\text{Clear}(u, s) \,\&\, \text{Different}(u, y) \Rightarrow \text{Clear}(u, \text{Puton}(x, y, s))]$$

$$\forall u \forall v \forall x \forall y \forall s[\text{On}(u, v, s) \,\&\, \text{Different}(u, x) \Rightarrow \text{On}(u, v, \text{Puton}(x, y, s))]$$

Assume that you also have axioms stating that things like Different(A, B), Different(A, C), and Different(B, C) are all TRUE.

In clause form the frame axioms are as follows:

$$\neg\text{Clear}(u_8, s_8) \lor \neg\text{Different}(u_8, y_8) \lor \text{Clear}(u_8, \text{Puton}(x_8, y_8, s_8)) \tag{8}$$

$$\neg\text{On}(u_9, v_9, s_9) \lor \neg\text{Different}(u_9, x_9) \lor \text{On}(u_9, v_9, \text{Puton}(x_9, y_9, s_9)) \tag{9}$$

7-7a

Explain both of the frame axioms in English.

7-7b

Show that the following state can be achieved. Do this by using set-of-support resolution.

$$\exists s[\text{Clear}(C, s)]$$

A good way to start is to use axiom 4. At each step in the proof, indicate which clauses are being resolved. Rename variables consistently to ensure that the variable names in the clauses you resolve are mutually exclusive. Note that the proof requires fewer than ten steps.

7-7c

Repeat using Green's trick to find the plan that achieves the indicated state.

Exercise 7-8 (Tomás Lozano-Pérez)

This exercise explores the STRIPS problem solver developed principally by Richard E. Fikes, Nils J. Nilsson, and Peter Hart [Fikes and Nilsson 1971]. The key to STRIPS is the way it deals with the frame problem. Rather than using situation variables to indicate in what states statements are true, STRIPS maintains a single set of expressions, its *world model*, that represents what is true *now*. STRIPS's procedures, called operators, modify the current state by adding new expressions and deleting old ones. In particular, we can now assume that an operator will remove any expressions that are not true in the world after the operator is used. Therefore, all the other expressions are still true. Thus, STRIPS embodies the heuristic that things do not change unless some operator explicitly affects them. This is not always true, but is, in many cases, a good approximation to reality.

The other components of STRIPS operators are their preconditions, the conditions that must be true before the operator may be performed. Here are some operators for moving blocks:

PICKUP(x)
precondition: EMPTYHAND& Clear(x) & On(x, y)
     delete: EMPTYHAND, Clear(x), On(x, y)
        add: INHAND(x)

PUTDOWN(y)
precondition: INHAND(y)
     delete: INHAND(y)
        add: EMPTYHAND, Clear(y), On(y, TABLE)

UNSTACK(u, z)
precondition: EMPTYHAND& Clear(u) & On(u, z)
     delete: EMPTYHAND, Clear(u), On(u, z)
        add: INHAND(u), Clear(z)

STACK(v, w)
precondition: INHAND(v) & Clear(w)
     delete: INHAND(v), Clear(w)
        add: EMPTYHAND, Clear(v), On(v, w)

STRIPS uses two basic data structures: the state description (a set of literals) and a goal stack. Each entry in the goal stack contains either a single-literal goal, a conjunction of literals, or an operator with its arguments.

The basic **STRIPS** procedure is as follows:

To prove a theorem using **STRIPS**:

1   Initialize the state description using the initial state and initialize the goal stack using the desired goal, which may be a compound goal.

2   Using depth-first search to continue from choice points on failure, until succeeding or exhausting the choice points, examine the item at the top of the goal stack:

    2a   If the top item *matches the state*, apply the unifying substitution to the goals on the stack and pop the stack.

    2b   If the top item is a *single-literal goal*:

        2b1   Find an operator that has that literal in the Add formula. If no relevant operator exists, then fail. This is a choice point.

        2b2   Obtain a unifying substitution of the Add formula and the goal. This is a choice point.

        2b3   Push the operator on the stack.

        2b4   Push the operator's precondition formula on the stack.

    2c   If the top item is an *operator*, then remove literals from the state that match its Delete list and add the Add formula (after binding variables specified by the operator arguments). Pop the operator off the stack.

    2d   If the top item is a *compound goal*, then push each of the conjuncts on the stack in some order. This is a choice point.

    2e   If the goal stack is *empty*, then succeed.

Thus, whenever failure occurs, the process backs up to one of the choice points and tries a new alternative. Note that step 2d leaves the compound goal on the stack as well as placing its literals on top of it. This ensures that possible goal interactions do not interfere with achieving the compound goal.

Now, finally, the problems. You are given the initial state and goal state shown in figure E-18. Simulate **STRIPS** as it solves the problem. Whenever a compound goal is placed on the stack, add its conjuncts to the stack in left-to-right order. At other choice points, simplify your work by choosing a favorable option.

7-8a

Show the stack at each point when it reaches a local maximum depth. For each of your snapshots, show how much of the stack is popped before pushing starts.

7-8b

Show the sequence of operators required to reach the goal.

Exercise 7-9

7-9a

Consider the following to be axioms:

$$P \Rightarrow R$$
$$Q \Rightarrow R$$
$$P \vee Q$$

Show that R is a theorem using resolution.

7-9b

Repeat, if possible, using the constraint-propagation proof procedure. If you fail, explain why.

EXERCISES FOR CHAPTER 8

Exercise 8-1 (Karen A. Prendergast)

Snow White, a famous fairy-tale character, knows a number of dwarfs. These dwarfs include Blimpy, Crazy, Grumpy, and Happy.

Snow White knows nothing about these dwarfs except what can be derived from the semantic net shown in figure E-19.

8-1a

Add IS-A links, AKO links, other links, and if-needed procedures to the semantic net, as appropriate, so as to capture the following statements:

1 Weightlifters have high strength.
2 Professors have low strength.
3 Dwarfs have small size.
4 Gourmets have large size.
5 Businessmen and athletes are competitors.
6 Competitors like contests.
7 The salary of an employed person is high if he likes contests.
8 The personality of a businessman is unfriendly.
9 The personality of a dwarf is friendly if the dwarf has small size.

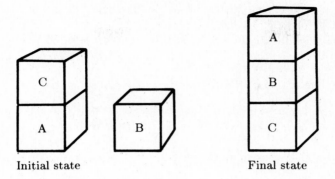

Figure E-18. A problem for **STRIPS**.

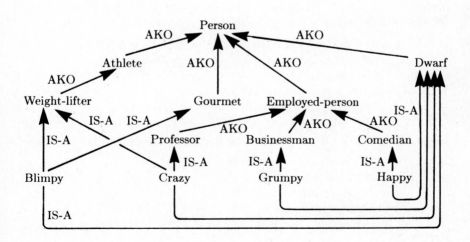

Figure E-19. Snow White's dwarfs.

Write the if-needed procedures, if any, in the condition-action style illustrated in the following model:
For the businessman node, for the health slot the if-needed procedure is:

If   heavy is the value in the weight slot
then   put bad in the health slot

The meaning intended is: if you need to know the health of a businessman, then see if his weight is heavy; if so, his health is bad.

8-1b

Using N inheritance, determine answers to the following questions, if any. Assume that the breadth-first search involved is done in clockwise order, starting at 9 o'clock.

1   What is Grumpy's personality?
2   What is Happy's personality?
3   What is Blimpy's personality?
4   What is Grumpy's salary?
5   What is Crazy's salary?
6   What is Grumpy's strength?

8-1c

Now suppose the nodes for the dwarfs are split into two perspectives each, the work perspective and the play perspective. Work perspectives are connected to the professor, businessman, and comedian classes. Play perspectives are connected to the weightlifter and gourmet classes.

1   From the work perspective, what is Grumpy's salary?
2   From the work perspective, what is Crazy's salary?

Exercise 8-2

Show that if-needed procedures, carelessly used, can lead to infinite loops.

Exercise 8-3

Suggest some heuristics for using news stories to fill slots in frames of the following types:

8-3a

A hurricane.

8-3b

A wedding.

Exercise 8-4

If a story writer uses pronouns freely, it may be hard to fill in frames. Consider the following story:

A Birthday Party

Robbie and Suzie were going to Marvin's birthday party. <u>One</u> of <u>them</u> wanted to buy a kite. "But <u>he</u> already has <u>one</u>," <u>he</u> said to <u>her</u>, "if <u>you</u> give <u>him</u> <u>one</u>, <u>he</u> will ask <u>you</u> to take <u>it</u> back."

In this version, unraveling the pronoun references is a real chore. Rewrite the story in the form of news, circumnavigating the pronoun reference problems.

Exercise 8-5

Consider the sentence "Robbie comforted Suzie." Reducing the sentence to primitive acts and state changes, and then generating English from the reduced primitive acts and state changes, we have a paraphrase, "Robbie did something that caused Suzie's mood to become happy."

8-5a

What paraphrases would be generated for the following sentences:

1   *Robbie angered Suzie.*
2   *Robbie killed a fly.*
3   *Robbie opened the door.*
4   *Robbie walked to town.*
5   *Robbie gorged on ice cream.*
6   *Robbie hurled a stone into the stream.*

8-5b

Would it be significantly more difficult to generate the paraphrases in another language?

Exercise 8-6

As described, summaries are built starting with the most connected abstraction unit in the story to be summarized. Specify two or three other abstraction units to start with.

Exercise 8-7

One way of describing the similarity between two stories is to name the most connected top-level abstraction unit appearing in both stories. Another is to enumerate all the top-level abstraction units appearing in both stories. Specify two or three other ways.

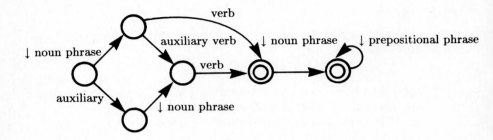

Figure E-20. An ATN.

EXERCISES FOR CHAPTER 9

Exercise 9-1 (Mark Lavin)

Consider the following sentences. Identify those that can be parsed by the net shown in figure E-20. Note that words like *do*, *can*, and *have* can be auxiliary verbs.

1   John cried.

2   He cursed the fates.

3   He tore his hair with abandon.

4   He had defaulted.

5   He could not pay the rent.

6   Crafty John thought he could bribe the landlord with a $20 bill.

7   Did that work?

8   Did the landlord give quarter?

Exercise 9-2

Exhibit the parse trees produced by the WASP parser given the following sentences. Note that *has*, *will*, and *been* can serve as auxiliary verbs.

Robbie takes Suzie to school. Robbie has taken Suzie to school. Robbie will take Suzie to school. Suzie has been taken to school

Exercise 9-3

Consider the following story:

Cinderella

Cinderella went to the ball by coach. The Fairy Godmother had
made the coach for her out of a pumpkin. During the evening,
Cinderella danced with the Prince. She flew down the steps at
midnight. The Prince found her with a glass slipper. She went
from misery to happiness ever after.

9-3a

Identify the thematic role of all the noun phrases.

9-3b

Understanding the thematic role identity of the noun phrases involved in
the previous problem enables answers to some simple, direct questions.
For the following questions, indicate the answer and the thematic role that
supplies the answer.

1   *When did Cinderella dance?*

2   *Where did Cinderella go?*

Exercise 9-4

From the perspective of thematic-role grammar, what advice would you
give to someone who wishes to learn quickly to converse about everyday
things in a foreign language.

Exercise 9-5

Modify the Question and Attribute transition nets given in the text so that
they handle the following sentences:

1   *What are the sales of Sears?*

2   *Show me General Motor's sales and earnings.*

3   *How many items does IBM buy from Intel?*

4   *How many companies are there with sales greater than $1 billion?*

474

a   Wide filter

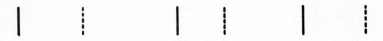

b   Narrow filter

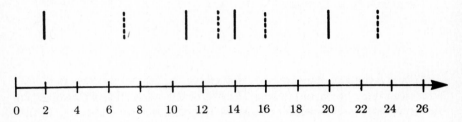

Figure E-21. Some zero crossings to be matched.

EXERCISES FOR CHAPTER 10

Exercise 10-1

In the language of generalized cylinders, a wedge can be described as a constant-size triangle moving along a straight axis. Give another description.

Exercise 10-2 (Ellen C. Hildreth)

Consider the zero crossings found with wide and medium sombrero filters shown in figure E-21. Note that there are fewer lines in the coarse-scale result.

10-2a

Match the coarse-scale zero crossings.

10-2b

Match the fine-scale zero crossing. Ignore the previous results from coarse-scale matching.

10-2c

Match the fine-scale zero crossings again. This time exploit the previous results from coarse-scale matching.

10-2d

What are the disparities?

Exercise 10-3

This exercise explores the stereo procedure invented by Hans P. Morevec [1977].

10-3a

Suppose you want to find that part of the right image that best matches a particular small square patch, P, of the left image. You propose to do this by maximizing the following measure of correlation:

$$\max_{\Delta i, \Delta j} \sum_{P} L_{i,j} \times R_{i+\Delta i, j+\Delta j}$$

where the $L_{i,j}$ are the left-image intensities and the $R_{i,j}$ are the right-image intensities.

After some experiments, you determine that your measure is flawed: your procedure tends to get sucked toward those parts of the right image with high average intensity. How would you fix this problem?

10-3b

Matching by correlation works best in areas that have high variability. Morevec calls such areas *interesting*. Suggest a measure for locating interesting areas.

10-3c

Unfortunately, for high resolution, you would like to correlate using small areas, but to avoid local maxima in the correlation measure, you would like to correlate using large areas. How can you get the best of both small and large areas?

Exercise 10-4

Note that for the PQ projection, the projecting line is normal to the surface of the sphere since it goes through the center of the sphere. This makes it easy to write an expression for a surface normal vector corresponding to the (p, q) point on the PQ plane. Show that the surface normal is given by $(p, q, -1)$.

Exercise 10-5

10-5a

In addition to the surface normal vector, $(p, q, -1)$, two other vectors are of consummate interest. One of these vectors points to the light source. This vector will correspond to some particular values of p and q. Let us call these values p_s and q_s, where the s is to suggest s̲un, corresponding to the vector pointing to the sun, $(p_s, q_s, -1)$. Another interesting vector is the one pointing to the viewer. This is the vector $(0, 0, -1)$.

With surface normal, sun, and viewer vectors in hand, it is possible to derive some useful formulas relating the emergent, incident, and phase angles to p and q. Show that the following formula holds:

$$\cos i = \frac{pp_s + qq_s + 1}{\sqrt{p^2 + q^2 + 1}\sqrt{p_s^2 + q_s^2 + 1}}$$

10-5b

Derive similar formulas for $\cos e$ and $\cos g$.

Exercise 10-6

Now recall that the brightness of a Lambertian surface is $\rho \cos i$. If the light source is directly behind the viewer, $p_s = 0$ and $q_s = 0$. Exploiting the general formula for $\cos i$, we have this formula relating brightness to p and q:

$$E = \rho \cos i$$

$$= \rho \times \frac{1}{\sqrt{p^2 + q^2 + 1}}$$

This is a constant when $p^2 + q^2 + 1$ is a constant. But since $p^2 + q^2 + 1 = c$ is an equation for a circle on the PQ plane, we conclude that the isobrightness lines on a PQ reflectance map are circles when the light source is behind the viewer. Show that the shadow line, when present, is straight.

Exercise 10-7

Secure a basketball or other sphere and examine it in a room illuminated by a single small light source to your rear.

10-7a

How does its intensity vary?

10-7b

Why does the full moon look flat?

Exercise 10-8

Treatises on makeup often suggest using facial makeup to compensate for excessively flat-looking appearance. Explain why this makes sense. Should people with flat-looking faces use dark or light makeup?

Exercise 10-9

Suppose Martians generally have spherical heads and Lambertian skin. The really beautiful Martians have egg-shaped heads, with the long axis of the egg horizontal and pointed in the direction the Martian is looking. Describe where you would advise a Martian with a spherical head to place dark makeup, given that the Martian wishes to look like it has an egg-shaped head. You may assume the light source is behind the viewer at all times.

Exercise 10-10

Consider a Lambertian cube standing in front of a Lambertian wall as shown in figure E-22. In principle, the light intensity along the *ab* line can look like what you see in figure E-23a. But if the corners of the cube are rounded, the intensity is more likely to look like what you see in figure E-23b.

10-10a

In PQ space, show the exact location of the surface normals of the visible cube faces.

10-10b

Show a plausible location, in PQ space, for the direction to the light source.

10-10c

Sketch the intensity profile along the *cd* line assuming the edge is sharp.

10-10d

Sketch the intensity profile along the *cd* line assuming the edge is rounded.

Exercise 10-11

A scanning electron microscope works because beam electrons crash into surfaces, whereupon secondary electrons are emitted, collected, and counted, as suggested in figure E-24.

The steeper the surface, the more electrons are emitted. In fact, when the electron beam hits a surface perpendicularly, the secondary electron emission goes to zero. For our purposes here, assume that the actual observed brightness, E, is given by $E = \rho \sin i$, where i is the incident angle. Curiously, pictures made with a scanning electron microscope do not impress people as weird in spite of the strange reflectance function involved.

Suppose the electron beam is scanned across a surface with the cross section shown in figure E-25. Sketch the resulting image intensity.

478

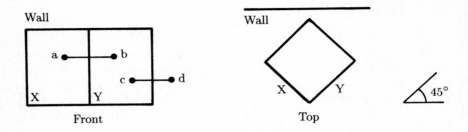

Figure E-22. A Lambertian cube.

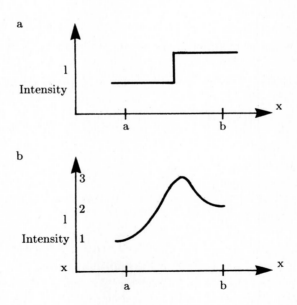

Figure E-23. Intensity profiles for sharp and rounded edges.

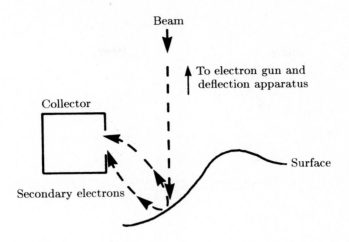

Figure E-24. A scanning electron microscope.

Exercise 10-12

You have learned a well-kept secret that there are three oddly shaped mountains of unknown origin somewhere on the equator. When seen from the side, these mountains look as shown in figure E-26a.

Alphonse, an intrepid explorer, arranges a flight to go directly above these mountains to photograph them. Wishing to capture them in their glory, he arranges the overflight for noon, when the sun is directly overhead. His flight path is shown in figure E-26b.

10-12a

Using three PQ spaces, indicate the surface normals exhibited by each of the three mountains.

10-12b

Alphonse is disappointed in the view, for two of the mountains look the same. Describe what he sees, assuming the mountains are made of a Lambertian material.

Exercise 10-13

In the array below, we note p, q, and the observed brightness, E_r, for an array of points in an aerial-photograph image:

−1	−1	.23		+1	−1	.23		+1 −1 .17
−1	−1	.23		+1	−1	.17		0 0 .3
0	0	.3		0	0	.3		0 0 .3

480

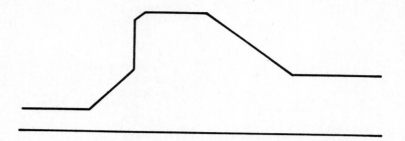

Figure E-25. A surface cross section for the scanning electron microscope.

a

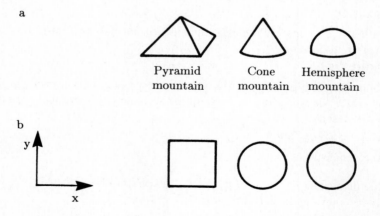

Pyramid mountain

Cone mountain

Hemisphere mountain

b

y

x

Figure E-26. Three mountains.

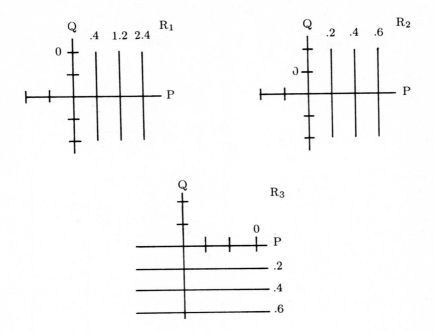

Figure E-27. Three reflectance maps.

Assume the observed brightness, E_r, is $\rho(x,y)R(p,q)$, where $R(p,q)$ corresponds to the isobrightness lines of the Lambertian reflectance map with the sun directly behind the viewer and $\rho = 1$.

Classify each point in the image as rock, tree, or grape, assuming that the albedo factor is .7 for rocks, .5 for trees, and .3 for grapes.

Exercise 10-14

A surface patch has unknown albedo, ρ. It is illuminated at different times from three separate light sources. For surfaces with $\rho = 1.0$, the three lights yield reflectance maps as shown in figure E-27. The brightness observed when the various lights are on is as follows:

$$I_1 = .2 \qquad I_2 = .1 \qquad I_3 = .1$$

10-14a
Draw lines in PQ spaces representing loci where I_1/I_2 equals 2, 3, and 4. Similarly, draw lines for I_2/I_3 equals .5, 1, and 2.
10-14b
What is the value of ρ?

482

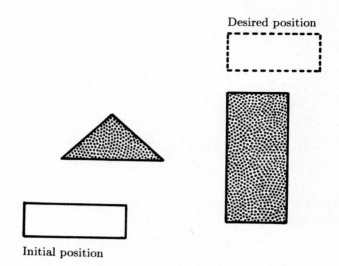

Figure E-28. A path-finding problem. How can we move the object to its destination through the strait between the shaded obstacles?

Exercise 10-15

Consider cantelopes, cherries, eggplants, oranges, papayas, and watermelons.

10-15a

Using the pattern-recognition approach, prescribe a two-feature system for differentiating among them.

10-15b

Would your system degrade gracefully as the number of types to be recognized increases?

Exercise 10-16

Why does the CONSIGHT system use two light sheets instead of just one?

Exercise 10-17

Why is force-and-position control needed to open a door?

Exercise 10-18

Consider figure E-28.

10-18a

Create a configuration space for the object and obstacles shown. Do this for the object as shown and for the object rotated 90°.

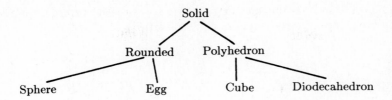

Figure E-29. An AKO tree.

10-18b

Describe a procedure, using configuration space, to find collision-free paths. Confine yourself to two-dimensional problems without rotation.

10-18c

Show the paths that your procedure would find through the configuration spaces you derived for figure E-28.

10-18d

Describe how you would generalize your solution to deal with problems requiring rotations.

EXERCISES FOR CHAPTER 11

Exercise 11-1

The Martians have landed. Taking a strict fundamentalist position, you decide they should learn about apples before it is too late.

You assume that the Martian's perceptual system builds semantic nets with only the following information:

- An object's color is red, green, blue, purple, white, or black.

- An object's weight is a number.

- An object's shape is anything in the tree given in figure E-29.

- An object may be inedible, fragrant, or smelly. There are no other properties.

You elect the following teaching sequence. For each sample, note what heuristic is applied and explain what is learned.

Color	Red	Example 1
Shape	Sphere	
Weight	4	
Quality	Fragrant	

Color	Red	Example 2
Shape	Sphere	
Weight	4	

Color	Red	Near miss 1
Shape	Sphere	
Weight	4	
Quality	Inedible	

Color	Green	Example 3
Shape	Sphere	
Weight	4	

Color	Green	Example 4
Shape	Sphere	
Weight	7	

Color	Red	Example 5
Shape	Egg	
Weight	5	

Color	Red	Near Miss 2
Shape	Cube	
Weight	4	

Exercise 11-2

Suppose a learning procedure is told to consider something six feet tall, with a long neck, long legs, and black feathers. The learning procedure is told that the thing is an ostrich.

A teacher can specify that a penguin, a tall black crane, a crow, an elephant, a giraffe, a gazelle, and a kiwi are not ostriches. The teacher knows that not all ostriches are black.

11-2a

The teacher wants to convey the idea that ostriches cannot fly. Which animal does the teacher use? What heuristic does the learning procedure use?

11-2b

Next, what should the teacher specify to persuade the learning program to drop a descriptor?

11-2c

Finally, suppose the teacher specifies that a four-foot ostrich is an ostrich. What does the learning program do? What heuristic does it use?

Exercise 11-3

This exercise explores the near-miss group idea, invented or reinvented by me, which is closely related to the one-disjunct-per-lesson idea conceived by Kurt A. VanLehn [1983]. The problem is that it is hard to construct a near miss that has just one critical difference with the evolving model. For example, taking the top off of an arch deletes two SUPPORT relations but introduces two RIGHT-OF relations at the same time. One way to cope with this is to rank the importance of various relations. Another is to use several near misses collectively.

11-3a

Explain how to use several near misses collectively.

11-3b

Show how using two near misses collectively can deal with the problem of the spurious RIGHT-OF relations.

Exercise 11-4

Create a decision tree for animal identification. Use the animals considered by the IDENTIFIER system in chapter 6.

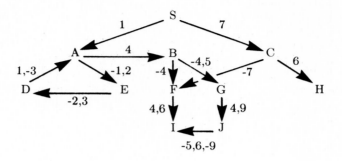

Figure E-30. A similarity net.

Exercise 11-5

In figure E-30, a similarity net connects object models that are collections of properties. The labels on the arcs are difference descriptions that indicate which properties are dropped and which are added when moving in the direction of the arrowhead. For example, the label $(-1, 2)$ indicates that property 1 is dropped and property 2 is added. The following procedure can be used to traverse such nets:

To identify an unknown using a similarity net:

1   Until there is reason to stop, calculate the difference between C and U, $d(C, U)$.

    1a   If the difference description is empty, stop, announcing success.

    1b   Otherwise, compute the difference, $d(C, M)$, between C and each neighboring model, M.

        1ba   Compare $d(C, U)$ with each $d(C, M)$ by counting the number of identical items in the difference descriptions. If there is no count greater than zero, stop, announcing failure.

        1bb   Otherwise, let the current node be the neighbor corresponding to the highest count in the comparison of differences.

11-5a

What kind of search does the procedure do?

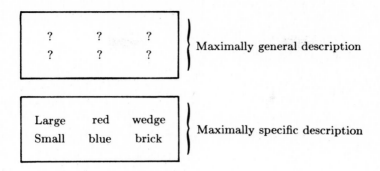

Figure E-31. A maximally general and a maximally specific description.

11-5b

Assuming that the starting node, S, has no properties, determine the properties of the other nodes. Then use their properties to make a table of differences between the nodes and unknowns with the following properties:

1   1, 2, and 3
2   1, 4, and 5
3   1, 4, and 6
4   1, 4, 5, 6, and 9

11-5c

What are the paths followed when identifying the unknowns?

Exercise 11-6 (Karen A. Prendergast)

This exercise explores a learning procedure invented by Tom M. Mitchell [1982]. To keep things simple, we take the domain to be collections of blocks. They are either small or large, red or blue, and bricks or wedges. The thing to be learned is a description of a set of blocks such as "there is one red block and one other block that is a wedge."

Mitchell's procedure takes the first example to be the *maximally specific* description. If the first example is a pair of objects, one a large red wedge and the other a small blue brick, then the maximally specific description is the one shown in the lower part of figure E-31. At the same time, Mitchell's procedure creates a *maximally general* description in which the properties of the objects are replaced by question marks. For this example, there are two objects with three properties each, so the maximally general description has two objects with three question marks each. This is shown in the upper part of figure E-31.

The overall strategy of Mitchell's procedure is to make the maximally general description more specific using negative examples and to make the

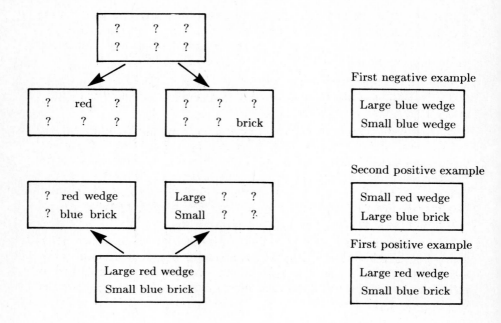

Figure E-32. An emerging version space.

maximally specific description more general using positive examples. Thus the negative examples and the positive examples cause the maximal descriptions to sprout trees that grow toward one another. Taken together, all these descriptions are called a *version space*.

Let us go on to some details. If we present a positive example, Mitchell's procedure matches the objects in the positive example with the existing specific descriptions, forming new descriptions in which each clashing property is replaced by a question mark. Of these new descriptions only those that match a description connected to the maximally general description are retained.

In our example, if the next positive example is a small red wedge and a large blue brick, then there must be two new descriptions, one for each way of matching the objects together. One of these corresponds to matching the small red wedge of the positive example with the large red wedge in the specific description. The other corresponds to matching the small red wedge to the small blue brick. Once clashing properties are replaced by question marks, we have the descriptions connected to the maximally specific description shown in figure E-32.

On the other hand, if we present a negative example, Mitchell's procedure matches the objects in the negative example with the existing general descriptions, forming new descriptions in which only enough question marks are converted to properties so as to exclude the negative example. Of these new descriptions, only those that match a description connected to the maximally specific description are retained.

In our example, the negative example consists of a large blue wedge and a small blue wedge, yielding two possibilities, both connected to the maximally general description in figure E-32.

Negative examples also enable pruning out bad specific descriptions. Whenever a negative sample matches a specific description, that specific description is eliminated. In the example, the negative example matches the description specifying a large block and a small block, so that description is eliminated. Symmetrically, positive examples enable pruning out bad general descriptions. If a positive example fails to match a general description, that general description is eliminated.

An unknown is definitely a member of the class described by the version space if it matches all the descriptions ascending up from the maximally specific description. An unknown is definitely not a member if it fails to match any of the descriptions descending from the maximally general description. Otherwise, an unknown cannot be classified.

11-6a

What heuristics best describe the generalization and specialization parts of Mitchell's procedure?

11-6b

Form a version space representing what is learned about the following sequence of lunches. Assume lunches always have two items that are either delicious or unpalatable, hot or cold, cheap, medium-priced, or expensive.

1   A typical lunch: A delicious hot cheap item and an unpalatable cold expensive item.

2   A typical lunch: A delicious cold expensive item and an unpalatable hot cheap item.

3   An atypical lunch: A delicious cold cheap item and an unpalatable cold cheap item.

11-6c

Given the learning sequence, how will the following things be classified:

1   An unpalatable hot cheap item and a delicious cold expensive item.

2   A delicious cold cheap item and an unpalatable cold medium-priced item.

3   An unpalatable hot expensive item and an unpalatable cold expensive item.

490

EXERCISES FOR CHAPTER 12

Exercise 12-1

Criticize the following statements:
12-1a
A procedure has not really learned until it surprises its programmer. There-fore, no procedure has really learned.
12-1b
Most learning leads to major additions to what is known already.
12-1c
Learning systems must have powerful procedures for correcting mistakes made when they leap to conclusions with too little to go on.
12-1d
A computer can only do what some programmer explicitly tells it to do.

Exercise 12-2

The META-WASP procedure was said to adhere to Martin's Law. Does it also adhere to other learning principles?

Exercise 12-3

Given that precedents can, in principle, supply all that learned rules can, why have rules?

Exercise 12-4

Given that rules can be given explicitly, what practical advantage is there to having them learned?

Exercise 12-5

Characterize the domains that should be susceptible to learning using the MACBETH procedure.

Exercise 12-6

Consider the following problem:

An Exercise

This is a problem concerning a noble and a domineering greedy lady. The noble is married to the lady. Show that the lady is able to influence the noble.

Show the rule produced by solving the problem using the *Macbeth* and *Linda and Dick* precedents.

Exercise 12-7

Consider the following precedent:

Adam and Eve

This is a story about Adam and Eve and an apple. Adam is greedy because Eve is foolish. Adam wants to eat a forbidden apple because he is greedy. God punishes Adam and Eve because Adam eats the forbidden apple.

Consider also the following problem:

An Exercise

This is a problem concerning a foolish noble and a domineering lady. The noble is married to the lady. Show that the lady may persuade the noble to want to be king.

Show the rule produced by solving the problem using information from the *Macbeth*, *Linda and Dick*, and *Adam and Eve* precedents, as necessary.

Exercise 12-8

This exercise explores an idea introduced by me for making rules in the absence of the usual AND/OR tree [Winston 1981]. Consider the situations shown in figure E-33. The problem is to show that Tom should take insulin by virtue of the precedent involving John.

12-8a

The analogy procedure fails. Why.

12-8b

How would you generalize the analogy procedure so that it can produce the following rule:

The Insulin Rule:

If   A person is a diabetic
        the person's blood's sugar is high
then   the person should take insulin

Exercise 12-9

Consider the MATCH procedure. Why does it make sense to modify the first step such that the CAUSE link configurations are at the front of L1, the link configurations at the head or tail of CAUSE link configurations are in the middle, and all other link configurations are at the end?

Exercise 12-10

Show that a link may be useful in matching even if there are many others of the same type in the same situation.

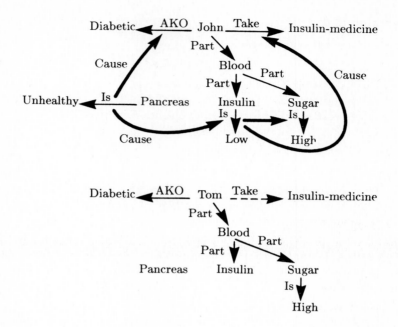

Figure E-33. A medical problem. Heavy links are **CAUSE** links.

Exercise 12-11

It has been said that censors form a sort of fence around each rule. As the number of censors increases, the fence contracts. Are there circumstances in which the fence gets larger?

Bibliography

This bibliography contains items directly cited in the chapters as well as some related items of special interest. To keep length manageable, I generally list only the earliest publication together with the most recent or most easily accessible publication for each concept.

Abelson, Harold, and Andrea diSessa, *Turtle Geometry*, MIT Press, Cambridge, MA, 1981.

Aikins, Janice S., "A Theory and Methodology of Inductive Learning," *Artificial Intelligence*, vol. 20, no. 3, 1983.

Allen, James, "Recognizing Intentions from Natural Language Utterances," in *Computational Models of Discourse*, edited by J. Michael Brady and Robert C. Berwick, MIT Press, Cambridge, MA, 1983.

Amarel, Saul, "On Representation of Problems of Reasoning about Actions," in *Machine Intelligence 3*, edited by Donald Michie, Edinburgh University Press, Edinburgh, Scotland, 1968.

Ambler, A. P., H. G. Barrow, C. M. Brown, R. M. Burstall, and R. J. Popplestone, "A Versatile System for Computer Controlled Assembly," *Artificial Intelligence*, vol. 6, no. 2, 1975.

Bajcsy, Ruzena (editor), *Representation of 3-Dimensional Objects*, Springer-Verlag, New York, 1982.

Ballard, Dana H., and Christopher Brown, *Computer Vision*, Prentice-Hall, Englewood Cliffs, NJ, 1982.

Barlow, H. B., "Summation and Inhibition in the Frog's Retina," *Journal of Physiology*, vol. 119, 1953.

Barr, Avron, Edward A. Feigenbaum, and Paul R. Cohen, *The Handbook of Artificial Intelligence*, 3 vols., William Kaufman, Los Altos, CA, 1981.

Barrow, Harry G., and Jay M. Tenenbaum, "Recovering Intrinsic Scene Characteristics from Images," in *Computer Vision Systems*, edited by A. Hanson and E. Riseman, Academic Press, New York, 1978.

Barrow, Harry G., and Jay M. Tenenbaum, "Computational Vision," *Proceedings of the IEEE*, vol. 69, no. 5, 1981.

Baudet, Gerard M., "On the Branching Factor of the Alpha-beta Pruning Algorithm," *Artificial Intelligence*, vol. 10, no. 2, 1978.

Beckman, Lennart, Anders Haraldson, Osten Oskarsson, and Erik Sandewall, "A Partial Evaluator, and Its Use as a Programming Tool," *Artificial Intelligence*, vol. 7, no. 4, 1976.

Berliner, Hans J., "Some Necessary Conditions for a Master Chess Program," *Third International Joint Conference on Artificial Intelligence*, Stanford, CA, 1973.

Berliner, Hans J., "Chess as Problem Solving: The Development of a Tactics Analyzer," PhD Thesis, Carnegie-Mellon University, Pittsburgh, PA, 1975.

Berliner, Hans J., "A Chronology of Computer Chess and Its Literature," *Artificial Intelligence*, vol. 10, no. 2, 1978.

Berliner, Hans J., "Computer Backgammon," *Scientific American*, June 1980.

Berliner, Hans J., "An Examination of Brute-Force Intelligence," *Seventh International Joint Conference on Artificial Intelligence*, Vancouver, British Columbia, Canada, 1981.

Berwick, Robert C., "Introduction: Computational Aspects of Discourse," in *Computational Models of Discourse*, edited by J. Michael Brady and Robert C. Berwick, MIT Press, Cambridge, MA, 1983.

Berwick, Robert C., *Locality Principles and the Acquisition of Syntactic Knowledge*, MIT Press, Cambridge, MA, in preparation. Based on a PhD thesis, Massachusetts Institute of Technology, Cambridge, MA, 1982.

Berwick, Robert C., and Amy Weinberg, *The Grammatical Basis of Linguistic Performance*, MIT Press, Cambridge, MA, 1983.

Binford, Thomas O., "Visual Perception by Computer," *Proceedings IEEE Conference on Systems Science and Cybernetics*, Miami, 1971.

Binford, Thomas O., "Inferring Surfaces from Images," *Artificial Intelligence*, vol. 17, August 1981. Volume 17 is also available as *Computer Vision*, edited by J. Michael Brady, North-Holland, Amsterdam, 1981.

Binford, Thomas O., "Survey of Model-Based Image Analysis Systems," *International Journal of Robotics Research*, vol. 1, no. 1, 1982.

Bledsoe, W. W., "Non-Resolution Theorem Proving," *Artificial Intelligence*, vol. 9, no. 1, 1977.

Bobrow, Daniel G., and Allan Collins, *Representation and Understanding*, Academic Press, New York, 1975.

Bobrow, Daniel G., and Bruce Fraser, "An Augmented State Transition Network Analysis Procedure," *First International Joint Conference on Artificial Intelligence*, Washington, D. C., 1969.

Bobrow, Daniel G., and Terry Winograd, "An Overview of KRL, a Knowledge Representation Language," *Cognitive Science*, vol. 1, no. 1, 1977.

Bobrow Daniel G., Ronald M. Kaplan, Martin Kay, Donald A. Norman, Henry Thompson, and Terry Winograd, "GUS, A Frame-Driven Dialog System," *Artificial Intelligence*, vol. 8, no. 2, 1977.

Boden, Margaret A., *Artificial Intelligence and Natural Man*, Basic Books, New York, 1977.

Bogen, Richard et al., "MACSYMA Reference Manual," unnumbered report, Laboratory of Computer Science, Massachusetts Institute of Technology, Cambridge, MA, 1975.

Boley, Harold, "Directed Recursive Labelnode Hypergraphs: A New Representation-Language," *Artificial Intelligence*, vol. 9, no. 1, 1977.

Brachman, Ronald J., "On the Epistemological Status of Semantic Networks," in *Associative Networks—Representation and Use of Knowledge by Computers*, edited by Nicholas V. Findler, Academic Press, New York, 1979.

Brady, J. Michael, "Toward a Computational Theory of Early Visual Processing in Reading," *Visible Language*, vol. 15, no. 2, 1981.

Brady, J. Michael (editor), *Computer Vision*, North-Holland, Amsterdam, 1981.

Brady, J. Michael, "Representing Shape," in *Robotics*, edited by Lester Gerhardt and J. Michael Brady, Springer-Verlag, New York, 1983.

Brady, J. Michael, and Robert C. Berwick (editors), *Computational Models of Discourse*, MIT Press, Cambridge, MA, 1983.

Brady, J. Michael, John M. Hollerbach, Timothy L. Johnson, Tomás Lozano-Pérez, and Matthew T. Mason (editors), *Robot Motion: Planning and Control*, MIT Press, Cambridge, MA, 1982.

Brand, D., "Analytic Resolution in Theorem Proving," *Artificial Intelligence*, vol. 7, no. 4, 1976.

Brooks, Rodney A., "Symbolic Reasoning among 3-D Models and 2-D Images," *Artificial Intelligence*, vol. 17, August 1981. Volume 17 is also available as *Computer Vision*, edited by J. Michael Brady, North-Holland, Amsterdam, 1981. Based on a PhD thesis, Stanford University, Stanford, CA, 1981.

Brooks, Rodney A. "Planning Collision Free Motions for Pick and Place Operations," *International Journal of Robotics Research*, vol. 2, no. 4, 1983.

Brooks, Rodney A., "Solving the Find-Path Problem by Good Representation of Free Space," *IEEE Transactions on Systems, Man, and Cybernetics*, vol. SMC-13, 1983.

Brooks, Rodney A., and Tomás Lozano-Pérez, "A Subdivision Algorithm in Configuration Space for Findpath with Rotation," *Eighth International Joint Conference on Artificial Intelligence*, Karlsruhe, Federal Republic of Germany, 1983.

Brou, Philippe, "Finding the Orientation of Objects in Vector Maps," PhD Thesis, Massachusetts Institute of Technology, Cambridge, MA, 1983.

Brown, Malloy F., "Doing Arithmetic without Diagrams," *Artificial Intelligence*, vol. 8, no. 2, 1977.

Buchanan, Bruce G., and Richard O. Duda, "Principles of Rule-Based Expert Systems," *Advances in Computers*, vol. 22, 1983.

Buchanan, Bruce G., and Edward H. Shortliffe, *Rule-Based Expert Programs: the MYCIN Experiments of the Stanford Heuristic Programming Project*, Addison-Wesley, Reading, MA, 1984.

Bundy, Alan "Will It Reach the Top? Prediction in the Mechanics World," *Artificial Intelligence*, vol. 10, no. 2, 1978.

Campbell, A. N., V. F. Hollister, Richard O. Duda, and Peter E. Hart, "Recognition of a Hidden Mineral Deposit by an Artificial Intelligence Program," *Science*, vol. 217, no. 3, 1982.

Carbonell, Jaime G., "Learning by Analogy: Formulating and Generalizing Plans from Past Experience," in *Machine Learning — An Artificial Intelligence Approach*, edited by Ryszard S. Michalski, Jaime G. Carbonell, and Tom M. Mitchell, Tioga Publishing Company, Palo Alto, CA, 1983.

Card, Stuart, Thomas P. Moran, and Allen Newell, *The Psychology of Human-Computer Interaction*, Lawrence Erlbaum Associates, Hillsdale, NJ, 1983.

Charniak, Eugene, "Toward a Model of Children's Story Comprehension," PhD Thesis, Massachusetts Institute of Technology, Cambridge, MA, 1972.

Charniak, Eugene, Christopher K. Riesbeck, and Drew V. McDermott, *Artificial Intelligence Programming*, Lawrence Erlbaum Associates, Hillsdale, NJ, 1980.

Chester, Daniel, "The Translation of Formal Proofs into English," *Artificial Intelligence*, vol. 7, no. 3, 1976.

Chomsky, Noam, *Syntactic Structures*, Mouton, The Hague, 1957.

Chomsky, Noam, *Lectures on Government and Binding*, Foris, Dordrecht, Holland, 1981.

Clark, Keith L., and Sten-Åke Tärnlund, *Logic Programming*, Academic Press, New York, 1982.

Clarke, M. R. B. (editor), *Advances in Computer Chess 1*, Edinburgh University Press, Edinburgh, Scotland, 1977.

Clarke, M. R. B. (editor), *Advances in Computer Chess 2*, Edinburgh University Press, Edinburgh, Scotland, 1980.

Clocksin, William F., and Christopher S. Mellish, *Programming in Prolog*, Springer-Verlag, New York, 1981.

Clowes, Maxwell, "On Seeing Things," *Artificial Intelligence*, vol. 2, no. 1, 1971.

Cohen, Brian L., "The Mechanical Discovery of Certain Problem Symmetries," *Artificial Intelligence*, vol. 8, no. 1, 1977.

Cohen, Brian L., "A Powerful and Efficient Structural Pattern Recognition System," *Artificial Intelligence*, vol. 9, no. 3, 1977.

Colmerauer, Alain, "Prolog and Infinite Trees," in *Logic Programming*, edited by Keith L. Clark and Sten-Åke Tärnlund, Academic Press, New York, 1982.

Colmerauer, A., H. Kanoui, R. Pasero, and P. Roussel, "Un Système de Communication Homme-Machine en Français," internal report, Groupe d'Intelligence Artificielle, Université Aix-Marseille II, 1973.

Davis, Larry S., and Azriel Rosenfeld, "Cooperative Processes for Low-level Vision: A Survey," *Artificial Intelligence*, vol. 17, August 1981. Volume 17 is also available as *Computer Vision*, edited by J. Michael Brady, North-Holland, Amsterdam, 1981.

Davis, Martin, "The Mathematics of Non-Monotonic Reasoning," *Artificial Intelligence*, vol. 13, no. 1&2, 1980.

Davis, Randall, "Teiresias: Applications of Meta-Level Knowledge," in *Knowledge-Based Systems in Artificial Intelligence*, edited by Randall Davis and Douglas B. Lenat, McGraw-Hill Book Company, New York, 1982. Based on a PhD thesis, Stanford University, Stanford, CA, 1976.

Davis, Randall, "Expert Systems: Where are we? And Where Do We Go from Here," Report AIM-665, Artificial Intelligence Laboratory, Massachusetts Institute of Technology, Cambridge, MA, 1982.

Davis, Randall, and Jonathan King, "An Overview of Production Systems," in *Machine Intelligence 8*, edited by Edward W. Elcock and Donald Michie, John Wiley and Sons, New York, 1977.

Davis, Randall, and Douglas B. Lenat, *Knowledge-Based Systems in Artificial Intelligence*, McGraw-Hill Book Company, New York, 1982.

Davis, Randall, and Reid G. Smith, "Negotiation as a Metaphor for Distributed Problem Solving," *Artificial Intelligence*, vol. 20, no. 1, 1983.

Davis, Randall, Bruce G. Buchanan, and Edward H. Shortliffe, "Production Rules as a Representation for a Knowledge-Based Consultation Program," *Artificial Intelligence*, vol. 8, no. 1, 1977.

Davis, Randall, Howard Austin, Ingrid Carlbom, Bud Frawley, Paul Pruchnik, Rich Sneiderman, and Al Gilreath, "The Dipmeter Advisor: Interpretation of Geological Signals," *Seventh International Joint Conference on Artificial Intelligence*, Vancouver, British Columbia, Canada, 1981.

DeJong, Gerald F., II, "A New Approach to Natural Language Processing," *Cognitive Science*, vol. 3, no. 3, 1979.

de Kleer, Johan, "Qualitative and Quantitative Knowledge in Classical Mechanics," PhD Thesis, Massachusetts Institute of Technology, Cambridge, MA, 1975.

de Kleer, Johan, "Causal and Teleological Reasoning in Circuit Recognition," Report TR-529, Massachusetts Institute of Technology, Cambridge, MA Artificial Intelligence Laboratory, 1979.

Dietterich, Thomas G. and Ryszard S. Michalski, "Inductive Learning of Structural Descriptions," *Artificial Intelligence*, vol. 16, no. 3, 1981.

Duda, Richard O., and Peter E. Hart, *Pattern Recognition and Scene Analysis*, John Wiley and Sons, New York, 1973.

Duda, Richard O., Peter E. Hart, and Nils J. Nilsson, "Subjective Bayesian Methods for Rule-Based Inference Systems," Report TR-124, Artificial Intelligence Center, SRI International, 1976.

Duda, Richard O., Peter E. Hart, Nils J. Nilsson, and Georgia L. Sutherland, "Semantic Network Representations in Rule Based Inference Systems," in *Pattern Directed Inference Systems*, edited by Donald A. Waterman and Frederick Hayes-Roth, Academic Press, New York, 1978.

Dyer, Michael G., *In-depth Understanding—A Computer Model of Integrated Processing for Narrative Comprehension*, MIT Press, Cambridge, MA, 1983. Based on a PhD thesis, Yale University, New Haven, CT, 1982.

Ernst, George, and Allen Newell, *GPS: A Case Study in Generality and Problem Solving*, Academic Press, New York, 1969.

Evans, Thomas G., "A Heuristic Program to Solve Geometric Analogy Problems," in *Semantic Information Processing*, edited by Marvin Minsky, MIT Press, Cambridge, MA, 1968. Based on a PhD thesis, Massachusetts Institute of Technology, Cambridge, MA, 1963.

Fahlman, Scott E, *NETL: A System for Representing and Using Real-World Knowledge*, MIT Press, Cambridge, MA, 1979. Based on a PhD thesis, Massachusetts Institute of Technology, Cambridge, MA, 1979.

Feigenbaum, Edward A., "The Art of Artificial Intelligence: Themes and Case Studies in Knowledge Engineering," *Fifth International Joint Conference on Artificial Intelligence*, Cambridge, MA, 1977.

Feigenbaum, Edward A., and Julian Feldman, *Computers and Thought*, McGraw-Hill Book Company, New York, 1963.

Feigenbaum, Edward A., and Pamela McCorduck, *The Fifth Generation*, Addison-Wesley, Reading, MA, 1983.

Fikes, Richard E., and Nils J. Nilsson, "STRIPS: A New Approach to the Application of Theorem Proving to Problem Solving," *Artificial Intelligence*, vol. 2, no. 3&4, 1971.

Fikes, Richard E., Peter E. Hart, and Nils J. Nilsson, "Learning and Executing Generalized Robot Plans," *Artificial Intelligence*, vol. 3, no. 1-4, 1972.

Fillmore, C. J., "The Case for Case," in *Universals in Linguistic Theory*, edited by E. Bach and R. Harms, Holt, Rinehart, and Winston, New York, 1968.

Findler, Nicholas V. (editor), *Associative Networks—Representation and Use of Knowledge by Computers*, Academic Press, New York, 1979.

Finkel, Raphael A., and John P. Fishburn, "Parallelism in Alpha-Beta Search," *Artificial Intelligence*, vol. 19, no. 1, 1982.

Follett, Ria, "Synthesizing Recursive Functions with Side Effects," *Artificial Intelligence*, vol. 13, no. 3, 1980.

Forbus, Kenneth D., "Qualitative Reasoning about Physical Processes," *Seventh International Joint Conference on Artificial Intelligence*, Vancouver, British Columbia, Canada, 1981.

Forbus, Kenneth D., "Qualitative Process Theory," Report AIM-664, Artificial Intelligence Laboratory, Massachusetts Institute of Technology, Cambridge, MA, 1982.

Forgy, Charles L., "Rete: A Fast Algorithm for the Many Pattern/Many Object Pattern Match Problem," *Artificial Intelligence*, vol. 19, no. 1, 1982.

Freeman, P., and Allen Newell, "A Model for Functional Reasoning in Design," *Second International Joint Conference on Artificial Intelligence*, London, 1971.

Freuder, Eugene C., "A Computer System for Visual Recognition Using Active Knowledge," PhD Thesis, Massachusetts Institute of Technology, Cambridge, MA, 1976.

Freuder, Eugene C., "Synthesizing Constraint Expressions," *Communications of the Association for Computing Machinery*, vol. 21, no. 11, 1978.

Freuder, Eugene C., "A Sufficient Condition for Backtrack-Free Search," *Journal of the Association for Computing Machinery*, vol. 29, no. 1, 1982.

Frey, Peter W. (editor), *Chess Skill in Man and Machine*, Springer-Verlag, New York, 1977.

Frey, Peter W. (editor), *Chess Skill in Man and Machine (second edition)*, Springer-Verlag, New York, 1983.

Funt, V. Brian, "Problem-Solving with Diagrammatic Representations," *Artificial Intelligence*, vol. 13, no. 3, 1980.

Gaschnig, John, "Performance Measurement and Analysis of Certain Search Algorithms," Report CMU-CS-79-124, Department of Computer Science, Carnegie-Mellon University, Pittsburgh, PA, 1979.

Gelperin, David, "On the Optimality of A*," *Artificial Intelligence*, vol. 8, no. 1, 1977.

Gentner, Dedre, "Structure-mapping: A Theoretical Framework for Analogy," *Cognitive Science*, vol. 7, no. 2, 1983.

Gentner, Dedre, "The Structure of Analogical Models in Science," Report 4451, Bolt, Beranek and Newman, Cambridge, MA, 1980.

Gentner, Dedre, and Albert L. Stevens (editors), *Mental Models*, Lawrence Erlbaum Associates, Hillsdale, NJ, 1983.

Gillogly, James J., "The Technology Chess Program," *Artificial Intelligence*, vol. 3, no. 3, 1972.

Goldstein, Ira P., "Summary of MYCROFT: A System for Understanding Simple Picture Programs," *Artificial Intelligence*, vol. 6, no. 3, 1975. Based on a PhD thesis, Massachusetts Institute of Technology, Cambridge, MA, 1973.

Green, Claude Cordell, "Theorem Proving by Resolution as a Basis for Question Answering," in *Machine Intelligence 4*, edited by Bernard Melzer and Donald Michie, Edinburgh University Press, Edinburgh, Scotland, 1969.

Green, Claude Cordell, *The Application of Theorem Proving to Question-answering Systems*, Garland, New York, 1980. Based on a PhD thesis, Stanford University, Stanford, CA, 1969.

Griffith, Arnold K., "A Comparison and Evaluation of Three Machine Learning Procedures as Applied to the Game of Checkers," *Artificial Intelligence*, vol. 5, no. 2, 1974.

Grimson, W. Eric L., *From Images to Surfaces*, MIT Press, Cambridge, MA, 1981. Based on a PhD thesis, Massachusetts Institute of Technology, Cambridge, MA, 1980.

Grosz, Barbara J., "Natural Language Processing," *Artificial Intelligence*, vol. 19, no. 2, 1982.

Guzman, Adolfo, "Computer Recognition of Three-Dimensional Objects in a Visual Scene," PhD Thesis, Massachusetts Institute of Technology, Cambridge, MA, 1968.

Haralick, Robert M., Larry S. Davis, and Azriel Rosenfeld, "Reduction Operations for Constraint Satisfaction," *Information Sciences*, vol. 14, 1978.

Harris, Larry R., "A High Performance Natural Language Processor for Data Base Query," *ACM SIGART Newsletter*, vol. 61, 1977.

Hart, Peter E., "Progress on a Computer Based Consultant," *Fourth International Joint Conference on Artificial Intelligence*, Tbilisi, Georgia, USSR, 1975.

Hart, Peter E., Richard O. Duda, and M. T. Einaudi, "PROSPECTOR—A Computer-based Consultation System for Mineral Exploration," *Mathematical Geology*, vol. 10, no. 5, 1978.

Hayes, Patrick J., "In Defense of Logic," *Fifth International Joint Conference on Artificial Intelligence*, Cambridge, MA, 1977.

Hayes, Patrick J., "The Naive Physics Manifesto," in *Expert Systems in the Micro-Electronic Age*, edited by Donald Michie, Edinburgh University Press, Edinburgh, Scotland, 1979.

Hayes-Roth, Frederick, "Using Proofs and Refutations to Learn from Experience," in *Machine Learning — An Artificial Intelligence Approach*, edited by Ryszard S. Michalski, Jaime G. Carbonell, and Tom M. Mitchell, Tioga Publishing Company, Palo Alto, CA, 1983.

Hayes-Roth, Frederick, Donald A. Waterman, and Douglas B. Lenat (editors), *Building Expert Systems*, Addison-Wesley, Reading, MA, 1983.

Hedrick, L. Charles, "Learning Production Systems from Examples," *Artificial Intelligence*, vol. 7, no. 1, 1976.

Hendrix, Gary G., Earl D. Sacerdoti, Daniel Sagalowicz, and Jonathan Slocum, "Developing a Natural Language Interface to Complex Data," *ACM Transactions on Database Systems*, vol. 8, no. 3, 1978.

Hewitt, Carl E., "PLANNER: A Language for Proving Theorems in Robots," *First International Joint Conference on Artificial Intelligence*, Washington, D. C., 1969.

Hewitt, Carl E., "Viewing Control Structures as Patterns of Passing Messages," *Artificial Intelligence*, vol. 8, no. 3, 1977.

Hewitt, Carl E., and Peter de Jong, "Open Systems," Report AIM-691, Artificial Intelligence Laboratory, Massachusetts Institute of Technology, Cambridge, MA, 1982.

Hildreth, Ellen C., "The Detection of Intensity Changes by Computer and Biological Vision Systems," *Computer Vision, Graphics, and Image Processing*, vol. 22, 1983. Based on a MS thesis, Massachusetts Institute of Technology, Cambridge, MA, 1980.

Hildreth, Ellen C., "The Measurement of Visual Motion," PhD Thesis, Massachusetts Institute of Technology, Cambridge, MA, 1983.

Hillis, W. Daniel, "The Connection Machine," Report AIM-646, Artificial Intelligence Laboratory, Massachusetts Institute of Technology, Cambridge, MA, 1981.

Hillis, W. Daniel, "A High Resolution Imaging Touch Sensor," *International Journal of Robotics Research*, vol. 1, no. 2, 1982. Based on a MS thesis, Massachusetts Institute of Technology, Cambridge, MA, 1981.

Hobbs, Jerry R., and Stanley J. Rosenschein, "Making Computational Sense of Montague's Intensional Logic," *Artificial Intelligence*, vol. 9, no. 3, 1977.

Hofstadter, Douglas R., *Gödel, Escher, Bach: Eternal Golden Braid*, Vintage Books, New York, 1980.

Holland, Stephen W., Lothar Rossol, and Mitchell R. Ward, "CONSIGHT-I: A Vision-controlled Robot System for Transferring Parts from Belt Conveyors," in *Computer Vision and Sensor-based Robots*, edited by George G. Dodd and Lothar Rossol, Plenum Press, New York, 1979.

Hollerbach, John, "Hierarchical Shape Description of Objects by Selection and Modification of Prototypes," MS Thesis, Massachusetts Institute of Technology, Cambridge, MA, 1976.

Hollerbach, John, "Dynamics," in *Robot Motion: Planning and Control*, edited by J. Michael Brady, John M. Hollerbach, Timothy L. Johnson, Tomás Lozano-Pérez, and Matthew T. Mason, MIT Press, Cambridge, MA, 1982.

Hollerbach, John, "A Recursive Lagrangian Formulation of Manipulator Dynamics and a Comparative Study of Dynamics Formulation Complexity," in *Robot Motion: Planning and Control*, edited by J. Michael Brady, John M. Hollerbach, Timothy L. Johnson, Tomás Lozano-Pérez, and Matthew T. Mason, MIT Press, Cambridge, MA, 1982.

Horn, Berthold K. P., "Obtaining Shape from Shading Information," in *The Psychology of Computer Vision*, edited by Patrick H. Winston, McGraw-Hill Book Company, New York, 1975. Based on a PhD thesis, Massachusetts Institute of Technology, Cambridge, MA, 1970.

Horn, Berthold K. P., "The Binford-Horn Line Finder," Report AIM-285, Artificial Intelligence Laboratory, Massachusetts Institute of Technology, Cambridge, MA, 1971.

Horn, Berthold K.P., "Understanding Image Intensities," *Artificial Intelligence*, vol. 8, no. 2, 1977.

Horn, Berthold K.P., "Sequins and Quills—Representations for Surface Topography," in *Representation of 3-Dimensional Objects*, edited by Ruzena Bajcsy, Springer-Verlag, New York, 1982.

Horn, Berthold K. P., *Robot Vision*, MIT Press, Cambridge, MA and McGraw-Hill Book Company, New York, 1984.

Hubel, D. H., and T. N. Wiesel, "Receptive Fields, Binocular Interaction and Functional Architecture in the Cat's Visual Cortex," *Journal of Physiology*, vol. 160, 1962.

Huffman, David, "Impossible Objects as Nonsense Sentences," in *Machine Intelligence 6*, edited by Bernard Meltzer and Donald Michie, Edinburgh University Press, Edinburgh, Scotland, 1971.

Hummel, Robert A., and Steven W. Zucker, "On the Foundations of Relaxation Labeling Processes," *IEEE Transactions on Pattern Analysis and Machine Intelligence*, vol. PAMI-5, no. 3, 1983.

Hunt, Earl B., *Artificial Intelligence*, Academic Press, New York, 1975.

Ikeuchi, Katsushi, and Berthold K. P. Horn, "Numerical Shape from Shading and Occluding Boundaries," *Artificial Intelligence*, vol. 17, August 1981. Volume 17 is also available as *Computer Vision*, edited by J. Michael Brady, North-Holland, Amsterdam, 1981.

Inoue, Hirochika, "Force Feedback in Precise Assembly Tasks," Report AIM-308, Artificial Intelligence Laboratory, Massachusetts Institute of Technology, Cambridge, MA, 1974.

Kahn, Kenneth, and Anthony G. Gorry, "Mechanizing Temporal Knowledge," *Artificial Intelligence*, vol. 9, no. 1, 1977.

Kanade, Takeo, "A Theory of Origami World," *Artificial Intelligence*, vol. 13, no. 3, 1980.

Kanade, Takeo, "Recovery of the Three-Dimensional Shape of an Object from a Single View," *Artificial Intelligence*, vol. 17, August 1981. Volume 17 is also available as *Computer Vision*, edited by J. Michael Brady, North-Holland, Amsterdam, 1981.

Kaplan, Jerrold., "Cooperative Responses from a Portable Natural Language Database Query System," in *Computational Models of Discourse*, edited by J. Michael Brady and Robert C. Berwick, MIT Press, Cambridge, MA, 1983.

Kaplan, Ronald M., "Augmented Transition Networks: Psychological Models of Sentence Comprehension," *Artificial Intelligence*, vol. 3, no. 2, 1972.

Katz, Boris, and Patrick H. Winston, "A Two-way Natural Language Interface," in *Integrated Interactive Computing Systems*, edited by P. Degano and Erik Sandewall, North-Holland, Amsterdam, 1982.

Knuth, Donald E., and Ronald W. Moore, "An Analysis of Alpha-Beta Pruning," *Artificial Intelligence*, vol. 6, no. 4, 1975.

Kornfeld, William A., and Carl E. Hewitt, "The Scientific Community Metaphor," *IEEE Transactions on Systems, Man, and Cybernetics*, vol. SMC-11, no. 1, 1981.

Kowalski, Robert, *Logic for Problem Solving*, North-Holland, Amsterdam, 1979.

Kulikowski, Casimir A., and Sholom M. Weiss, "Representation of Expert Knowledge for Consultant," in *Artificial Intelligence in Medicine*, edited by Peter Szolovits, Westview Press, Boulder, CO, 1982.

Langley, Pat, Gary L. Bradshaw, and Herbert A. Simon, "Rediscovering Chemistry with the BACON System," in *Machine Learning — An Artificial Intelligence Approach*, edited by Ryszard S. Michalski, Jaime G. Carbonell, and Tom M. Mitchell, Tioga Publishing Company, Palo Alto, CA, 1983.

Lauriere, Jean-Louis, "A Language and a Program for Stating and Solving Combinatorial Problems," *Artificial Intelligence*, vol. 10, no. 1, 1978.

Lehnert, Wendy, "Plot Units and Narrative Summarization," *Cognitive Science*, vol. 5, no. 4, 1981.

Lehnert, Wendy G., Michael G. Dyer, Peter N. Johnson, C. J. Yang, and Steve Harley, "BORIS—An Experiment in In-Depth Understanding of Narratives," *Artificial Intelligence*, vol. 20, no. 1, 1983.

Lenat, Douglas B., "AM: Discovery in Mathematics as Heuristic Search," in *Knowledge-Based Systems in Artificial Intelligence*, edited by Randall Davis and Douglas B. Lenat, McGraw-Hill Book Company, New York, 1982. Based on a PhD thesis, Stanford University, Stanford, CA, 1977.

Lenat, Douglas B., "The Ubiquity of Discovery," *Artificial Intelligence*, vol. 9, no. 3, 1977.

Lenat, Douglas B., "The Nature of Heuristics," *Artificial Intelligence*, vol. 19, no. 2, 1982.

Lesser, Victor R., and Lee D. Erman, "A Retrospective View of the Hearsay-II Architecture," *Fifth International Joint Conference on Artificial Intelligence*, Cambridge, MA, 1977.

Lettvin, Jerome Y., R. R. Maturana, W. S. McCulloch, and W. H. Pitts, "What the Frog's Eye Tells the Frog's Brain," *Proceedings of the Institute of Radio Engineers*, vol. 47, 1959.

Levi, Giorgio, and Sirovich Franco, "Generalized And/Or Graphs," *Artificial Intelligence*, vol. 7, no. 3, 1976.

Levy, David, *Chess and Computers*, Computer Science Press, Woodland Hills, CA, 1976.

Lindsay, Peter H. and Donald A. Norman, *Human Information Processing*, Academic Press, New York, 1972.

Lindsay, Robert, Bruce G. Buchanan, Edward A. Feigenbaum, and Joshua Lederberg, *Applications of Artificial Intelligence for Chemical Inference: The DENDRAL Project*, McGraw-Hill Book Company, New York, 1980.

Lozano-Pérez, Tomás, "Robot Programming," Report AIM-698, Artificial Intelligence Laboratory, Massachusetts Institute of Technology, Cambridge, MA, 1982.

Lozano-Pérez, Tomás, "Spatial Planning: A Configuration-space Approach," *IEEE Transactions on Computers*, vol. 71, no. 7, 1983. Based on a PhD thesis, Massachusetts Institute of Technology, Cambridge, MA, 1980.

Mackworth, Alan K., "Interpreting Pictures of Polyhedral Scenes," *Artificial Intelligence*, vol. 4, no. 2, 1973.

Mackworth, Alan K., "Consistency in Networks of Relations," *Artificial Intelligence*, vol. 8, no. 1, 1977.

Marcus, Mitchell P., *A Theory of Syntactic Recognition for Natural Language*, MIT Press, Cambridge, MA, 1980. Based on a PhD thesis, Massachusetts Institute of Technology, Cambridge, MA, 1977.

Marr, David, *Vision*, W. H. Freeman, San Francisco, CA, 1982.

Marr, David, "Artificial Intelligence—A Personal View," *Artificial Intelligence*, vol. 9, no. 1, 1977.

Marr, David, and Tomaso Poggio, "A Theory of Human Stereo Vision," *Proceedings of the Royal Society of London*, vol. 204, 1979.

Martelli, Alberto, "On the Complexity of Admissible Search Algorithms," *Artificial Intelligence*, vol. 8, no. 1, 1977.

Martin, William A., "Descriptions and the Specialization of Concepts," Report TM-101, Laboratory of Computer Science, Massachusetts Institute of Technology, Cambridge, MA, 1978.

Mason, Matthew T., "Compliance and Force Control for Computer Controlled Manipulators," *IEEE Transactions on Systems, Man, and Cybernetics*, vol. SCM-11, no. 6, 1981. Based on a MS thesis, Massachusetts Institute of Technology, Cambridge, MA, 1979.

Mason, Matthew T., "Manipulator Grasping and Pushing Operations," PhD Thesis, Massachusetts Institute of Technology, Cambridge, MA, 1982.

Mayhew, John E. W., and John P. Frisby, "Psychophysical and Computational Studies towards a Theory of Human Stereopsis," *Artificial Intelligence*, vol. 17, August 1981. ·Volume 17 is also available as *Computer Vision*, edited by J. Michael Brady, North-Holland, Amsterdam, 1981.

Mazlack, Lawrence, J., "Computer Construction of Crossword Puzzles Using Precedence Relationships," *Artificial Intelligence*, vol. 7, no. 1, 1976.

McAllester, David A., "An Outlook on Truth Maintenance," Report AIM-551, Artificial Intelligence Laboratory, Massachusetts Institute of Technology, Cambridge, MA, 1980.

McCarthy, John, "Epistemological Problems of Artificial Intelligence," *Fifth International Joint Conference on Artificial Intelligence*, Cambridge, MA, 1977.

McCarthy, John, "Circumscription—A Form of Non-Monotonic Reasoning," *Artificial Intelligence*, vol. 13, no. 1&2, 1980.

McCarthy, John, and Patrick J. Hayes, "Some Philosophical Problems from the Standpoint of Artificial Intelligence," in *Machine Intelligence 4*, edited by Bernard Melzer and Donald Michie, Edinburgh University Press, Edinburgh, Scotland, 1969.

McCorduck, Pamela, *Machines Who Think*, W. H. Freeman, San Francisco, CA, 1979.

McDermott, Drew, and Jon Doyle, "Non-Monotonic Logic I," *Artificial Intelligence*, vol. 13, no. 1&2, 1980.

McDermott, John, "R1: A Rule-Based Configurer of Computer Systems," *Artificial Intelligence*, vol. 19, no. 1, 1982.

McDonald, David D., "Natural Language Generation as a Computational Problem," in *Computational Models of Discourse*, edited by J. Michael Brady and Robert C. Berwick, MIT Press, Cambridge, MA, 1983.

Michalski, Ryszard S., "Pattern Recognition as Rule-Guided Inductive Inference," *IEEE Transactions on Pattern Analysis and Machine Intelligence*, vol. 2, no. 4, 1980.

Michalski, Ryszard S., "A Theory and Methodology of Inductive Learning," *Artificial Intelligence*, vol. 20, no. 3, 1983.

Michalski, Ryszard S., and Richard L. Chilausky, "Learning by Being Told and Learning from Examples: An Experimental Comparison of the Two Methods of Knowledge Acquisition in the Context of Developing an Expert System for Soybean Disease Diagnosis," *International Journal of Policy Analysis and Information Systems*, vol. 4, no. 2, 1980.

Michalski, Ryszard S., and Robert E. Stepp, "Learning from Observation: Conceptual Clustering," in *Machine Learning — An Artificial Intelligence Approach*, edited by Ryszard S. Michalski, Jaime G. Carbonell, and Tom M. Mitchell, Tioga Publishing Company, Palo Alto, CA, 1983.

Michalski, Ryszard S., Jaime G. Carbonell, and Tom M. Mitchell (editors), *Machine Learning—An Artificial Intelligence Approach*, Tioga Publishing Company, Palo Alto, CA, 1983.

Michie, Donald, *On Machine Intelligence*, John Wiley and Sons, New York, 1974.

Michie, Donald (editor), *Expert Systems in the Micro-Electronic Age*, Edinburgh University Press, Edinburgh, Scotland, 1979.

Michie, Donald, "Chess with Computers," *Interdisciplinary Science Reviews*, vol. 5, no. 3, 1980.

Miller, G. A., E. Galanter, and K. H. Pribram, *Plans and the Structure of Behavior*, Holt, Rinehart, and Winston, New York, 1960.

Minker, Jack, Daniel H. Fishman, and James R. McSkimin, "The Q* Algorithm—A Search Strategy for a Deductive Question-Answering System," *Artificial Intelligence*, vol. 4, no. 3&4, 1973.

Minsky, Marvin, *The Society of Mind*, book in preparation.

Minsky, Marvin (editor), *Semantic Information Processing*, MIT Press, Cambridge, MA, 1968.

Minsky, Marvin, "Matter, Mind, and Models," in *Semantic Information Processing*, edited by Marvin Minsky, MIT Press, Cambridge, MA, 1968.

Minsky, Marvin, "A Framework for Representing Knowledge," in *The Psychology of Computer Vision*, edited by Patrick H. Winston, McGraw-Hill Book Company, New York, 1975.

Minsky, Marvin, "Plain Talk about Neurodevelopmental Epistemology," *Fifth International Joint Conference on Artificial Intelligence*, Cambridge, MA, 1977.

Minsky, Marvin, "K-lines: A Theory of Memory," *Cognitive Science*, vol. 4, no. 1, 1980.

Mitchell, Tom M., "Generalization as Search," *Artificial Intelligence*, vol. 18, no. 2, 1982. Based on a PhD thesis, Stanford University, Stanford, CA, 1978.

Moore, James A., and Allen Newell, "How Can Merlin Understand?," in *Knowledge and Cognition*, edited by L. Gregg, Lawrence Erlbaum Associates, Hillsdale, NJ, 1974.

Morevec, Hans P., "Towards Automatic Visual Obstacle Avoidance," *Fifth International Joint Conference on Artificial Intelligence*, Cambridge, MA, 1977.

Moses, Joel, "Symbolic Integration," PhD Thesis, Massachusetts Institute of Technology, Cambridge, MA, 1967.

Nau, Dana S., "An Investigation of the Causes of Pathology in Games," *Artificial Intelligence*, vol. 19, no. 3, 1982.

Nevatia, Ramakant, *Machine Perception*, Prentice-Hall, Englewood Cliffs, NJ, 1982.

Nevatia, Ramakant, and Thomas O. Binford, "Description and Recognition of Curved Objects," *Artificial Intelligence*, vol. 8, no. 1, 1977.

Newborn, M. M., "The Efficiency of the Alpha-beta Search on Trees with Branch-dependent Terminal Node Scores," *Artificial Intelligence*, vol. 8, no. 2, 1977.

Newell, Allen, and Herbert A. Simon, *Human Problem Solving*, Prentice-Hall, Englewood Cliffs, NJ, 1972.

Newell, Allen, John C. Shaw, and Herbert A. Simon, "Preliminary Description of General Problem Solving Program-I (GPS-I)," Report CIP Working Paper 7, Carnegie Institute of Technology, Pittsburgh, PA, 1957.

Nilsson, Nils J., *Principles of Artificial Intelligence*, Tioga Publishing Company, Palo Alto, CA, 1980.

Nishihara, H. Keith, "Intensity, Visible-surface, and Volumetric Representations," *Artificial Intelligence*, vol. 17, August 1981. Volume 17 is also available as *Computer Vision*, edited by J. Michael Brady, North-Holland, Amsterdam, 1981. Based on a PhD thesis, Massachusetts Institute of Technology, Cambridge, MA, 1978.

Ogden, C. K., *Basic English: International Second Language*, Harcourt, Brace, and World, New York, 1968.

O'Gorman, Frank, "Edge detection using Walsh Functions," *Artificial Intelligence*, vol. 10, no. 2, 1978.

Ohlander, Ronald B., "Analysis of Natural Scenes," PhD Thesis, Carnegie-Mellon University, Pittsburgh, PA, 1975.

Ohlander, Ronald B., Keith Price, and D. Raj Reddy, "Picture Segmentation Using a Recursive Splitting Method," *Computer Graphics and Image Processing*, vol. 8, 1979.

Palay, Andrew J., "The B* Tree Search Algorithm: New Results," *Artificial Intelligence*, vol. 19, no. 2, 1982.

Papert, Seymour, *Mindstorms*, Basic Books, New York, 1981.

Papert, Seymour, "Uses of Technology to Enhance Education," Report AIM-298, Artificial Intelligence Laboratory, Massachusetts Institute of Technology, Cambridge, MA, 1973.

Papert, Seymour, and Cynthia Solomon, "Twenty Things To Do with a Computer," Report AIM-248, Artificial Intelligence Laboratory, Massachusetts Institute of Technology, Cambridge, MA, 1971.

Pastre, D., "Automatic Theorem Proving in Set Theory," *Artificial Intelligence*, vol. 10, no. 1, 1978.

Patil, Ramesh, "Causal Representation of Patient Illness for Electrolyte and Acid-Base Diagnosis," PhD Thesis, Massachusetts Institute of Technology, Cambridge, MA, 1981.

Patil, Ramesh S., Peter Szolovits, and William B. Schwartz, "Causal Understanding of Patient Illness," *Seventh International Joint Conference on Artificial Intelligence*, Vancouver, British Columbia, Canada, 1981.

Paul, Richard P., *Robot Manipulators: Mathematics, Programming, and Control*, MIT Press, Cambridge, MA, 1981.

Pearl, Judea, "Knowledge versus Search: A Quantitative Analysis Using A*," *Artificial Intelligence*, vol. 20, no. 1, 1983.

Pednault, E. P. D., Steven W. Zucker, and L. V. Muresan, "On the Independence Assumption Underlying Subjective Bayesian Updating," *Artificial Intelligence*, vol. 16, no. 2, 1981.

Pereira, Fernando C. N., and David H. D. Warren, "Definite Clause Grammars for Language Analysis—A Survey of the Formalism and a Comparison with Augmented Transition Networks," *Artificial Intelligence*, vol. 13, no. 3, 1980.

Pitrat, Jacques, "A Chess Combination Program Which Uses Plans," *Artificial Intelligence*, vol. 8, no. 3, 1977.

Pople, Harry E., Jr., "On the Mechanization of Abductive Logic," *Third International Joint Conference on Artificial Intelligence*, Stanford, CA, 1973.

Pople, Harry E., Jr., "Heuristic Methods for Imposing Structure on Ill-Structured Problems: The Structuring of Medical Diagnostics," in *Artificial Intelligence in Medicine*, edited by Peter Szolovits, Westview Press, Boulder, CO, 1982.

Pylyshyn, Zenon W., "Literature from Cognitive Psychology," *Artificial Intelligence*, vol. 19, no. 3, 1982.

Raibert, Marc H., and Ivan Sutherland, "Machines That Walk," *Scientific American*, vol. 248, no. 1, 1983.

Raphael, Bertram, *The Thinking Computer*, W. H. Freeman, San Francisco, CA, 1976.

Reiter, R., "A Logic for Default Reasoning," *Artificial Intelligence*, vol. 13, no. 1&2, 1980.

Requicha, Aristides A., "Representations for Rigid Solids: Theory, Methods, and Systems," *ACM Computing Surveys*, vol. 12, no. 4, 1980.

Rich, Charles, and Howard E. Shrobe, "Initial Report on a LISP Programmer's Apprentice," *IEEE Transactions on Software Engineering*, vol. SE-4, no. 6, 1978.

Rich, Elaine, *Artificial Intelligence*, McGraw-Hill Book Company, New York, 1983.

Richter, Jacob, and Shimon Ullman, "A Model for the Temporal Organization of the X- and Y-Type Receptive Fields in the Primate Retina," *Biological Cybernetics*, vol. 43, 1982.

Rieger, Chuck, "On Organization of Knowledge for Problem Solving and Language Comprehension," *Artificial Intelligence*, vol. 7, no. 2, 1976.

Roberts, R. Bruce, and Ira P. Goldstein, "The FRL primer," Report AIM-408, Artificial Intelligence Laboratory, Massachusetts Institute of Technology, Cambridge, MA, 1977.

Robinson, J. A., "A Machine-Oriented Logic Based on the Resolution Principle," *Journal of the Association for Computing Machinery*, vol. 12, no. 1, 1965.

Robinson, J. A., "The Generalized Resolution Principle," in *Machine Intelligence 3*, edited by Donald Michie, Elsevier, New York, 1968.

Rosenbloom, Paul S., "A World-Championship-Level Othello Program," *Artificial Intelligence*, vol. 19, no. 3, 1982.

Rosenfeld, Azriel (editor), *Multiresolution Image Processing and Analysis*, Springer-Verlag, New York, 1983.

Rosenfeld, Azriel, and Avinash C. Kak, *Digital Picture Processing*, Academic Press, New York, 1976.

Rosenfeld, Azriel, Robert A. Hummel, and Steven W. Zucker, "Scene Labelling by Relaxation Operators," *IEEE Transactions on Systems, Man, and Society*, vol. 6, 1976.

Ruth, Gregory R., "Intelligent Program Analysis," *Artificial Intelligence*, vol. 7, no. 1, 1976.

Sacerdoti, Earl D., "Planning in a Hierarchy of Abstraction Spaces," *Artificial Intelligence*, vol. 5, no. 2, 1974.

Salisbury, J. Kenneth, Jr., "Kinematic and Force Analysis of Articulated Hands," PhD Thesis, Stanford University, Stanford, CA, 1982.

Salisbury, J. Kenneth, Jr., and John J. Craig, "Articulated Hands: Force Control and Kinematic Issues," *International Journal of Robotics Research*, vol. 1, no. 1, 1982.

Salisbury, J. Kenneth, Jr., and B. Roth, "Kinematic and Force Analysis of Articulated Mechanical Hands," *Journal of Mechanisms, Transmissions, and Automation in Design*, vol. 105, 1983.

Samuel, Arthur L., "Some Studies in Machine Learning Using the Game of Checkers," *IBM Journal of Research and Development*, vol. 3, no. 3, 1959.

Samuel, Arthur L., "Some Studies in Machine Learning Using the Game of Checkers II. Recent Progress," *IBM Journal of Research and Development*, vol. 11, no. 6, 1967.

Schank, Roger C., "Conceptual Dependency: A Theory of Natural Language Understanding," *Cognitive Psychology*, vol. 3, no. 4, 1972.

Schank, Roger C., *Dynamic Memory*, Cambridge University Press, Cambridge, England, 1982.

Schank, Roger C., and Kenneth Colby (editors), *Computer Models of Thought and Language*, W. H. Freeman, San Francisco, CA, 1973.

Schubert, L. K., "Extending the Expressive Power of Semantic Networks," *Artificial Intelligence*, vol. 7, no. 2, 1976.

Shannon, Claude E., "Automatic Chess Player," *Scientific American*, vol. 182, no. 48, 1950.

Shannon, Claude E., "Programming a Digital Computer for Playing Chess," *Philosophy Magazine*, vol. 41, 1950.

Shirai, Yoshiaki, "Analyzing Intensity Arrays Using Knowledge about Scenes," in *The Psychology of Computer Vision*, edited by Patrick H. Winston, McGraw-Hill Book Company, New York, 1975.

Shortliffe, Edward H., *MYCIN: Computer-based Medical Consultations*, Elsevier, New York, 1976. Based on a PhD thesis, Stanford University, Stanford, CA, 1974.

Shortliffe, Edward H., and Bruce G. Buchanan, "A Model of Inexact Reasoning in Medicine," *Mathematical Biosciences*, vol. 23, 1975.

Shostak, Robert E., "Refutation Graphs," *Artificial Intelligence*, vol. 7, no. 1, 1976.

Sidner, Candace L., "Focusing in the Comprehension of Definite Anaphora," in *Computational Models of Discourse*, edited by J. Michael Brady and Robert C. Berwick, MIT Press, Cambridge, MA, 1983.

Simmons, Robert, "Semantic Networks: Their Computation and Use for Understanding English Sentences," in *Computer Models of Thought and Language*, edited by Roger Schank and Kenneth Colby, W. H. Freeman, San Francisco, CA, 1973.

Simon, Herbert A., *The Sciences of the Artificial*, MIT Press, Cambridge, MA, 1969.

Simon, Herbert A., "The Structure of Ill Structured Problems," *Artificial Intelligence*, vol. 4, no. 3&4, 1973.

Simon, Herbert A., and Joseph B. Kadane, "Optimal Problem-Solving Search: All-or-None Solutions," *Artificial Intelligence*, vol. 6, no. 3, 1975.

Slagle, James R., "A Heuristic Program That Solves Symbolic Integration Problems in Freshman Calculus," in *Computers and Thought*, edited by Edward A. Feigenbaum and Julian Feldman, McGraw-Hill Book Company, New York, 1963. Based on a PhD thesis, Massachusetts Institute of Technology, Cambridge, MA, 1961.

Stallman, Richard M., and Gerald J. Sussman, "Forward Reasoning and Dependency-directed Backtracking in a System for Computer-aided Circuit Analysis," *Artificial Intelligence*, vol. 9, no. 2, 1977.

Stefik, Mark, "Planning with Constraints (MOLGEN: Part 1 and Part 2)," *Artificial Intelligence*, vol. 16, no. 2, 1980.

Stepankova, Olga, and Ivan M. Havel, "A Logical Theory of Robot Problem Solving and Language Comprehension," *Artificial Intelligence*, vol. 7, no. 2, 1976.

Stevens, Albert L., R. Bruce Roberts, Larry S. Stead, Kenneth D. Forbus, Cindy Steinberg, and Brian C. Smith, "Steamer: Advanced Computer Aided Instruction in Propulsion Engineering," Report 4702, Bolt, Beranek and Newman, Cambridge, MA, 1981.

Sugihara, Kokichi, "Quantitative Analysis of Line Drawings of Polyhedral Scenes," *Proceedings of the Fourth International Joint Conference on Pattern Recognition*, Kyoto, Japan, 1978.

Sugihara, Kokichi, "Mathematical Structures of Line Drawings of Polyhedrons: Toward Man-machine Communication by Means of Line Drawings," *IEEE Transactions on Pattern Analysis and Machine Intelligence*, vol. PAMI-4, 1982.

Sussman, Gerald J., *A Computer Model of Skill Acquisition*, Elsevier, New York, 1975. Based on a PhD thesis, Massachusetts Institute of Technology, Cambridge, MA, 1973.

Sussman, Gerald J., and Richard M. Stallman, "Heuristic Techniques in Computer Aided Circuit Analysis," *IEEE Transactions on Circuits and Systems*, vol. CAS-22, no. 11, 1975.

Sussman, Gerald J., Terry Winograd, and Eugene Charniak, "Microplanner Reference Manual," Report AIM-203A, Artificial Intelligence Laboratory, Massachusetts Institute of Technology, Cambridge, MA, 1971.

Szolovits, Peter (editor), *Artificial Intelligence in Medicine*, Westview Press, Boulder, CO, 1982.

Szolovits, Peter, Lowell B. Hawkinson, and William A. Martin, "An Overview of OWL, a Language for Knowledge Representation," Report TM-86, Laboratory of Computer Science, Massachusetts Institute of Technology, Cambridge, MA, 1977.

Tenenbaum, Jay M., and Harry G. Barrow, "Experiments in Interpretation-Guided Segmentation," *Artificial Intelligence*, vol. 8, no. 3, 1977.

Terzopoulos, Demetri, "The Computation of Visible-Surface Representations," PhD Thesis, Massachusetts Institute of Technology, Cambridge, MA, 1983.

Thorne, J., P. Bratley, and H. Dewar, "The Syntactic Analysis of English by Machine," in *Machine Intelligence 3*, edited by Donald Michie, Edinburgh University Press, Edinburgh, Scotland, 1968.

Tversky, Amos, "Features of Similarity," *Psychological Review*, vol. 84, no. 4, 1977.

Ullman, Shimon, *The Interpretation of Visual Motion*, MIT Press, Cambridge, MA, 1979. Based in part on a PhD thesis, Massachusetts Institute of Technology, Cambridge, MA, 1977.

VanLehn, Kurt Alan, "Felicity Conditions for Human Skill Acquisition: Validating an AI-based Theory," PhD Thesis, Massachusetts Institute of Technology, Cambridge, MA, 1983.

Vere, Steven A., "Relational Production Systems," *Artificial Intelligence*, vol. 8, no. 1, 1977.

Waltz, David, "Understanding Line Drawings of Scenes with Shadows," in *The Psychology of Computer Vision*, edited by Patrick H. Winston, McGraw-Hill Book Company, New York, 1975. Based on a PhD thesis, Massachusetts Institute of Technology, Cambridge, MA, 1972.

Waltz, David, "Natural Language Access to a Large Data Base: an Engineering Approach," *Fourth International Joint Conference on Artificial Intelligence*, Tbilisi, Georgia, USSR, 1975.

Waters, Richard C., "The Programmer's Apprentice: Knowledge Based Program Editing," *IEEE Transactions on Software Engineering*, vol. SE-8, no. 1, 1982.

Webb, Jon A., and J. K. Aggarwal, "Structure from Motion of Rigid and Jointed Objects," *Artificial Intelligence*, vol. 19, no. 1, 1982.

Webber, Bonnie L., "So What Can We Talk about Now," in *Computational Models of Discourse*, edited by J. Michael Brady and Robert C. Berwick, MIT Press, Cambridge, MA, 1983.

Weizenbaum, Joseph, *Computer Power and Human Reason*, W. H. Freeman, San Francisco, CA, 1976.

Weyhrauch Richard W., "Prolegomena to a Theory of Mechanized Formal Reasoning," *Artificial Intelligence*, vol. 13, no. 1&2, 1980.

Wilks, Yorick A., *Grammar, Meaning, and the Machine Analysis of Language*, Routledge and Kegan Paul, London, 1972.

Wilks, Yorick, and Eugene Charniak, *Computational Semantics*, North-Holland, Amsterdam, 1976.

Winograd, Terry, *Understanding Natural Language*, Academic Press, New York, 1972. Another version appears as "A Procedural Model of Language Understanding," in *Computer Models of Thought and Language*, edited by Roger Schank and Kenneth Colby, W. H. Freeman, San Francisco, CA, 1973. Based on a PhD thesis, Massachusetts Institute of Technology, Cambridge, MA, 1971.

Winograd, Terry, "Frame Representations and the Declarative/Procedural Controversy," in *Representation and Understanding*, edited by Daniel G. Bobrow and Allan Collins, Academic Press, New York, 1975.

Winograd, Terry, "Extended Inference Modes in Reasoning by Computer Systems," *Artificial Intelligence*, vol. 13, no. 1&2, 1980.

Winograd, Terry, "Towards a Procedural Understanding of Semantics," *Revue Internationale de Philosophie*, vol. 3, no. 3-4, 1976.

Winograd, Terry, *Language as a Cognitive Process, Volume I: Syntax*, Addison-Wesley, Reading, MA, 1983.

Winston, Patrick Henry, "Learning Structural Descriptions from Examples," in *The Psychology of Computer Vision*, edited by Patrick H. Winston, McGraw-Hill Book Company, New York, 1975. Based on a PhD thesis, Massachusetts Institute of Technology, Cambridge, MA, 1970.

Winston, Patrick Henry, "The MIT Robot," in *Machine Intelligence 7*, edited by Bernard Meltzer and Donald Michie, Edinburgh University Press, Edinburgh, Scotland, 1972.

Winston, Patrick Henry (editor), *The Psychology of Computer Vision*, McGraw-Hill Book Company, New York, 1975.

Winston, Patrick Henry, "Learning by Creating and Justifying Transfer Frames," *Artificial Intelligence*, vol. 10, no. 2, 1978.

Winston, Patrick Henry, "Learning and Reasoning by Analogy," *Communications of the Association for Computing Machinery*, vol. 23, no. 12, 1980.

Winston, Patrick Henry, "Learning New Principles from Precedents and Exercises," *Artificial Intelligence*, vol. 19, no. 3, 1982.

Winston, Patrick Henry, "Learning by Augmenting Rules and Accumulating Censors," Report AIM-678, Artificial Intelligence Laboratory, Massachusetts Institute of Technology, Cambridge, MA, 1982.

Winston, Patrick Henry and Richard Henry Brown (editors), *Artificial Intelligence: An MIT Perspective, vol. 1*, MIT Press, Cambridge, MA, 1979.

Winston, Patrick Henry, and Richard Henry Brown (editors), *Artificial Intelligence: An MIT Perspective, vol. 2*, MIT Press, Cambridge, MA, 1979.

Winston, Patrick Henry, and Berthold K. P. Horn, *LISP*, Addison-Wesley, Reading, MA, 1981.

Winston, Patrick Henry, and Karen A. Prendergast (editors), *The AI Business: The Commercial Uses of Artificial Intelligence*, MIT Press, Cambridge, MA, 1984.

Winston, Patrick Henry, Thomas O. Binford, Boris Katz, and Michael R. Lowry, "Learning Physical Descriptions from Functional Definitions, Examples, and Precedents," *National Conference on Artificial Intelligence*, Washington, D. C., 1983.

Witkin, Andy, "Scale-space Filtering," *Eighth International Joint Conference on Artificial Intelligence*, Karlsruhe, Federal Republic of Germany, 1983.

Woodham, Robert J., "Analyzing Images of Curved Surfaces," *Artificial Intelligence*, vol. 17, August 1981. Volume 17 is also available as *Computer Vision*, edited by J. Michael Brady, North-Holland, Amsterdam, 1981. Based on a PhD thesis, Massachusetts Institute of Technology, Cambridge, MA, 1978.

Woods, William A., "Transition Network Grammars for Natural Language Analysis," *Communications of the Association for Computing Machinery*, vol. 13, no. 10, 1970.

Woods, William A., and Ronald M. Kaplan, "The Lunar Sciences Natural Language Information System," Report 2265, Bolt, Beranek and Newman, Cambridge, MA, 1971.

Woods, William A., "What's in a Link," in *Representation and Understanding*, edited by Daniel G. Bobrow and Allan Collins, Academic Press, New York, 1975.

Zucker, Steven W., "Early Orientation Selection and Grouping: Type I and Type II Processes," Report 82-6, Department of Electrical Engineering, McGill University, 1982.

Zucker, Steven W., Robert A. Hummel, and Azriel Rosenfeld, "An Application of Relaxation Labeling to Line and Curve Enhancement," *IEEE Transactions on Computers*, vol. 26, 1977.

Zucker, Steven W., Azriel Rosenfeld, and Larry S. Davis, "General Purpose Models: Expectations about the Unexpected," *Fourth International Joint Conference on Artificial Intelligence*, Tbilisi, Georgia, USSR, 1975.

INDEX